THE PUBLIC HOUSES AND INNS OF SALISBURY

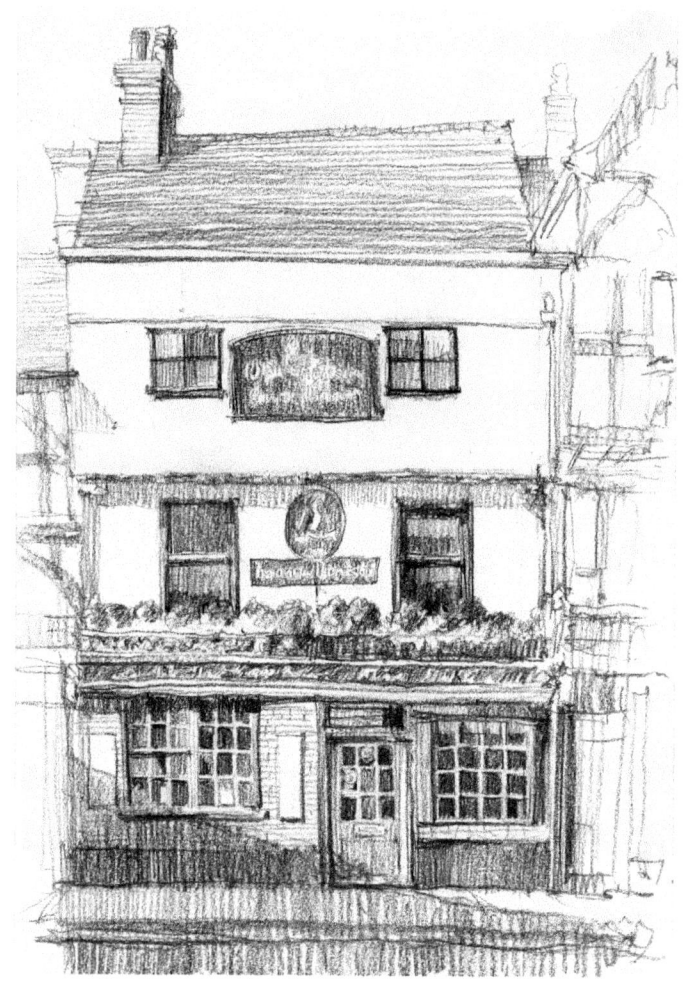

Haunch of Venison, Minster Street (Fred Fieber)

The Public Houses and Inns of Salisbury

A HISTORY

Edwin M Garman

Illustrations by Fred Fieber

First published in the United Kingdom in 2017

by The Hobnob Press,
30c Deverill Road Trading Estate, Sutton Veny, Warminster BA12 7BZ
www.hobnobpress.co.uk

© Edwin M Garman, 2017

The Author hereby asserts his moral rights to be identified as the Author of the Work.

All rights reserved. No part of this publication may be reproduced, stored in a retrieval system, or transmitted in any form or by any means, electronic, mechanical, photocopying, recording or otherwise, without the prior permission of the publisher and copyright holder.

British Library Cataloguing in Publication Data
A catalogue record for this book is available from the British Library

ISBN 978-1-906978-43-3

Typeset in Octavian 11/12.5 pt and Gill Sans. Typesetting and origination by John Chandler

Printed by Lightning Source

Cover illustration: Rose & Crown, Harnham (photo, author)

Contents

Author's Note	vi
Illustrations	vi
Acknowledgements	vi
Introduction	vii
Inns, Taverns and Ale Houses	vii
Coaching Inns	ix
Licensing and Licensed Hours	ix
Inns of Salisbury	x
The Old Inns of Salisbury	xi
Names of Pubs	xi
The Breweries of Salisbury	xii
Inventory of Inns, Alehouses and Public Houses	1
Map of Salisbury, 1797	232
Appendices	
1 Old Inns of Salisbury	233
2 A Dispute between Coach Masters	272
3 Street Names	280
4 Measurements	281
Notes	282
Bibliography	283
References	284
Pub Name Cross Reference	302

Author's Note
I would have liked to describe this volume as a definitive guide to the history of Salisbury Inns and Public Houses. However, there are still gaps in the licensing records which, at the time of publication, seem unlikely to be filled. In addition, the collection of the information that has led to this book has taken me far longer than I originally envisaged. Thus, I feel it is more important to publish it in the present form than to wait any longer. Suffice it to say that I will continue my researches and I welcome any additional information that any reader can provide. This may result in a second edition at a date sometime in the future! In the meantime, I apologise for any errors that have crept into my research.

Illustrations
The illustrations in this book are from a series of charcoal drawings by Fred Fieber. Fred has produced three posters featuring the pubs of Salisbury together with two posters showing lost pubs of Salisbury. A further poster shows pubs in the countryside in the Salisbury area. These posters are available either framed or unframed and the individual drawings of pubs are also available. Details of these and Fred's other artwork can be found at fredfieber.com.

Acknowledgements
The information in this document has been gleaned from a number of sources. Wherever possible, I have gone back to original documents. Hence the microfilmed copies of the *Salisbury Journal* have proved invaluable as have the licensing records kept at the Wiltshire and Swindon History Centre. More recently, the British Newspaper Archive has proved a valuable asset, allowing one to search the Salisbury newspapers via an excellent search engine. I have to thank the staff of the History Centre and also those of the Reference Library in Salisbury for their courteous and friendly help. Salisbury Museum has some very helpful collections, particularly of old photographs. Where the facts expressed in this document differ from those expressed in other, older publications, I have been very careful to verify the new interpretation before committing it to print. In addition, wherever possible, I have quoted the source of the information so that others may examine the evidence and make up their own minds. However, some of the connections between pub names and the locations of these pubs have been difficult to determine and errors may have occurred (for which I apologise).

Introduction

The first and most obvious question to answer is why write a book on the history of pubs and why confine it to the City of Salisbury? The answer to the first part is simply that Inns, Taverns and Public Houses form an important part of the social fabric of Great Britain and yet their history receives very little attention. To the second part of the question the answer is yet simpler: even in a city as small as Salisbury there is a vast amount of historical data that can be gathered to enlighten us and to handle a larger area would have taken more time than I could afford.

However, these simple answers do not do justice to the subject. Salisbury or New Sarum is a new town as far as British History is concerned but we find that inns were among the first buildings of the city and have throughout its history played an important role. Alongside the inns and taverns, there has always been an associated brewing industry together with malting of barley. Despite this, one finds in most historical accounts that the nobility, the clergy, the large houses and major industries are discussed but never the pubs. They were always there; forming a backdrop to all other historical events but always overlooked.

Another major factor that set me to start the research that has led to this book was the number of pubs in Salisbury that had some claim to be the oldest! It was quite obvious that some of the claimants had no substantial reason for their statements but once one started to examine the possible candidates, the beer became cloudier the closer one looked. I have answered the question in my own mind. I believe the oldest pub in Salisbury that has a continuous history in its current building is the Red Lion Hotel although it has not always been known by this name. Others may still disagree. I will ask the reader to examine the information I have managed to gather and make up their own mind!

Inns, Taverns and Alehouses

Originally, inns were houses that were licensed to sell beer and spirits (and wine). They were also obliged to serve bona fide travellers with food and refreshments at any time of day or night. They also possessed stabling for traveller's horses together with forage to feed the horses. Thus, inns also always had rooms for travellers to stay in. Inns were at the top of the tree as far as houses selling alcoholic beverages were concerned but to counter the privileges they possessed over other public houses, they were also the most closely regulated.

The term tavern was also used with regard to public houses that were licensed to sell spirits and wine. They may have had some rooms for travellers and would usually provide some food, But generally, they provided for local trade. In Salisbury, it appears to be rare for houses to be labelled as taverns. Over the years, the legal distinction between inns and taverns became less until both simply became fully licensed public houses. It should also be noted that in modern times, public houses that offered accommodation could be subject to additional hotel legislation

Besides the inns and taverns, there were numbers of alehouses. These were, generally, smaller establishments which were not licensed to sell wine or spirits. Alehouses often brewed their own beer but were little more than private houses that sold beer. As a reaction to the large-scale drinking of gin in the 18th and early 19th C., the Beer Act of 1830 introduced a lower tier of drinking establishment. Anybody could obtain permission to open a beerhouse by paying two guineas. But, essentially, a beerhouse was similar to the earlier alehouse apart from the certification. During the 19th C., the number of beerhouses expanded significantly and so, the Wine and Beerhouse Act of 1869 brought beerhouses under the same, strict licensing laws as inns and taverns, the significant difference being that beerhouses were not allowed to sell wines and spirits. However, it should be understood that for many periods, alehouses were not regulated under any licensing laws and, thus, do not appear in the magistrate's records of licensed premises. The result is an erratic record for these houses and also the sudden appearance of a house in the licensing records when there is no evidence that the house existed before.

After the 1869 Act, the number of Beerhouses gradually reduced with some closing as the owners did not wish to submit to the stricter regulations, while others applied for full public house licenses. The Duke of York in York Road was the last pub in Salisbury to hold a beer-only license until it gained a full license in 1951.

It must also be said that in recent years, the link between the a public house being described as an inn, tavern, bar or beerhouse and the function of the house has almost disappeared. I think that the landlord of a modern inn would not be amused by a traveller knocking on his door in the early hours of the morning and demanding food and accommodation!

Coaching Inns

There is a common fallacy that all very old (and wooden beamed) inns were coaching inns. In fact, a low fraction of inns actually providing facilities for coaches. This was partly due to the need to provide stabling for a large number of horses to allow the changing of teams of coach horses. In addition, a coach with four horses was a quite unwieldy vehicle and could not be turned around in a small yard. And in many towns and cities such as Salisbury, the streets were quite narrow and, if a coach changed its horses in the street, no other wagons would have been able to pass. In Salisbury, there were comparatively few inns that were regular stops for coaches. Most commonly, these premises had two coach entrances in order that a coach did not have to turn around in a small space. Thus, the most obvious coaching inns were the Black Horse (Winchester Street), Chough (Blue Boar Row), Three Swans (Winchester Street) and the Red Lion (Milford Street). Others had a separate entrance to the rear of the inn onto the road on the other side of the chequer from the front of the inn. Examples of these are the Antelope (Catherine Street) and the White Hart (St John Street). There were a few other inns where coaches stopped and passengers were taken on in the road outside the inn but these were few.

Licencing and Licenced Hours

It is largely a myth that restricted licensing hours were introduced into this country by the Defence of the Realm Act of 1914. This introduced a common system of restricted hours throughout the country but many towns and cities, including Salisbury, imposed restrictions on the opening hours of inns, alehouses and public houses many years before DORA.

As early as 1649, Eliza Heale at the Antelope Inn was convicted of allowing tippling to take place in her house. At that time, it appears that tippling referred to allowing drinks to be sold and consumed during the hours of church services on a Sunday.

In January 1803, the Mayor of Salisbury decided it was necessary to preserve decorum during church services in the City. He directed the High Constables to visit all the keepers of inns and public houses, requesting that they would make a point of not drawing any liquor, and of not giving admittance to any guests (except to strangers who may be travelling) during the hours of morning and afternoon service on Sundays.

Several occasions of breaking these rules are given below:

Mar 19 1821. 'William Sworn and Thomas Harding, two of the Sub-constables of this city appeared and made complaint against James Hibberd, Landlord of the Pelican Alehouse, for suffering Tippling therein, whereupon it is ordered that the said James Hibberd be summoned to answer the said complaint on Monday next, and also that Thomas Cooper and Thomas Conduit be summoned to answer for the complaint of Tippling alleged against them respectively'

Mar 26 1821. 'At this meeting James Hibberd, keeper of the Pelican alehouse in this City. appeared to answer the complaint of William Sworn one of the Sub-constables thereof for suffering Tippling in his said Alehouse whereupon after hearing the said William Sworn, Thomas Harding and John Harford, and the said James Hibberd thereon, the said Janes Hibberd is convicted of allowing Tippling in his house and hath forfeit the sum of 10/-'.

Dec 6 1824. Ordered that all Public Houses within this City be closed at Eleven o'clock at Night and that Notice to that effect be given to the different publicans.

Mar 15 1825. 'The Sub-constables having reported that on visiting the Mitre and the Ox Public Houses on Saturday last they found the same open after 12 at Night and that on the following day during Divine Service they found persons drinking and tippling in the Rose and Crown and Catherine Wheel Public Houses. It is ordered that the respective keepers thereof be Summoned to appear on Monday next. – Subsequently cautioned against repetition of the offence'.

May 24 1830. 'Ordered that the several Inns and Ale-Houses be Closed on Sunday in the Morning from ten till half past twelve o'clock and in the afternoon from two till four o'clock'.

In 1834, the Justices of Salisbury used the Beerhouse Act entitled "An Act to Amend an Act passed in the first year of this present Majesty, to permit the general Sale of Beer and Cider by Retail in England" to limit the opening hours of all houses selling Ale, Beer and Cider [6]. The limits were fairly generous in that from September to March pubs could open from 6:00 in the morning until 9:00 at night while from March to September they could open from 5:00am until 10:00pm. However, none were allowed to open before 1:00pm on Sundays, Good Friday, Christmas Day and any other day specified by the Justices.

Sep 6 1848. George Ings for opening his house, the Globe in Gigant Street, for the sale of beer before half past twelve on Sunday. To pay the expenses 3/-

Inns of Salisbury

The starting point for the research that has led to this current volume was the discovery in the Salisbury Reference Library of an unpublished manuscript entitled the Inns of Salisbury by Roland Graham Gordon. Mr Gordon had obviously searched through old copies of the Salisbury Journal and several other sources and had compiled a fairly comprehensive gazetteer of the pubs and inns in Salisbury. The document in the Reference Library in Salisbury is a photocopy of the original which is held in the Wiltshire and Swindon History Centre in Chippenham.

I used this document as my starting point for research and have added to it (and corrected in some cases) as I gradually found new sources of information.

The Old Inns of Salisbury

Between July 1886 and September 1894, a series of letters to the Editor of the Salisbury Journal were written by W. A. Wheeler and were printed in the newspaper, These articles are of some value to local historians as Mr Wheeler was able to talk to the older inhabitants of the city and thus extend our first-hand knowledge of the inns of Salisbury back into the early 1800s. These letters help to clarify, the position of many inns and the changes in names of inns. However, more recent research by the current author has shown that not all of Mr Wheeler's facts are correct and, thus, they need to be read with care.

The only W A Wheeler that I have been able to find in the 1881 Census was a William A Wheeler who was a Printer's Overseer living at the Cricket Field, Britford with his wife and two children. It seems feasible that he was the author of the articles, as he would have had the opportunity to arrange with the Editor to obtain space for the long letters!

The original letters appeared in the Journal on July 24 1886, July 31 1886, August 21 1886, December 24 1886, March 26 1887, July 23 1887 and August 20 1887 with a further letter on September 29 1894.

I have added the text of these letters as Appendix 2 of this volume. I have endeavoured to transcribe the letters accurately but apologise for any errors that have occurred.

Names of Pubs

Among the names of Salisbury pubs, are many that are nationally common such as the Rose and Crown, the King's Head and the Royal Oak. There are also some from the early days of New Sarum that have been transcribed from ancient manuscripts with greater or lesser accuracy such as Pynnok's inn, the Legge, and Tarent's Inn. There are others that although not common throughout the country are not unknown such as the Carpenter's Arms, the Maidenhead, and the India Arms. There are others that are distinctly unusual and possibly unique to Salisbury. It is not known how the Queen's and Plasterer's Arms acquired its unusual sign. Similarly, it is not known why the Archangel and the Crystal Fountain acquired their names. And this is not counting the modern tendency to invent unusual names such as the Slug and Lettuce and the Slurping Toad.

Some pubs have unusual names that do have a known origin. It is said that Noah's Ark gained its name from the first landlord being Noah Hayter. It may be obvious to many Salisbury folk that the two Radnor's Arms were a reference to a local peer and landowner, Lord Radnor. The Pheasant's earlier name of the Crispin Inn can be explained as St Crispin was the patron saint of shoemakers and the hall of that trade guild was adjacent to (if not within) the inn.

It is quite clear that the Royal George is named after the well-known naval vessel, but perhaps not so clear is why the landlord choose that name for his pub. Perhaps he had been a naval man in earlier days.

A full list of pub names is given in the cross-reference toward the end of this book together with the premises' later name if that is known.

The Breweries of Salisbury

In the earliest days of New Sarum, the inns and alehouses would brew their own ales. Brewing would take place in the spring and autumn as it would be too cold in the winter and too hot in the summer to achieve good quality ales. Consequently, the quantities brewed and stored in pubs was much greater than we see nowadays. This is exemplified by the Anchor & Hope in Winchester Street when it was put up for sale in December, 1789. Its stock consisted of 60 Hogshead of strong beer – an enormous quantity when it is realised that a hogshead contained 54 gallons (245.5 litres). In addition, the pub also had several large casks containing between 3 and 8 Hogsheads.

Although some inns probably supplied ales to their smaller neighbours and there were probably small, independent brewers, the first record we have of a brewery in Salisbury was the Communal Brewhouse project of 1623. A puritan group led by John Ivie decided to undertake a number of projects aimed at reducing poverty in the City. They built a brewery (in Rollestone Street) with the aim of supplying ale to inns and alehouses at a lower cost than other suppliers. They also intended to use the profits of the brewery to assist the poor. The brewery was apparently efficient and brewed large quantities of ale. But the inns and alehouses that brewed their own ale were reluctant to pay for alcohol from another supplier and the independent brewers also restricted sales from the Communal Brewhouse.

Thus, the brewery never made a profit and failed to repay the loans that funded its construction. This was despite a summons from the Council to attend a meeting in 1625 'to be treated touching their taking some of their beer of the communal brewhouse'. One benefit of this to the modern researcher is that a list was made of landlords who attended the meeting and which premises they represented. Nothing more is heard about the communal brewhouse.

Other Salisbury breweries that are known are:

Castle Street Brewery. This brewery was in business from 1851 when it was operated by George Pain & Son. By 1875 this was Pain, Lewer & Co and then Pain, Heath & Waters in 1880. Shortly after it became Herbert Mew & Co until this company moved to the Milford Street Brewery. It is not clear if the brewery continued beyond 1886 but by 1928 it was the Castle Auction Mart. In about 1968, the brewery buildings, including the prominent towers that flanked the entrance, were demolished to make way for a supermarket.

Endless Street Brewery. This brewery was started by Henry Macklin in 1809 to brew beer for his own alehouse known as Macklin's Tap. For a number of years, the brewery and tap continued under a number of owners: William Crumley (1820s), Thomas Chamberlain (c. 1829), Thomas Wolferstan (early 1830s), George Bridger (late 1830s and 1840s) until William Fawcett took control in about 1855. In 1898, the company was incorporated as W Fawcett & Sons. In June, 1914, the brewery was purchased by the Lamb Brewery of Frome together with the six pubs owned by Fawcetts and the brewery closed down although the associated pub continued (see Salisbury Arms).

Fisherton Street Brewery. The Fisherton Street Brewery appears to have commenced brewing sometime between 1861 and 1871. It probably retailed beer as well as brewing it and probably only brewed for its own consumption. Interestingly, in 1891, George Strong is noted as being a Steam Engine Maker & fitter as well as being the landlord of the Fisherton Brewery Inn. By 1911, Thomas Garland is described as being the Brewery Manager and a Traveller. This may imply that beer from the brewery was sold to other establishments. Before 1932, the pub & brewery were purchased by H & G Simonds of Reading and brewing ceased.

Gibbs Mew, Anchor Brewery, Gigant Street – Bridger Gibbs moved to Salisbury some time before 1851 having been born in Haslemere, Surrey in 1827. In the 1851 census, he is shown as being a Brewer's Clerk and living in Bridge Street, Salisbury. He was, presumably, working at the King's Head Brewery. He became the landlord of the Bell & Crown (the Cloisters) in 1855 and it is believed that he brewed at that pub. He moved to the Anchor Brewery in Gigant Street in 1858. Gibbs Mew & Co. Ltd was registered in 1898 to acquire Bridger Gibbs & Son and

Herbert Mew & Co (qv). Warehousing moved to a new site on Netherhampton Road in Salisbury but brewing remained in Gigant Street. In 1997, brewing of beer ceased. The Gibbs Mew estate was mostly sold to Enterprise Inns in 1998.

Gigant Street Brewery. This building appears to have been erected in about 1840 and was almost certainly a brewery and alehouse from the outset. It is not known for how long brewing was continued on the premises. In 1861, the census records a brewer living on the premises as well as the landlady of the Gigant Street Brewery Tap. But from the 1871 census onwards, the head of the household was referred to as a publican or innkeeper and there is no mention of a brewer. Despite this, the pub retained the name of the Gigant Street Brewery Tap until well after the pub was taken over by Eldridge Pope of Dorchester (before 1932).

Hopback Brewery, Wyndham Arms, Estcourt Road. John Gilbert started the Hopback Brewery in the cellar of the Wyndham Arms in 1987. Such was the success of the brewery that in 1993, new premises were found on a trading estate in Downton. Brewing ceased completely at the Wyndham Arms in 1995.

King's Head Brewery, Bridge Street. The King's Head inn in Bridge Street was often named as the King's Head Brewery & Inn. Certainly in 1841, the landlord was shown in the Census as a brewer & innkeeper and in 1861, there was a brewer alongside the innkeeper. In 1867, the brewery side of the business was known as Trubridge & Attwater and by 1880 it was Hicks & Co. Brewing ceased when the inn was demolished in the early 1890s. Brewing did not recommence when the County Hotel was opened on the site in 1895.

Lovibond's Brewery, St Anns Street. This brewery was started by John Lovibond in 1869 as an addition to Lovibond's brewery in Greenwich. The estate of the Salisbury branch of Lovibonds was sold to Courage Barclay & Simonds in 1962 and the brewery closed. Another member of the Lovibond brewing dynasty, Joseph Lovibond, invented the tintometer to assess the quality of beer by its colour. The company formed to market this device still exists in the Salisbury area as Tintometer Ltd.

Milford Street Brewery A brewery has existed on this site for a very long period. It lies behind the pub once known as the Milford Arms but more recently the White Rooms. The remaining buildings date back to the 15th C. but the earliest brewer known on the site was Maton & Co. in 1838 when Mr Maton proposed to open a bar called Maton's Tap. It was known as Maton's Tap until at least 1871. Herbert Mew moved from the Castle Street Brewery to Milford Street when the premises were known as the Malt & Hop Brewery as was the bar. Herbert Mew merged with Bridger Gibbs in 1898 to form Gibbs Mew (qv). The Milford Street Brewery seems to have closed at this time.

Old George Steam Brewery, Rollestone Street. The Old George was a pub from at least the 17th C. and undoubtedly brewed beer for its own use. In 1850, John Folliott took over the pub and its brewing concern. Alongside the Old George was the Brewery Tap, also owned by John Folliott which was the tap of the brewery. The brewery became John Folliott & Sons in about 1898. The company was acquired by Ushers of Trowbridge in 1919 together with its estate of 23 pubs. The site of the brewery and the Old George was redeveloped in 1989 but the buildings of the Brewery Tap and the Old George can still be seen.

Three Crowns Brewery, West Harnham. Samuel Dear certainly brewed beer at the Three Crowns on the Town Path in the last years of the 19th C. It is not known if this was solely to supply that pub or whether he supplied other pubs in the area.

Samuel Whitchurch & Co, Milford Street. Samuel Whitchurch brewed in Milford Street from at least 1783 until his death in 1835. This was probably at the Milford Street Brewery before that site was taken over by Maton & Co. but this has not been proven. Samuel Whitchurch either owned or leased many pubs in Salisbury but this estate was broken up on his death.

Woolfryes, Culver Street. William Woolfryes was brewing in Culver Street from at least 1795 until the 1820s. The brewery seems to have closed by the time of the 1841 census.

Anchor Inn and Anchor Brewery

The Inventory of Inns, Alehouses and Public Houses

Note that where an address is shown as 'nk' this is an abbreviation for 'not known' and indicates that the location of the public house has not been identified. The names Rowe, Wheeler, Gordon, Haskins & Hoare in the text are shorthand references to documents listed in the Bibliography as is the abbreviation 'RCHM'.

1 Abbey, nk

There are two references to Le Abbey in 1455; one stating it is Carternstrete (Catherine Street) and the other that it is in Culverstrete (Culver Street). This may be an error in transcription of these ancient records. Hoare states that it was on the corner of Endless Street and Chipper Lane. Suffice it to say that there was an inn of this name in Salisbury in the mid-15th C.

2 Albert, nk

So far, there is only a single reference to this public house in 1858 [22] It appears that it is somewhere between the Rising Sun in Castle Street and Stratford-sub-Castle. Suffice it to say that the landlady, Mrs Ridout, had two knives stolen but the evidence was insufficient to convict the two alleged offenders.

3 Anchor, Culver Street

Little is known of this alehouse apart from the fact that it is mentioned in City records as early as 1759. The Anchor is listed as one of the houses selling ale without a licence and the Town Clerk announces that the 'Mayor & Justices of the City will suppress all such Houses and prosecute any Brewer selling Ale & Beer without being duly licensed thereto". In 1778 the ownership of the alehouse was transferred from Joseph Hinxman to William Hibberd and the pub was then advertised as being to let and described as 'a good house with a large garden and back side'. Despite that, there is no further mention of the pub after 1779.

4 Anchor Inn, 38 Gigant Street.

This building has been described as being of 16th C. origin but rebuilt at later dates in brick [23]. Despite that, it does not appear in the licensing records until 1867 when in the ownership of Bridger Gibbs, the co-founder, with Herbert Mew, of the Gibbs Mew brewery. However, Bridger Gibbs moved to the Anchor Brewery from the Bell & Crown in Catherine Street at the beginning of 1859. It was probable that the brewery existed before Bridger Gibbs acquired it but there is no mention of a pub in that area apart from the Globe which was a quite separate house. Later in 1859, he applied for a license for the premises but this was refused on the grounds that there were sufficient public houses in the city [24]. The evidence on the numbers of pubs came from Superintendent Barber of the Salisbury Police. He stated that there were more public-houses in Salisbury in proportion to the number of inhabitants than in any other town or city in England,

and the annual returns of crime showed that there was more drunkenness than in any other city of the same size in the country. But the Editor of the *Salisbury and Winchester Journal* added a note to the end of the report of the court case in which he stated it would have been much more satisfactory to the public if this officer, in making the grave charge that Salisbury is the most drunken place for its size in this country, had quoted his authority for so sweeping an assertion!

Bridger Gibbs obtained a spirit licence at the annual licensing meeting in September, 1860. This suggests that the house was functioning as a alehouse before that date and it may well have been a brewery tap selling only beer before Bridger Gibbs acquired it. By any account, the 1861 Census shows that he is employing a barmaid, and the house always appears in the licensing records from 1861 onwards.

The pub remained the brewery tap of Gibbs Mew until that brewery closed in 1998. It was refurbished in 1987 while retaining the stone floor in the public end of the bar. It was called the Anchor Brewery Tap at the beginning of the 20th C. and later became the Anchor Tap before becoming the Anchor Inn. The pub soldiered on for a while until the Anchor brewery was demolished in 2001. It is said that he façade of the pub was preserved and may still be seen forming the front of the new residential properties, although it takes a little imagination to see this.

5 Anchor & Hope Inn, 59 & 61 Winchester Street

This fine timbered building is one of the older inns in Salisbury with the earliest record so far discovered dating back to 1620 when it was known as the Talbot. RCHM states that the building dates from the 16th C. although much of what can be seen dates from the 19th C. With its position on one of the major roads leading out of the City, it is likely that the site has been an inn since the earliest days of Salisbury although it is said that it started out as an inn, at a later date it became an alms house but then was further converted to be an inn and a cottage. It was known as the Talbot until 1760 when its name was changed to the Angel. In December 1805, it became the Lord Collingwood Arms in honour of Admiral Lord Collingwood who was Nelson's second-in-command at Trafalgar and commanded the fleet to victory after Nelson was mortally wounded [4]. By 1819, the name had been changed once more to the Anchor & Hope.

The pub has had its livelier moments as noted in the *Salisbury and Winchester Journal* of Sep 19 1781 – 'We hear that the Free and Easy Convivialists of this city intend to commence their social Winter meetings at the Angel Inn, in Winchester Street, next Saturday evening' [25]. But the trade cannot have been too brisk as in 1794, James Street, the landlord was made bankrupt [26] and the contents of the pub sold [27]. When the pub was sold again in 1805, the advertisement stated that it was that 'well-known old-established Public House called the Angel, situate in Winchester Street, together with a tenement adjoining; the Public House comprising two parlours, tap-room, two cellars, pantries, four bed-rooms, stabling for 12 horses, and a garden' [28].

In 1816, James White, the landlord, was convicted of selling beer and spirituous liquors by retail without a licence [29]. Since he had had his licence as a public house renewed in September of that year, this seems somewhat strange but may well be concerned with selling alcoholic beverages off the premises.

Later, in 1829, the pub was advertised as being available to let and it was stated that the new tenant would have the privilege of brewing. This indicated that the pub was not linked to any brewery at this date.

In 1898, William Hall became the landlord. He had been a Sergeant-Major in the Royal Artillery, based in Dorchester. In that year, he sued Major C B Watkins, the commanding officer of the 7th Field Battery, for £200 damages for alleged slander by implying he was dishonest while running the artillery canteen. The evidence showed that Major Watkins had implied that virtually all the past stewards of the canteen were dishonest and several past stewards gave evidence that the financial arrangements for the canteen were unsatisfactory as they did not allow for breakages, spillage and leakage from casks. Hence, by the Major's reckoning, all of the stewards did not collect sufficient funds and hence must be dishonest. The court found for William Hall but only awarded him £5 damages! [30]

Between 1932 and 1962 (and almost certainly earlier), the Anchor and Hope was a Lovibond's house before becoming a Courage pub. In 1972, Courage's public house estate was merged with that of Grand Metropolitan to form Inntrepreneur Estates. A part of this company became the Unique Pub Company which was taken over by Enterprise Inns. The Anchor and Hope remains an Enterprise Inn. It was closed for a short time in 2013 but was reopened following refurbishment.

6 Angel Hotel, 66 Fisherton Street

This was originally a small public house but was developed during the 19th C. into a substantial hotel although it is still referred to as the Angel Inn in 1872. It appears to have closed sometime during the First World War but was re-opened as a YMCA hostel in 1918. It closed again in 1935 and was purchased the next year by British Gaumont cinemas. It was demolished together with some adjoining buildings to allow the building of the Gaumont picture house which opened in 1937. This building survives as the City Hall.

Licensing records show it to have been in existence as a public house as early as 1741 and an entry in Hoare suggests it was in existence somewhat earlier than this when Mrs Cusse paid quit rent to the Cathedral of £1-8s (£1.40). In 1771, it was sold by Mr Street, the stock including '1350 gallons of exceeding good strong ale' [31]. When sold again in 1775, it was described as 'a well situated and good accustomed house; consisting of two parlours, a kitchen, bar, back-kitchen, a large new-built club room and 6 chambers; stabling for 40 horses, very good conveniences for brewing, good cellars & other offices; with a skittle alley, and a large garden behind the same' [32].

In 1773, a wrestling match is advertised to be held at the Angel, the prize being a silver bowl valued at 2 guineas [33].

The pub was still in the ownership of the Dean and Chapter of Salisbury Cathedral in 1850 but it is not known when they relinquished the premises [34].

In 1891, the Angel was put up for sale once more [35]. But this time, it is described as having a capital front bar with suitable commercial and family public and private rooms, a capital stock room, a billiard room, a spacious dining room to hold 100 guests and a suite of 28 well-lighted bedrooms approached by an easy staircase from wide and airy corridors. This is quite a change from 1775 and emphasises that the house was substantially rebuilt in about 1875 when it became known as the Angel Hotel.

It is not totally clear if the Victorian hotel was built on the same site as the earlier pub but it is unlikely that the sites are different.

7 Angel Inn, 42 & 44 High Street
This inn was on the west side of High Street to the south of Pynnok's Inn (qv). This puts it roughly where the Crown Hotel was in more recent times (the site most recently a discount store). However, it is definitely not the same house as the Crown Hotel as this inn was in existence before the Angel closed. In addition, a lease of 1815 shows that the Crown Hotel was to the south of the Angel and that the Angel ran back to the River Avon [36]. It was one of the earliest inns in Salisbury being first recorded in 1417 as 'Tarente's Inn in Ministrestret which is called hyestret'. However, Roger Tarent appears to have been in residence in 1410 and presumably he ran it as an inn! Bishop Beauchamp's Liber Niger of 1455 shows rent of assize collected for 'le Angel'. It continues as the Angel until well into the 18th C. However, in 1761 the landlord, William Long, was made bankrupt [37] and the house was let to a builder, Edward Whatmore, as a dwelling and timber yard [38].

The inn was one of the coaching inns in Salisbury with the Bath stagecoach starting from here in 1751 in opposition to that starting from the Oxford Arms in Catherine Street [39]. In 1752, the Salisbury Flying Stage Coach was advertised as travelling from the Angel Inn in Salisbury three times a week to the Bell Savage, Ludgate Hill [40]. This coach was operated by William Long & Thomas Massey with a note that the service ran if God Permitted. As a consequence of the stagecoach services, the Post Office moved to the Angel from the White Hart in 1756.

But inns of this time were not only suppliers of accommodation, food and drink. They were also the centre of social life and travelling shows set up in the inns for the entertainment of the public [41]: 'John Adams is just arrived from London & has brought with him, & to be seen at the long Room at the Angel in High Street, a new-invented Machine, which demonstrates all the surprizing Experiments of the Activity & Force of Electricity, both in Attraction & Repulsion etc. Producing Light and actual Fire from various Substances, especially human bodies. The Person electrified exits Fire from any part of his Body by the Approach of another; fires Spirits of Wine at a 100 Yards Distance, & causes an instantaneous sensation on a Number of Persons at once; it also darts Fire round the Room, and makes a Cock spew Fire round the Room. It causes a 1000 Figures to dance between two Pewter Plates at the Word of Command, & stop when ordered; & cures the Rhumatism, Augue, Gout, Tooth-Ach & Dullness of Hearing instantly. Attendance will be given from 10 in the Morning till 10 at Night. He will carry the Machine to any Gentlemen's House, on giving two hours' notice. Price 6d each Person.'

As stated above, William Long was made bankrupt in 1761 although the inn was kept open for at least a further year. But by 1766 we find Edward Whatmore advertising various sorts of Boards, Planks, Spokes, Laths, Fillies for Waggon Wheels and rough Timber for sale at his house 'being lately the Angel Inn'. He apparently let the spare rooms in the building but it never regained its status as an inn

8 Antelope Inn, 35 & 37 Catherine Street.

This was one of the principal inns of the City in the late 18th and early 19 C. It was on the east side of Catherine Street and lay either side of the walkway from that street into what is now the Brown Street car park. This walkway is still known as Antelope Passage and the Chequer bounded by Catherine Street, Ivy Street, Brown Street and Milford Street is known as Antelope Chequer. It is probable that the building immediately south of Antelope Passage is a remnant of the inn.

The first mention of the inn comes from it being the first of the city inns to entertain a royal guest when the Prince of Brunswick, nephew of Queen Ann of Denmark, stayed overnight on 28 Jan 1610. In 1625, Mrs S Lawrence attended the meeting arranged by the Council to discuss taking beer from the Communal Brewhouse. During the Civil War, the landlady, Eliza Heal, was convicted of keeping a tippling house (that is, allowing drinking during the hours of Church Services).

In 1664, the landlord, Francis Manninge, issued a farthing token which showed an antelope on one side and stated the inn was in 'Kathren Street, Sarum' [42]. These tokens were given in lieu of small change to customers with the advantage that they could only be redeemed at the named inn.

During the time when the Antelope was at the peak of its fame, the Best family ran the inn for over 50 years. Robert Best was the landlord from at least 1755 until his death in 1768 when his widow, Martha Best, took over. She ran the inn until she died in 1798 [43] when her daughter, also Martha Best, took over until early in 1805 when she died [44]. The inn was available to let in early 1806 and Jonathan Johnson applied for the license [4]. This application was refused and Samuel Jones, from Weymouth, applied for the license and this application was approved [45]. But in July, 1806, he places a notice in the *Salisbury and Winchester Journal* where he complains that there have been rumours that he is not really interested in the Antelope. He claims that as a consequence, many members of the royalty and nobility who he had known through his father-in-law in Weymouth had failed to use his premises when travelling through Salisbury [46].

By 1810 the inn sported a life-size white antelope on the roof of each of its two wings rivalling the Hart on the roof of the White Hart. Unusually, the landlord of that year, Samuel Jones, moved to the White Hart and the White Hart's landlord, Jonathon Johnson, reciprocated by moving to the Antelope.

In about 1810, the inn was renamed the Antelope Inn and Prince Regent's Hotel. This name is said to have derived from the Prince Regent, the future George IV, who often stopped at the Antelope to change horses and take refreshment on his way to and from Weymouth. The Prince Regent apparently conferred the second name on the inn himself and it was certainly known by this name before 1817.

In the meantime, the following advertisement appeared in the *Journal*: 'George Bidder, the Devonshire boy, so celebrated for mental calculation, is still in this city. As a proof of his wonderful prowess, he within the last few days gave immediate answers to the following questions: - If there are 9999 grains of corn in a half pint, how many are there in 99 sacks? Answer 505, 898,189. ... This extraordinary boy now sees company at the Antelope Inn, and we understand he will depart from hence on Wednesday next for Southampton [47].'

George Mill was the last landlord from 1836 until 1840. He advertises it as being for sale in September, 1839 [48], but then withdraws the advert in October stating that the Antelope remains open for business as usual [49]. A sale of the contents of the inn is announced in March 1840 including the horses and ponies used for mail coaches and post-chaises [50]. By December, 1840, the inn is closed but the Antelope Bazaar is advertised offering coaches and carriages for sale from the yard of the Antelope [51]. The premises are again offered for sale in February, 1841, by George Mill who is apparently living in East Harnham [52]. By the end of May, 1841, George Mill is advertising a "Genuine Drug Establishment", he having served an apprenticeship with a Chemist and Druggist in Exeter [53]. A printing office was housed in the north wing of the inn. The closure of the Antelope was too early to be a direct result of the coming of the railways as the first station in Salisbury was not built until 1847, but probably did reflect the decline of the stagecoach in the 19th C

9 Avon Brewery, 75, Castle Street

This well-known pub on the west side of Castle Street is noted for its wonderful, curved glass window. Little is known of its history with it first appearing in the licensing records in 1851. Leases for the site dating from 1814 are stored at the Wiltshire and Swindon History Centre but, of these, the earliest that records the name of the pub is from 1869 [54]. This lease is to Messrs Trubridge and Attwater who were brewers at the King's Head in Salisbury.

By 1877, the pub was owned by Pern, Heath & Waters who had taken over the King's Head Brewery. In turn, the inn was owned by Herbert Mew.by 1886 and Mew & Ellers by 1888. Herbert Mew had taken over the Castle Street Brewery before moving to the Milford Street Brewery in 1886. But in 1898, Mew's brewery had merged with Gibbs to form Gibbs Mew. Thus one would have expected the Avon Brewery to have become a Gibbs Mew house but it clearly became an Eldridge Pope house from 1932 at the latest. This possibly occurred in 1891 when the landlord, Thomas Sheppard, became bankrupt.

The pub had a beer only license until 1877, when the landlord, George Warren, was granted a spirit license [55], his application being aided by the owners of the pub, Pern, Heath & Waters.

An unusual prosecution occurred in 1889 when George Sturgess, who was the landlord at this time, was charged under the Explosives Act with having manufactured fireworks in unlicensed premises [56]. It appears that Sturgess had manufactured fireworks for his own use, as had his father before him, for at least 25 years in total. He claimed he was not aware that he was breaking the law and was very sorry that he had. The fine he was liable to pay under the Explosives Act was £100 but since he had only used the fireworks himself on Bonfire Night and had never sold any, the Magistrates fined him only £1 including costs

10 Baker's Arms, St Ann Street

Probably built in 1847 (if a date carved into a chimney breast in the roof is to be believed) and known as the Albion Inn. It was certainly a pub by 1851 and was almost certainly built as a public house. It gained a spirit licence in 1854 [57] and from that date onwards it appears in the public house licensing records. It was purchased by Lovibond's brewery in 1869. The brewery was in the Friary behind St Ann Street and, naturally, the pub became the brewery tap and was known as the Albion Brewery Tap. It later became the St Ann's Brewery Tap and in the early years of the 20th C. it was known as the St Ann Street Brewery Tap. When Courage, Barclay & Simonds bought Lovibond's brewery in 1962 the name reverted to the Albion Inn. It stayed that way until the Grand Metropolitan/Courage brewery/pub swap when it was sold as a free house becoming the Baker's Arms in 1993. Although it was opened out into a single bar, it retained much of the character of a typical Victorian back street pub. However, in late 2006 it closed as a pub to be opened in 2007 as St Anns House, a small hotel with a private dining room. The publicity for the hotel describes it as 'a magnificently restored Georgian town house' which may contain some poetic licence

11 Bar 44, 44 Fisherton Street

This pub was originally the brewery tap of the Fisherton Brewery which occupied the site from 1870 but most probably from an earlier date as in that year Elizabeth Bath took over the running of the brewery from her late husband [58]. In 1883, the pub and brewery were put up for sale [59]. It was described as 'comprising a Commodious Dwelling House, with two entrances, Public and Private Bars, Smoking Room, Two Cellars, Brewhouse, Yard in which is a Large Builder's Shop (let off), and good Garden, that whole having the unusual depth of 200 feet, with a Frontage of 30 feet to the important thoroughfare of Fisherton'. The brewhouse contained plant that could mash two and a half quarters of malt and there was an offer to give a new tenant lessons in brewing.

In 1908, the pub was again offered for sale [60]. This time it was described as having 'a front bar, a private bar, a smoking room, living room, lean-to greenhouse and kitchen on the ground floor, and a front sitting room and five bedrooms on the first floor, whilst it also possesses useful adjuncts to the business in the way of a two and a half quarter plant brewery and stabling for twenty-one horses'. It was also stated that it was one of the few free houses in Salisbury. On this occasion, the pub failed to meet its asking price, with the highest bid being £1200 which the auctioneer described as being very close to the reserve price. It was most probably sold by private contract shortly after this auction and since it became a Courage house in later years, it could well have been purchased by Lovibonds as, in a roundabout fashion, their pubs eventually ended up in Courage's hands.

Until February 1949, the pub had a beer-only licence and was known as the Fisherton Brewery Inn but at this time it gained a full licence and was renamed the Fisherton Arms. For some time from 1962, it had a separate off-licence. It retained that name as a Courage's house but changed from that ownership to that of the newly independent Usher's Brewery in 1992. In 1997, it was closed for a while being refurbished and re-opened as the Ale and Cider Press. In late 2005, it was renamed yet again to Bar 44. It closed again in 2009 with a notice saying this was due to 'high street competition and government interference'. In mid-2011, the pub was still closed with the windows and door boarded over and has since become a shop

12 Barley Mow, 71 Greencroft Street

The Barley Mow was in Greencroft Street just to the south of Salt Lane and facing on to the Greencroft. The earliest reference to the Barley Mow is 1742 when it applied for, and was refused a licence [61]. However, this application would have been for a full licence and it is presumed it was an alehouse before that time and certainly continued as an alehouse after this date. The licence refusal had a handwritten note on it which stated 'home brewed'. In 1759, the City Clerk, W Swanton, announced that the Mayor & Justices of the City will suppress 'all such Houses and prosecute any Brewer selling Ale & Beer without being duly licensed thereto'. He also stated that 'the houses at present selling Ale without license are the Leopard's Head, Valiant Soldier, Anchor and the New Barley Mow' [62].

Whatever the condition of the licence, the Barley Mow continued in existence albeit it was noted in the licencing records of 1768 that it was not a very reputable house. Samuel Lawes had the licence transferred to him from Thomas Burnett in December 1819 [63] but he was declared bankrupt in 1829, although the reasons for his monetary loss are not described [64]. But in 1821, a stranger stayed the night in the pub but left behind him in his room a purse containing bank notes. Samuel Lawes made detailed enquiries but was unable to find the man. He advertised that he had the purse and offered to return it to the owner if his expenses were paid [65]. It is not known if the purse ever reached its owner. In 1838, the house was advertised to let, and the adjoining malt house was included as part of the premises. The malt house was the single storied building immediately to the north of the pub.

In 1847, the Barley Mow is advertised for sale and is described as the "newly-erected Freehold Inn or Public-House" [66]. The premises included a skittle alley and the malthouse is described as being capable of wetting ten quarters of barley. Since Thomas Andrews was the landlord from 1845 through to 1849, one wonders how extensive the re-build was and whether the inn actually closed during this period. The RCHM describes the construction of the Barley Mow as being from the early 19th C. so it does appear that the building does date from about 1847.

An advertisement for sale of the Barley

Mow in June 1859 describes the house as having a newly fitted up Front Bar, Smoking Room, Sitting Room, Seven Bedrooms, Brewhouse, Cellars, enclosed Skittle Alley and Yard [67]. The 10-quarter malthouse was included in the sale although it is noted that it was occupied by William Fawcett, who at that time owned the Endless Street Brewery.

In the 1860's, the landlord, Albert Noyle, held regular annual Bean Feasts [68]. Between 40 and 70 people attended these events although it is not stated exactly what food constituted a bean feast. The reports in the *Salisbury and Winchester Journal* describing these events describes them as being annual events which does not match with the 5th being held in 1862, the 6th in 1865, the 8th in 1866 and the 12th in 1869. Perhaps the *Journal* reporter attended the feasts and could not recall how many there had been!

By the middle of the 20th C. it was an Usher's house which had a long, thin public bar on the right of the entrance and a small square saloon bar on the left. In 1974, it became a Chef and Brewer house within the Watney Mann Group. In about 1988, the licence transferred to Gibbs Mew and the pub was rebuilt as a single bar. After the demise of Gibbs Mew, the pub continued on until 2004 when it was closed and put up for sale as private housing

13 Belfry, Cathedral Close

The belfry of Salisbury Cathedral was contained in a separate bell tower (a campanile) to the north of the Cathedral on the edge of the churchyard. The outline of its foundations can still be seen during dry summers owing to the thin layer of soil above the remaining stonework. The bell tower was demolished in 1789, partly because, it is said, it was being used as a tavern! Not a conventional pub but an interesting part of the history of drinking in Salisbury.

14 Bell Inn, 70 Exeter Street

The first mention of this inn that has been found was from 1598 when the master, John Cannons, died. In 1625, Thomas Chiffinge, the landlord of the Bell, attended the meeting called by the Council, to discuss taking beer and ale from the Common Brewhouse.

In 1660, the landlord, John Gilbert, issued a farthing token showing a Bell on the obverse [69]. These tokens were often issued by inns owing to a shortage of small coins of the realm – the tokens being redeemable at the named inn for goods and services. The connection of the token to this particular Bell Inn is not certain but seems very probable.

A Lease of 1696 is about a property near the Bell and states 'adjoining to the Inn called the Bell situate or lying and being in the City of New Sarum aforesaid in a certain street or place now called commonly Dragon Street also Drakehall Street' [70].

Between 1718 and 1737, the pub was known as the Coach and Horses and this seems to match the period when Richard Reeves was the landlord [71] [72]. There is also an entry in the licensing records in 1760 for the Coach and Horses in Catherine Street (qv) and this may be another reference to the Bell.

The inn continued in operation throughout the 18th and 19th C. although it changed hands many times. An advertisement in the *Salisbury and*

Winchester Journal of 21 May 1792 announced the sale of 'All the Household Furniture, Stock of Beer, etc. at the Bell Inn, Draghall Street, consisting of bedsteads with cotton and other furniture; feather beds, blankets, and quilts; chests of drawers, tables and chairs; an eight-day clock, kitchen furniture, a brewing copper, almost new, that holds about 140 gallons; several large casks, from 12 hogsheads each down to four; square coolers, large mash tub and about 4500 gallons of strong beer' [73].

In 1812, the sale was advertised of 'A Freehold Estate, "comprising the Bell Inn, situate the corner of St Ann Street, and Exeter Street; roomy premises, containing six chambers on the first story, and lofts over, on the ground story, are two parlours, bar, tap-room, two cellars and offices, large yard, with shed and brew-house, store-cellar, with loft over, in the occupation of Mr Wild [74]. The annual rent was 10 shillings!

In 1862, the pub was for sale again, but the items for sale included 100 Hogsheads of Store Casks. Since a hogshead was equivalent to between 48 and 54 gallons (according to the exact nature of the contents), this meant that this pub could store upwards of 4,800 gallons of beer in its cellar!

In 1886, the bell ringers of Salisbury held their annual dinner at the Bell. As well as singing later in the evening, the ringers 'rendered various selections of music on their hand bells [75]'.

In 1931 and later, the inn was known as the Old Bell and sported a large bell hanging from a wrought iron support on the corner of the street. From this date until 1954, it is shown in the licensing records as being a free house. It was then purchased by Matthews brewery from Gillingham. In 1963 it became a Hall & Woodhouse pub when that brewery merged with Matthews. In 1971, it reverted to private ownership. However, in the 1990s, the opening of the pub became a little erratic. In the summer of 1996, it showed signs of a resurrection as it re-opened as a free house but this did not last long and the Old Bell reverted to being a hotel. By 2005, it had closed permanently as a public house and in early 2006, planning permission was sought to convert the buildings into private dwellings. The wrought iron work that supported the bell that was the pub sign is still present but, unfortunately, the bell itself is missing

15 Bell, Milford

An Indenture of 1849 covers the sale of a piece of meadow land to the north side of the road or highway near Milford Bridge, called the Bell Mead adjoining a Messuage or Tenement theretofore called the Bell Inn. An earlier indenture of 1833 also describes the tenement 'as heretofore called the Bell Inn' [77]. One of 20 Sept 1783 does not mention the Bell Inn at all. However, a notice of sale in 1780 covers the Bell Inn and the Bell Mead [76]

16 Bell, Milford Hill

The sign of this house appears in an engraving published in Hall's Picturesque Monuments entitled 'A Shakespeare scene – Old Houses at the top of Milford Street'. The map produced for Salisbury City Council in 1851 in connection with the construction of the sewerage system shows the Bell to have been on the north-eastern corner of the junction between what is now Milford Hill and Rampart Road.

It was advertised for sale in 1772 when it was a 'good, accustomed Public House' [78]. In 1774, Francis Jones was granted the license of the Bell. Between then and 1781, the pub was advertised as being for sale several times. From this date until 1822 when Martha Berry was granted a license for the Bell, there is no mention of this pub. It is possible that it was known as the King of Prussia during this period as Martha Berry was granted a license for that pub in 1811. However, a connection between the King of Prussia and the Bell cannot be proved

In 1835, the Bell was advertised for sale as part of the estate of Samuel Whitchurch and it was stated that the pub was held under a copy of the Court Roll of the Lord Farmer of the Manor of Milford [79].

James Kite, the landlord of the pub from 1836, was also noted as being a Veterinary Surgeon. As such, he was sued in court, in 1844, for the value of hay supplied to him by John Kitto [80]. Mr Kitto wanted to charge Kite 55 shillings a ton for the hay while Mr Kite claimed the hay delivered was of insufficient quality to warrant that price. There was conflicting evidence during the case and the jury was obviously confused. They returned a verdict in favour of Mr Kite, but after questioning by Mr Kitto's attorney, the foreman of the jury admitted he had made a mistake and the verdict was in favour of Mr Kitto! By that time, the Clerk to the Court had already written down the original verdict and much argument took place as to whether the Sheriff, the chairman of the bench, had the authority to alter the written verdict. It was decided to send the jury out to reconsider their verdict. On the return of the jury, the foreman repeated his original verdict in favour of Mr Kite, causing uproar in the court and the *Salisbury and Winchester Journal* commented that it was doubtful if the members of the jury understood one another. In the end, it was decided the verdict was in favour of Mr Kite, as the jury believed the hay was not worth the original sum of money. Naturally, Mr Kitto announced he was going to appeal against the verdict but, unfortunately, the result of the appeal is not recorded.

Later in 1844, John Hobbs announces that he has moved from the Bell, Exeter Street to the Bell in Milford Street [81]. This is just the sort of change that appears to have been made solely to confuse future local historians!

At the annual Brewster Session of September, 1854, no application was made to renew the licence of the Bell and there was no further mention of the house

17 Bird in Hand, 18 North Street

The Bird in Hand appears to have opened in 1865 during the development of Fisherton Anger following the arrival of the railway in Salisbury (North Street was referred to as New Road, Fisherton in 1865). An advertisement in February 1865 described the pub as "recently erected" and situated in Arthur Street, Fisherton [82]. George Cribb appears to have been installed as a temporary licensee and he was still in occupation at the time of an auction later in 1865 [83]. Joseph Best becomes the landlord after the auction. Confusingly, when the licence was transferred in 1869, the pub is said to be in North Street, Dent's Nursery, Fisherton [84].

In 1875, an application was made for a spirit license for the Bird in Hand [85]. The Magistrates were told that the house had

Bird in Hand, North Street

been built for 20 years and had had a beer license for ten years. While the time that the license had been held agrees with the licensing records, the age of the building does not seem to match the statement that it was newly erected in 1865! However, the licensee, Joseph Daniel Powell, had previously run the Globe in Gigant Street for three years without any issues and had been in the Salisbury Police Force and before that in the Police Department of the South West Railway. He also had many letters from neighbours supporting his application. Thus, the spirit license was grant to Mr Powell.

By 1878, the landlord was James Elliott who was described as being a horse breaker. As well as advertising his presence in the Bird in Hand, he also stated that he would still break horses for riding and also for use in harness [86]. Mr Elliott did not stay in the pub for very long and David Marjoram took over the premises in April, 1879. However, two years later he was convicted for having his pub open for selling drinks during closing hours on a Sunday morning [87]. A police constable visited the pub after complaints against the landlord and found him leaving the smoking room with two glasses on a tray. Four men with beer were found in the pub. Mr Marjoram was fined £5 but as it was his first offence, the Magistrates did not endorse his license with the offence which could have led to him losing his license at the next annual licensing session.

A fire broke out in the pub in 1893 [88]. It appears that there was a fault in a chimney in the building which resulted in a chest of drawers becoming heated and catching fire. The fire brigade managed to confine the fire to the room in which it started with no further damage done to the premises.

In 1904 a boy of 13 was convicted for stealing money from the pub {89}. The landlady was working in the bar but went to the kitchen for a short time. On returning to the bar, she found the boy behind the counter. The boy asked for a halfpennyworth of cigarettes which Mrs Salter refused to give him. The boy rushed out of the pub and then Mrs Salter found that the till was open and six shillings was missing. She rushed out of the pub and asked a cabman to go after the boy and bring him back to the pub. This the cabman succeeded in doing and the boy produced the money from his pocket. A police constable took charge of the boy. The boy said he would not do such a thing again if he was let off but his father said he had had a lot of trouble with the boy lately and this was due to the bad company he kept (a story that would be heard many times right up until today!). In Court the boy was found guilty but the Magistrates decided to be lenient and sentenced him to six strokes with a birch rod!

From at least 1932, the pub was owned by Eldridge-Pope of Dorchester and stayed in that ownership until at least 1975. It continued until 2006 as a small, local public house although without the skittle alley that was at one time in regular use. In 2007 it closed and was converted to housing

18 Bird in Hand, Trinity Street

This public house was on the corner of Trinity Street and Love Lane and was known by many names over the years. It was owned by the Tailor's Company and seems to have been first licensed between 1651 and 1685 as the Pot and Limbeck (a limbeck or alembic was a type of still used for distilling wine and other liquors). It was certainly in existence in 1691 when Thomas Clarke was granted a lease [90]: 'At this assembly it is voted that Thomas Clarke shall have a lease of the Pott & Lymbeck, in Love Lane, for the term of 31 years, to commence after the end of a former lease, for £35 fine by vote of the corporation.'

It may have been closed for a while as in 1715, Richard Marsh was granted a lease of a tenement formerly called the Pot & Limbeck, provided the previous lease-holder, Thomas Clarke, agreed to surrender his lease [91]. It then became the Flower De Luce (sometimes recorded as the Fleur de Luce) in 1763 when it was advertised for sale with a shop, brewhouse, stables & garden and retained that name until at least 1794.

In 1794, the landlord, William Sworn, was in trouble with the City Magistrates for assaulting two spinsters, Elizabeth Hibberd and Elizabeth Dourse, in his house. He was reprimanded by the Magistrates for his impertinent manner and his licence was not renewed at the annual licensing session in September 1794 [3]. In his defence, the presence of two spinsters in a pub on the corner of Love Lane might be considered proof of the reputation of that street!

By 1802 it was the Talbot before becoming the Bird in Hand in 1822. In 1852, although the pub was still licensed to Richard Sutton, the whole of the brewing plant and store casks were offered for sale

[92]. By 1854, John Clark purchased a malt house that was formerly the Bird in Hand but also late the Fleur-de-Lis and late the Pot and Limbeck [93].

19 Bishop Blaze, Milford Street

This pub name is normally spelled 'Bishop Blaise' and the name derives from that of a martyr who was reputed to have been killed by having his flesh torn with iron combs. Consequently, he became the patron saint of woolcombers and hence the connection with the wool trade in Salisbury. It was licenced from 1786 but may well have been an alehouse before that time, possibly under a different name. The landlord in 1793, Thomas Sellwood, was bound over to keep the peace towards his wife and others [3]. But later in that year, Sellwood dies and the furnishings of the pub are put up for sale. [94]

In August, 1794, Lawrence Flemington was granted the transfer of the licence of the Bishop Blaze to the Duke of York, Milford Street (qv) on the condition that the Bishop Blaze was discontinued as a public house

20 Bishop's Palace, Cathedral Close

During the Commonwealth, the Cathedral Close came under the control of the civil Parliamentary Trustees. One of their first acts was to sell the Bishop's Palace to William and Joseph Barter in 1648 for a sum of £880 2s. Parts of the Palace were demolished and the remainder became an inn and some small tenements. At the Restoration in 1660, the Palace returned to the control of the Bishop and rebuilding commenced. In 1667, Dr Seth Ward, Bishop of Exeter, was appointed to the see of Salisbury. The following is taken from an account of his reception, as given by Dr Pope [95]:

'His next care was to repair, I might almost say rebuild, his palace, which was much ruined; the hall being pulled down, and the greatest part of the house converted to an inn, having a passage opened through the Close Wall, to give entrance to the market people, and other travellers, who came through Harnham, from the western parts. What remained of the palace was divided into small tenements, and let out to poor handicraft men. The dilapidation and spoil was the work of one van Ling, a Dutchman, by trade a tailor, who bought it of the Parliament, when Bishop's lands were exposed to sale.'

It is not known what the relation was between van Ling and the Barters.

21 Black Bear, Castle Street

This pub was in Castle Street just to the north of Chipper Lane but had a large yard behind the inn buildings with an entrance off Chipper Lane. This left a plot between the Black Bear and Chipper Lane which is approximately that now occupied by what was the Post Office until early 2016. The inn was in existence from at least 1566 when Thomas Asheby was admitted as the tenant. A lease from 1676 exists at the Wiltshire and Swindon History Centre that shows that, at that time, the inn was owned by the Mayor and Commonalty of New Sarum and they leased the inn to Andrew Roberts [96].

For the remainder of its existence, the inn was in the ownership of the Mayor and Commonalty of New Sarum but the leaseholders then rented the property to landlords who were their under-tenants.

A lease of 1771 to Thomas Bucknall of Portsmouth shows that he paid £70 for the lease followed by an annual rent of £4 [97].

The inn was leased to Thomas Long in 1783 but when the lease was transferred to William Coster in 1797, on the death of Thomas Long, it was referred to as 'formerly called or known by the name of the Black Bear' [98]. A lease of 1804 also states that the buildings were used as a Clothing Manufactory after it closed as an inn.

A building exists in Castle Street nowadays at what was most likely the site of the Black Bear. This lies just to the north of the old Post Office and it lies slightly back from the road with railings enclosing a small forecourt. Records show this to have been occupied since 1808 and it is probable that it was built on the site of the inn.

22 Blackbird, 30 Churchfields Road

Sarah Jebbett gained a licence for the beerhouse that would become the Blackbird in August 1870. This seems to be the earliest reference to the Blackbird, and Sarah remained the landlady until 1887. In the 1881 Census the pub is called the Churchfields Beerhouse. By 1901 it was known as the Blackbird and it continued by that name until it closed. For many years it was owned by the Lamb Brewery of Frome until that brewery was taken over by Ushers of Trowbridge in 1957. In the 1980s it was closed but reopened as a Whitbread house in 1989. It closed yet again and was once more reopened as a free house in about 1995. Finally, in 2000 it closed as a public house and was converted into two dwellings.

23 Black Boar, Market Ward

This is mentioned in a list of brandy dealers of 1721 with Leonard Flacher shown as the licensee. Otherwise, nothing is known of this pub.

24 Black Horse Inn, 134 Castle Street

The Black Horse was on the east side of Castle Street nearly opposite Mill Stream Approach. The pub appears under this name in 1865 but it may well have been known by another name before this time. George Hopkins appears to be the first landlord of this pub. The situation is confused by there being two pubs of the same name at this time and by the Castle Street Black Horse displaying, in recent years, posters relating to the Winchester Street Black Horse. However, this Black Horse was technically in Milford parish and thus there were not two pubs of the same name in the same licensing area.

In 1868, when a railway train crashed on the branch line from Salisbury station to the Market House (now the Library), it was reported that it demolished a shed belonging to Mr Hopkins of the Black Horse, Castle Street [99].

In 1890, the brewer's assistant died at the Black Horse when he fell into the mash tub when it was boiling [100]. He was throwing away a bucket full of hot water and put his foot on the edge of the mash tub. His foot slipped and he fell into the mash tub. He was rushed to the infirmary but was so badly scalded that he died the same evening.

The pub was put up for sale in 1893 [101]. At that time it was described as a substantially-built dwelling that was split into two tenements. However, when it was put up for sale again in 1898, it was said to have been entirely rebuilt to meet the requirements of the trade [102]. It is presumed that this changed the form of the pub to that which it retained until it closed (and the external form of the building remains the same today).

This was an Usher's house until 1974 when it became a Chef and Brewer house within the Watney Mann group. In 1988, it was sold to Gibbs Mew being sold on again on the demise of that brewery. In 2010 it closed after a period of uncertainty and in June, 2011 it was announced that it was available as a retail unit with separate accommodation above. It was actually converted into a private house.

25 Black Horse Inn, 18 Winchester Street

This was one of the main coaching inns of Salisbury and it occupied the whole of the south-east corner at the junction of Brown Street and Winchester Street. One can still see the bricked-up coach entrance above the shop front of 18, Winchester Street.

A manuscript shows that between 10/5/1624 and 26/3/1625, William Gold at the Black Horse took 18 barrels of beer and 16 couls of ale from the Common Brewhouse.[17] William Gold also attended a meeting in 1625 that was called to persuade the innkeepers and alehouse-keepers to take beer from the Common Brewhouse.[18] The Common Brewhouse was a valiant attempt to provide funds for the poor of the City by supplying beer to the pubs. But as most pubs brewed their own beer in those days, few houses took beer from the Common Brewhouse and it was never a profitable venture.

It appears that this inn may have been called the Star and Garter for a time as it is recorded that in 1775 its name was changed back to the Black Horse by the new landlord, George Webb. However, it was certainly called the Black Horse from 1755 until 1767 so the name could only have been changed for a short period.

Several coaches are recorded as having run from the Black Horse including the Flying Machine to the Angel, St Clements Danes in 1762 [103], the Salisbury, Andover, Whitchurch & Overton Machine to the Golden Cross, Charing Cross in 1767 [104], the Exeter Diligence in 1780 [105], Cooke's original Salisbury Coach to the Bell Savage, Ludgate Hill in 1782 [106] and the Balloon Coach from Exeter via Salisbury to the Saracen's Head, Snow Hill in 1789 [107].

Fire was always a hazard in these old inns with candles and lanterns supplying light and stables holding quantities of hay and straw for horses. A fire was discovered in the stables in January, 1781 but was extinguished without major damage with the help of soldiers stationed at the inn [108]. Yet again, the stables caught fire in October, 1797 and four horses would have perished if the local butcher, Mr Marks, had not rushed in and driven them out. Once again, the military were of assistance with members of the 2nd Regiment of Dragoon Guards protecting the premises after the fire was put out [109]. However, the military were not always helpful as the landlord, Mr George Webb laid a complaint before the Magistrates of the City against 'the privates of the Queen's Bays, quartered at his house, for injuring his bedding, breaking the windows of the room where they slept, littering up their horses with his hay, which cost him four guineas the ton, and other misdemeanours' [110].

Whatever the success of the Black Horse during the heyday of coaches, there is no doubt that it suffered from their demise. In 1837, there were 19 different coaches running from the Black Horse, most of these being daily services with those to London generally running through the night to arrive early in the morning [111]. But in October 1838, a new coach, The Railroad, was leaving the Black Horse at 1:30 in the afternoon to meet the London railway train at Basingstoke, arriving in London at nine in the evening [112]. Not only was this a much faster journey, but in these early days of the railway, the coach, with its passengers, was loaded onto a railway wagon and continued its journey to the traditional inns in London on arrival at the railway terminus. This trend continued in 1840 with coaches leaving Salisbury for Southampton to meet the London trains [113]. The problem for the coaching inns was that these new, short services did not require the many teams of horses required to maintain the speed of horse-drawn long distance coaches. In addition, the short journey times meant that the inns lost the revenue from providing food and refreshments to passengers as they waited for horses to be changed, or stayed overnight before the next leg of their journeys. Some inns adapted to the changes but the Black Horse was not one of them.

In the middle of 1840, the landlord, Thomas Rogers was declared bankrupt [114]. Thus in August, 1840, there was a large auction of "About 350 Dozen of superior choice Wines, in bottle and in wood; 200 Gallons of Spirits; fifty-three excellent fast Coach and Post-Horses, with their harness; Post-Chaise, Chariot, Fly, Phaeton, and Gig; excellent Cow; extensive assortment of Plate, Plated Articles, Linen, China, Household Furniture, and other Effects" of the Black Horse Inn [115]. However, it appears that the creditors of Thomas Rogers decided that it would be more beneficial to themselves to keep the inn open and the sale was postponed [116]. In addition, they voted in favour of employing Thomas Rogers to run the inn on their behalf! [117] By August, 1841, the creditors received 5 shillings and a penny for every pound of their debts [118]. Although this does not appear to be a great deal of money, Thomas Rogers seems to have been discharged from his bankruptcy, getting married shortly afterwards [119], and continuing as landlord until October, 1843. The new landlord, Francis Hackman, ran the Black Horse until, in October 1845, it was declared that the inn was closed, and that there would be a sale of the furniture and other property of the inn [120].

For a few years, it appears that the large rooms of the inn were hired out for meetings. For example, in August, 1848, Joseph Stamford, a shoemaker, was reprimanded and fined 3 shillings for disturbing a religious congregation, the Latter Day Christians, assembled in a room at the Black Horse Inn [8]. But eventually in May, 1852, the owner, Sir Benjamin Brodie, offered all the premises of the Black Horse for sale [121]. This was sold in four lots including the Falcon Inn (qv) in Brown Street!

However, in October, 1869, Henry Carslake was granted a licence for the Black Horse in Winchester Street although this was at a special licensing session for granting certificates for beer-house licences rather than full public house licences [122]. The new pub was certainly much smaller than the original inn, being what had been described as a dwelling house fronting on to Winchester Street in the sale of 1852.

In January, 1881, Thomas Jones was charged with vagrancy [123]. It appears that he had been begging in the city for two days. He went to the Black Horse and asked the landlord, Alfred Dominey, for relief. Mr Dominey refused to give him any assistance and told the court that his house had been made the 'object of the attentions of the fraternity'. Jones denied that he had been begging but the Police Superintendent said he had been watched by a plain-clothes policeman and his evidence was irrefutable. It was stated that the number of vagrants visiting the City had decreased recently probably because of 'the stringent repressive measures adopted by the Bench'. The Bench sentenced Jones to 14 days imprisonment with hard labour in line with their policy. One wonders if a vagrant in January might have welcomed the bed and food provided in gaol even with hard labour!

In 1902, Mary Sullivan, who was described as an Irish woman of no fixed abode, was charged with being drunk and disorderly and also smashing a pane of glass at the Black Horse [124]. The landlord said he had served Sullivan with half a pint of beer but after she had sat down she started using foul language. He asked her to leave the pub and when she refused to leave, he threw her out. As he returned indoors, Sullivan shattered the pane of glass. She was found guilty by the Magistrates who imposed a fine of five shillings, But the fine would not be imposed if she left Salisbury by noon on the day of her court appearance!

But by the early 20th C. it was even further run down. In May 1923, the application for renewal of the licence was opposed by the Salisbury and District Temperance Society, supported by the Salisbury Free Church Council [8]. It was stated that there were 21 other licensed premises within 200 yards of the Black Horse and that it was impossible for any tenant to make a living out of the small trade done by the house. What is more, the house had been closed for several months without any apparent inconvenience to the inhabitants of Salisbury! Not surprisingly, the renewal of the licence was refused and in October, 1923, it was closed with £28 10s compensation being paid to the landlord and £541 10s being paid to Eldridge Pope, the owners of the inn.

26 Black Lion, Market Ward

This is another of the pubs mentioned in a list of brandy dealers of 1721 with George Marsh shown as the licensee. Otherwise, nothing is known of this inn.

27 Black Swan, St Martin's Parish

Haskin's states that the Black Swan in St Martin's Parish was granted a license as an alehouse in 1758 when John Fellon was the landlord. No other information about this house has been found although there is a possibility that this was another name for the White Swan in Payne's Hill.

28 Blue Boar, Blue Boar Row

Sometimes described as the Boar Inn, this inn gave its name to its surrounding chequer. The site of this inn is covered by Debenham's store but a small part remains hidden within the building (the restaurant at the rear of the shop). A written contract of 1444 almost certainly refers to these remains as the dimensions of the wooden framework of the restaurant match that shown on the contract for its building! Other documents show this site to have belonged to the Ludlow family in 1448 and to have been called the Blue Boar by 1451.

In 1595, the inn belonged to Anthony Parry and George Story was the innkeeper. It then comprised of a hall, two parlours, a kitchen, a buttery, a cellar, seventeen chambers, eight shops or warehouses, other small rooms and a garden [125]. The courtyard extended right through the chequer to Chipper Lane.

An indenture of 1636 describes the sale of a building in Blue Boar Row that was next door to the Blue Boar [126]. It also clearly shows that the Blue Boar and the Saracen's Head were different buildings on either side of the building being sold.

It appears that the inn started to go downhill after the opening of the Three Lions in the early part of the 18th C. The last landlord was Robert Read who ran it from 1721 to 1756 and it closed after his death in 1756 [127]. A further notice in the *Journal* shows the Blue Boar as having been shut up and the Excise Office moved to the Red Lion in Milford Street [128]. It seems probable that at least part of the inn was pulled down at that time. In 1819 we find that Dr Fowler built himself a house on part of the site. By 1825 we find this house being used as a Library and Reading rooms upstairs with a shop below. It is likely that the living rooms of this private residence are still intact as the offices of the modern store

There is a small yard to the north of this building leading off Chipper Lane which is probably the original yard of the Blue Boar and is now the covered loading bay of the store. In this yard are three round stones set in a triangle with two iron studs in the centre. This is supposed to mark the place of execution of Henry Stafford, Duke of Buckingham in 1483. Although it is recorded that Stafford was executed in the Market Place, it is very possible that the site is correctly marked as the Market Place was originally much larger than it is nowadays. The open area of the market gradually reduced in size as market stalls became permanent structures that later became shops and houses. In August 1839, a skeleton was found beneath the kitchen floor of the Saracen's Head which stood alongside the site of the Blue Boar. This was said to have been Stafford's as the head and right arm were missing, supposedly removed after the execution to be sent to the King and then displayed at Temple Bar. It is said that his ghost has been seen regularly since his death. When the three stones were moved to allow building work, many things went wrong in the adjoining store. These happenings ceased when the stones were replaced.

29 Blue Post, Milford Hollow

This pub is known from several records dating from the 18th C. but it is not clear when it ceased to be a pub. Milford Hollow is the track which runs down towards Milford Mill alongside the Godolphin School and it undoubtedly follows the original route from Salisbury to Clarendon Palace. The house is still standing as part of Brome House and is used by the school.

It appears it may have been an unlicensed alehouse prior to 1775 when it received a licence from the City authorities, as shown when it was advertised for sale in that year [129]. At that time, it was occupied by John Chaunt and the pub was also known as the Cheesecake House. The latest record of it as a pub that has been found so far was in 1786 when it was broken in to and the thief stole a bottle of rum, another of brandy, and a loaf of bread [130]. It does not appear in the licensing records for 1798. It was certainly closed as a pub by 1856 when the road through Milford Hollow was stopped up beyond the Blue Post, which was shown in a legal notice as 'formerly the Blue Post' [131].

30 Boathouse, Millstream Approach.

This was converted in 1984 from a boat keeper's cottage to provide a bar and restaurant called appropriately the Boathouse. An attraction of the bar was the doors opening onto the riverside where one could hire rowing boats in the summer. In 2000, it was refurbished and re-opened as the Afon with an emphasis on it being a brasserie.

Since then it has reverted to the name of the Boathous

31 Bowling Green, Castle Street

This was just north of the Castle Street Gate and hence was in Milford Parish rather than the City of New Sarum. This gave it the advantage of escaping some of the strictures of the City Corporation and the Church. It was in existence from some time before 1763 when the following advertisements appeared [132]: "This is to acquaint the Curious, That there is now at the Bowling Green, near this City, A Person who after spending many years, with a great Expense & Trouble, has collected the following ancient and valuable Curiosities, viz:- the original Watch of Mary Queen of Scots, presented to her by Francis the French King; the Crucifix carried before her when she went to execution; two Egyptian Gods 4000 years old, one buried with King Pharaoh in the mummy shape; several curious manuscripts on vellum; an Egyptian sea-horse taken out of the Red Sea; a collection of putrefactions; upwards of 100 medals; a most curious piece of workmanship by a blind man; a scalp and scalping knife of an Indian Chief;'

It was still open in 1778 [133] and may have been in operation in 1784 when a balloon was apparently launched in its vicinity [134]. After that date, no definite reference to it can be found.

32 Bowling Green, Crane Bridge Street

This pub still has a small connection to modern Salisbury in that the house near the car park in this street is called Bowling Green House. It was in existence from at least 1748. In 1764, the owner, John Rogers, complained that his garden wall had been broken down or damaged several times and he offered two guineas reward if he received information about the culprits leading to their conviction [135]. It was still in existence in 1783 when it was available to let with the stock and furnishings being for sale to the new tenant [136]. But no record can be found of it after this date.

33 Brewery Tap, 5 Rollestone Street

This pub originated as the Tap of the

Rollestone Street brewery which became Folliott's Brewery sometime in the 19th C. The pub was licensed up until 1972 and in its later life it was always referred to as the 'cider house'. This is not surprising as in 1971, it was noted that despite being a very small pub having a single small bar, it was selling 150 gallons of scrumpy cider a week!

From 1870, the pub was licensed as part of the Old George and hence was known as the Old George Tap, as the Old George on the corner of Rollestone Street and Winchester Street was also owned by John Folliott [137]. The building was also described as 'newly erected'. Consequently, this pub is missing from the licensing records for most of the 20th C. as it was still considered to be part of the Old George. In its last years, Ushers Brewery had been taken over by Watney Mann (West) Ltd. They stated that 'The company will not promote the sale of scrumpy in any way, and will certainly not take active steps to move its trade to surrounding houses'. This can be taken to mean that they would not move the sale of scrumpy to any other Watney Mann house. In line with this policy, the pub closed in January, 1972, thus finishing the sale of draft scrumpy in Salisbury. It was re-built in 1989 and used as a doctor's surgery.

34 Bricklayer's Arms, Market Ward

This was probably known as the Carpenter's Arms as Robert Rowden, the last recorded landlord of the Carpenter's in 1811, is the landlord of the Bricklayer's from 1812 to 1814. Apart from this, the site of the pub is not known. The Carpenter's first appears in records in 1803 and has a rapid succession of landlords until 1811. The Bricklayer's disappears from the licensing records after the 1814 annual licensing.

35 Bridge, nk

John Morgan is recorded as holding the licence for the Bridge in 1795 but it has not been possible to link this to a building or a pub of a different name. There vis a small possibility that it may have been an alternative name for the Shoulder of Mutton.

36 Brown Bear, Castle Street

This pub is mentioned in the *Salisbury and Winchester Journal* of 21st March, 1774, as an auction of houses near Castle Gate was being held there. It has not been possible to link this to a building or another pub, unless this was an accidental misnaming of the Black Bear.

37 Bugle, Blue Boar Row

This inn appears to have been in existence in 1624/5 when innkeepers were summoned to a meeting to discuss them taking beer from the Common Brewhouse.[18] Thomas Elton from the Bugle in Blue Boar Row attended. All the other references to this inn come from the period 1756-1760 when the house was almost continually advertised as being to let or to be sold. The last reference to it is in 1760 although Wheeler, writing in the *Salisbury and Winchester Journal* in 1894 was of the opinion that it became the Parade Coffee Tavern (qv) [138].

38 Bull Hotel, 11 Fisherton Street

This inn was in Fisherton Street, nearly opposite Malthouse Lane. It was in existence from at least 1713 although much of the building one can see is of a later date. In 1769, it was described as being large and commodious and freehold with adjoining stabling for 80 horses [139]. In 1805, the *Salisbury and Winchester Journal* reported [140]: 'During the last week, our expectation of seeing their Majesties had been excited by the continual passing through of the King's servants, horses, carriages, and baggage. Ten of the cream-coloured state horses, and five other of his Majesty's favourite horses, rested here on Wednesday night, in the excellent stables of the Bull Inn, Fisherton. It appears evident that his Majesty means to have more of the state of a King this season, than he has heretofore been accustomed at Weymouth '

The King referred to was George III who usually spent his summers at Weymouth when he was not suffering one of his bouts of madness.

In 1820, Thomas Thomas, who had been the landlord since 1798, died and his widow took over the pub [141]. But in a short while, the pub was advertised as available to rent with the incoming tenant expected to pay for the household furniture, stock, casks and fixtures at an agreed valuation [142]. It is unclear whether the house was let at this time or Mrs Thomas stayed on but the next recorded landlord was Robert Samuel Hibberd who obtained the license in March 1822. In April of that year, he announces that he has entered the inn and that he has stocked it with 'good home-brewed Strong Beer, draught and bottled Cyder, excellent Foreign and other Spirits, and fine-flavoured old Wines' [143]. Mr Hibberd stays at the Bull until 1828 when a solicitor requests that his creditors provide details of the sums owed to them and also for any debtors to pay their accounts [144]. This would normally indicate that Mr Hibberd had been made bankrupt but in this case, there is no indication that this was so. Perhaps Mr Hibberd left before his creditors could catch up with him?

In September, 1887, William Hicks & Co, who had been operating the King's Head Brewery since at least 1880, announced that they were retiring from business. In consequence, the brewery and the King's Head Inn were put up for sale as were four public houses including the Bull Hotel [145]. This was described as the 'well-known and well-situate old Market Inn, within a stone's throw of the Brewery, with extensive Stabling in Fisherton Street'. For whatever reason, this sale was postponed and was advertised as being for sale by auction again in December, 1888. Again, whether these properties were not sold or were withdrawn from sale is not known but the whole set of premises were again offered for sale in March 1891 [146]. At this time, the Bull was described as being recently rebuilt.

But in April, 1891, the furnishings and other effects of the Bull were advertised for sale by auction as a result of the bankruptcy of a Mr Stroyan [147]. Whether he purchased the Bull in March but went bankrupt almost immediately after or whether he had been the landlord of the hotel to a different owner is not known although an A D Stroyan is shown to have been manager of the King's Head Brewery just before it was demolished in October of 1891.

Suffice it to say, in November, 1892, the license of the Bull was transferred to Mr Woodhouse of the brewers in Blandford Forum [148]. It is noted elsewhere that the

Bull was purchased by Hall & Woodhouse of Blandford Forum in 1901. So it is possible that the earlier license transfer indicated that the hotel was first rented by the brewery before it was purchased. It continued as a 'Badger' pub up until 1997. It closed for a while at this time being refurbished at the same time as the adjacent Infirmary site. However, it was sold and closed in 2004 and re-opened as a turf accountant's premises in 2005.

39 Bush, Market Ward

It is not known where this pub was in the vicinity of the Market Place. Richard Caplyn is recorded as being the landlord in 1620 & 1626. In addition, a farthing token inscribed 'AT THE BVSH IN' on the obverse and 'SALSBVRY 1657' on the reverse has been recorded [149]. This token has a hoop of hop vine on the obverse and the landlord's initials, 'T.R.' on the reverse.

40 Butt of Ale, 49 Sunnyhill Road

This pub was opened on the Paul's Dene estate in 1965. It was situated high on the north side of the city with fine views across to the cathedral. It gained a provisional licence in May 1963 when it was shown as going to be the Dorchester Inn [13]. The licence was finalised in June 1964 with it taking its eventual name of the Butt of Ale. For many years, it was operated by Eldridge-Pope of Dorchester but in later years became a free house. It was closed and it became clear that the owner wished

Butt of Ale

to demolish the pub and use the resultant large plot of land to build several houses. A long battle involving a local resident's group and Salisbury District Council opposing the plans eventually resulted in the pub re-opening in 2005. However, after further troubles it closed again, but re-opened again on 1 July 2009. It did not last long again this time and the Council eventually gave permission for it to be demolished and replaced by domestic houses.

41 Cactus Jack's, Water Lane

This bar opened as Reuben Langford's in 1984 with an emphasis on wine and food with occasional live music. It later changed its name to Maxwell's before becoming Cactus Jack's on a change in ownership in 1994. It is now more of a bistro with Mexican food than a pub.

42 Cartwells, Minster Street

There is a single entry in the licensing records for 1817 showing a licensed premise of this name in Minster Street. There is no connection with the much earlier inn of this name (see under Countewell's Inn) and no other record of this premises can be found

43 Cat Tavern, 115 South Western Road

This pub dates from about 1870 although there is a possibility that it existed at an earlier date. It was then known as the Engineer's Arms and may well have originated when Fisherton Street and Fisherton Church Street were altered to accommodate the new railway in 1859.

In 1872, the pub was advertised as available to let, called the Engineer's Arms, and owned by the Castle Street Brewery [150]. Four years later, the brewing plant from the pub was advertised for sale as a consequence of that brewery supplying the pub with beer [151].

In 1877, an application was made for a spirit license for the pub [152]. The solicitor applying for the license on behalf of the owners, stated that it had had a beer-only license for as long as he could recollect. Considering that the pub had only been open for less than ten years, his memory seems very poor for an advocate! The pub was described as belonging to Pern, Heath and Waters of the Castle Street Brewery but let to the Misses Parsons for £10 per year. The pub was then sublet to the landlord, Samuel Reanor for £30 per year. The only objections to the license came from neighbouring pubs. A magistrate said he thought these objections were a matter of personal interest on the part of the landlords and therefore of no great interest! Therefore the magistrates granted the license.

By 1891, the pub was owned by Styring's Brewery of Tisbury [153]. In November of that year, the landlord, James Courtney, applied for permanent transfer of the license of the pub to himself, having been granted a temporary transfer in September. The Police Superintendent pointed out that Mr Courtney did not live at the pub all week as he was still employed by the London and South Western Railway Company, as he had been for the last 33 years. So, the question was put to the Magistrates as to whether the responsible person who held a pub license was required by law to reside on the premises. The pub was actually run by the landlord's wife with the help of her two grownup daughters and her 22-year-old son. Rather than transfer the license to the landlord's son (as, in fact, did happen in 1899), the Magistrates decided to continue with a temporary transfer but reminded Mr Courtney that if anything untoward occurred at the pub, he would be required to live permanently at the pub even if that meant resigning from the railway.

As stated above, Mr James Courtney, Junior took over the pub in 1899. But in 1904, he was brought before the Salisbury Bankruptcy Court [154]. He had borrowed £200 from his mother when he took over the pub, of which £120 was still owing, and paid his father £30 for the good will of the business. Mr Courtney claimed £30 as being a credit to his accounts as an incoming landlord would pay this for the good will of the business. The Court was somewhat surprised that a new tenant would pay for the good will to a business that had gone bankrupt! The main reason Mr Courtney stated for his inability to make a profit was that in earlier times, the porters at the railway station and the crew of the trains used to come out of the station to get a drink when they were still on duty. But this had been stopped by the railway company to the detriment of his trade. As a consequence of Mr Courtney's bankruptcy, the furnishings of the pub were put up for sale.

The Engineer's Arms came under the ownership of Eldridge Pope of Dorchester in 1912 when that brewery took over Styrings. However, Mr Frederick Styring retained some level of ownership of the premises. It continued as the Engineer's until 1999 when it became the Swinging Cat Tavern with an emphasis on live music. More recently, its name has been curtailed to the Cat Tavern.

44 Cathedral Hotel, 7 & 9 Milford Street

The central part of this hotel is of 18th C. construction but an additional bay was added on each side, probably when the hotel opened in 1879 (or at least, later than 1875). In December, 1879, a dinner was provided at the hotel for the builders and men who had completed a new school on the London Road paid for by the Reverend W C Baker [155] (it is not clear where this school was). By 1880, Mr Wilkes, of the hotel, was providing refreshments for the County Ball held at the Assembly Rooms in Salisbury [156]

The Salisbury Chess Club held its meetings at the Cathedral Hotel in the late 1880s, but in 1892, they decided to move their meetings from the Cathedral Hotel to a restaurant in High Street [157]. Despite that, in 1894, the Chess Club held a simultaneous chess match at what were described as the Salisbury Chess Rooms at the Hotel [158]. At this match, Mr Schonberg (the Honorary Secretary of the Wilts County Chess Association) played fifteen members of the Salisbury and Wilton Chess clubs simultaneously, winning six matches, drawing five and losing four.

In 1897 it was described as being a temperance hotel although it is not clear for how long it retained this designation. In 1909, the hotel was advertised for sale by private contract [159]. It was described as being 'expensively Furnished, and replete with every comfort; about 20 rooms, Confectioner's Shop, Large Dining-Room, Good Domestic Offices, Bakery, etc.'

In 1923, an additional floor was added. In 1931, an advertisement stated it as being entirely redecorated and refurnished with electric passenger lift to all floors (proprietors Captain and Mrs W Gilbert King). By 1938 its advertisements state that it has running hot and cold softened water and radiators in bedrooms, steel balconies and safety ladders from the roof to the ground and lights over beds and dressing tables

By the second half of the 20th C the bar was a busy and popular meeting place. From the late 1970s, the bar fluctuated between being open, closed, with or without music and of various themes! It was closed to the public in the early 1990's with the bar reopening in 1996 as a resident's lounge for the hotel. But in 1997 the complete hotel was closed and boarded up. In 2000, the hotel was re-opened with the bar once more serving customers and providing live music.

45 Chapter House, St John's Street

This pub is at the southern end of St John's Street near to the corner with St Ann Street. The two, southern gable ends of this inn date from the late 16th C. but the current building is dominated by the large gable of the north range which was built in the first half of the 17th C. A deed of 1569 records a group of tenements known as the Seven Deadly Sins being leased to Richard Symond [160]. But by 1638, the King's Arms is leased to William Symons together with a new house on the site of the former seven tenements, although the licensee was Henry Hewett [161]: 'THIS INDENTURE made the Eighth day of September Anno Domini 1638 And in the fourteenth year of the Reign of our Sovereign Lord Charles By the Grace of God of England Scotland France and Ireland King Defender of the Faith etc. Between the Dean & Chapter of the Cathedral Church of Sarum in the County of Wilts of the one part, And William Symons of the City of New Sarum in the County aforesaid Gentleman of the other part Witnesseth that the said Dean & Chapter as well for and in consideration of the Surrender of a former Lease heretofore made of the Tenements and other things hereunder Specified heretofore demised to Richard Symons of the City of New Sarum aforesaid Innholder deceased, whereof Thirty years & more are yet to come, as also for & in consideration of the sum of Ten pounds of lawful English money now in hand paid by the said William Symons to the said Dean & Chapter in the name of assign, with their whole assent consent & agreement Have demised granted and to farm lett, and by these presents for them and their Successors do demise grant and to farm lett unto the said William Symons, All that their Inn now commonly called the Kings Arms, situate in the City of New Sarum aforesaid now in the tenure of Henry Hewett, of the City aforesaid Innholder and a new erected house adjoining thereunto now in the tenure of Robert Edmonds of the said City gentleman, being heretofore seven several tenements lying together with the appurtenances, then commonly called the Seven Deadly Sins, and all and singular houses, edifices, shops, Cellars Solars stables buildings Orchards gardens, backsides easements profits commodities & advantages to the same Inn, newly erected house & seven tenements & to each or any of them belonging or in anywise appertaining or with them or any of them held & enjoyed as part & parcel thereof ...'

In June 1651, Henry Hewett was still

the landlord and is said to have let the inn be used by Royalists as a secret rendezvous while Charles II was concealed at Heale House. It was later used as a secure asylum as Lord Wilmot and others laid plans for the King's escape to France.

In 1739. the inn developed its trade by hiring out 'Coaches, Chariots and Chaises' [162]. The ostler at this time must have been a character as in 1752 an advertisement stated [163]: 'This Day is Published (Price 6d) The Wiltshire New Phaenomenon; Or The Free-Thinking Christian Philosopher. Being the Philosophical Essays of Charles White, Hostler, at the King's Arms at Sarum. On the following subjects: - I The Being and Attributes of God. II Accidents & Comets. III The Resurrection. London; Printed for J Robinson, at the Golden Lion in Ludgate St, & sold by B.Collins, Bookseller, in Salisbury.'

By 1755 the Flying Machine coach was running from the King's Arms to the Angel Inn in the Strand in London three times a week [164]. In 1756, a recruiting party for the King's Own Regiment of Foot was at the King's Arms where volunteers 'shall receive a Guinea Advance, & a Crown to drink H.M.'s Health; and at the arrival of the Regiment, new Clothes etc., fitting to compleat a Gentlemen Soldier, in his Majesty's own Regiment' [165].

The Post Office was moved to the King's Arms in 1763 from the White Hart [166]. The inn was described as 'a large & commodious Inn & in the direct Post Road from London to the West of England' which seems to be quite a good description of the White Hart as well as the King's Arms!

The inn was undoubtedly a house of good quality at this time as in 1765, it was reported that [167]: 'On Friday about eleven o'clock, their Royal Highnesses the Dukes of York and Gloucester, came from Southampton to the King's Arms in this city, where, after taking some refreshment and changing horses, they proceeded with a post chaise and six, and three postillions to Warminster in their way to Bath. Soon after, arrived at the same inn, the Earl of Northampton and family, where they stop'd to change horses, and then proceeded to Devizes, in their way to Bath.'

Of note during this period is that John Shergold took the inn in 1755. He dies in November, 1773 [168] after 18 years as the landlord. His wife, Mary continues to run the inn until 1795 when [169]: 'She returns her most sincere thanks to the Nobility and Gentry frequenting the said Inn, and to her Friends and the Public in general for all past favours, and informs them she has declined business in favour of Mr James Ball, on whom she places the greatest confidence of giving general satisfaction, and requests that they will in future please to favour him with their commands, which will be ever most gratefully acknowledged by their obliged and very humble servant.'

In 1799, Richard Richardson and Frances Webb place the following notice in the *Salisbury and Winchester Journal* [170]: 'We whose Names are hereunto subscribed, being two of the Commissioners named and appointed in and by a certain Act of Parliament made and passed in the thirty-ninth year of the reign of his present Majesty King George the Third, intitled, "An Act for dividing and allotting the open and common fields, and other commonable lands and grounds, in the parishes of Stratford under the Castle and Milford, in the county of Wilts." Do hereby give Notice, that we have set out such public and private roads and ways through and over the lands by the said Act directed to be divided and allotted; as in our judgement appear to be necessary and convenient; and have ordered our Surveyor to stake out the same, and to place direction posts in such places where the same are necessary for the information of the public. Whoever may be aggrieved, or have any objection to make to the roads set out, or omitted to be set out, may state the cause of complaint to us at our next meeting, to be held at the house of James Ball, the King's Arms Inn, in the city of New Sarum, on Monday the 7th day of October next, at twelve o'clock at noon.'

Presumably, these enclosures did take place.

In 1852, William Potto moves from the Ship Inn in Winchester Street to the King's Arms [171]. As a consequence, the Salisbury Unity of Loyal and Independent Modern Order of Foresters moved their lodge to the King's Arms from the Ship [172]. But this move cannot have taken place without some level of dissension. In 1853, a letter to the *Journal* stated that the newspaper had reported a meeting of the Loyal and Independent Modern Order of Foresters at the Ship [173]. The letter complained that the only true Lodge of the Foresters was that at the King's Arms. It was admitted that several expelled members of the Parent Lodge did work on the feelings of a few persons to open a benefit society at the Ship, and designated it the Modern Order of Foresters. However, they were not identified with, or had any connection either directly or indirectly with the Lodge at the King's Arms.

By 1858, the character of the inn seems to have slipped [174]. The Police were called to the inn and found about 40 persons in the road by the inn with some of them making a great deal of noise. One of them tried to get the crowd to throw a policeman into the ditch but the Sergeant of Police arrived and attempted to disperse the crowd. Some people did leave but a hard core of people refused to move. The Police determined that Thomas Bryant was the main culprit and he was detained at the Police Station. In Court, Bryant called two witnesses who claimed that Bryant was no more disorderly than anybody else in the crowd. The Police replied that one of the witnesses was himself very disorderly. They also said that there had been many complaints of disorderly conduct at the inn and that they should have summoned all those who had been present, including the two witnesses who had given evidence. Bryant was found guilty and was fined 20 shillings plus costs.

In 1869, there was a dispute between the King's Arms and the White Hart over the ownership of a cellar at the King's Arms [175]. It was stated that the inn had been part of the property of the White Hart at an earlier time and that, when it was sold, the White Hart retained use of the cellar. As a consequence, in early 1870, the Directors of the White Hart Hotel Company announced at their annual general meeting that they had purchased the King's Arms for £750 so that they would be free of the inconvenience and annoyance to which they had been subject [176]. This explains why the King's Arms has no significant yard behind the inn and that, nowadays, the car park of the White Hart extends behind the inn almost to St Anns Street.

In the 19th C. a large dining room was

constructed to the north of the carriageway through the inn. In later years, the lower floor of this part of the building was let as a shop. To the south of the pub was William Osmond's stonemason's shop and works built in 1820. This later became a newsagent before being bought by the King's Arms in about 1997. The shop and the adjoining area were converted into a new bar/bistro known as the Vestry.

Despite the earlier ownership of the inn by the White Hart, it came under the ownerships of Ushers Brewery in the 20th C. and in 1963, it was leased to Berni Inns although Ushers confirmed that they still controlled the hotel. It stayed with Ushers until 1974, when it became a Chef and Brewer House within the Watney-Mann Group.

In 2011, the whole hotel and bar were closed while a great deal of building work was conducted. It opened towards the end of 2011 with the name of the whole premises changed to the Lazy Cow, much to the dismay of many local people. By 2015, the pub had again been renamed as the Chapter House.

46 Checkers, Endless Street

In 1455, there is a reference to Le Checkers in Endlestrete. It is believed to have been an inn but nothing more is known of the house.

47 Chequers, nk

An alehouse of this name applied for a full licence in 1742 and had its application refused. It is not known if it continued on as an alehouse or whether it changed its name and was granted a licence at a later date.

48 Cherry Tree, Brown Street

This alehouse was on the north corner of Brown Street and St Ann Street. Haskins states that it was licensed as an alehouse sometime between 1635 and 1685 [18] but at the same time he states that Robert Shafflin obtained a license for the Cherry Tree in 1771.[20] The pub was still in operation at the time of the 1821 Licensing Sessions with the landlady being Elizabeth Swift. The inn is advertised for sale in March 1822 [177] and the inn does not appear in the September, 1822, annual licensing session. However, on 25th September 1822, William Needle applied for a licence of the house formerly called the Cherry Tree but the Magistrates adjourned the discussion [4]. He does not seem to have been successful as he was granted a licence for a pub called the Bell & Crown (this not being the premises now called the Cloisters as that was known as the White Lion at that time) on the 30th September 1822. If this was a renamed Cherry Tree, then this was for only a short time as the White Lion became the Bell & Crown sometime in 1823! So a minor mystery remains and nothing more is heard of the Cherry Tree after these dates.

49 Chough, Blue Boar Row

The current building that was the Chough dates from the 16th C. although there is little of this age that is visible. It was entered through the yard leading off Blue Boar Row. The main part of the inn lay to the east of the yard, the buildings to the west of the yard originally being stables and stores.

The earliest record of it comes from 1626 when it was known as the Cornish Chofe [178]. The name probably originates from the Arms of St Thomas Beckett which had three Choughs on them (a chough is also sometimes referred to as a Beckit in heraldry). The Parish Church near to the Chough is dedicated to St Thomas Beckett.

For many years the Chough had a large room available for the sale of goods or for travelling exhibitions. This results in some interesting entries in the *Salisbury and Winchester Journal*:

14th February 1780: 'Just arrived in this city, from the Great Room in Panton-street, Hay-market, and to be seen at the large Room at the Chough Inn, Sieur Manuelli's Great Mechanical Exhibition. In three Different Divisions. Part I. Several new and amazing Deceptions. Part II. The Italian Fantocini, never performed here before, the Scenes & Figures being in the Italian taste, and brilliant, beyond description. Part III. Les Ambres Chinoises or Lilliputian Theatre – The particulars of the exhibition may be seen in hand-bills [179].'

22nd October 1787: 'However striking a Curiosity may be, there is generally some difficulty in engaging the attention of the public; but even this was not the case with that graceful couple in Miniature, Mr James Harris and Lady Morgan, the celebrated Windsor Fairy, who is now in the thirtieth year of her age, and only eighteen pounds weight; for no sooner were they arrived at their apartments at the Chough Inn, in the Market Place, than the curious of all degrees resorted to see them, being sensible that prodigies like these never made their appearance amongst us before; and the most penetrating have frankly declared that neither the tongue of the most florid orator, or pen of the most ingenious writer, can sufficiently describe the beauty and elegance of these phenomena of nature; and that all description must fall infinitely short of giving that satisfaction which may be obtained on judicious inspection [180].'

14 July 1788: 'Positively for Six Nights Only. At the Chough Large Room, in the Market Place, Salisbury, this present Monday Evening, and every Evening during the week, and no longer; - The Undeceiving Exhibition, or Dissertations on Deception; discovering the Modes of Deceiving practised by Jugglers, Sleight of Hand men, Fortune Tellers, and Natural Magicians; also detecting the Frauds of Mountebanks, Quack-Doctors, etc. To conclude with a Collection of the most celebrated Deceptions, such as are usually practised on Cards, Money, Boxes, etc with their agreeable discoveries, in such a manner, that every person in the room may be capable of doing them immediately themselves. – To begin at seven. Tickets Two Shillings and One Shilling – to be had of the Printer, at the Bar of the Chough, and of Mr. Mexville, at Mr. Hackets, hostler, next door to the Chough [181].'

17 November 1807: 'Ganter's Universal Museum. Comprising the greatest variety of Curiosities of Nature and Art ever seen, will be exhibited from Ten in the Morning until Nine in the Evening, commencing Monday, Nov 16 at the Chough Inn, Market Place, Salisbury. The Proprietors have been nearly twenty years in collecting this Exhibition, and can safely assure the public, that a more Interesting and Pleasing Spectacle does not at this time travel the United Kingdom. The proprietors have also just received an extensive collection of some of the rarest Curiosities, which they purchased at the late sale of the Leverian Museum, - It

should be impossible, in the compass of an advertisement, to enumerate half the articles this Museum consists of, there being nearly 2000 Natural and Artificial Curiosities of the most valuable and pleasing kind, - In short, the Proprietors are bold to assert, that such an Exhibition was never before offered to the inspection of the public at so low a price. Admission, One Shilling [182].'

16 October 1809: 'Gigantic Youth. To be seen at the Chough Inn, Market Place, Salisbury. – That most wonderful and surprising Yorkshire Youth, Seventeen years of Age, Seven Feet Six Inches High, and who weighs upwards of Twenty Four Stone; who has had the honour of being introduced to their Majesties and the Royal Family, at Windsor, when he was most graciously received and entertained. A more surprising instance of gigantic stature was never beheld or was exhibited in this or any other kingdom, being proportional in all respects and equal to his gigantic stature; the sight of whom never failed to give entire and universal satisfaction, and fill the beholders with wonder and astonishment. Now allowed by the first judges to surpass all men ever yet seen. Admission One Shilling; children and servants Sixpence [184].'

The Chough was a coaching inn with one entrance in Blue Boar Row and another in Castle Street. One tends to associate coaching with a genteel way of life that we have lost but in fact competition in this trade was as ruthless as in any modern business. The advertisements and letters concerning a dispute in 1808 between two coach companies can be found at Appendix 2.

As with many inns around the Market Square, the Chough made special arrangements for the trade on market days. It advertised 'An ordinary every Tuesday at one o'clock', an ordinary being a complete meal at a fixed price [185].

In June, 1878, James Macklin sold the Chough to Frederick William Miller for £2500 [186]. James Macklin had been the owner of the inn since 1834 when John Lodge occupied the house. As such, James Macklin had never been the licensee of the Chough but let it to tenants who were the licensees. Frederick William Miller had been the last tenant under Mr Macklin's ownership before purchasing the hotel. But in August of this year, Mr Miller leased the inn to Bridger Gibbs for 15 years at an annual rent of £200 [186]. Thus the house ran as a Gibbs pub for the next few years.

For many years in the late 1800s and into the 20th C., the Chough was the headquarters of the Salisbury Football League. By 1905, the Salisbury & District Senior Football League held their annual general Meeting at the Chough [187]. This league seemed to have a strange geographical spread for its six teams comprising three civilian clubs (Salisbury City, Andover Town and Eastleigh Athletic) but also three military teams (26th Brigade RFA, 28th Brigade RFA and 2nd Battery, Scots Fusiliers). It is presumed that the Fusiliers team was based at Larkhill as the term Battery is associated with artillery. It is also believed that the RFA referred to was the Royal Field Artillery (also based at Larkhill) not the modern designation of the Royal Fleet Auxiliary.

In March, 1896, Frederick William Miller died and he left the inn to his daughter Eva Ellen. Two years later, she mortgages the inn to William Herbert Jackson for £1000 [188]. For some reason,

Mr Jackson then passed on the mortgage to the Wiltshire and Dorset Banking Company. In 1903, this bank leased the inn to Gibbs Mew and Co for 14 years from September, 1909 [189].

In 1923, on completion of the lease to Gibbs Mew, the Chough was sold to Strong's brewery of Romsey by Lloyd's Bank, who had taken over the Wilts & Dorset Bank in 1914, for £7500 [190]. In 1924, Strong's applied for planning permission to convert the stables and stores fronting Castle Street into a bar with a restaurant on the first floor [191]. Permission was granted and the building on Castle Street was changed to what we see today.

In 1957, the Chough was advertising that all the bedrooms had hot and cold running water and electric fires demonstrating that these conveniences were not common at that time.

The original bar of the Chough was on the east side of the yard entered by a few steps up from the yard followed by more steps down into the bar. This latter bar could become rowdy on Saturday nights as it was the haunt of Salisbury Rugby Club. The pub also had a skittle alley at the rear of the yard.

In 1969, the pub came under the ownership of Whitbread Wessex Ltd when that brewery acquired Strongs of Romsey. In 1989, the inn was extensively re-built with a 'glass wall' across the end of the yard adding a new bar immediately behind it and becoming a Beefeater Inn. Sometime before 2004, the pub became known as Alchemy@ the Chough.

In 2007, the pub closed for a short time before re-opening under the ownership of the Hidden Brewery from Wylye. Quite a lot of refurbishment was done but the pub never reached the potential that the brewery expected. In late 2009, Hidden left the Chough and it was taken over by Gusto. Finally, in 2013 the pub finally closed opening in 2014 as a restaurant, part of a chain named Bill's.

50 City Hall, Fisherton Street

The City Hall in Salisbury was built as the New Picture House in 1937. Its entrance was in an Art Deco style immediately to the east of Summerlock Approach. In 1961, the cinema was purchased by the District Council and converted into a public hall. During a later modernisation, the entrance to the City Hall was moved to the side of the building in Malthouse Lane. This left the old entrance redundant and it was used by a number of retail shops but in early 1990s it was used as a café and bar known as the Café Bar Circolo. This closed in 1999 leaving the old entrance once more as an unused space.

51 Cloisters, Catherine Street

This pub, on the north-east corner of Catherine Street and Ivy Street, has been known as the Cloisters since 1986 when it was extensively re-built by Gibbs Mew, the brewer, to create one large bar and a restaurant area. Before that it was known for many years as the Bell & Crown. But it only took that name in 1824. It had been known as the White Lion from 1772 to 1824 and before that it was the King of Prussia. Even earlier names were the Duke's Head (1757), the Duke William (1755), the Rose & Horseshoes (1743) and, possibly, the Horseshoes (1626).

Assuming that the attribution of the

Horseshoes to this public house is correct, then there is a reference to this inn in 1625-26, the landlord being John Layland. He attended the meeting to discuss the supply of beer and ale from the Common Brewhouse to the inns in the city [18].

In the 18th C. it was a regular venue for cock fighting [192]: 'A main of cocks will be fought each morning during the Races at the house of Jas. Imber, the sign of the King of Prussia in Cath St., between the Gentlemen of Wilts & Dorset, for 4 guineas a battle, & 20 the odd battle, to shew three cocks each for the main, & 10 for bye battles. To be pitted each morning at 10 o'clock. Hurst & Peake, Feeders.'

The White Lion seems to have fallen foul of some nefarious dealings in 1793 as it is recorded in the City Magistrates minutes that Arthur Smith, the landlord, was 'convicted in the penalty of 5s on the oath of Jno Robinson a private in the Buckinghamshire Militia of selling one pint of Cyder in the said City to the said Jno Robinson on Sat last 29th June, the said pint of Cyder not being of the Statute [3].' Since the Antelope in Catherine Street was also convicted of the same offence, at the same Magistrate's sitting on the oath of the same soldier, one wonders who instigated the charges? But perhaps Arthur Smith was not totally innocent as he had been convicted in 1791 of having 32 gallons of foreign brandy in his stock which had not been notified to the Excise (i.e. it had been smuggled) and had the Brandy confiscated [3].

In 1808, Jane Cook, the landlady, was convicted and fined £20 for not keeping good order at the White Lion and also allowing gambling to take place [4]. She left the pub later in the same year and William Knight became the landlord.

In January, 1821, it was advertised in the *Salisbury and Winchester Journal* that one half of a £20 note, from the bank of Brodie and Dowding in Salisbury, had been found on the pavement at the corner of High Street in November 1820 [193]. In January, the other half of the note had been found in a cupboard at the White Lion. The advertisement stated that if the owner went to the bank, giving the number of the note, they would be paid, less the expenses and a reward to the finders. In March of the same year, it was further advertised that if the owner of the note had not been able to find the number of the note, if they went to the bank and explained the circumstances whereby the two halves of the note had been found, they would be recompensed [194]. No further advertisements related to the note appeared in the *Journal*, and thus it is not known if the original owner was ever found.

In 1824, the following advertisement appeared in the *Salisbury and Winchester Journal* [195]: 'Salisbury, Bell and Crown Inn, Late the White Lion, Catherine-Street. To be Let, and entered on immediately, this the above Inn. It has been lately fitted up at considerable expense. Its vicinity to the principal Inns, and its long established reputation, secures it a constant and regular supply of Custom. The draught in Spirits is very great: in Beer, the consumption is Six Hogsheads per week. It is a Home Brewed Beerhouse, and has maintained its character for excellence in both. It possesses all the Accommodations which the first-rate Inns can supply, and presents a source of Speculation, which cannot fail of being eventually advantageous. For further particulars apply, personally or by letter (post-paid), to Messrs Maton and Co, High-street, Sarum. N.B. The Casks and Brewing Utensils may remain the property of the Proprietors.'

One notable landlord of the 1850s was Bridger Gibbs, the co-founder of Gibbs Mew, who brewed at the Bell & Crown between 1852 and 1858 before moving to the Anchor brewery site in Gigant Street [196]. But the Bell & Crown remained associated with Gibbs' brewery in the future and with Gibbs Mew after the 1898 merger of Gibbs' and Mew's breweries.

In late 1859, it was announced that the Salisbury Select Harmonic Society had been formed at the Bell and Crown and a celebratory dinner was held [197]. It was said that the dinner was of the "most sumptuous and recherché character", and reflected the highest credit on the host, Mr Colbourne. In keeping with the nature of the Society, some songs were sung by the members, and some members of the Cathedral choir, assisted by the Mr Colbourne, executed several catches and glees, amongst the latter of which were "Strike the Lyre", "The Mighty Conqueror", "Life's a Bumper" and "Sleep Gentle Lady"

David Rogers was charged with hawking without a certificate in 1875 [198]. A police constable saw him offer a tobacco pipe to a man in Ivy Street and accept money for it, before going into the Bell & Crown. The constable followed him into the pub and asked Rogers what he had been selling. He replied that he had sold nothing and confirmed that he had no license to sell as a pedlar. The police superintendent explained that Rogers was in the habit of buying a pipe for 6 pence and then offer it to people at the railway station for 3 shillings and sixpence. He made sure that he only had one pipe with him at a time and thus the police had great trouble in proving that he was a hawker. The Magistrates said that there was no law preventing a man from selling his own pipe. To be called a pedlar, a man must go from town to town or house to house selling items. This Rogers had not been doing and thus the case against him was dismissed.

The pub remained a Gibbs Mew pub until the demise of that brewery in 2000. Before that, in 1988, the pub was remodelled to provide one large bar plus a kitchen and an eating area on the ground floor of the pub. At that time its name was altered to the Cloisters and it has retained that name up until the present day.

52 Coach and Horses, Castle Street

Haskins notes this as being an alehouse, with Thomas Penny being the landlord, in 1743.[20] It may well be an inaccurate entry for the Coach & Horses in Catherine Street.

53 Coach and Horses, Catherine Street

Nothing more is known about this pub apart from an entry in the *Salisbury and Winchester Journal* in 1760 [199]: 'A middle size Man, dressed in a dark gray Coat" on July 13th, hired a light Chestnut Mare of Nathaniel Lane, at the Coach and Horses in Catherine Street. Reward to anyone securing the said Mare.'

This may have been referring to the Bell in Exeter Street which was known as the Coach & Horses earlier in the century and at this time St John Street was known as part of Catherine Street.

54 Coach and Horses, 39 Winchester Street

This building dates from the late 15th or early 16th C. This matches a record of an early deed relating to the pub dating back to 1482 when it was sold to William Kensington as the Cokk Inn. In 1560, it was said to have been known as the Tolbott but this name is almost certainly an earlier name for the Anchor and Hope(qv). It is also said that it was later known as the Running Horse but by the time the Coach and Horses was definitely in Winchester Street (see below) the Running Horse was also established in Winchester Street. It has also been said that it was the Three Tuns in 1780 but by this date, the Three Tuns was clearly established on the corner of Endless Street and Winchester Street.

The earliest records of the Coach and Horses clearly show that it was either at the very east end of Winchester Street or in the London Road An article in the *Salisbury and Winchester Journal* in 1765 states that the Coach & Horses was above Winchester Gate [200] and an advert of 1783 states it was at the upper end of Winchester Street on the turnpike road leading to London [201].

In 1787, the landlord, James Olden, was convicted of harbouring and concealing in his house two men and one woman, who were suspected to have committed a robbery in the shop of Mr Gillo, salesman, in this City [202]. He had his licence revoked and was prohibited from selling ale for three years. Again, this article states that the Coach and Horses was in the parish of Milford, adjoining the city of New Sarum which suggests that the pub was still outside of the Winchester Gate.

Thus there is some doubt whether the earlier references to the Cokk refer to the site near Winchester Gate or to the more recent site of the Coach and Horses in the middle of Winchester Street.

Not until 1795 do we find references which refer to the Coach and Horses being in Winchester Street in the city of New Sarum and thus confidently being attributed to the current premises [203]. Suffice it to say that there has been a pub on the current site from the late 1400s even if we are unsure of its name!

In 1879, the ostler at the Coach & Horses had a pair of boots stolen [204]. The alleged culprit was Ralph Downs, but at his court appearance the police asked for a further remand of Downs in order that further enquiries about him could be made. The following week, he appeared in court again. When asked to plead, he said that 'I must plead guilty, on my own innocence'. What he meant by this was that he admitted having the boots in his possession but he did not admit stealing them, suggesting that another man was involved. From police evidence, it emerged that Ralph Downs was also known as Alfred Downs and also as George Williams. He had been found to be a deserter from the 76th Regiment of Foot from which he had absconded in July, 1877. He had subsequently, fraudulently, enlisted with the Royal Wilts Militia. Owing to his guilty plea, he was sentenced to four months' imprisonment with hard labour. Presumably he was handed over to the military authorities when he had completed his sentence.

In 1884, the pub was put up for sale by Charles Holloway who was retiring from business on account of ill health [205]. The pub was described as having on the

Coach and Horses

ground floor an entrance gateway, a front bar, with a smoking room adjoining, a tap room, a kitchen, a large front market room or dining room, a capital beer cellar, a compact brew house and a hop loft over it, a spirit cellar, a larder, a coal cellar and a WC. On the first floor was a private sitting room, six bedrooms and a WC. There was also a Coach House and stables for 20 horses.

It appears that the pub was purchased by Folliott's brewery. That brewery was purchased by Usher's Brewery of Trowbridge with whom it remained for many years.

After 1991, it was run by Inntrepreneur after the Grand Metropolitan/Courage pub swap. In 1986 it was re-modelled with a single bar and rooms opening off what was the original carriageway through the building. In early July 2015, the pub was closed. A new leaseholder came forward and it was hoped to reopen the pub for the August Bank Holiday weekend. Later in 2015, the pub was closed again and its future fate is not known.

55 Cock, nk

An alehouse that applied for a licence and had it granted in 1743. It was described as being 'overight St Edmund's Church'.

56 Comb Pot, Milford Street

Another pub that is known via a single reference in an advertisement in the *Salisbury and Winchester Journal* in 1740. This described John Grove, a corn-cutter, as living at the sign of the Comb Pot [206].

His trade was the removing of corns from feet etc. not cutting arable crops!

57 Commercials, 131 South Western Road
Licensed in the 1920s and 30s and believed to be a small hotel with a public bar.

58 Cope, High Street
This is mentioned in a document of 1476 as being in the High Street next to the Helme. The Helme was part of what had formerly been Pynnock's Inn which was on the west side of High Street. Thus, the Cope could have been a forerunner of the Crown Hotel.

59 Cornmarket Inn, Cheese Market
This new pub opened as the Slurping Toad early in 1998 on the corner of the walkway next to the library, virtually on the site of the Maidenhead. It was part of a chain of inns owned by Eldridge Pope of Dorchester. It was re-worked as a pub in 2002 and renamed the Cornmarket Inn (presumably because it is next door to the Library which was originally built as the Corn Market). Closed in late 2006 and became a restaurant.

60 Countewell's Inn, High Street
This inn was immediately to the north of Pynnoks Inn and on the north side of the Town ditch in High Street. This places it as being on the west side of High Street immediately north of the junction with New Canal. It was owned as a private house by Geoffery of Warminster in 1335. Richard Furbour owed 2 shillings in rent on his building in 1406 which was noted as being above the ditch next to Countwelle Inn.

There is a Cartwell's Inn noted in the City Domesday of 1442 but no street is given. It is presumed this is the same inn with the variability of spelling that was common at that time.

Geoffrey of Warminster's heir, Reginald de Kyngesbrugge, leased the building as "Countwell's Inn" to a person unknown in 1455. An entry in the city Ledgers of 1474 seems to refer to it as the Cup Inn.

61 Crane, Crane Street
John Chandler, in the notes appended to his book, Endless Street, states that Crane Street was named after an inn (Notes to Chapter 4: Note 7). In a more recent volume [207], he equates it with Rechabite House in Crane Street. A reference in 1455 mentions a house called Le Crane, owned by Sir John Lysle, that was near to the Lower Bridge in Fisherton. Sir John Lysle (1406-1471) was Sheriff of Wiltshire in 1438-39 but most of his business was in Hampshire. It is likely that this was the town house of Sir John which would have also been used by his staff when visiting Salisbury on his business. It would have had a sign or badge outside of it, to assist those who could not read, which led to its name. Whether this was actually at any time an inn in the conventional meaning of the word is uncertain.

62 Cricketers Arms, Rampart Road
From an entry in the 1861 census, this pub appears to be immediately adjacent to the Winchester Gate public house, on the south side. Henry Forward obtained a full

licence for it in 1855, but it may well have been a beer-only house before that date. It disappears from the licensing records after the 1866 annual licensing session. There is a possibility that it was incorporated into the Winchester Gate as the southern extension of the public bar of that pub does appear, externally, to be a different building.

63 Cross Keys Inn, Queen Street

This inn was in Queen Street where the entrance to the Cross Keys Chequer shopping mall is now. The exact form of this building and the adjoining Plume of Feathers inn is difficult to ascertain as the whole site has been rebuilt. Parts of the buildings have been rebuilt using original materials, others have been rebuilt in modern materials and others have been completely remodelled. The inn was certainly in existence by 1649 and was present up to at least 1865 but had gone by the 1871 Census. It would appear that the Cross Keys was to the south of the present entrance with the Plume of Feathers to the north. An etching of the old Council House, which burnt down in 1780, clearly shows a sign of the Cross Keys in the background with the landlord being shown as J Page. This was published in Peter Hall's 'Picturesque Memorials of Salisbury' [208] in 1834 but unfortunately the etching is undated.

The life of a landlord in the centre of a busy city had its ups and downs as it does nowadays [209]: 'Whereas on Whit-Sunday last, between One & Two o'clock in the morning, Capt. Clements, of the Regiment now lying in Salisbury, did encourage one of his Soldiers to beat & abuse one John Webb, Landlord of the Cross Keys Inn (and is bound over to the Assizes for the same) and the said Soldier did thereupon threaten with several oaths that he would beat me to Death. That he may also be brought to Justice for the said offence, and to prevent the like again, I do hereby offer a Reward of Half a Guinea to any Person who will discover to me the Name of and Place where the said Soldier is now to be found. John Webb.'

One may deduce that life did not get any easier for a publican in later years [210]: 'A Meeting will be held at the Cross Keys Inn, in Sarum, on Tuesday the 22nd day of April instant, at two o'clock in the afternoon, to establish an Association for the prevention of Robberies and Thefts, the preservation of Private Property, and the protection of Persons of Individuals. At this Meeting, Proper Articles will be ready for the inspection and approbation of all Persons who choose to become Members thereof.'

In February 1808, an unusual advertisement was placed by George Fry, the landlord of the Cross Keys, for the sale of gypsum for the use as a fertiliser for crops such as Clover, Sainfoin and Lucerne [211]. What is particularly strange is the advertisement offers to ship the gypsum to any part of the country which would be appropriate for the other advertiser, the Gypsum Company, but seems strange for the landlord of a town inn!

Single Stick was a common and popular form of competition in earlier years. It is sometimes stated to be an early form of fencing but using a stick which was held with one hand. A bout was advertised in the *Salisbury and Winchester Journal* in 1808 [212]: 'Single Stick. There will be a

Match played at Salisbury, on Wednesday and Thursday Mornings, July the 27th and 28th, being the last two days of the Races, for Twenty Guineas each day. To play without pads Wednesday and with pads Thursday, in order that the Somersetshire men may have an opportunity of playing in the practice of their county as well as the Wiltshire. The play to be conducted by able judges, and the greatest care taken that the prizes be properly contested and fairly won. Each Player to enter his name at the Cross Keys – as early on the morning of playing, as the play must be arranged so as to terminate before one o'clock, when the Races begin.'

The landlord in 1814, John Butt, who had been at the Cross Keys for only three years, died. The following obituary appeared in the *Journal* [213]: 'With feelings of the deepest regret we record the death of Mr John Butt, of the Cross keys Inn, in this city, who departed this transitory life on Tuesday se'nnight, at Blandford; a young man whose exemplary good conduct throughout life endeared him, not only to his immediate relatives and friends, but to all who knew him. To the inexpressible grief which this melancholy circumstance produced in the minds of his brothers and sisters, was added the afflicting loss of their second brother, Mr William Butt, who died on Monday last, after having suffered most severe attacks of epilepsy for ten successive years. – We hesitate not to add, that society a loss by the death of these excellent and much-respected young men.'

His father, also John Butt became landlord of the inn in 1786 and ran it until he died in 1793 [214]. His wife, Martha then ran the Cross keys until 1802 when she married George Fry [215] and, in accordance with the practice at the time, George became the landlord. George Fry died in 1811 after falling down the stairs at an inn in Devizes [216]. John Butt, junior took over the running of the inn.

That the Cross Keys was an important inn cannot be doubted after reading the following advertisement which appeared after the death of John Butt, junior [217]: 'Capital Inn to be disposed of. Cross Keys Inn, Salisbury. To be Sold by Auction, by Mr Elderton, on the premises, on Tuesday the 6th day of September next, at four o'clock in the afternoon, (unless previously disposed of by Private Contract) – All that very valuable and long established Inn, called the Cross Keys, situate in the Market Place of the City of Salisbury, in the County of Wilts, late in the occupation of Mr John Butt, deceased, with excellent newly built Wine Vaults, (which, being very capacious, render the premises peculiarly eligible for the business of a wine merchant), roomy cellars for spirits and beers, brew-house, malt rooms, ware rooms, coach houses, stabling for nearly fifty horses, stable yard, a separate house for soldiers, and various other accommodations – Also a Messuage on the right of the front gateway of the said Inn, and another Messuage on the left of the said gateway, in the respective occupancies of Mr Back and Mr Harding. The premises are most desirably situated for business, being near the Council House where County Assizes and Quarter Sessions are held, and on the great Western Road from London to the Land's End. This Inn is one of the most respectable and best accustomed in the West of England, its trade is very extensive and increasing. The late proprietor and his family have been in the occupation of it 29 years and it is now to be disposed of on account of his decease. The Purchaser will be expected to take all the Household Furniture, Stock of Wines, Spirits, beer etc etc by Appraisement.'

James Morris, a Wine and Brandy merchant took over the premises and advertises that he has a well selected stock of wines and spirits [218]. In December, 1829, John Perry announces that he has taken the Cross Keys, but in the same edition of the *Salisbury and Winchester Journal*, a sale is announced of all the brewing equipment and household furniture of the inn. But immediately after, in January, 1830, the matter is clarified as the sale is of the property belonging to James Morris, who has left the Cross Keys. What is more, the furniture has been removed from the inn to another building so, presumably, John Perry has installed his own furniture and fittings.

In 1865, there is a complex series of advertisements that amount to the Cross Keys being sold, either as a whole or in parts, along with all the contents of the inn [219]. It appears that different parts of the inn were sold to different people as, in March, 1867, James Mitchell announces that he still keeps the Cross Keys Corn Store, which apparently had access from Brown Street [220]. The inn appears to have been kept running as a Mr Lodge announces the sale of all the contents of the inn, also in March, 1867 [221], including the brewing plant, as he is moving to the Shoulder of Mutton. However, the inn does not appear in the licensing records after 1865, so for the short period of two years, it may have operated simply as a beer-only house.

64 Cross Keys Tap, Brown Street

In the mid-19th C, this was at the back of the Cross Keys Inn, a little south of the junction between Winchester Street and Brown Street.om the west side of Brown Street. It was licensed in its own right from 1841 until 1865 and appears to be still operating as a pub in late 1866. It is probable that the Cross Keys Tap acted as the public bar whereas the bar in the inn was for the use of guests and travellers alone.

In 1853, the daughter of the landlord, Mr Smart, was found drowned in the water channel running down Brown Street [222]. The report is the *Salisbury and Winchester Journal* was headlined 'The Open Channels Again' which suggests that death resulting from falling into the water channels or canals in Salisbury was not an unusual occurrence.

That the Tap was considered to be part of the premises of the Cross Keys Inn can be seen from a notice of sale with the latter inn in 1865 [223]. It seems likely that the Cross Keys Tap was sold separately from the rest of the Cross Keys as a later advertisement does not mention the Tap [224]. However, in 1866, the household furniture, fixtures and effects of the Cross Keys Tap were put up for sale as Mr Ireland, the landlord was moving to the Waggon and Horses in Brown Street [225]. The pub stayed open for some time as late in 1866, two men were charged with having tendered a forged coin in payment for beer at the Tap [226]. However, in the following week when the men were brought before the court, they were discharged as there was doubt as to the identity of the coin produced in court as it had been handled by several people who had determined that it was a forged coin.

The Cross Keys Tap does not appear in any later licensing records and is presumed to have been closed in late 1866 or 1867.

65 Crown, Castle Street

This alehouse was described as being 'without Castle Gate'. In other words, it was in Castle Street but just to the north of the old gate. It was in existence in 1625 when the landlord, Richard Toppyn, attended the Council meeting that discussed inns taking beer and ale from the Common Brewhouse.[18] In 1666, Thomas Shergold issued a halfpenny token showing a crown on the obverse [227]. This has been linked to this pub possibly because the Crown in High Street may have been known as the Rose and Crown at that time.

The alehouse seems to have had a poor reputation. This culminated in August 1788 with the events being described in the *Salisbury and Winchester Journal* [228]: 'Friday last Samuel Edwards and Martha Williams were brought hither from Bath, and on Saturday they were committed to Fisherton gaol, by the Magistrates of this city, to take their trial at the next Lent Assizes, charged on the oath of Matthias Jenneway, with a violent suspicion of having privately and feloniously stolen out of his breeches pocket, in the night of the 4th of August inst. at the Crown alehouse in this city, a leather purse, and seventeen guineas in gold, and half a crown and sixpence in silver. These are the two persons mentioned in our last, as having been concerned with Sarah Verriner in the said robbery, besides whom there appears to have been other accomplices, who are not yet taken. The Crown alehouse abovementioned has long been a receptacle for the most infamous and abandoned characters of both sexes; the master of it is at present a convict in Fisherton gaol, but the business of the house, as conducted by his wife, suffers little diminution from this circumstance; on the contrary, it affords almost one continual scene of riot, debauchery, and the most abandoned profligacy. We are happy to hear that in consequence of the many complaints preferred against it, the Magistrates have resolved to discontinue the licence, and we also have good reason to hope that several other houses in the city of bad repute will meet with a similar fate.'

The house does seem to have closed at this time as no more is heard of a Crown in Castle Street. However, there is no mention of the Rising Sun (qv) in Castle Street until about 1795 and it is quite possible that the Crown was re-opened as that pub.

66 Crown, Fisherton

Haskins states that this alehouse was granted a license in 1752 with the landlord being Thomas Bury.[21] No other mention has been found of this house

67 Crown Hotel, 46/48 High Street

Certainly one of the earlier inns in Salisbury, the Crown seems to have been called the Rose in 1411 when it was given by John Goweyn to the Procurator and Commonalty of the Cathedral. The Crowne Inn is mentioned in the instructions of the Tailors Guild in 1450, showing it to be in High Street although it appears to have covered the whole corner between High Street and Crane Street. In 1624, a new house appeared in Crane Bridge Street called The Rose which had stabling for 30 horses [229]. This appears to be part of the Crown Inn.

In the late 18th and early 19th C, the inn in High Street was known as the Rose & Crown and some early photos of Crane Bridge Street clearly show an entrance with the sign saying the Crown Hotel. Thus, about all one can say is that the inn in High Street extended around the corner in Crane Bridge Street and was variously one or two establishments known as the Rose, the Crown or the Rose & Crown!

In 1624, John Morrys of the Rose and Crown took 2 Hogsheads and 1 Barrel of beer from the Common Brewhouse. [17] He also took 6 couls of ale but it has not been possible to identify the size of a coul. John Morrys also attended the meeting in 1625 of innkeepers and ale-house keepers called by the Council to discuss their taking beer and ale from the Common Brewhouse. [18]

In December 1772, there was a robbery at the Rose and Crown [230]. A person unknown, while the family was busy in the kitchen, went up into the chamber & broke open a chest of drawers, and took away out of the small drawer £18 14s; also a purse with £11 16s and another purse with 3 pieces of eight, 3 Queen Anne's half-crowns; four crown pieces, 2 of King William's, one of Queen Elizabeth's & the other of King Charles'; with a great many 2d 3d & 4d pieces; one gold wedding ring, the posy of which is "In thee my choice, I do rejoice"; one pair of stone buttons, & one link of plain silver buttons. The landlord of the inn, William Biddlecombe, offered a reward of five guineas for information leading to the apprehension of the criminal but it is not known if this reward was successful in arresting the villain.

In 1785, the lease of the inn was advertised for sale [231], it being described as the Rose and Crown in High Street. It was held on a 40-year lease from the Vicars of the Cathedral Church of New Sarum.

In 1834, the Salisbury Lodge of the Ancient Order of Druids held their tenth anniversary dinner at the Rose and Crown [232]. Members of another lodge attended the meeting and members of both lodges visited Stonehenge.

In early 1848, the Rose and Crown was advertised as available to rent [233]. It was stated that the House had undergone a compete repair and made more compact, the rent and general out-goings considerably reduced, and the coming-on can be rendered easy. This may have been a precursor to the events later in the year.

In August 1848, the Messrs Brodie were declared bankrupt. As a result, there was a sale of their property [234] which included ownership of the *Salisbury and Winchester Journal*. Also included was a leasehold inn called the Rose and Crown Inn, in Crane Bridge Street but which was connected to the Rose and Crown Inn in High Street, this inn being unoccupied at the time of the sale. To confuse matters more, in April 1849, there was an advertisement in which the lease of the Rose and Crown Inn in High Street, occupied by William Fawcett, was offered for sale [235]. In addition, there was a lease for sale of a dwelling house in Crane Bridge Street, described as being newly constructed, that had been occupied by the Rose and Crown in High Street but was unoccupied at the time of sale.

By 1862, the lease of the inn was again offered for sale as the Crown Inn [236]. It possessed a commodious billiard-room, parlour, smoking, and other convenient rooms; together with a most excellent brewhouse, large and commodious cellar; and fitted up with every convenience for carrying on a General Tavern Business. No mention is made at this time of the premises in Crane Bridge Street. The advertisement notes that the inn was still held under a lease from the Vicars of Salisbury Cathedral but confusingly, the premises are described as occupying the corner of Crane Street and High Street.

In 1872, the hotel was taken over by Edmund Whitby Wells. Shortly afterwards, he starts to advertise the sale of home brewed ales which were described as being the cheapest, purest and best in Salisbury [237]. Apart from his own ales, he also sold Guinness's Dublin Stout and Allsopp's Pale Ales, this being from Burton-on-Trent. By 1878, he advertises that he has opened a wine and spirit department in Crane Street [238], this being the part of the hotel that later became the Old Ale House (qv). By 1882, he becomes the agent in Salisbury for Groves' brewery of Weymouth [239] The beer from this brewery appears to replace Mr Well's home brewed ales.

In 1884, Mr Wells announces that he is retiring from business and that in consequence the household furniture and the brewing plant were put up for sale [240]. Charles Frederick Chubb becomes the new landlord but by the emphasis in his advertisements on his being the agent of Groves' brewery [241], it seems likely that this is the date when the brewery became the owners of the premises. It continued to be owned by that brewery until 1960 when Devenish took over Groves.

The Crown survived as a hotel well into the 20th C and in 1938 described itself as a 'well-known Hotel, fully licensed and open all the year round and noted for its excellent cuisines, quick service and comfort.' There was hot and cold running water in all bedrooms, electric light and two billiard tables. The garage had room for 15 cars on the premises and hence must still have had access from Crane Bridge Street. It closed in about 1969. (but see entry for the Old Ale House)

It is of interest that remnants of the inn still exist in that a shop in High Street still has a goods entrance in Crane Bridge Street.

68 Crown & Anchor Inn, 108 Exeter Street

The Crown and Anchor was on the east side of Exeter Street well down the street towards the Exeter Street roundabout. The building appears to date from the 16th C. and this matches the earliest records of the pub in 1625 when it was known as the Griffin. By 1664, a farthing token issued by George Clemens has a creature upon it that has been described as a dragon. In 1727, the pub appears to have been known as the Dragon. In 1782 & 1787 it was known as the Flower Pots [242] although in 1791 we once again find it called the Griffon with the landlord being Clement Miller. Perhaps a succession of landlords was not able to distinguish between a griffin and a dragon!

By 1803 the pub was known as the Northumberland Arms and it retained that name until Thomas Newport changed it to the Horse & Jockey in July, 1808. The pub was known as the Crown and Anchor in 1813 and retained that name until it closed.

In August, 1817, William Lawrence, the landlord, announces that he will have a booth at the Salisbury Races, near the starting post, where he will sell Wines,

Spirits, and Home-Brewed Beer [243]. In 1820, he then announces that his friends and gentlemen may become members of his Annual Cucumber Society, provided they pay their subscription for at least three months. The next annual show of cucumbers was held in March, 1821, when the first prize was a piece of plate valued at £2 10s.

In 1823, a not uncommon event occurred at the Crown and Anchor. A Mr Park had sent a horse to the pub for stabling but the landlord had heard nothing from Mr Park for four months. Consequently, he advertised that if the horse was not collected and the expense of its keep paid, the horse would be auctioned in Salisbury Market to defray the expenses. There is no indication as to whether the horse was collected or sold.

In May, 1855, George Blake was summoned for obstructing Exeter Street by leaving three horses and a donkey unattended. The police constable giving evidence said he found Blake in the Crown and Anchor and warned him that if he did not move them in fifteen minutes, he would be prosecuted. The constable returned in an hour and a half to find the animals still outside the pub. Part of Blake's defence was that he had only two horses and no donkey! He was fined 5 shillings and costs but warned that if he was summoned a second time, he would be fined the full amount of £5.

In 1880, an able bodied seaman from HMS Duke of Wellington at Portsmouth, Emmanuel Robbins, was charged with refusing to quit the pub but also with attempting to stab the landlord, James Elliott. While in the pub, Robbins started quarrelling with a woman and struck her two or three times. The landlord interfered in the argument and Robbins assaulted him, drew a knife, and attempted to stab him. After he was thrown out of the pub, he broke two panes of glass. Robbins offered no explanation for his behaviour and the court sentenced him to one month's imprisonment with hard labour.

The Crown and Anchor was an Usher's house for many years. By the end of the 20th C. its trade was declining and it was only open intermittently. It closed permanently in about 2002 and since then has been converted into three dwellings. However, the gate into the old pub yard still retain the initials 'C' and 'A'.

69 Crown & Guns, Market Place

This alehouse was in the Market Place but its exact location is unknown. It may also have been known as the Cross Guns. The only records of its existence are from the 1790s. In June 1794, William Munday who was licenced to keep the Crown and Guns in the Parish of St Thomas appeared at a meeting of the Magistrates and voluntarily surrendered his licence [3]. No more is heard of this alehouse.

70 Crown & Slipper, Fisherton

An alehouse that was in the parish of Fisherton and is known from a few references dating from the middle part of the 18th C. A sale of timber took place at the premises in 1746 and it is said that Thomas Smith was granted a licence for it as an alehouse in 1762. It may not have been an establishment of very high class as in June, 1755, Daniel Cornish who was lodging at the Crown and Slipper was committed to the Salisbury Gaol for stealing a horse!

71 Crystal Fountain, 45 Milford Street

This pub was on the north side of Milford Street between Pennyfarthing Street and Guilder Lane. It appears to have been built in 1840 and plans dating from 1849 show extensive brewery buildings behind it in Swayne's Chequer. It has been described as being a large three-storeyed building with a prominent bay window on the first floor.

Emma Higgins applied for a spirit licence in September, 1852, but it was refused. She reapplied in 1853 and had the licence granted. It is assumed that the pub was an alehouse before this.

In 1857, the pub is put up for sale and described as "newly erected" but that it had had a good beer and spirit trade since it had opened as an inn. Presumably this good trade had been since 1853, but if it was built in 1840, it seems a long time for it still to be described as recently built.

At the annual licensing session in September, 1870, the Crystal Fountain was one of eight pubs that had been complained against. The Mayor said that all eight licenses would be granted provided the landlords gave undertakings that their houses would be run in an orderly and peaceable fashion.

In October of the same year, the landlord, Edmund Decamp, was charged with wasting water supplied to him by the Board of Health. It appeared that there was water continuously running from a fault in the pipes in the toilet. Mr Decamp had been warned about this leak but a month later the water was still running. That this leak was considered a serious matter was more to do with mains supplied water being a rarity at this time and the source of water being somewhat limited. Suffice it to say, Mr Decamp was fined five shillings and costs.

At the annual licensing session in 1889, the Salisbury Temperance Society objected to the license of the Crystal Fountain being renewed on the grounds that the landlord had allowed drunkenness on his premises. As might be expected, the Temperance Society wished to reduce the total number of pubs in the City, but on a previous occasion, they had been advised that rather than petitioning for a reduction in numbers, they would be better opposing individual licenses when there was good reason for the objection. In fact, there had only been one previous referral of the pub to the Magistrates and, in that case, the landlord pleaded guilty and paid the fine. The police stated that after that incident, the pub had been much better managed. Consequently, the Magistrates overruled the objection and granted renewal of the license.

However, four years later, the landlord of the pub, David Bissett, was summoned for allowing drunkenness in his house. Mr Bissett did not appear in court and a doctor's certificate was produced showing that he was seriously ill and might die. Consequently, the summons to appear in court had not been served. The case was adjourned for three weeks, by which time Mr Bissett had died and a new tenant for the pub had been found. No notice of objection to the renewal of the license had been served and thus the Magistrates granted renewal of the license. However, they made it quite clear that if Mr Bissett had still been alive and had attended the court, his license would not have been renewed.

From the 1930s it was an Ushers house and it remained under that ownership until it closed on 25th August, 1968. Its license lapsed at the Brewster sessions on 2nd February 1970. It was demolished in 1970 and replaced by modern office buildings. For some years afterwards, there was small commemorative sign with the name of the pub outside of these offices.

72 Cups, 111/113 South Western Road

This was a small hotel in South Western Road with a bar that was open to the public at its front. It appeared in the licensing records from 1927 until 1964. It seems to have closed as an hotel in about 1970.

73 Danny's Craft Bar, 2-4 Salt Lane

This building was formerly the Liberal Club for many years and was on the south side of Salt Lane, near to the junction with Rollestone Street, opposite the Pheasant Inn. It became the Café Prague in early 1997. A little later its name was changed to the Café Pride with the hope of establishing a gay bar in Salisbury. It was then changed to Mojito, a bistro and tapas bar.

It became Conran's Bar in 2007. This was an Irish themed bar, serving food with live music often being played. In January 2015, it was announced that Conran's was to be closed. In August 2015, the premises were refurbished and opened as Danny's Craft Bar, with a range of craft beers and cocktails.

74 Deacons, Fisherton Street

This pub was open in 1871 and possibly a little earlier when it was known as the Star. As this was technically in Fisherton village, there was no apparent conflict with the Star in Brown Street which was in New Sarum.

Mr Edward Wortley, the landlord, applied for a spirit license for the pub in 1875, his solicitor stating that the pub had held a beer license for at least ten years. He also stated that the pub had been purchased by Lovibond's brewery the previous year and they had spent much money in converting the pub to be used as a hotel. The premises now had seven bedrooms, which were often let to commercial travellers, but also had two rooms especially for soldiers when they were billeted there! Since there had been no objections from persons in the locality and that the police stated that they had had no complaints since the pub opened, the Magistrates granted the license.

The Star remained a Lovibond's house until 1962 when that brewery was taken over by Courage's. It was converted in about 1987 to provide space for an additional bar and carvery and became known as the Rare Joint. It did little trade in this form and it was sold in 1989 to become the Deacon's Alms, a free house which specialised in having a variety of real ales. More recently, the name has been shortened to Deacons. In August, 2015, the pub was closed for a while but it reopened in 2016.

75 Devizes Inn, 55 Devizes Road

This pub dates from about 1881 when it was known as the Devizes Road Hotel. It initially held a six-day license which meant that it could not open on Sundays. In 1886, an application was made on behalf of the landlord for a full seven day's license. The Mayor, as Chairman of the Magistrates, stated that he did not consider that the arguments put forward to support the application were sufficient to overturn the understanding from when the house was first licensed that its license should be for six days only.

A year later a Coroner's inquest was held at the pub. It was the normal practice for inquests to be held at public houses at this time as pubs had the room to accommodate a jury and other interested parties. In this case, the inquest was on the death of a three-month-old baby. His mother put him to bed in the morning and when she checked on him one or two hours later, she found him lying on his face, quite dead. It was stated that it was quite evident that the baby had suffocated and hence a verdict of accidental death was returned. It is doubtful that such a verdict would be so easily arrived at these days!

In 1898 and 1899, further attempts to gain a seven days license were made. In both cases, the application was refused. In the second case, the Salisbury Temperance Society joined in with their objections to the extension of drinking on Sundays. However, in 1900 yet another attempt to gain the extended license was made. On this occasion, the solicitor making the application was said to represent both the landlord and Messrs Styring & Co, brewers of Tisbury and Poole, who were now the owners of the hotel. A particular part of the application was that the Devizes Road Hotel was the only licensed premises in Salisbury to have a six days license. This time, finally, the license extension was granted.

The pub remained as a Styring's house until that brewery was taken over by Eldridge Pope of Dorchester in 1916. But it appears that Mr Frederick Styring retained some interest in the pub as between 1932 and 1975, the licensing records show joint ownership between the brewery and Mr Styring. The pub remained in Eldridge Pope hands until that brewery sold its pub estate in 1997.

It was one of the few pubs in Salisbury to retain an off-trade counter until recent years. It was also unusual in having an entrance to the public bar on one side of the building and a separate entrance to the saloon bar on the opposite side. It was known by the name of the Devizes Inn from 1979. By 2015, the pub was closed up and advertised for sale but reopened in 2016.

76 Dolphin, Dolphin Street (Little Culver Street)

This pub was in Dolphin Street which was formerly known as Little Culver Street and is clearly a different house from the other two Dolphins. Haskins states that Thomas Thomas was granted a licence for an alehouse called the White Swan in Payne's Hill in 1743. As with many of these alehouse licences, it is probable that the White Swan had been a pub before this date.

John Jones, an 'operator of the teeth' from London, lodged at the White Swan in July 1757 [244]. He said he could be spoken with at any time of the day!

In May 1776, the White Swan was put up for sale by auction at the Three Lions and it was advertised that it had 'a much-esteemed vault or cellar under the same' [245]. The pub was still available for sale in 1777. Gordon states that in 1778, the White Swan had been closed and its licence transferred to a house in Brown Street that had not been previously licenced. It is thought that this new public house may well be the White Swan in Brown Street. Although it has not been possible to verify Gordon's statement, Joseph Rogers is shown in the licensing records as being the last landlord of the White Swan on Payne's Hill in 1777 and the first landlord of the White Swan in Brown Street in 1779 so this change of license is believed to be correct.

In 1788, Mr Woolfry and Captain Mount, who both lived in Payne's Hill requested that the Justices did not to grant a license for the house which had been Mr Roger's [2]. This was clearly the White Swan and the Justices acquiesced with the request. There is a little confusion at this time as a notice of sale in 1801 describes the Dolphin as being occupied by Joseph Rogers, the malthouse adjoining the Dolphin also being for sale as also were the three tenements adjoining the malthouse that had at one time been a house known as the White Swan! {246}. But a conveyance of 1849, associated with the sale of the Dolphin, clearly states that this pub had formerly been known as the White Swan [247]. This conveyance clearly shows the Dolphin to have been on the south-east corner of Payne's Hill and Dolphin Street.

In 1801 once again, Joseph Rogers is shown to be the landlord. He, published the following notice in the *Journal*: 'Dolphin Inn, Salisbury. Joseph Rogers begs leave to return his most sincere Thanks to his Friends for their past favours for the many years last in the Public and Malting Business, and informs them that he still continues the above Businesses, and humbly hopes for a continuance of their favours, which will be ever esteemed and gratefully acknowledged by their most obedient servant, Joseph Rogers.' [248]

In 1832, the pub held its first annual cucumber show in April [249] followed by a carnation show in August [250]. In 1840, there was an auction at the Dolphin of 50 quarters of malt [251]. There was a warning that the malt was "slightly smoked" as a result of a fire at the maltsters and hence the malt was sold with no reserve price.

The following year there was a demonstration of New Zealand cookery [252]. A Mr Wood was to prepare a meal for fifty persons without the use of fire or any cooking utensil! The food was warranted to be superior to any cooked by the traditional methods of boiling or roasting. There is a slight clue as to how this was to be achieved in that the guests, by paying an extra sixpence on top of the price of the meal, they could see the provisions being taken out of the earth!

There had been a Friendly Society at the Dolphin since 1808. In December, 1842, there was a meeting held to dissolve the society on the grounds that the remaining members had become old and could not run the Society with efficiency [253]. It was reported that during the 34 years of the Society, it had paid for the burial of 45 members, for the burial of 36 women (wives of members), and paid £1284 1s to members when they were sick.

A notice of sale of the furniture and fittings of the inn in 1846 described it as having nine bedrooms, two parlours, a club room, a kitchen, a bar and a shop [254]. A week later, the inn itself was advertised as available to rent.

Throughout the 1850s, the pub appears to have become rather down at heel. In 1851, two men and two women were convicted of behaving in a riotous and disorderly manner in and near the Dolphin at one o'clock on a Sunday morning [255]. The Superintendent of Police commented that disorderly behaviour was a frequent occurrence at the Dolphin. In 1853, Robert Safe was convicted of being disorderly and resisting the police after he refused to leave the Dolphin when told to by the landlord [256]. Again, the Superintendent stated that there had been numerous complaints about the disorderly behaviour at the Dolphin. The Mayor also said that he had cautioned the landlady twice and that if the behaviour continued, she might have to leave the pub. By 1859, when there was a request to transfer the licence of the Dolphin to a new landlord, there was an objection by the police on the grounds that he was not a fit person to be entrusted to a licence [257]. However, it was pointed out that if the licence was refused, the Dolphin could only be opened as a beer-house, in which case the police would have less legal reasons to regulate the pub. Thus the licence was granted.

The pub appears for the last time in the licensing records in the autumn of 1861. In February 1862, the pub was put up for sale [258]. It appears that if it was sold, it did not continue as a pub as later in that year the contents of the pub were sold [259]. Nothing more is heard of the Dolphin.

77 Dolphin, Fish Row

This pub was close to the site of the Guildhall in the Market Square. It is said that it was known as the Royal Oak in 1743. However, the Royal Oak was said to have changed its name to the Dolphin in 1779. In 1788, the *Salisbury and Winchester Journal* stated [260]: 'The men employed in pulling down the houses upon the site of our intended new Council House, discovered on Thursday a very ancient stone chimney piece, most curiously carved, in the house adjoining the Dolphin ale-house. It is not improbable that this piece of work once adorned a great man's house in Old Sarum, and we hope it will not be defaced.'

Since there is no mention of this pub after that date, it is presumed it was one of the houses demolished to make way for the Council House.

With regard to the relation between this inn and the Dolphin in New Street, that inn closed in 1740 and thus there is no conflict with this later inn.

78 Dolphin, New Street.

Haskins attributes John Durneford, who attended the Council Meeting regarding inns taking beer from the Common Brewhouse in 1626, as being the landlord of the Dolphin in Fish Row. It is more likely to have been this Dolphin as the other inn was probably known as the Royal Oak in that year. It should also be noted that Haskins points out that he has added the names of the streets in which the inns lie and he clearly adds the street name of a later inn in several cases. Haskins also places this Dolphin on the corner of New Street and Catherine Street in 1718.

The Will of John Trowman, a tailor, dated 19 January, 1648 shows that he bequeathed to his son (also John) 'the house in the lower end of New Street known by the sign of the Dolphin' [261]. However, an indenture of 1658, in the same bundle of documents as John Trowman's will, is concerned with the sale of two buildings in Ivy Street that had been the property of John Trowman the son. But in this later Indenture, there is no mention of the Dolphin so it is not possible to link these properties with the Dolphin mentioned in the will. However, it does state that John Trowman the elder had occupied the premises in Ivy Street since 1621 and it should be noted that Ivy Street was considered to be part of New Street in past years.

However, Vaughan Richardson issued a farthing token in 1666 [262]. This token shows the name Vaughan Richardson with the image of a dolphin on the obverse with 'Katherine Str in Sarum' on the reverse. Rowe attributes this token to the Dolphin being on the corner of Catherine Street and New Street following Haskins.

In 1718, Haskins states that a Mr Button gained a license for the Dolphin. In the same year, it was said that a bridge was needed from Dolphin corner to White Hart corner. This would have been a simple wooden structure bridging the open stream (sewer) that ran down New Street and was joined by another stream coming down Catherine Street. This would have had to be a strong structure if it truly ran diagonally across the junction of New Street and Catherine Street as it would have to have stood up to the coach and waggon traffic on the Exeter road! Thus, if this report is correct, it casts some doubts about the exact location of the Dolphin.

By 1740, the premises, now described as 'formerly the Dolphin Inn', were available to let for other business but it is not stated where this house was situated apart from being on the corner of Catherine Street. An advertisement published in October of the same year states that the former inn had good stabling with out-buildings and a large courtyard. This is the last that is heard of this Dolphin Inn.

Thus there is some doubt as to the exact location of this Dolphin except that it is associated with New Street and Catherine Street.

79 Draggon, St Martin's Church Street

The Draggon is mentioned in the will of Ric' Spencer in 1414 and is described as being in Saynte Martynstret. It was also mentioned in the City Domesday of 1442. It is not known if this was a precursor to either the Tollgate Inn or the World's End.

80 Duchess of Albany, 1 Ox Row

The history of the site of this pub is rather complicated and I hope I have managed to unravel it accurately. The site was alongside the Half Moon, which was next to the old Council House on the north side of Ox Row, backing on to the Market Place. The Half Moon was closed in 1776 and became a shop and then was burned down in 1823, leaving a vacant plot between this pub and the new Guildhall.

The earliest mention of a pub which later became the Duchess of Albany was in 1743 when it was known as the New Roebuck before changing to be the Black Dog in 1782. It changed to be the Greyhound by 1801 until between 1835 and 1838, it appears to have been called the Black Swan. In 1839, the pub's name changed to the Elephant and Castle, the name it retained before becoming the Duchess of Albany in 1889. Thus, the sequence appears to be:

1743-1782 New Roebuck
1782-1795 Black Dog
1801-1834 Greyhound
1835-1838 Black Swan
1839-1889 Elephant & Castle

Duchess of Albany

1889-1968 Duchess of Albany

Haskins states that in 1743, this house appears to have been granted a licence as the New Roebuck, with the landlord being Thomas Carter. It should be noted that the Old Roebuck apparently received a licence at the same time but this is attributed to the Roebuck (qv). In 1762, the pub was advertised as being to let and described as "the Roe-Buck, a Public-House next the Half-Moon Tavern, in the Market Place" [263].

In 1782, the house is available to let complete with all its furniture and other goods and named as the New Roebuck [264], But in October of that year, all the household furniture and other effects of the Black Dog are for sale [265]. And a week later, the Black Dog is available to rent. No direct evidence of the change of name has been found but the coincidence of one pub disappearing from the licensing records and another appearing in a short period of time with both being in the Market Place is sufficiently strong to make this assumption. Moreover, Mr W A Wheeler, writing in the *Salisbury and Winchester Journal* in 1886 (see part II of Appendix 1) links the names of this pub as shown above.

In 1785, Robert Russell, who had broken out of Winchester gaol on the 21st of June, was apprehended in bed at the Black Dog ale-house in the Market Place [266]. He was committed to the Fisherton gaol and then transferred back to Winchester. It also became known that he had robbed a farmer named Drake of three guineas while on the run from Winchester, and that he had worked for Mr Drake in earlier times. It was also stated that he had broken out of the Salisbury town gaol some years earlier.

The Black Dog is last heard of in 1795 [267] and by 1801, the pub was known as the Greyhound when all the household furniture was put up for sale [268].

In 1823, the Greyhound was described as being greatly injured when Mr Wheeler's premises (originally the Half Moon inn) burned down and the adjoining pub, the Packhorse, was pulled down to prevent the fire from spreading [269]. But the Greyhound was rebuilt as it continued in the licensing records, with the landlord being Joseph Carter (from 1819 until 1827).

In December, 1835, the Greyhound is offered as available to rent [270]. It is noted that the incoming tenant has the unusual opportunity to provide his own furniture, casks, and beer as the pub has none, although the building had been extensively repaired. Just over a year later, the Black Swan, in the Market Place is available to rent. Charles Elliott announces he has taken the inn [271] but only three months later, John Felton announces that he is re-opening the Black Swan and, unusually for these times, he will supply tea and coffee every morning in addition to the usual products sold at an inn [272].

Adding further confusion about the naming of this pub, in March, 1840, an advertisement shows that the Elephant & Castle is available to let [273]. But on May 4 of this year, the Black Swan, late the Greyhound, is to be sold [274]. Then, on May 11, the Elephant & Castle is again available to let, either as a private house or as a shop [275]! Suffice it to say, from this time onwards for a number of years, the Elephant & Castle appears in the licensing records with no further mention of the Black Swan or the Greyhound (or at least, not in the Market Place).

The landlord of the Elephant & Castle was summoned to the Magistrates Court in 1861, for removing the street sign for Ox Row from his pub [276]. He explained that the sign was fastened below his windows and illiterate people intending to go to the Ox Inn next door, might mistake the street sign and enter his house instead. It was agreed that when the sign was replaced, it would be at first floor level, where in fact it was more conspicuous than before!

The Bloody British History volume concerning Salisbury states that there had been five suicides at the Elephant and Castle. In January, 1872, a young man named William Croom hanged himself in a garret at the pub [277]. He was the son of the landlady, Sarah White, by her first husband, a former landlord of the pub. He had returned from his place of work in Aldershot a few days earlier and had had what were described as several nervous fits. He was found hanged by a servant girl at the pub and the inquest on his death returned a verdict of 'Temporary insanity'. In August, 1877, Mary Ann Batten, the wife of the landlord of the Elephant and Castle committed suicide by cutting her throat [278]. She left five children, the youngest being only thirteen months old. At some time soon after, Mr Alfred Batten remarried, presumably to provide a mother for his children. But in July, 1879, Superintendent Mathews of the Salisbury Police was called to the pub, where he found Mr Batten hanged from a rope in the cellar [279]. It was said at the inquest that Mr Batten had been 'very strange' since his first wife died and thus the inquest gave a verdict of 'Death committed whilst in a state of temporary insanity'. It is said in the book that a further case of suicide two weeks after Mr Batten's death was connected to the Elephant and Castle. Apart from the means by which Thomas Colleman killed himself and that he had showed some morbid interest in the death of Alfred Batten there seems to be little connection as Mr Coleman committed suicide in his house in Bedwin Street [280]. As to the fifth suicide, the current author has been unable to find any record of it.

In May, 1889, the pub was put up for sale. It appears to have been purchased by Bartlett & Co of Warminster as that brewery were granted permission in August of that year to change the name of the pub to the Duchess of Albany [281]. The Duchess of Albany was the Princess Helene of Waldeck Pyrmont who married Prince Leopold, the Duke of Albany in 1882. Prince Leopold was Queen Victoria's youngest son. Unfortunately, Prince Leopold died suddenly in 1884. The Duchess visited Salisbury on several occasions and it is of interest that a pub in Upton Lovell, to the west of Salisbury, is named after Prince Leopold.

The following year, Bartlett's brewery asked for a license for Thomas Pavitt to take over the Duchess [282]. The police objected to the application on the grounds that Mr Pavitt had been convicted of allowing drunkenness on his premises. That had occurred at the Royal Oak in Culver Street and Mr Pavitt's defence was that he was not aware that a customer in the smoking room was drunk and, in any case, the man in question left the pub on his own accord without being thrown out by Mr Pavitt. The Mayor, as chairman of the magistrates, said that he did not think this to be a serious case and fined Mr Pavitt 10 shillings and did not endorse his license. This seemed to contradict the police objection to the new license, and the Bench approved the license for the Duchess of Albany.

From 1898, the Duchess was an Ushers house, this brewery having taken over Bartlett's of Warminster. However, the Duchess of Albany that was trading in 1900 must not be mistaken for the building in the Market Place that proudly bears that name nowadays. The Duchess of Albany was a tall narrow building that was next door to the similar Ox Inn which, in turn, stood next to the building which is now a fish and chip shop. The Ox was closed in 1924 and the Duchess of Albany took over the premises. It is not clear at present whether the two buildings were demolished to allow the current building to be built or whether the Ox was remodelled to match the Duchess. Something quite close to the latter is the most probable as a step in the frontage of the Duchess building in Butcher Row matches one that can be seen in an early photograph of the Ox.

The enlarged Duchess continued to trade into the 1960s but it is interesting to note that a license was granted on 12th February 1962 for new premises [13]. This was probably when the building was altered to its current form. The pub appears to have closed on 17th November 1968 although the license was retained until February, 1972 [14].

81 Duck, Duck Lane, Laverstock

The Duck sits in Duck Lane and it would be reasonable to assume that it is an ancient site for an inn. The earliest record of it is from 1862 when the landlord, Henry Rattue applied for a new license but had it refused [283]. One presumes that this application was for a full public house license as in 1869 he was granted a beerhouse certificate under the Wine and Beerhouse Act of that year. In the 1861 Census, there are a William Rattew and a David Rattew recorded who were both brewers, but their addresses were simply recorded as being in Laverstock with no mention of the Duck or any other beer-house. But it is likely that they were brewing for a predecessor of the Duck.

The pub was advertised for sale in 1871 when Henry Rattue was still the landlord [284]. Henry Rattue dies in late 1882 and David Rattue, presumably his son, took over the pub.

By 1906, there was a Slate Club operating from the Duck and the annual dinner of the club occurred in November of that year [285]. Apart from the dinner, it was noted that a selection of music was played on a gramophone as part of the entertainment.

In 1934, the pub was owned by Gibbs Mew and a licence to sell wine was granted to the landlord, Cecil James Macklin [286]. In 1948, that licence was further extended to include spirits and Mr Macklin gained a full publican's licence [9].

After the demise of Gibbs Mew in 1997, the pub soldiered on a few more years before being bought by Hopback Brewery in 2003. At that time, it was extensively re-modelled with a terrace and improved parking.

82 Duke of York, Milford Street

This is one of the few pubs that we can definitely state the date of its opening. It is recorded in the records of the City magistrates: 'Aug 11 1794. Lawrence Flemington. On Condition to keep good

Order at the House wherein he now lives and for which he has a licence; at the corner of Culver Street, opposite Guilder lane and to be the Sign of the Duke of York – This is the first Licence and the House is put up in lieu of the House in Milford Street late the Sign of the Bishop Blaze & discontinued as a Public House [3].'

Unfortunately, nothing more is heard of this inn!

83 Duke of York, 34 York Road

Evidence in a court case of 1902 concerning the ownership of some fencing states that the fence originally surrounded the plot of land where the Duke of York was built [287]. The evidence stated that the building started in 1900 with the fence surrounding the plot being removed at that time. The pub was built for Folliott's brewery of Rollestone Street and appears to have been completed by 1902. However, the earliest record found of it as a pub was in 1905 when a Miss B Newman was the landlady. Folliott's brewery was taken over by Ushers of Trowbridge in 1919 and the pub remained with Usher's for many years. It appears to have been a beer-only pub until 1951 when it was granted a full pub license [12]. It was remodelled in about 1988 to have a single bar. Became a gay bar in the early part of the 21st C. but often had a closed door with entry controlled via a TV camera. It closed in early 2010 but reopened in July 2011 as a more traditional pub with real ales.

84 Eagle Inn, 31 Fisherton Street

The Eagle was on the south side of Fisherton Street and was originally one of a group of buildings, built in the early 19th C. that included four adjoining shops. It was certified as a beerhouse in 1869 but may have been in existence before that date. Between the Licensing Acts of 1830 and 1869, there was not a legal requirement to register alehouses and hence it is probable that the Eagle was a beerhouse from the time the row of shops was built.

In September, 1875, Eli Thick applied for a spirit license of the pub [288]. He stated that he had been the landlord for 8 or 9 years and he was certainly shown as being at the address in the 1871 Census. He had spent more than £500 improving the premises including fitting out a large club room on the first floor. Since there were no objections to the license, the application nwas granted.

In 1888, a Professor Richard G Sayers was staying at the Eagle and offered consultations in Phrenology (the study of the shape of the head including its bumps and hollows which some believed could allow analysis of a person's character) [289]. He said he would read anybody's character for 1 shilling but would write out the result for 5 shillings or more and would produce the reading in a book for £1. It would appear that the man was a professor by his own estimation as was not unusual for quack doctors!

By 1891, the Eagle was owned by Eldridge Pope of Dorchester although it is not clear when they acquired the pub.

The Licensing Acts of 1902 and 1904 allowed local authorities to refuse to renew the licence of pubs that were deemed not to be needed to satisfy the requirements of the population and to compensate the owner of the pub for its closure. The Eagle fell foul of this legislation in 1913 and a report of the Renewal Authority for Salisbury stated

[10]: 'Fully licensed Public-house since 1876, prior to which date it was an ante 1869 on Beerhouse. Poor Rate Assessment £24 gross. The present tenant has held the Licence since 1901.

'This house is situated in Fisherton Street, Salisbury, at the following distances from other licensed premises in the same street: -

"Shoulder of Mutton" (Fully licensed) 270 yards

"Fisherton Brewery" (On Beerhouse) 35 yards

"Angel" Hotel (Fully licensed) 40 yards

"Star" Hotel ditto. 183 yards

"Plume of Feathers" ditto. 253 yards

"King's Arms" ditto. 220 yards

"Lamb" Inn ditto. 160 yards

"Bull" Hotel ditto. 60 yards

All the above houses (including the "Eagle" and one other, the "County Hotel") are contained in a distance of about 520 yards.

'The house and premises are long, but narrow and inconvenient as a licensed house. There is no sleeping accommodation for travellers and no stabling. The house generally is in need of repair.

'Of the other licensed houses referred to, all are of better and more suitable structure, and have better accommodation for the public; while all except the "Star Hotel" have stabling.

"The Eagle" has the lowest assessment to Poor Rate.'

No evidence was offered on behalf of the Tenant to show the amount of trade done at the "Eagle", but observation made upon the house showed that the number of people using the premises was small; and evidence was given of complaints by the Licensee as to the slackness of business, and a statement by him that he had by arrangement with the Owners, become simply the Manager of the place.

Hence in June 1913 the licence was refused and the owner, Eldridge Pope of Dorchester, did not oppose the closure and received compensation of £387 18s 9d.

85 Eagles, Cathedral Close

The Eagles was on the site of the outbuildings and stables to the east of Mompesson House on Chorister's Green in the Close. It was reputed to have been a mid-17th C building but it was acquired by Sir Thomas Mompesson in about 1680 and replaced by the existing buildings.

86 Elephant & Castle, Brown Street.

Two advertisements in December, 1837, refer to the Elephant and Castle in Brown Street. One advert calls for the creditors of Richard Billet to pay their bills in order that a dividend of his estate can be prepared [290]. It is not clear if Mr Billet was dead or bankrupt! The second advert in the same edition of the *Salisbury and Winchester Journal*, gives notice of the sale of the stock-in-trade of Mr Billet plus some items of furniture. No other mention can be found of this pub but shortly after the date of these adverts, the name was taken by the inn that later became the Duchess of Albany (qv)

87 England's Glory, nk

The England's Glory is known from licensing records from 1810 to 1814 with the landlord being John Yeates but its location is not known [4]. It may well have had another name in earlier times. However, at the end of 1814 the following note is found in the *Salisbury and Winchester Journal* [291]: 'City of New Sarum. Notice is hereby given, - That the Mayor and Justices of this City, will, at their next meeting, to be holden in the Council Chambers, on Monday the 2nd day of January, 1815, take into consideration the propriety of granting a Certificate, to William Mitchell, to keep a common Inn or Alehouse, now called or known by the sign of England's Glory, and to be hereafter called or known by the sign of the Green Man, in the parish of St Edmund, in the City aforesaid.'

The Mayor and Justices did grant a licence [5] but there is no record of either an England's Glory or a Green Man after this date.

88 Falcon, Brown Street

This pub appears to be at or very close to the south-western corner of the junction between Winchester Street and Brown Street. It appears to have been the Black Horse Tap between 1829 and 1832, when it held a licence in its own right separate from the Black Horse. During that time, Sarah Larkham is noted as being the licensee. It may have been on the site of the Greyhound, Brown Street (qv) that became a wine merchant in 1790 and could possibly have been purchased by the Black Horse Inn to provide more space.

The Falcon appears in the licensing records from 1834 until 1848 and since the dates of it and the Black Horse Tap are contiguous, there are assumed to be one and the same place. In June, 1846, the contents of the pub were put up for sale [292] and it is probable that it did not operate as a pub for a few years. But in October, 1851, the first of a monthly sale of agricultural live and dead stock was held at the Falcon Inn, which was advertised as being "late part of the Black Horse at the back of the Cross Keys" [293]. The landlord in 1851, John William Edginton, was described as an engineer and brassfounder! These sales certainly continued until February, 1853, and possibly longer. But it is of note that the Falcon was put up for sale in 1852, as part of the sale of the Black Horse in Winchester Street [294]. In this notice of sale, John Edginton is said to be in occupation of the inn but that the extensive yard and stabling was held under a lease of seven years from Michaelmas, 1851 by John Waters.

George Stainer, the landlord in 1857, was summoned to the Magistrates Court charged with knowingly allowing persons of notoriously bad character to assemble in his house [295]. The evidence was that the police entered the house and found fifteen to twenty navvies and four women drinking in the tap room. There were very noisy and none appeared to be sober. In addition, it was said that some of the women were prostitutes. However, after questioning the police, the Magistrates formed the view that none of the men had been arrested for drunkenness and that no proof of disorderly behaviour had been presented. Thus, the case was dismissed.

However, two years later, George Stainer was once again in court on a similar charge [296]. This time, the police gave evidence that convicted thieves and prostitutes had been seen entering the premises. The Superintendent of Police described the pub as being a brothel of the worst description. George Stainer was fined two shillings plus costs, a fairly low fine which may have represented a fairly sceptical view by the Magistrates.

The pub last appears in the licensing records at the annual licensing session of September, 1861. Nothing more is heard of the Falcon or any possible record of an inn on this site after this date.

89 Falcon, Crane Street
There is a reference in 1455 to Le Falcon, near the Lower Bridge in Fisherton. It is often quoted that the Falcon survives as part of Church House in Crane Street. There is a little confusion in this area and one cannot be sure about the accuracy of earlier transcriptions from the source documents.

90 Faucon, Castle Street
Records of the City of New Sarum in 1455 refer to Le Faucon in Castelstret. It is stated that the proprietor is John Hill having previously been William Marchal. There is no other mention of this inn but there is some confusion as Faucon is French for Falcon and a few texts consider that this is the same inn as the Falcon.

91 Fiddle & Trumpet, nk
There is a reference to this house in 1742 when a licence was applied for and refused [297]. Presumably it was an alehouse and was attempting to gain a full public house licence. There is no indication as to where the house was in Salisbury.

92 Fisher's Stalls, nk
There is a reference in 1455 to a tavern in which Nicholas Sagen dwells at the Fisher's Stalls. It is not known what was the proper name of the tavern but it is possible it was in Fish Row.

93 Five Bells, Corn Market
There is a single reference to the Five Bells from 1759 which describes William Armstrong opening a Linen Drapers shop opposite the Five Bells in the Corn Market [298]. This is two years before the Five Bells in Salt Lane gained its licence and the Corn Market is generally considered to have been on the north side of the Market Place adjacent to Blue Boar Row. Thus, this appears to have been a different establishment to that in Salt Lane but one cannot be completely certain.

94 Five Bells, Fisherton
A single reference to the Five Bells in Fisherton is found in the *Salisbury and Winchester Journal* in 1799, when Mr Whitmarsh, the Coroner, held an inquest at this pub into the death of a Mr Joseph Payne, whose body was found in the river [299].

95 Five Bells, 28 Salt Lane
Haskins states that this pub was licensed as an alehouse in 1761 but was almost certainly in existence earlier owing to the lack of a requirement to licence alehouses in the Licencing Act of 1730. It was known as the Druid and Five Bells around 1825 and was the Ring of Bells at the time of the 1851 Census but it always reverted to its original name after a while.

From 1760 up to at least 1791 it was home to an annual Carnation Feast. Rather than eating carnations, gentlemen attended to display flowers they had grown and had a meal at the pub as part of the festivities [300]: 'The Annual Carnation Feast will be held at the Sign of the Five Bells on Friday the 30th of July 1762. That Person who produces 12 of the best Blossoms of whole blowing Carnations, one of a sort, of his own blowing & propagating from the Layer, shall be entitled to a Silver Bowl of One Guinea & a ½ value ... The Person who produces 10 of the best Blossoms, one of a Sort, of whole blowing Carnations, of his own blowing & propagating from the Layer, shall be entitled to the 2nd Prize, a Punch Ladle of One Guinea value. The person who produces 8 of the best Flowers ... shall be entitled to the 3rd Prize, a Silver Spoon of 15 shillings' value. The Person who produces 6 of the best Flowers, of his own rising this year, shall be entitled to the 4th Prize, a Silver Spoon of ½ a Guinea Value. No Person to win but one Prize; and every Person, except a Subscriber, before he has Liberty to shew for any Prize, is to subscribe 2/6 towards the next year; but if he wins the First Prize, then to subscribe a Crown. Mr Roger Yeats & Mr Archibald Shuter, Stewards.'

Like many pubs of its time, the Five Bells brewed its own beer as can be seen from the following advertisement in the *Salisbury and Winchester Journal* in 1813 [301]: 'Five Bells Inn, Salisbury. To be Sold by Auction, on the Premises, by J. F. Gerrard, on Wednesday April 20, 1813, - All the Household Furniture, iron-bound casks, brewing utensils, and fixtures, the property of Mr J Tewkesbury, who has removed from the above Inn; consisting of 4-post, tent and other bedsteads, with cotton and check furniture; feather beds, mattresses, blankets, and counterpanes; mahogany dining, card, and tea tables; mahogany and other chairs, chests of drawers, pier and dressing glasses, kitchen range and stove grates, brass and copper articles, and kitchen requisites; beer machine, with two motions and pipe to ditto, 170 hogsheads of capital well-seasoned casks, from three to twenty hogsheads each; 170-gallon copper and grate, a capital mash tub and underback, three coolers and a number of other articles, which will be sold without reserve. The sale to begin at eleven o'clock.'

Considering that a hogshead contained 54 gallons, this meant that this fairly small pub had storage available for around 5000 gallons of beer, enough to provide up to ten 18 gallon kilderkins of beer a week for the whole year! A modern pub would be pleased to sell this much beer. However, it was not possible to keep a brew sufficiently warm during the winter months or sufficiently cool during the summer so all brewing was done in the spring and autumn. What was considered to be 'good Strong Beer' in those days might not find appreciation by modern connoisseurs of real ale.

A burglary took place at the Five Bells in 1817 [302]: 'Burglary – Five Guineas Reward. Whereas early on the Morning of Sunday the 1st instant, the House of Mr Leonard Jesse, the sign of the Five Bells, in the City of Salisbury, was broken open (the sash of the bay window at the back of the house being removed) and robbed of £7 in Bank-notes (one of them a Ringwood £2 note), about £6 or £7 worth of Silver, a crooked Half-Guinea, 6 Silver Tea-Spoons (marked AG) and two old Silver Watches, one of which was marked with the name of James Hookey, Headley, No. 5191. This is to give Notice that a reward of Five Guineas will be given by L Jesse to any person giving such information as will lead to the conviction of the offender or offenders.'

The *Salisbury and Winchester Journal* of the following week stated that Daniel Tabor and Richard Tabor had been charged with the crime.

In June of the same year, the first annual Pink Feast was advertised at the Five Bells [303]. These were held until at least 1822. Presumably the Pink was in fashion as the flower to grow compared with the Carnation a few years earlier.

The Five Bells often had a booth at Salisbury Races to provide refreshment to the race goers as did other Salisbury pubs. In 1840, Philemon Witt of the Five Bells, along with four other publicans, complained of the high prices charged them for having booths on the race course [304]. Consequently, they announce that they have rented some ground adjacent to the course and will supply refreshments from the new site as usual.

Philemon Witt announces in 1845 that he is leaving the Five Bells owing to his ill health [305]. This cannot have been too bad a state of health because he actually soldiers on until 1858! But Mr Witt does then appear several times at the Magistrates Court for selling beer outside of the legal hours. When he was found guilty in June, 1858, he was only fined £3 and costs because there had been no previous convictions [306]. The Magistrates must have forgotten that he had been found guilty of a similar offence in 1849 [9]. What is more, he had been found guilty in 1854 of selling beer without a licence at Britford Fair [307]. It seems that occasional licences were granted for booths at the Fair for whatever length of time a landlord requested. Unfortunately, Mr Witt had only requested a licence for the Fair day (a Saturday), and he was found selling beer on the Sunday. But he was described as being "potations pottle deep" at the time and when he was found guilty in Court, it was said that his "rubicund visage glowed with indignation when he was made to comprehend the nature of the sentence, and he energetically expressed his determination not to pay 'one farden'". One suspects this throws light on the nature of is ill health!

Suffice it to say, in August, 1858, the Five Bells is advertised as being available to rent owing to illness in the family of Mr Witt [308] and a week later the household furniture, stock-in-trade, brewing plant, casks and other effects are offered for sale in September. Also in September, 1858, Mr Witt was found guilty of assaulting and threatening to shoot Mr Pain of Laverstock [309]. He was fined £5 and costs and ordered to find two sureties of £20 and bound over to keep the peace for three months at a cost of £20. By 1859, Mr Lavery is landlord of the inn.

By 1861, Mr Lavery is advertising a Ball at the pub [310]. He stated that he was throwing open his spacious and well-ventilated club room for the event and would be providing a 6-piece band to play music for the dancing. But by 1865, Henry Hayward was the landlord. He could not have been very successful as the following year, all the household furniture, bar and gas fittings and other effects of the pub were put up for sale in order to pay off his creditors [311]. In consequence, Charles Rambridge takes over the pub and advertises he is selling 'Fine Sparkling Ales and Dublin Stout' amongst other produce [312]. He also stated that he would continue his previous business as a Boot and Shoe Maker as usual. He does not stay long at the Five Bells as in April, 1867, the pub is advertised as being available to let with immediate possession [313].

In 1906, there is an advertisement for the products of the Sarum Wrought Iron Works in Rampart Road [314]. One example of their work was stated to be the support for the pub sign of the Five Bells and this can still be seen at the Five Bells.

Throughout the 20th C, the Five Bells was a Gibbs Mew house until the closure of that brewery in 1997. It has been an Enterprise Inns house since that time.

96 Fleece, nk

An alehouse that applied for a full licence in 1742 and had it refused.

97 Flower Pots, Culver Street

This pub is known to have been in existence in Culver Street from 1742 to 1762. A note in a bundle of documents at the WSHC states that the Flower Pots applied for a license and had it granted with conditions [315]. Unfortunately, this note is not dated but probably was from 1742-43. The pub was offered to let in 1755 and was described as having 'a Brewhouse, an exceeding good Cellar, and a large Garden walled in [316].

An advertisement in the 1760 offered for sale "A Curious Piece of Clock-Work Machinery, representing a Lady, which moves about a large Room in a very easy genteel Manner" [317]. The pub was named in that advertisement as the Three Flower Pots but when the pub was advertised as available to rent later in that year, it had reverted to its original name [318].

The pub seemed to be available to let for the whole of the known period and was last advertised in 1762. By the 1780s, the Crown and Anchor in Exeter Street was known by this name so either the Culver Street pub had closed or had changed its name.

98 Fountain, High Street

This pub was on the east side of High Street at its junction with New Canal. Its history is entwined with that of the Assembly Rooms on the corner of New Canal and High Street which has been a bookseller's premises for many years. The current building was built in 1802 but before that time the Fountain and an earlier Assembly Room occupied the site.

Little is known about the Fountain before 1751, but in October of that year it was advertised that there would be a Ball in the Great Assembly Room and that there would be further Balls on each Tuesday throughout the season [319]. In the same edition of the *Salisbury and Winchester Journal*, it was also advertised that on Saturday, November 2nd, there would be Badger Baiting at the Fountain Tavern. It was stated that the badger was a 'large and beautiful Beast of the Kind'. It was clear from these two adverts that the Fountain must have been in existence for some time prior to 1751

In January, 1752, it was advertised that 'A large Quantity of useful & ornamental China & engraved Glasses etc. to be sold under Prime Cost at the New Assembly Room in High Street' [320] and in March of that year 'Monday next the 9th and Weds the 11th (being the Assizes) will be a Ball at the Great Assembly Room at the Fountain in High St, where Tickets may be had at 2/6 each' [321]..

By 1755 we find [322]: 'Alfred & Mary Tokett, who formerly kept the Assembly Room in New Street, Salisbury, have now taken the Fountain in High Street, where Assemblies will be kept as usual, & the greatest care taken to have the best attendance & most genteel accommodation ... Monday & Wednesday, the 21st and 23rd inst, being the Assizes, will be a Ball. Tickets 3/-.'

For the years following, the Assembly Room accommodated many Balls and other grand social occasions with little mention of the associated inn until in 1772 it was advertised [323]: 'John Lavenu, late cook to the Hon. Stephen Fox and since pastry-cook & poulterer in this City, has taken the Assembly Rooms in High Street, with the dwelling house late the Fountain which he intends opening as a Tavern & Coffee House.'

Events at the Assembly Room and at the Fountain (sometimes referred to as a Coffee House and sometimes as a Tavern) continue to be advertised until in 1781 we find [324]: 'To be Sold by Auction, on the premises, in one lot, by Messrs Smith & Son, on Thursday the 16th inst, precisely at twelve o'clock. All that capital Freehold Tavern and Coffee House, situate in the High Street and New Canal, known by the name of the Fountain, with the elegant Room adjoining; its size about 72 feet long, 30 wide, 26 high, where the assembly, concerts, and other public diversions are kept; the whole in the renting of Mr John Lavenu on a lease, of which two years are unexpired at Lady Day next.'

John Lavenu obviously extended his lease as he is still found running the two premises in 1788 and possibly until 1791 [325]: 'Fountain Tavern, Salisbury. Henry Roles begs leave to inform the Nobility, Gentry, and his friends and the Public in general, that he has taken the above Tavern, with the Concert and Assembly Room adjoining, lately occupied by Mr Lavenu, situate in the High Street, Salisbury, and purposes entering on the same on the 24th instant. – He has laid in a compleat stock of the most genuine wines and other liquors which he flatters himself will meet with the approbation of a generous and liberal Public; assuring them, at the same time, that no attention on his part shall ever be wanting at deserve their Favours, which will be ever gratefully acknowledged, by their respectful and obedient servant H Roles. N.B. An exceeding good Billiard Table.'

But in November 1792, John Roles dies suddenly and in January 1793, Walter and Philpott, Leather Breeches-Makers, Glovers, Tailors, and Habit-Makers advertise that they had moved to new premises, formerly the Fountain Coffee House [326]. By 1795, apartments in the former inn were advertised to let and in 1798, the whole of the former Fountain and the Assembly Room are advertised for sale [327]. It is not clear if it was sold at that time but it is advertised for sale again in 1801 [328] and in January 1802 [329]. In May 1802, a subscription is started to build a new and larger Assembly Room as a consequence of the decay of the former premises and the site of the Fountain is chosen for the new construction. It is this new building that can be seen today.

99 Fox and Goose, nk

It is not known whether there was a pub of this name in Salisbury but George Hughes issued a farthing token in 1658 showing a fox & a goose on the obverse and stating he was of Sarum [330]. Similar tokens from outlying villages show the village name correctly thus it is likely he was a trader in Salisbury. However, many of these tokens used standard dies and he may have

100 French Horn, nk

This may have been a house with an off-licence as its name never appears in any lists of public houses or inns. But, in March 1834, 'William Gill, Licensed Retailer of Beer, was convicted in the sum of 40/- and 10/- costs for permitting Beer to be consumed and drank in his House called the French Horn situate in the parish of St Edmund' [6].

101 George, Fisherton

Haskins states that Humphrey Marchant gained a license for this house in 1713. There are further mentions of these premises at various dates up until 1736 but no more of it is known.

102 George Inn, High Street

The remains of this inn form the High-Street entrance to the Old George Mall with the ground floor having been removed to create a pedestrian thoroughfare. The building dated from the 14th C. although there were possibly remnants of an earlier 13th C. building incorporated in its structure. The structure remaining has been much altered over the centuries.

It has been suggested that it was originally built in the period 1307-27 as faces carved into the beams of the hall are said to represent Edward II and Isabella of France. It may have been a pilgrim's hostel dedicated to Saint George but it is more likely that it is connected to the Guild of St George, the fraternity of the Mayor and Corporation that originated in 1306.

The building appears to have originally belonged to the Teynterer family but it is not clear whether it was at that time a private house or an inn. William Teynterer Jnr was Mayor in 1361 and 1375 and, when he died in 1376, he left the property to the Guild of St George subject to the life interest of his widow Alesia. The General Entry Book has an entry that states 'Order that the house called George's Inn, surrendered by Alice, wife and executor of William (Teynterer?), be granted to William Warmwell' [331]. This entry is undated owing to the poor state of the original manuscript but is estimated to be from 1394-95. The following folio in the General Entry Book appears to record the forfeiture of the George by the Mayor and Commonalty from Alice Teynturer and William Warmwell to be held by the Fraternity of St George.

In 1404, the inn was intended to be purchased by the Mayor and Commonalty of Salisbury [332]. However, it is doubtful that this purchase was completed as in 1410, it was determined that the Mayor and Commonalty had no right to the George inn as it was held by feoffees [333] The use of feoffees was, in effect, a medieval form of tax avoidance whereby the feoffees held the ownership of land or premises while a beneficial holder had full use of the property. If the beneficial holder died, the feoffees determined who would become the new beneficial holder and this would normally be the person specified in the original holders will. This prevented the property being confiscated by the Crown if there was no will or if the heir to the property was under age. The use of feoffees was becoming widespread in the late 1300s but eventually was made obsolete by the formal end of feudalism in 1660. But in 1412, the Mayor and Commonalty finally purchased the inn [334].

From 1414 to 1669, the George belonged to the Corporation of Salisbury. The Corporation spent a considerable sum on the property after acquisition resulting in it being let to John Burton in 1418 for £20 per annum. Many entries are found in the Corporation records including "20s for the making one baye wyndowe at Georgys Yn". It was damaged by fire in about 1457 and the lease passed to John Gryme in 1474. An inventory exists that was attached to his lease showing it to have 14 chambers each containing 2 or 3 beds, a buttery and a tavern or wine cellar containing the tuns of ale.

In 1569, the free grammar school founded by the City Council started in a room in the George but after criticism in 1608 it finally moved to its own premises in Castle Street in 1624 ('The Sculehouse removed from the George because of the inconveniency of cominge to the schollers by the Taphouse and inne') In 1579, the landlord of the George was forgiven a debt of £22.10.0 outstanding rent because no visitors were allowed into the city on account of the Plague.

It is said that Shakespeare and his players came here and, indeed, in 1624, it was agreed that "henceforth all players shall make their plays from the George Inn, the size and form of the quadrangle being well adapted for that purpose". In 1645, Cromwell slept here on his way to join his Army. In 1661 it was recorded that Roger Bedbury "to have a new lease of the Inne called the George in High Streete" [335]. (Note there is a slight problem here as some documents count the Regnal years of Charles II from the death of Charles 1 whereas others count them from his succession to the throne in 1660. Hence this lease might be dated 1672) He was the son of the previous landlord George Bedbury and was noted as a Royalist being fined £10 in 1646 for taking the King's Oath. He issued a farthing token in 1664 owing to the lack of national coinage [336]. This showed George and the Dragon on the obverse.

Samuel Pepys stayed at the inn in 1668. He recorded [337]: 'Jun 10 1668. So all over the Plain by the sight of the steeple; to Salisbury by night; but before I came to the town I saw a great fortification, and there light, and to it and in it, and find it prodigious, so as to fright me to be in it all alone at that time of night, it being dark. I understand since it to be that, that is called Old Sarum. Came to the George Inn, where lay in a silk bed, and very good diet. To supper, then to bed.'

Jun 11 1668. 'Up, and W Hewer and I up and down the town, and find it a very brave place. The river goes through every street, and a most capacious market-place. The City great; I think greater than Hereford. But the Minster most admirable; as big, I think, and handsomer than Westminster, and a very large Close about it, and houses for the officers thereof, and a fine palace for the Bishop. So to my lodgings back, and took out my wife and people, to show them the town, and church, but, they being at prayers, we could not see the choir. A very good organ; and I looked in and saw the Bishop, my friend Dr Ward. Thence to the Inn, and there not being able to hire coach horses, and not willing to use our own, we get saddle horses very dear. Boy that went to look for them 6d. So the three women behind Mr Hewer, Murford, and our guide, and I single to Stonehenge, over the plain, and some great hills to fright us.

George

Come hither and find them as prodigious as any tales I ever heard of them, and worth going this journey to see. God knows what their use was. They are hard to tell, but yet may be told. Gave the shepherd woman for leading our horses 4d. So back by Wilton, my Lord Pembroke's house, which we could not see, he being just coming to town, but the situation I do not like, nor the house promise much, it being in a low and rich valley. So back home, and there being light, we to the church, and there find them at prayers again, so could not see the choir. But I sent the women home, and I did go in, and saw very many fine tombs, and among the rest some very ancient of the Montagues. Home to dinner, and that being done, paid the reckoning, which was so exorbitant, and particular in rate of my horses, and 7s.6d for bread and beer, that I was mad, and resolve to trouble the master about it, and get something for the poor, and come away in that humour.'

A series of leases from 1672 up until 1733 [335] show the inn to still be the property of the Mayor and Corporation and was almost certainly still being run as an inn.

In 1721, changes were made to Salisbury Races with the races being held on 'the new round course'. A plate valued at £18 was presented to the winner of the principal race at the George Inn. This association between the races and the

George seems to have continued to at least 1756 when an auction of paintings was held at the inn on the first day of the races.

In 1769, the inn was put up for sale, presumably by the Mayor and Corporation, as persons wishing to purchase it were required to apply to the City Chamberlain at the Council Chamber [338]. It was described as being 30 feet wide on the High Street with the total plot being 201 feet deep and 147 feet wide with stabling for 50 horses. Whether it was actually sold is in some doubt as in 1842, it is still described as being the property of the Mayor and Corporation with the leaseholder being Mr James Trowbridge. The inn does not appear in the licensing records from this date and for many years.

It seems that the inn was now used as one or more shops with accommodation over them. From at least 1851, it was largely occupied by George Sydenham, a boot and shoe maker. In 1864, he advertises that he is a Gentleman's Boot Maker and that he has sold his Ladies' business to Mr J D Courtenay [339]. This part of the business seems to have occupied all of what had been the George Inn. In 1887, Mr Courtenay requested tenders for repairs and alterations to a portion of the buildings that formed the Old George Inn [340]. It seems likely that by this time, Mr Courtenay, and possibly, Mr Sydenham before him, actually owned the property. Mr Courtenay advertised regularly in the *Salisbury and Winchester Journal* up until his death in 1894.

Dealing with the estate of Mr Courtenay must have taken some time as it was not until 1899 that the Trustees of his estate advertised the buildings as being for sale [341]. They were described as 'all those Very Valuable Freehold Business and Residential Premises, formerly the Old George Inn, and now known as Nos 15 and 17, High Street, Salisbury, in which for many years the late Mr Courtenay carried on the business of Boot and Shoe Maker. The property, which is situated in the very best position in the City, Comprises: - Two Large Well-Lighted Shops having Bow Windows, and measuring 42 ft by 13 ft and 49 ft by 13 ft respectively. The Residential Portion contains Fifteen Bedrooms viz., Four Large Rooms about 21ft by 17ft with Bay Windows, and Rooms 22ft by 14ft, 18ft by 16ft, 16½ft by 15ft 6in, 19ft by 17ft and 15ft by 14ft 6in respectively; together with the Dining Room, formerly the Banqueting Room of the Old George, containing beautifully carved Oak Panelling and Beams, Bath Room with Hot and Cold Water, 5 wcs, 2 Kitchens, and Offices, and capital Underground Cellars. In the pleasant Gardens at the back are 2 Greenhouses with Potting Shed and a Two Storey Workshop.' It was said that the premises were ideally suited to be adapted as a private hotel or for letting as apartments and this latter is what seems to have happened.

By 1905, Mr and Mrs Mursell advertise the Old George House for sale [342]. The advertisement sates that they have been running the business for several years and that they wished to retire. It appears that they have been letting the promises as a number of apartments. They also state that the premises would be ideally suited to be a boarding house or a private hotel, and that there were six reception rooms, sixteen bedrooms, two bathrooms and six wc's. By this time, it even had electric light and a telephone.

The inn was now opened as a private hotel and re-appears in the licensing records. It seems to have been in the same family ownership from 1911 until 1957 (the Holland-Youngs). In 1957, an advertisement showed that a modern wing had been added and that the hotel now contained '46 letting bedrooms, all with H & C; some are oak timbered; the majority face the garden, formerly the courtyard. It has been equipped with modern conveniences, such as interior coil-spring mattresses, lights over beds and basins, central heating in public rooms, passages and some bedrooms (others have gas or electric fires), some private bathrooms'.

As far as I can determine, the George continued in use until it was remodelled again in 1967 to form the entrance to the Old George Mall as we see it today. The left hand wooden pillar as one faces into the Mall dates from the 14th C and originally flanked the carriage entrance to the inn. I think it would be true to say that the alterations in 1967 would be considered to be vandalism nowadays and it is a shame that such a fine building exists only as an entrance to modern shops.

103 George & Dragon, 85 Castle Street

The George and Dragon stands on the west side of Castle Street about halfway between Avon Approach and Millstream Approach. The building dates from the 16th C. but it appears to have been altered in the 18th C when it became a pub. This pub was known as the Silent or Quiet Woman up until 1822 when it became the George and Dragon. The original pub sign showed a decapitated woman carrying her head under her arm. Wheeler states categorically that the pub had no written sign only the picture of the decapitated woman and this was the reason that the name of the pub varied between quiet and silent! It is said to have been first licensed in 1709. Shortly afterwards, the landlady of the Silent Woman was indicted for keeping a disorderly house

The pub first appears in the licensing records in 1819 when William Walker was the landlord of the Quiet Woman [5]. It is possible that Mr Walker had been the landlord for a longer time as a list of Innkeepers in the licensing records of 1815 shows a William Water. Unfortunately, there is no list of licensees with pub names between 1814 and 1819 and the Quiet Woman does not appear in the licensing records in 1814 and one presumes it was just an unlicensed alehouse. Philip Blatch appears as landlord of the Quiet Woman in 1821 but at the 1822 annual licensing session he is shown as being at the George and Dragon [5]. The pub is known by this latter name from this date onwards.

When Robert Tink prepares to leave the George and Dragon in 1846, he announces that as he has a very large stock of beer "he is willing to sacrifice his superior Strong Beer (for which he has been so justly celebrated), at 4d per Quart, by Retail, Out of Doors. A liberal allowance made by wholesale for ready money" [343]. But he does not leave the pub until July, 1848, so he may not have gone ahead with this sale.

George Creed, the landlord in 1856, was charged with keeping his house open after 11 o'clock on the night of Good Friday [344]. He said that he was ill that night and left his wife in charge of the pub. A police constable stated that he had gone to the George and Dragon at about a quarter to twelve o'clock and found 12 or 13 persons drinking. Mrs Creed said that she could not get them out of the pub. She called her son to assist to no avail. The Mayor said that if she had gone to the police station straight away, he would have been able to find a policeman to help clear the pub. Mr Creed said that policemen are never to be found when they are wanted. The Bench fined him 20 shillings plus costs.

In the early 1880s the pub appears to have been rented by Lovibond's Brewery as Mr Lovibond's agent held the license in early 1881. But the actual ownership of the pub is related to the King's Head in Bridge Street, as the George and Dragon was put up for sale at the same time as that inn [345]. Folliott's brewery of Rollestone Street seems to have purchased it as John Folliott is shown as the licensee from late 1891 until mid-1892. Folliott's brewery was acquired by Ushers of Trowbridge in 1919. The pub remained in Ushers hands until 1974 when it became a Chef and Brewer house in the Watney-Mann group. Later it became a member of the Enterprise Inns group. The sign outside the pub was changed to read 'G & D's' in 2010 but reverted to the George and Dragon in 2014. In August 2015, the pub was closed with Enterprise Inns advertising it as available at an annual rent of £29,000. It has since re-opened under a new tenant.

104 Globe, Gigant Street

This pub was on the west side of Gigant Street to the south of what became Gibbs Mew & Co.'s Brewery. The buildings on the site were demolished when the 'road to nowhere' was built in the 1970s and has since been covered by new housing.

Haskins suggests that this pub may have been called the Lamb in 1742 when it was granted a license as an alehouse. This seems unlikely as the Lamb in Catherine Street was well established by this date.

It is recorded that Robert Tuffin was granted a licence for it as the Star and Garter, an alehouse in 1765. In that same year, Tuffin placed the following advertisement in the *Salisbury and Winchester Journal* [346]: 'Robert Tuffin at the Star & Garter in Jiggin Street at Salisbury Begs leave to acquaint the Public that he is possessed of a valuable Receipt of the late Dr Thompson's, King's Physician, by which he has acquired a Method of healing sore legs, occasioned by accident or ulcerous Humours, be they of ever so long standing, in either Sex, no Cure no Pay: And to remove any apprehensions the Afflicted may entertain of their Sores returning again, he hereby assures them, that they may be perfectly easy on that Head, as he will make a perfect and sound Cure. If any of the Fair Sex should object to his attendance, his Mother, who is perfectly acquainted with the Receipt, will wait on them. Several Cures that he has performed in Town can be attested by the Persons. N.B. The said Robert Tuffin intends selling Capons of his own cutting this Summer, or will cut for anyone that pleases to employ him.'

By 1785, Thomas Heazel was advertising that he was operating a Common Stage Cart from his premises, the Star & Garter, to carry goods from Salisbury to Shaftesbury on Tuesday afternoons, returning to Salisbury the next day [347].

Haskins states that the pub was renamed the Golden Fleece in 1770. This does not seem to tie up with the licensing records, but from 1803 to 1805 the house does seem to have been named the Golden Fleece.

In 1806, the pub was renamed the Nelson's Arms. It remained with that name until 1819 when William Lawrence had a renewal of his licence refused for some unspecified reason [5]. However, it may be that William Lawrence never entered the Nelson's Arms as a William Lawrence is noted as being the landlord of the Crown & Anchor in Catherine Street from 1813 to 1819, and of the Three Crowns in Brown Street in 1820, Richard Kitchell applied for the licence but this was discussed by the Mayor and Justices of the city, and since his name never appears in the licencing records, one can assume that this application was refused. William Kitchell became the landlord in June, 1820, when it became known as the Globe [5].

In September 1848, the landlord, George Ings, was fined 3/- for opening his pub before 12:30 in the morning on a Sunday. Very different from the opening hours in recent years! In 1867, there was a strange case of attempted robbery at the Globe [349]. Alfred Wells was charged with being in a bedroom of the Globe with the intent of stealing the money, goods and chattels of Martha Stevens, the landlady of the inn. He was found after a servant in the house came across a man in Mrs Stevens' bedroom. The man ran down the stairs and escaped when the servant ran to get assistance. When the police arrived, they went upstairs and found Wells hidden under the bed. At his trial, Wells pleaded guilty but then was interviewed by the Recorder of the Court. It transpired that Wells came from Shaftesbury to find work but had been unable to find a permanent position [350]. It appears he had never been to school and had been persuaded to go up the stairs by a second man, Henry Langridge. It seems that Wells was the innocent dupe and that Langridge was the real criminal. Wells was sentenced to three months' imprisonment with hard labour but was warned that if he ever committed similar offences in the future, he would be sentenced to penal servitude in the colonies.

In May, 1872, the pub was advertised as available to let [351] and a month later, the brewing plant was advertised as to be sold by auction [352]. In that same month the license of the pub was transferred to Joseph Daniel Powell, although it is not known whether he took over the brewing plant or intended to obtain his beer from elsewhere.

However, by October, 1875, Henry Dibsdale had taken over the license. He took Joseph Powell to Court for the rent of furnished rooms at the Globe occupied by Mr Powell and his family [353]. It appears that when Henry Dibsdale took over the pub, he agreed to rent the rooms to Mr Powell until he moved to his new premises, the Bird-in-Hand in North Street. But the money paid by Mr Dibsdale to Mr Powell for the Globe was late in being honoured at the bank. As the Judge said, Mr Powell was paying rent for rooms in a pub that he still owned! As a consequence, the Court found for Mr Powell and the rent that he had paid into the Court before the hearing, which was smaller by the rent for the period that Mr Powell had not been paid for the pub than that claimed by Mr Dibsdale, was accepted as the correct amount.

By December, 1877, the Globe was owned by Messrs Bailey, brewers from

Frome, and may have been so for some time previously. In that year, they applied for a temporary license for the pub as the last tenant had absconded [354]. This application was approved but it seems that problems continued. In the following April, the brewery again asked for a temporary license as the tenant was 'elsewhere' [355]. This was again granted with the license being held by Mr Jacob Barlow of Andover. By February, 1879, the pub was put up for sale [356] and it does not appear in the licensing records after this date. It appears as a private house in the 1881 Census.

105 Glove, nk
This was an alehouse mentioned in records of 1625 with Edmond Snow as the landlord, when he took 24 barrels of beer and 6 couls of ale from the Common Brewhouse. Haskins states that the Glove was granted a licence in 1720, but there is no indication that this was the same house.

106 Goat Inn, 24 Milford Street
The Goat was mentioned as early as 1590. Building work in 1976 showed the north range facing onto Milford St was rebuilt in c.1820 after a fire. The south of the building has been dated to c.1500 although it was rebuilt in the 18th C and in c.1820. There was a small yard leading off to the E of the pub. In 1796, it was advertised for sale when it was described as 'that commodious and good-accustomed House known by the name of the Goat Inn, in Milford Street, with Stabling for upwards of 40 horses.'

Between May, 1624, and March, 1625, Christopher New, the landlord of the Goat, took 43 barrels of beer from the Common Brewhouse. Mr New was also one of the forty publicans who attended a Council meeting in 1625 to discuss taking beer from the same source.

In 1783, a woman from outside of Salisbury extorted money from the Ostler at the Goat by claiming that he had raped her. He paid her ten shillings (all he could afford) and she withdrew her warrant for his arrest [357].

Although the Goat was never a coaching inn, it does appear to have been a regular terminus for carrier's wagons as described in 1803 [358]: 'London and Salisbury Carriage Waggon. A Waggon sets out from the Goat, Milford Street, Salisbury, every Tuesday morning; gets into London on Thursday night; inns at the Saracen's Head, in Friday Street, Cheapside; and sets out on its return to Salisbury every Friday morning – calls at the Black Bear, Piccadilly, going in and out of London. Performed by William Dear, who solicits the favours of the Gentlemen, Tradesmen, etc. of Salisbury, and the intermediate towns, for which he will be truly grateful, and take the utmost care of all goods entrusted to his conveyance.'

Joseph Chinn, from Portsmouth, became the landlord of the Goat in 1814 [359]. He was obviously a keen gardener as he soon started a series of annual Pink Feasts at the Goat. These events enabled other horticulturists to display their flowers and sit down to a dinner after the judging of the blooms. These events continued at the Goat until at least 1829. Mr Chinn often won one of the prizes at these competitions. In the later years, he does not seem to have entered his own Pink Feasts but he was still winning prizes at other feasts held within the City.

In 1817, there was a robbery at the

Goat where it was supposed that the thief concealed himself in the pub during opening hours, and then broke into the bar and stole £8 in pennies and halfpennies and a bottle of rum. Mr Chinn offered a reward of £10 if the thief could be apprehended. Instead he received the following letter [360]: 'Mr Chinn, In reply to your handbills dated 1st I shall only contradict you in one or two circumstances that is you say there was £8 worth of Copper taken, I deny that for there was £7 5s 6d only in Copper. I am the Man that entered your house – I did not conceal myself but unlock'd the doors, you may depend upon it you will never Pick out the Rogue there is but one concerned in it, take care your house is not open'd again, Yours etc., P.S. I live in the town.'

The handwriting of the letter was said to be very good and Mr Chinn now offered a reward of £5 if the writer of the letter could be identified. Mr Chinn died in 1832. His wife, Mary Ann Chinn, continued to run the pub as well as providing a booth to supply alcoholic refreshments at Salisbury Races in order to support herself and her children [361].

William Holloway took over the inn from Mary Chinn in 1833. He ran the inn until he died in 1836 and his wife, Eliza, continued to run the Goat. She married Richard Dudman in 1840, and as was the practice at that time, he became the landlord. It seems likely that Eliza actually ran the pub and so, when she dies in early 1853, her son Francis becomes the landlord. This must have been a temporary arrangement as another son, Charles Holloway, takes over the pub shortly after. He runs the pub until 1856 when he moves to the New Inn in Milford (the Tollgate qv). Thus, ended a family concern that operated for 23 years.

In 1853, a Frenchman by the name of Franque Behrends was arrested for assaulting Miss Holloway, the landlady of the Goat [362]. He apparently arrived at the pub at half past eleven on a Saturday morning and demanded a bed for the night. Miss Holloway told him that she did not have a vacant room. On hearing this, Behrends became very abusive and spat in the landlady's face, leaving the pub before assistance could arrive. He then went to the Three Swans where he bought a glass of stout, walking around the room and demanding to be allowed to go through a locked door. The barmaid called the Ostler and Behrends was put out of the pub but later returned and put his fist through a glass window pane. He was arrested on account of his actions at the two pubs and several other complaints from around the City. In the Court, he declared that the two women witnesses were great liars and that he would take them to London to be judged before the Lord Mayor. He also began gesticulating violently and swearing at the Mayor and the other Magistrates. He refused to listen to any pleas to behave himself and, in the end, the Mayor fined him £1 and costs for the assault on Miss Holloway and 5s 6d for his behaviour at the Three Swans. Even then, the police had to remove him from the Court as his behaviour was described as being close to madness.

The furniture and brewing plant of the Goat were put up for sale when Charles Holloway left the inn [363]. It appears that a Mr Mullins purchased some of the furniture on behalf of Mr Onslow who became the landlord in early 1858. But Onslow ran out of money and Mullins was not paid for the furniture. Furthermore, Onslow assigned all his assets to his creditors to avoid bankruptcy and they took possession of the inn including the furniture purchased by Mullins who had still not been paid. There followed a complex court case between Mullins and Onslow [364] but unfortunately the verdict of the court, which was deferred to a later sitting, is not recorded in the *Salisbury and Winchester Journal* but it seems likely that Mr Mullins won his case although whether he was ever paid seems doubtful considering the financial situation of Onslow.

The Goat seems to have lived an uneventful life as an ordinary city pub for the remainder of the 19th C until it fell foul of the Licensing (Consolidation) act of 1910. This gave Magistrates the power to refuse renewal of a licence if it was considered that the pub was unnecessary to provide for the needs of the public. Compensation would then be paid both to the owner of the premises and the licensee. The Goat was referred to the Compensation Authority in May 1924 by Salisbury Magistrates.

The report on the pub stated [10]: 'This is situated in one of the most congested districts in the City as regards licensed properties. Milford Street is about 340 yards in length, and within this distance there are 9 licensed houses. The distances of the other licensed houses from "The Goat" were given as follows: -

"Malt and Hop Tap"   Practically opposite
"Catherine Wheel"   40 yards
"William IV"   27 yards
"Round of Beef"   48 yards
"Oddfellows Arms"   61 yards
"Red Lion Hotel"   76 yards
"Cathedral Hotel"   82 yards
"Crystal Fountain"   104 yards

In addition to these there are two other houses, the "Anchor Brewery Tap", and the "Waggon and Horses", (another house referred by me) just off Milford Street.'

The rateable value of "The Goat" for Poor Rate purposes is £29 15s 0d.

The premises were stated to be in a good state of repair. A ground floor plan of the house was put in, and accompanies this Report. On the first and second floors, there are nine bedrooms furnished, and on the first floor there is a spacious club-room.

Evidence from the sanitary point of view was given by the Sanitary Inspector for the City, and speaking generally, except for a complaint as to a defective fitting in one water closet, such evidence was not actually unfavourable to the house.

Evidence was also given of Police observations from the 7th to the 13th February, both inclusive, and showed that during the period 600 persons entered the house, the daily totals being: -

7th	61
8th	72
9th, Saturday	135
10th	77
11th	63
12th, Market Day	131
13th	61
	600

On behalf of the Owners it was pointed out that Salisbury had a large floating population apart from census figures. The following figures of trade were given in evidence: -

	a	b	c	d	e
1921	204	763	96	65½	99
1922	179	593	27	48	200

1923	160	419	15	26½	171
Total	543	1775	138	140	470
Average	181	591	46	47	157

[Note: a = Beers, bulk; b = Bottled beers, dozens; c = Wines, bottles; d = Spirits, gallons; e = Spirits bottles]

'After careful consideration of all the evidence we decided to refer to you the question of the renewal of the License on the ground of redundancy, and provisionally renewed the same to the tenant.'

Thus, although the Goat appears to have been well run, in good order and with a thriving trade (at least, in comparison with some other pubs elsewhere as will be seen in other entries in this volume), it was recommended for closure. In June, 1924, this recommendation was upheld and in October that year, total compensation for its closure was agreed at £1315. It closed shortly thereafter.

107 Goate, Fisherton

The Goate is mentioned twice in records of 1737 and 1756 but its site and what its life as a pub was is not known.

108 Golden Lion, Endless Street.

It is not clear where the Golden Lion was in Endless Street. It is possible that it was a later incarnation of either the Labour in Vain in Endless Street or the Three Tuns on the corner of Endless Street and Winchester Street. However, the licensing records for the period of interest are sparse and the records of the annual licensing meetings note the names of licensees without the names of their houses. So, it is difficult to be precise about changes in the names of public houses.

Haskins states that John Brettel was granted a license for an alehouse called the Golden Lion, in Endless Street, in 1779. If this statement is accurate, John Brettel could have only been the licensee for a short time as the pub was advertised in 1779 by William Whitchurch & Son as available to rent [365]. The following year, Gray and Lively, coach and harness makers, advertise a chaise and a diligence (both types of carriage) for sale, stating that they are at the Golden Lion, in Winchester Street [366]. This reinforces the view that the Golden Lion was a later name for the Three Tuns.

In 1794, William Whitchurch was granted a lease of 40 years for 'the corner tenement called the Golden Lion, in Endless Street. It was said that he had possessed a former 40 year lease for the premises of which ten years had expired. Unless he had had an even earlier lease, the number of years expired must be incorrect if he had owned the lease in 1779!

In 1810, the household furniture and fixtures of the Golden Lion were put up for auction as Thomas Brownjohn, the landlord, was leaving the premises [367]. Haskins states that the following year, the lease of the pub was transferred to Samuel Whitchurch. The following year, 1812, the licensing records show John Goddard to be the landlord [4], but in 1813, the records describe the pub as 'shut up'. No more is heard of this pub.

109 Grange Hotel, St Mark's Avenue

This was a large late-Victorian house which became a hotel. The bar was open to the public in the 1970s. There was a large ballroom built onto the rear of the premises which became a popular nightclub in

110 Grasshopper, Winchester Street

Nothing is known of this pub apart from a single, intriguing advertisement in the *Salisbury and Winchester Journal* in 1739 which states [368]: 'To be seen to Morrow, and every Day during its Stay in Town, (Sundays excepted) from Ten in the Morning, till Eight at Night, by Five or more, at One Shilling each, in a large Room at Mr Cooper's, late the Sign of the Grasshopper in Winchester Street. The Microcosm; Or the World in Miniature. Lately invented and made by Henry Bridges of Waltham Abby in Essex. It is the most curious and magnificent Piece of Mechanism ever made of this Kind; and has been shewn before the Royal Family, and most of the Nobility and Gentry, with the greatest applause. Its Height is ten Foot, and Breadth in the Base six Foot: The Whole is most beautifully compos'd of Architecture, Sculpture, Painting, Musick and Astronomy, according to the Best Rules and Principles, with great Variety of moving Figures. To give a particular Description of this Machine, in all its Parts, would here take up too much Room; those who have seen it declare, that the Entertainment surpasses thought. It equally delights and surprises All who see and hear it; and is allow'd to be the most finish'd Piece that appear'd in Europe.'

This is almost certainly an earlier name of an inn better known in later years but no connection has been made so far. However, the Plough on the corner of Chipper Lane and Castle Street was known as the Grasshopper in the late 18th C. and so there is always the possibility that the advertisement misplaced the pub.

111 Great Western Tavern, Fisherton

This pub was undoubtedly connected with the Great Western Railway that reached Salisbury in 1856 with a terminus in Fisherton Anger. The only mention of the Tavern found so far is from 1865 [369] by which time the tunnel connecting Fisherton with the London and Southampton lines had been opened. In late 1865, the building materials of the tavern were advertised for sale so, presumably [370], it was demolished together with some adjoining buildings. Its exact location is not known.

112 Gredire, Catherine Street

This was referred to in 1455 as the Le Gredire in Cartenstrete. A Gredire appears to be Old English for a Griddle or Gridiron.

113 Green Dragon, Fisherton

The landlord of this house in 1737 was a Mr Hall. It appears that in 1737, Mr Hall was also the curate in charge of the old Church in Fisherton. John Wesley, the famous preacher, was the brother-in-law of Mr Hall. It is recorded that Mr Hall preached a sermon in the coach-house of the Green Dragon [371]. An advertisement for the lease of two houses in Fisherton Anger in 1741 refers to them 'lying in Fisherton Anger on the East side of the house formerly the Green Dragon' [372]. No more is known of this pub.

114 Green Man, nk

A farthing token issued in 1658 by Edward Mason shows a naked man with some sort of headgear on the obverse [373]. This sign is usually associated with the Green Man of legend but there is no indication of the trade of Mr Mason. Thus it may or may not have been a pub in Salisbury! The entry in Rowe is a little confusing as the text is partially referring to a different farthing token featured on the previous page of the book. The other premises that may have been known as the Green Man is covered under the England's Glory (QV).

115 Grey Fisher, Ayleswade Road

This pub was mostly shown as the Swan up until 1980 but occasionally was shown as the White Swan. It then became the Grey Fisher. Interestingly, in most advertisements and notices in the local papers, the pub was almost always shown as the Swan.

Until 1903, the pub was on the east side of Ayleswade Road in Harnham, very close to St Nicholas bridge, but in that year the licence was moved to the newly-built premises on the current site further along Ayleswade Road. The earliest records of the inn are from 1760 but, as it was outside of the City limits of New Sarum, information from the earlier years is a little sparse. A notice from 1762 is for a creditor's meeting to be held at the White Swan [374]. It is very likely that the pub was in existence some time before that date. At that time, Ayleswade Road was the main road to Fordingbridge and Ringwood so the resultant traffic benefitted from an inn on that route.

In 1821, Samuel Nash, the landlord, put a notice in the *Salisbury and Winchester Journal* offering a 20-guinea reward for information leading to the identification of the person who had been circulating anonymous letters which claimed Mr Nash encouraged poachers, thus bringing his character into disrepute [375]. It said the letters did this by suggesting that he had made his house 'the receptacle for poached game of all descriptions'.

In March, 1828, the pub was advertised for sale [376]. The sale included about two acres of meadow and pasture land. The pub was actually owned by the Earl of Radnor. In April of that year, George Bowns became the landlord and he continued until his death in 1851. His widow, Ann Bowns, then ran the pub for four years [377], followed by her son, also George Bowns, who continued as landlord until 1877 when he died by falling headlong into a cask of beer! [378] It was thought he was overcome by the fumes from the beer. It appears that the family continued to run the pub until April 1879 when Alfred Pope became the landlord.

By 1849, the lease of the pub was once again up for sale [379]. The premises being sold consisted of the pub itself "together with the neat and compact Brewery, commodious Cellar, good Stabling, large Yard, and Garden, with Skittle-alley, under cover, and a Piece of Pasture Land on the south side of the said premises, called "The Orchard", and also that Meadow, called "Three Corner Ground", containing, by estimation, about 1 acre". The Bowns continued in residence.

It appears that the brewer, Gibbs Mew, acquired the lease in about 1899, and operated the pub until in 1902, when they agreed with the Earl of Radnor that a new pub was built on part of the land held under the lease. This was presumably the paddock adjoining the Swan. So Gibbs Mew built a new pub and in April, 1903 it was recorded [10]: 'On reading a Licence granted at the adjourned General Annual Licensing meeting for the Division of Salisbury and Amesbury on the 10th March 1903 to William James Webb of East Harnham (being the removal of the Licence of the Swan Inn at East Harnham to new premises recently constructed adjacent thereto) authorising him to hold any of the Excise Licences that may be held by a publican for the sale by retail at the said new premises of intoxicating liquors and on hearing Mr Henderson of counsel for the said William James Webb this Committee doth order that the said Licence be and the same is confirmed.'

With the new pub in operation, the old building was demolished and a row of houses was built on the land and the meadow land adjoining the river. This row of house can still be seen today between the pub and the river.

The new pub continued in trade for many years with a saloon bar to the left of the entrance and a public bar to the right. There was also a small jug & bottle bar between the two main bars inside the entrance. In about 1980, the pub was remodelled to have a single bar with the adjoining barn connected to the main building to provide an extension suitable for serving food. At the same time, it was renamed the Grey Fisher with a pub sign showing a heron.

In 2000, the pub was further remodelled after it was acquired by Greene King on the demise of Gibbs Mew. An extension was added to the rear of the pub to provide a large dining area and the pub was marketed as a Hungry Horse pub. The pub sign was changed to show, for some strange reason, a Kookaburra! More recently, the pub sign was changed to a Greene King generic 'Hungry Horse' sign which includes the name 'Greyfisher'.

116 Greyhound, Brown Street

This pub has variously been described as being in Brown Street, as being in Winchester Street & Brown Street and backing on to the Three Lions (which was on the corner of Winchester Street and Queen Street. It was probably on the south-west corner of the junction of Brown Street with Winchester Street. If so, it is likely that the whole of the south side of Winchester Street between Brown Street and the Market Square was occupied by the Greyhound and the Three Lions.

In Hoare's History of Modern Wiltshire, it is stated [380]: 'In 1624 it is recorded that the mayor, Robert Joles, In the time of his mayoralty, and towards the expiration of his office, he was much distempered with drink; and in the night time, about eight o'clock, as he was getting towards Mr Harnes's house, he being at Gaunt's Kyve, which is the filthy miry ditch that runneth through the Greyhound, could not get over the bridge, but fell into the same gutter, and getting out with much adoe, thinking to get over the stupples, he walked through the river, and then went into Mr Harne's house at the back door.'

William Naish's map of Salisbury printed in 1751 clearly shows one of the city's ditches running through the corner where the Greyhound is supposed to have stood. In relation to Robert Joles, there were many complaints about his behaviour. Not the least of his antics was to steal the Common Seal of the City in 1623 and apply it to Orders authorising the formation of a Brewer's Company despite this action having been refused by the Corporation.

At some time in the 18th C., the Greyhound came into the possession of John Gast who also owned the Three Lions. John Gast rented the Three Lions to an innkeeper while running the Greyhound up until 1783. He then advertised both properties for rent with an option to buy the freehold of the Greyhound. It appears that the Greyhound might have been let for a few more years until in 1790, William Gast, son of John, advertised that he had opened a Wine Cellar that had belonged to the Greyhound [381]. Here he sold wine both retail and wholesale. There is no further mention of the Greyhound as a pub. The name was taken over in 1803 by the pub that later became the Duchess of Albany. Note also that this may have become the Black Horse Tap (qv) and the Falcon (qv) at a later date.

117 Greyhound, Greencroft Street

This alehouse was recorded as having applied for a licence in 1742 and had it refused. If it had been granted, it would appear to have resulted in two pubs with the same name in the city which has not been seen at any other time (although pubs in Fisherton, outside of the city, did have names the same as those within the city). Thus, it is possible that this Greyhound became or was before, known by a different name.

118 Half Moon, Bedwin Street

This pub was near to St Edmond's Church and is variously described as being in Beaden Row or opposite St Edmond's Church. It appears to have been licensed in 1743 but may have been an unlicensed alehouse before this date. The last year in which this pub is recorded is 1746. It could possibly be an earlier name for the Vine in Bedwin Street.

119 Half Moon, Castle Street

This pub appears in the licensing records from 1791 [3] until October 1802 when Richard Tewkesbury acquired the licence [4]. He is next recorded as being the master of the Carpenter's Arms and it is possible that these are one and the same pub. The exact location in Castle Street is not known.

120 Half Moon, Ox Row

The Half Moon was in Ox Row next door to the Old Council House which burned down in 1780. As far as one can tell it was opposite Rutherford Walk which leads between Ox Row and New Canal near the Guildhall. It is clearly seen in an old engraving of the Council House that has been published elsewhere [382]. Note that this engraving shows the premises as being Mr Wheeler's shop which was not possible as the Council House burned down in 1780 and Mr Wheeler did not take the shop until 1783!

The Half Moon was in existence for many years but closed down some time before 1739 when Robert Cooper, Linen Draper, had his shop at the Half Moon [383]. However, in 1761 it was re-opened as a tavern [384]: 'The large House, near the Counsel House, lately inhabited by Mr

Cooper, Linen Draper, & formerly known by the name of the Half Moon Tavern, is now fitting up in a very elegant and convenient Manner, & will very soon be opened again as a Tavern ... The Coffee Room of the said House, allowed to be a very genteel & convenient one, is this Day opened, & the following Papers are provided, viz: - the Gazette, London & General Evening, & the Daily Advertiser; Lloyd's Chronicle & the Votes of the House of Commons, will also be provided, and nothing shall be wanting, to make it agreeable to the Public in General, & to Subscribers to the said Room in Particular, by their most obliged & very humble Servant, Mr Bailey.'

It did re-open in May 1761 and was once again known as the Half Moon. It quickly became re-established as one of the most important taverns in the centre of Salisbury owing to its proximity to the Market Square. By July 1762, it is advertised [385]: 'By order of the Steward of the Races, There will be an Ordinary on Wednesday & Friday next at the Half Moon Tavern & Coffee House; where Gentlemen may be supplied with the following neat Wines, viz. Champagne, Burgundy, Claret, Old Hock, Frontiniac, Rhenish, Mosell, Madeira, Florence, Port, Mountain & Lisbon. – Dinner to be on Table each day at 2 o'clock. The Public may depend on always meeting, at the above Tavern, with the genteelest accommodations, a good Larder, & the best of Wines etc.'

Many public meetings were held at the Half Moon during this period including establishment of a scheme to provide Salisbury with a regular supply of fresh fish [386], starting a subscription to open a smallpox hospital in Bugmore (the site of the Friary estate) [387], to discuss the building of a number of turnpikes in the Salisbury area [388] and many others. By July 1767 it was advertised that [389]: 'The Half-Moon Tavern, Salisbury, Is at the request of many Gentlemen provided with exceeding good Stall Stables, and opened for the Reception of Company travelling the Road. Such who please to make use of the said House, may depend upon having good beds, genteel and reasonable accommodations of every Kind, a constant Endeavour to meet a Continuance of their Favours, and the greatest Care taken of their Horses. The Half-Moon stands in the most pleasant part of the Market Place, almost adjoining to the Council House, and though but a few Yards from the great Road, is entirely free from the Noise of Carriages etc. A genteel public Coffee Room in the front of the House, furnished with all the Evening Papers etc etc. Neat Post Chaise.'

In 1768, Morris Bailey considered moving to the Three Lions in Queen Street but he stated that 'having by the Persuasion of many of my Friends declined all thoughts of going to the Three Lions, which is taken by another Person, I think it incumbent upon me to return my most grateful Acknowledgments to the Nobility, Gentry & Public in General for the many favours they have been hitherto pleased to confer upon me at the Half Moon' [390]. By July 1771, the Half Moon is also described as 'Bailey's Hotel' and was said to be 'greatly improved & enlarged' [391].

But perhaps this last action by Mr Bailey stretched his finances too far as the Half Moon is advertised to let with 'the household goods, stock, post-chaises

& horses to be sold to the person who will take the same' [392]. In March 1772, it is advertised that a commission of bankruptcy against Morris Bailey will meet at the Three Lions [393]. In April 1772, it is announced that Daniel Pearce Safe, the Post Master of Salisbury, has purchased the lease of the Half Moon and moved the Post Office to it from the Red Lion [394].

Morris Bailey must have been an excellent landlord as after his demise, the Half Moon rapidly moves between a number of landlords. Daniel Pearce Safe leaves in April 1774 although he retains the Post Office which he moves to his own house. William Schuldham takes over the tavern but by July 1774, the apparently thriving business is advertised [395]: 'Half Moon Tavern & Coffee House. To be sold to the Highest Bidder the valuable Lease of the said Tavern & Coffee House, on which 8 years were to come at Ladyday last, at an exceeding low rent. The whole is in thorough repair, £400 having been expended on it a few years since. Enquire of the present occupier, who quits it on account of his ill health, or of Messrs Smith in High St. The house is large & exceedingly convenient; the ground floor consists of the Public Coffee Room and two parlours in front; one large bar and one small ditto, two kitchens with many other conveniences; on the first floor is one large dining-room & one smaller ditto, a billiard room & three good bedchambers; on the second floor are six other good bed-chambers etc, over which is a large laundry and many good rooms for servants etc, & under the whole there is excellent cellarage. There are several clubs held weekly at the house of the principal gentlemen & tradesmen of the city; besides which there are 79 annual subscribers to the coffee room at 10/6 each, being more than sufficient to pay the whole rent and taxes, which will be made very easy to a newcomer & very great encouragement given.'

It is not clear if the house was actually let at this time as in March 1775, all the furniture and fittings are advertised for sale including the billiard table [396]. But in June 1775, James Ravenscroft announces that he has opened the Half Moon Tavern and Coffee Room [397]. This effort does not last long as Mr Ravenscroft's furniture is sold in February 1776 and later in the same month Messrs Benson & Fort, Hatters, announce that they have become Benson & Son and will 'carry on the same trade at the house late the Half Moon Tavern' [398]. Benson's business later became Wheeler's until, in 1823, the whole premises were destroyed in a fire.

121 Halfway House, 225 Wilton Road

This pub, in the Wilton Road just to the east of Skew Bridge was originally called the Sun and became commonly known as the Halfway House some time about 1781. However, even as early as 1760, the pub was referred to as 'the Sun, commonly called the Halfway House'.

The pub would have had some land attached to it before the railway was built as otherwise, bull baiting would be difficult [399]: 'Jun 1 1761. The famous Game Bull, from Hilperton Common, will be baited at Thos Hazard's, the Sun, near Fisherton Brick Kilns, commonly called the Half Way House, on Thursday next, being His Majesty's Birthday. The Owner

Halfway House

of the Dog which plays best & fairest, will be entitled to a Hat of 10/- Value. Also at the same Place will be baited a large Badger. To begin at ten o'clock. N.B. The above Bull will be lent to any Person within 25 miles of Salisbury, on reasonable Terms. Enquire at the Bell at South Newton, near Wilton.'

Smallpox was a common illness in the late 18th C. but already, inoculation was becoming a common means of protection from the disease as shown by this advertisement from 1781 [400]: 'Inoculation is now continued by E. Rolfe, at the Halfway House, at Bemerton, near Salisbury, with the greatest success. People in the natural Small-pox taken in, and whole parishes or companies inoculated and attended on the most reasonable terms. It being confidently reported that great numbers have lately died of inoculation in and near Salisbury, E. Rolfe begs leave to assure the Public, that he has not lost one patient, although he has inoculated near three hundred people within the space of two months.'

It seems likely that an alehouse known first as the White Horse and later as the Victoria was what later became the Halfway House again. This pub is shown as being one mile from Salisbury on the Wilton Road and in Bemerton parish. It first appears in the licensing records in 1831 with Thomas Griffin being the landlord [6]. But this entry in the records does not show it to be a new license and hence it is presumed it was in existence before this date. In July, 1833, it was put up for sale, the notice stating [401]: 'All that well-accustomed Public-House, called the

White Horse, with capital Garden, Timber-Yard, Cooper's and Hoopmaker's Shops thereto belonging, situate at Bemerton, adjoining the turnpike road leading from Salisbury to Wilton, now and for many years past occupied by Mr Griffin.'

Mr Griffin stayed at the inn until 1837 when the contents of the house including all the stock, household furniture and brewing equipment was put up for sale [402]. A week after this notice of sale, the inn itself is offered to let including the timber yard where the businesses of timber dealer, cooper and hoop maker had been run for over thirty years. The new tenant could also take an orchard of four acres' area adjoining the site of the inn.

The pub appears to have been renamed the Victoria Arms when William Jefferis became the landlord in August, 1838, a year after Victoria became Queen [8]. In the spring of 1839, Mr Jefferies advertised that he would be providing a series of entertainments on Easter Monday that would include donkey racing, jumping in sacks and jingling (whatever this might be!) [403].

Mr Jefferis ran the pub until July, 1839, when he assigned all his property to John Richardson, a grocer, Caleb Brunwin Caplin, landlord of the Rose Inn in Bridge Street, and John Croft Carly, landlord of the Old George in Winchester Street [404]. An assignment of this nature was intended to ensure that all the assignee's debts would be paid without making the person bankrupt. As a result, the contents of the Victoria Arms was put up for sale [405] and it appears that Benjamin Cooke took over the pub. But in December, 1840, the following advertisement appeared in the *Salisbury and Winchester Journal* [406]: 'Freehold, On The Wilton Road, Near Salisbury. To be Sold by Auction, at the Black Horse Inn, in the City of New Sarum, by Mr Brownjohn, on the 17th instant, at one o'clock pm, subject to such conditions as will then be produced, - All that Messuage or Tenement, lately known by the sign of the "Victoria Arms", and now in the occupation of Mr Cooke, with the Stables, Yard, Offices, and Garden thereto adjoining and belonging. And also all that productive Orchard adjoining, and containing, with the site of the house and above-described premises, Five Acres, or thereabouts. For further particulars, apply to Mr Alford, solicitor, Salisbury.'

The license was renewed in August 1841 with Mr Cooke still being the licensee but in August, 1842, the licensing records show that no application for renewal was made [8]. Nothing more is heard of the Victoria.

Speculating on the fate of this pub, one wonders if it was on the site of what is now the Halfway House. It is noticeable that the present pub backs onto the railway line. The line from Salisbury to Warminster has its origin in the proposal for the Wiltshire and Somerset railway line that was approved in 1844 (heavily backed by the Great Western Railway). It could be possible that the Victoria Arms was purchased to provide the land for this railway line to enter Salisbury. After many difficulties, this line was finally opened in 1856. The Halfway House was ready to reopen in 1862 and with what was most probably a new building that we see today. If this speculation is correct, it would appear that the Sun, which became commonly known as the Halfway House became the White Horse sometime after 1802, then became the Victoria Arms in 1838 before closing in 1842. A new building was opened as the Halfway House in 1862.

Thus, in 1862, Alfred Brown applied for a new licence and had his application refused. A licence was refused again in 1863 and 1864 but in 1865, the pub was issued with a new licence. But even then, the pub is missing from the licensing records in 1866-67 and when it reappears in 1868, it is once again described as a New House.

In 1867, the Alfred Brown, described as a beerhouse keeper, applied for a spirit licence but this was refused as the West End Hotel had such a licence and this was considered sufficient to fulfil the needs of the neighbourhood. However, in 1868, when William Bishop Wilson had become the landlord, the pub did receive a spirit licence [407].

The pub continued in trade for many years and was in later days owned by Usher's Brewery of Trowbridge. At a later date, it was taken over by Gibbs Mew of Salisbury until in 1995, it was purchased by Goldfinch Brewery of Dorchester. Like all of their pubs, the Halfway House was renamed Tom Brown's. In 2008, the pub was sold and returned to its old name of the Halfway House as a free house.

122 Hampton Inn, Pearce Way

A new public house opened as the Bishopdown, built in 2002 to service the Bishopdown estate. It is also well positioned for the A30 London road. Now called the Hampton Inn which was part of the Table Table group but is now listed as a Premier Inn.

123 Hatterestaverne, Castle Street

One of the earliest inns in Salisbury, this is described in 1396 as being in Mynsterstrete which is called Castelstrete. Its exact location has not been determined. But it should be said that Minster Street was the original name of what is now High Street, and at that time, the street continued past the west front of St Thomas' Church and continued as Castle Street,

124 Haunch of Venison, Minster Street

The current building occupied by the Haunch of Venison dates from the mid-15th C. but it is often said that the inn dates from 1320. It is also reputed to have been used to house workers employed on the building of the Cathedral spire in the 14th C. Whether this is true is not clear but there is a connection with the cathedral as the floor tiles in the bar were purchased from the Cathedral in the 18th C. for £11!

Whatever the origin of the building, there is virtually no record of the inn until Samuel Fawconer was the landlord in 1741 and little is recorded about the Haunch throughout the 18th C. However, it was stated in November 1784 that [408]: 'On Friday, about noon, a bureau in the house of Mr Merryweather, at the Haunch of Venison, in this city, was broke open, and robbed of between £60 and £70 by John Lamb, a Negro, who lodged in the house, and is since gone off.'

In or before 1803, Thomas Cheater became landlord of the inn and started a long dynasty. He was landlord until his death in 1830 when his widow, Maria Cheater continued to run the pub. In 1833, Firmin Potto, her son-in-law took over the pub and ran it for over 40 years [409]. His widow, Mrs Louisa Potto, continued with the pub before handing over to her son, Alfred Potto who continues up until 1903. It is possible that the succession was even longer as the landlord from 1903 was Firmin Sidney Bradbeer although the unusual first name may be purely coincidental. But in 1894, an assistant to Louisa Potto was a Francis Henry Bradbeer, and Mrs Potto was described as being his aunt.

In 1938, an advertisement states that the Haunch is noted for its antiquity, and also for its Grill room which supplies the best of English Meat. It also says that it has well-selected wines at moderate prices and good ale on draught or in bottle

For many years, the pub was supplied with beer from the Simond's Brewery in Reading. This brewery was acquired by Courage in 1960 and brewing ceased at the old brewery in 1979. The Haunch was then supplied from Courage, Bristol until the Grand Metropolitan/Courage brewery/pub swap in 1991. Since that time the Haunch has moved between a number of pub companies.

125 Horns, Market Place

This was an alehouse that was somewhere in the Market Place in the mid-1700s. It appears to have gained a licence as an alehouse in 1721. It was probably a different name for another, known pub but has so far not been connected to a different house.

126 Horse, Castle Street

This is known from a single reference in 1455 which referred to Le Horce in Castelstrete.

127 Horse's Head, High Street

Another 1455 reference to an inn called Le Horshed in what is now High Street.

128 Horse & Groom, nk

A licence was applied for and refused for this alehouse in 1742. It is believed that this licence would have upgraded the pub from an alehouse to a fully-licenced public house.

129 Horse & Groom, 54 Wilton Road

In 1864, Samuel Naish left the Malmesbury Arms in Wilton Road and moved to the West End Hotel. It seems probable that this pub had run as an alehouse before this year and hence does not appear in the records of public houses.

In 1868, a fire broke out in a bedroom in the West End Hotel [410]. A young man had gone to bed at about midnight and left a candle burning on a chair next to his bed. At about two o'clock in the morning, he was woke up by heat and smoke and found the curtains of his bed on fire. He called the landlord who, with the help of neighbours, managed to extinguish the fire, although the furnishings of the room were destroyed. The young man was severely burned on his face and hands and was considered to have had a lucky escape. It was noted that the landlord was insured with the London, Liverpool and Globe Insurance Office.

In 1870, Samuel Middleton had moved to the hotel from Netherhampton [411]. Amongst other attractions mentioned in an advertisement, he stated that he had pleasure and tea gardens. In 1872, Mr Middleton was charged with keeping his house open after eleven o'clock at night

[412]. He pleaded that he was ignorant of the change in the law and the provisions of the 1872 Licensing Act. This Act introduced universal closing hours throughout the country being eleven o'clock on weekdays and Saturdays and ten o'clock on Sundays. The Magistrates were eventually satisfied that the new requirements on landlords had not been made well known and, hence, Mr Middleton escaped without a fine although he had to pay the costs of the proceedings.

In April, 1889, a pigeon shooting match was advertised to take place in a field near the West End Hotel [413]. The matches were open to Wiltshire persons only. There was a new, breech-loading pigeon gun as a prize in a match for 20 persons at 20 shillings' entry fee and a handicap match with the winner receiving a sterling silver cup valued at 5 guineas. Refreshments were supplied by the hotel and a dinner was held there in the evening.

Isaac Deverill, the landlord since 1878, died in August, 1902. The pub was put up for sale by his Executors [414]. It seems likely that this was when the pub was purchased by Grove's brewery of Weymouth who owned it until 1960 when that brewery was purchased by Devenish brewery. It remained a Devenish house until at least 1976. Its name was changed to the Horse & Groom in the early 1980s and it appears to have become a free house at about this time.

130 Horse & Jockey, Scots Lane

This pub was noted as being an alehouse in 1741. It also appears as a single entry in the licensing records for 1810. Apart from this, nothing more is known of the pub.

131 Horseshoe, High Street

The shop and offices on the east side of High Street adjacent to the Close Gate were once an inn. In 1475, there is a reference to Marshall's inn or the Horseshoe, in High Street.

A Lease of October 1576 appears to name it as the White Horse. Certainly, in 1609, it was leased to John Lowe when it was stated that it was 'a capital messuage and garden adjoining, sometime an Inne called the Horseshoe, afterwards the White Horse' [415]. In 1649, when it was leased to James Underhill it consisted of a hall, parlour, kitchen, solar, two butteries, coalhouse, taphouse, two drinking rooms, stable, woodhouse, a fair dining room, four fair chambers, three chambers for servants, a shop and a garden of ten perches. There was also a small tenement adjoining next to the close wall consisting of a shop with a room above which is probably the same as the current premises.

In 1682, when it was leased to Robert Westbury, it was referred to as the Sunn and it appears that it was rebuilt at this time [416]. The rent of the main building was £4 per annum and that of the small tenement £1. By 1751, the lease for the building from the Dean & Chapter no longer showed its past history as a pub and thus we must surmise that it was by then a private house [417].

132 Horseshoes, Britford

An auction was held at the Three Swans in Salisbury on July 19 1780 in which Lot 5 was a 'Messuage or Tenement called the Horse-Shoes, in the Parish of Britford' [418]. Since the parish of Britford included what is now East Harnham, it is not possible to identify the site of this pub. The tenant was Anne Goodright.

133 Horseshoes, Fisherton
Haskins notes this house as having been licensed in 1713 [419]. Gordon notes it as being in Fisherton and suggests that John Layland was the landlord in 1624. However, it seems likely that the Horseshoe occupied by John Layland was what later became the Cloisters (qv).

134 Huntsman Tavern, 125 Gigant Street
This pub was built in about 1840 and was originally known as the Gigant Street Brewery Tap. However, there does not appear to be any mention of it being used as a pub before 1850. In that year, Charles Connor was charged with being drunk and disorderly and for assaulting Mr Clark of the Gigant Street Brewery [420]. Mr Connor stated in his defence that he was "the worse for liquor and when that was the case, he lost all self-command". Since it was stated in Court that it was his thirteenth appearance, he was bound over to keep the peace under his own surety of £10, and two other sureties of £10 each. He was also fined 10 shillings and costs.

Mr Clark remained as landlord of the pub until in January, 1860, he went in a carriage by himself to Plaitford even though he was "rather worse from liquor" [421]. He returned in the evening and was still suffering the effects of alcohol. As he got out of the carriage, he fell down. Before anybody could help him, he got up by himself but fell down on his back across his doorstep. He was helped to his bed and a doctor was called. The doctor attended him the next day but late in the day he died. A post mortem showed he had ruptured his bladder and hence the Coroner's Jury gave a verdict of Accidental Death.

It is not clear when the pub came under the ownership of Eldridge-Pope from Dorchester but it was certainly was by 1887. In that year, Eldridge-Pope sold the brewing equipment and store casks of the pub, as they were supplying the pub with beer directly from their brewery [422].

It continued to be known by variations of this name until about 1974 when it became the Huntsman Tavern. This latter name seems to derive from the fact that it was an Eldridge-Pope house for many years with a Huntsman being the trademark of that brewery. The Brewery's pubs were sold off in 1997 and the Huntsman is now a free house

135 Hynde, Winchester Street
This is described in Bishop Beauchamp's Liber Niger of 1455 as being in Wynchestrestret. It is believed to have been an inn but no more is known of it.

136 India Arms, Culver Street
The earliest record of tis pub was when it was known as the Nags Head in 1721 when Haskins states that the landlord, William Anets was granted a license as an alehouse [20]. The pub was still the Nags Head in 1799 when it was put up for sale along with some other property [423].

It continued in operation throughout the 18th C. The house is shown in the licensing records as the India Arms up until 1821 [5] when John Pratt becomes the landlord but in the 1821 annual licensing session, the name Nags Head is crossed out and the India Arms inserted.

However, in 1822 when it was sold it was referred to as the Nags Head [424].

In the licensing records, the pub remains named as the India Arms until 1824 when William Haskell becomes the landlord and the name of the house reverts to the Nags Head! . When William Morris took over the pub in 1827, the entry in the licensing records has Nags Head crossed out and India Arms written in [6]. The last record of the India Arms in licensing records is in 1832 when the landlord was still William Morris. William Morris appears to move to the Greyhound (later the Duchess of Albany) in the Market Place. It has been suggested that the India Arms later became the Royal Oak in Culver Street but there appears to be a thirty-year gap between the last mention of the India Arms and the first mention of the Royal Oak so this is unlikely

137 Joiners Arms, Milford Street

This alehouse is known from a series of advertisements in the *Salisbury and Winchester Journal* from 1775 until 1780. During this period, it seems to have been continually changing hands and being advertised to let. Finally, in September 1780, it was advertised thus [425]: 'The Joiner's Arms, a Public-House, conveniently situated in Milford Street, Salisbury, is now to be disposed of upon advantageous terms to a purchaser, there is no stock, brewing utensils, or household furniture, to be sold. Not more than half the purchase-money will be required to be immediately deposited. The premises are good in respect to estate as fee-simple, renewable upon terms certain, and have been lately renewed; nor will the purchaser be under obligation respecting brewing his liquor.'

As the house does not appear in later licensing records it is supposed that it was sold for purposes other than as a public house.

138 King's Arms, Fisherton Street

The origins of the King's Arms in Fisherton appear to be in the 16th C although the building was much altered in the 19th C... In 1760 it was known as the Cross Keys and Haskins states that Mr Oak was the landlord [21].

By 1824, the Cross Keys was put up for rent. Thomas Durnall (sometimes spelt as Devenall) advertised that the stock, brewing equipment and some furniture would be required to be purchased by the incoming tenant [426]. He emphasised that the new tenant must have £250 available in ready cash to immediately purchase the stock. The earliest advert for the pub in May of that year stated that the premises were newly built, explaining the age of the structure that still stands in Fisherton Street. It became the Nag's Head in June, 1829, when William Rossiter took over the pub [6]. It became the King's Arms in 1831 when James Compton became the landlord [6]. At this time, there was still the inn in St John's Street that was also known as the King's Arms, But that inn was in the City of Salisbury whereas this pub was in the parish of Fisherton Anger and thus there was no conflict.

In 1857, Asher Ratty was summoned for assaulting Abula Saunders in the tap room of the King's Arms [427]. Saunders stated that he had gone into the pub to borrow a shilling from a man named Burrows and was assaulted by Ratty. But witnesses stated that Saunders had taken off his coat before entering the pub and had, obviously, the intention of fighting. The Magistrates dismissed the case with a warning to both parties to be careful with their conduct in the future. But the court expenses of six shillings were charged to Saunders.

A stranger came to the King's Arms in December, 1890 and asked for a bed for the night [428]. The landlord was able to accommodate him and the stranger sat in the smoking room for the rest of the evening, smoking a cigar and drinking whisky. He retired to bed with a bottle of lemonade and a glass. The landlord was woken up at four in the morning by the most horrible groans and he quickly ascertained that they came from the stranger's room. The stranger admitted taking poison and the landlord summoned a doctor. Despite his efforts, the stranger died in agony. The remains of some Battle's vermin Powder were found and this substance contained strychnine, and it was clear that the stranger had taken the poison.

The landlord of the inn, Joseph Lonnen, appeared in court in February, 1906, having accused his wife, Janet, of stealing £10 from him [429]. When the hearing started, Mr Lonnen stated that he wished to withdraw the charge. The police opposed the withdrawal and the case was adjourned. At the adjourned hearing, the police agreed to drop the proceedings on the theft charge. However, the lawyer representing the police stated that his purpose was to obtain a warrant for the arrest of Mrs Lonnen on a charge of bigamy. He said that it appeared that Jenny Moore had married Joseph Lonnen in London the previous August while knowing that her husband, William Moore, was still alive. Jenny Moore was remanded on bail and the bigamy case came before the court in June, 1906. At that hearing, it was proved that Jenny Moore had married Joseph Lonnen, becoming Mrs Janet Lonnen, while her husband was still alive [430]. The jury found her guilty of bigamy but recommended mercy for her. She was sentenced to three month's imprisonment.

In later years The King's Arms was a Gibbs Mew house, continuing under this ownership until the brewery closed.

In 2010, the pub was closed and then the interior completely stripped down to bare brick walls. It was rebuilt to re-open as the Safari Garden which intended to serve a range of food (mainly Indian) plus cocktails and cask ales. It was open for a very short time and in 2011, the premises were stripped bare, its signs removed or painted over and advertised to let. It became a restaurant at a later date.

139 King's Head Hotel, Bridge Street

The first mention of an inn on the site now occupied by the King's Head was in 1426 soon after it was acquired by the Mayor and Corporation when it was referred to as a messuage at the Upper Bridge at Fisherton [431]. In 1456, repairs were ordered by the Corporation "at the tenement which Bover lately inhabited called Le Lyon". Consequently, it was referred to in the city records as Bover's Place. By 1483 it is being called Le Ramme and was let at a rent of 60 shillings a year. The ram appears in the arms of the Clothworkers Company and other livery companies associated with the wool trade. In 1509, the Corporation records show the words Le Ramme underlined and a later entry stating "The Kingishead" written alongside. These records record the inn as "Le Ramme ad superiorem pontern de Fisherton". In 1526, we find an entry "The Kings Head ad superiorem pontern de Fisherton Ancher". The change in name is said to have been in honour of King Henry VIII who came to the throne in 1518.

In 1623, John Taylor rowed his wherry up the Avon from Christchurch to demonstrate that the river could be navigable, having already brought his boat from London to Christchurch [432]. He recorded that he moored above Fisherton Bridge and lodged at the King's Head Inn. Richard Easton, the landlord, was his cousin. John Taylor was from London and is often referred to as the Water Poet.

Between May, 1624, and March, 1625, Richard Easton took 20 barrels of beer and one barrel plus one coul of ale from the Common Brewhouse. He also attended the meeting of the Council in 1625 to discuss the landlords of the City taking beer from the Common Brewhouse [18].

In 1647, the Mayor and Corporation sold the King's Head to William Wilson, an apothecary.

In 1783, the *Salisbury and Winchester Journal* recorded that the King's Head was 'a well-situated, good-accustomed Inn', was for let and could be entered immediately [433]. It also stated that the landlord's only reason for quitting was that 'it is his being arrived at a time of life when he thinks it is too great a fatigue'. This landlord was probably Mark Godden although this fact cannot be verified.

It was probable that the King's Head always brewed its own beer but the earliest reference to this fact is in 1804 when an advertisement of its sale included 'all the brewing utensils, stock of beer and liquors, etc. which is very good and extensive, and will be put up in small lots for the convenience of housekeepers; together with a number of casks, from 15 to 20 hogsheads each, as good as new' [434].

In 1846, the Quicksilver stagecoach left the King's Head on the last complete run of any regular stagecoach from Salisbury to London [435].

By 1865, the landlord was Thomas Trubridge who was a brewer by trade and by 1867 the inn was owned by the brewers Trubridge and Attwater.

In 1868, it was established that under the deed of sale of the King's Head to William Wilson in 1647, the owner of the inn was responsible for repairing and maintaining the hatch that controlled the flow of water from the River Avon into the Town Ditch [436]. The Clerk to the Council was instructed to inform Mr Woolfryes, who appears to be the landlord at that time, of his responsibility to maintain the hatch. Mr Woolfryes agreed with the instruction and repaired the hatch.

By 1880, the owners were the brewers Hicks & Co and they seem to have continued ownership of the King's Head and its brewery until the early 1890s. The inn was demolished in late 1891 [437] to be replaced by the County Hotel which opened in May 1895, having been built by Mr G Richardson [438]. At that time, it was the largest hotel in Wiltshire and it is this building which now stands on the site. However, it should be noted that the building to the east which now houses a bank, another bar and the majority of the bedrooms of the current hotel was originally built as wine vaults and only later incorporated into the County Hotel.

In 1957, the inn advertised that Peter Twiss, described as the fastest man on earth, had slept at the County Hotel. Peter Twiss had recently broken the world air speed record in a Fairey Delta 2, being the first such record over 1,000 mph. In the same advertisement, it said there was the Moonraker Cocktail Bar and the Sarum Saloon Bar. There was a television lounge and hot and cold running water in all the bedrooms.

In 1995 the hotel was closed for a while and the main bar opened again in 1996 as the Town House. Also at that time, the old snug bar entered from Fisherton Street was open as the Hogshead Bar despite protests from Gibbs Mew who owned the Hogshead in Wilton Road. As a result of Gibbs protests, the bar was renamed the Spire Bar. In 2002, the Town House was purchased by J D Wetherspoon. In 2004, it was re-modelled as a Lloyd's No 1 House, with the Spire Bar being deleted, and its name reverted to the King's Head.

140 King and Queen, 21, Chipper Lane

The King and Queen was an alehouse in Salisbury in the mid-1700s and Haskins states it was granted a license as an alehouse in 1739 [20]. The Kingdom & Shearm map of Salisbury, showing the proposed layout of the new sewer system, shows the King and Queen as being on the north side of Chipper Lane. This map was produced in 1854 and the 1861 census shows Henry Jones as being the landlord of the King and Queen at 21 Chipper Lane. There is no mention of the pub in the licensing records between the 1740s and the 1820s and so it is likely that this pub remained as an alehouse, unlicensed for wines and spirits, throughout this time. However, it must be said that a lease of 1823 [439] does not mention the name of the pub or even suggest it was an alehouse so there is some doubt as to this being an alehouse until James Everett became the tenant in 1833.

In 1858, James Wiltshire applied for a spirit license of the house [440]. This application was granted as the Magistrates said they had every confidence in the character of the applicant, and they hoped the house would be respectably conducted. In 1871 it was advertised for sale and shown as "formerly the King and Queen" [441]

141 King of Prussia, Milford Hill

Martha Berry became landlady of the King of Prussia in November, 1813 [442]. The only other mention of this pub comes from an entry in the *Salisbury and Winchester Journal* of October 23, 1815 [443]: 'A singular robbery was committed on Tuesday night last at a public-house called the King of Prussia, on Milford Hill, near this city; the landlady on Wednesday morning found, to her astonishment, that two fixed coppers had been removed and stolen from her house in the course of the night. Two travelling men who lodged in the house, and who decamped in the morning, are strongly suspected of the theft.'

As no other records can be found under this name and location, one can only assume that it was known by another name at other times. It is possible that this was the Bell, Milford Hill, as Martha Berry is shown as the landlady of that pub from 1822.

142 Labour in Vain, Endless Street

This was an alehouse that is recorded as being leased by the Tailor's Company to Timothy Edwards in 1723, for 31 years [444]. No other record of it has been found.

143 Lamb, 16-20 Catherine Street

The Lamb was a prosperous inn on the west side of Catherine Street about 50 yards from the junction with New Canal. As with many pubs in Salisbury, the earliest record of it is when Philip Seymour attended the meeting to discuss taking beer from the City's communal brewery in 1625 [18].

It is possible that Christopher Willmott issued a farthing token from the Lamb in 1666 [445]. These tokens were given as small change from an inn owing to a lack of small coins of the realm. C M Rowe in his book on Salisbury's local coinage states that Williamson, in his general catalogue of tokens, attributes this token to a clothier as a lamb is shown on the token. However, clothiers generally use the Paschal Lamb (the 'lamb and flag') as their mark, whereas the lamb on this token is a realistic picture of a lamb. Hence, Rowe attributes it to this inn.

It is next heard of in 1750 when the Salisbury Flying Cart, a stage coach service, was advertised as leaving the Lamb on Mondays, Wednesdays and Fridays to go to the Black Bear in Piccadilly, London [446]. The coach returned from London to Salisbury on Tuesdays, Thursdays and Saturdays with the journey being completed in a day.

Generally, the Lamb was not a coaching inn, but several carriers operated from the inn. In 1799, John Martin advertised that carriers left the Lamb Inn to go to Ringwood (Tuesdays and Fridays), Romsey (Tuesdays), Downton (Tuesdays, Thursdays and Saturdays), Manningford and Pewsey (Tuesdays) and Wimborne (Tuesdays). The preponderance of Tuesdays is clearly related to the Market in Salisbury [447].

In 1801, Edward Joy announced that he was giving up the business of carrier between Salisbury and Lymington [448]. John Martin, of the Lamb Inn, and Mr Mitchell, of the Nag's Head, Lymington, stated that they would continue the service and that they would also accommodate passengers. In December, 1802, William Jefferd advertises that he hopes people will continue to use his carrier service to Lymington from the Lamb Inn so he presumably took over from Messrs Martin and Mitchell some time in that year [449].

In June, 1803, the Lamb is advertised for sale with particulars of the house being available from John Martin [450]. But in July, he advertises that he is continuing the business as usual [451]. But all was not well as in the following May, all the furniture of the Lamb, the property of John Martin, was put up for sale [452]. This was followed by a notice in August, 1804, that the creditors of John Martin, late of the Lamb Inn, should meet at the Lamb to receive their dividends from his estate [453].

For the next few years, the Lamb is regularly advertised for sale or to let until William Garrett takes the inn in January 1824 [454]. Despite the sale of the inn in 1831 as a result of the death of the owner,

William Garrett remains the landlord [455]. In the following year, he advertises that coaches to London, Weymouth and Southampton leave the Lamb every day except Sundays [456]. By 1835, J Wheeler advertises an Omnibus service to Bristol from the Lamb on alternate days with it returning from Bristol to Salisbury on the other days [457]. James Cocks advertises his Packet Coach to Southampton in June, 1837 [458], and this continues until 1842 when James Cocks starts a new service using a "Commodious Conveyance" which he states is partly constructed as an omnibus to carry passengers at a new low fare of 3s 6d [459]. But, not only does this conveyance meet up with other coach services in Southampton, it now meets the London railway trains.

The effect of the new railway services continued to have more effects on the coaches. By July, 1847, James Cocks service has been replaced by the Red Rover, which runs between the railways stations in Southampton and Bath via the Lamb Inn [460]. This new approach was obviously not successful as by August, seventeen coach horses are advertised for sale at Salisbury Market as a consequence of the discontinuation of the Red Rover coach [461]. By 1850, William Garrett, junior, who has taken on the Lamb from his father, sells off the horses, carriages, dog-carts and gigs that were the property of the inn [462].

The reduction in coach services seems to have affected the Lamb more than other inns in Salisbury. By February, 1854, all the contents of the inn are offered for sale including the furniture, brewing equipment and kitchen utensils [463]. However, the inn remains licensed to James Rickards in 1854 and 1855. But by February, 1856, the inn is advertised for rent and it does not appear in any future licensing records [464]. In 1859, Thomas Aubrey announces that he is moving his veterinary infirmary and shoeing forge from Brown Street to the Lamb Inn [465]. By 1867, it is noted that Thomas Aubrey occupied it as a private and commercial hotel and that his son used the premises for his veterinary business when it closed as a hotel.

144 Lamb Inn, 81 Fisherton Street

The Lamb was a small pub on the south side of Fisherton Street between Water Lane and North Street. It appears to have opened before 1819 when it was known as the Fisherton Tap, as in that year the household furniture, brewing plant and stock were put up for sale [466]. In 1820, when the pub was advertised for sale, it was stated that the cost of entering the pub was low as there was no stock to purchase [467]. This may suggest that the pub had been unoccupied since 1819.

The pub became known as the Lamb by at least 1824 when Thomas Simper became the landlord. But there is a draft indenture of the 22nd March 1828 [468] stating that the house was formerly called the Lamb but now called the Red Bull. Since there is no other record of a pub called the Red Bull, it must be assumed that the sale described in the Indenture never took place or that it was decided not to rename the pub. Thomas Simper stayed at the Lamb until 1867, a substantial period of 43 years! Little more is mentioned about the pub over the following years until 1926 when it came under scrutiny from the Renewal

Authority for the City of New Sarum which considered whether pubs should be closed under the provisions of the 1910 Licensing Act. This Act allowed pubs to be closed if the Local Authority considered there to be too many pubs for the needs of that area.

The report on the Lamb states [8]: 'The question of a further reduction in the number of public houses in Salisbury has been receiving the consideration of the Licensing Justices. During the past year, a small sub-committee of such Justices have made a careful inspection of all on-licensed premises in the City, with one or two exceptions, such as large hotels, refreshment houses, etc.

'The sub-committee have made a full and detailed report to the Licensing Justices, and although for the most part such report has been favourable to the licensees as regards the cleanliness and management of their houses, the fact remains that the number of licensed premises is disproportionate and far in excess of what is really required to supply the needs of the City. Accordingly, in pursuance of the method adopted in 1924, the Magistrates have directed their attention to another district of Salisbury where congestion exists as regards the number of licensed houses, i.e. Fisherton Street. They selected one house, the Lamb Inn, as being most suitable compared with other houses in the vicinity, for closing, and as before, requested the Chief Constable to take formal objection to the renewal of the Licence on the ground of redundancy. This was done, and the necessary notice given, a copy whereof accompanies this Report. The objection was fully heard at

Lamb Inn, Fisherton Street

the Adjourned General Annual Licensing Meeting for the City on Monday the 22nd February, 1926.

'The Owners and the Tenant were represented by Mr F.H. Trethowan, of the Firm of Trethowan & Vincent, Solicitors, Salisbury.

'Evidence was given that the population of the City, according to the last census, is 22,867, and that there are within the City: -

- 65 Fully licensed Ale-houses
- 4 On-Beer-houses
- 3 Off-Beer-houses
- 2 Refreshment Houses, and
- 12 Wine Merchants', Grocers', and Chemists' Licences:

'A total of 86, or one to about 265 of the population. A plan of a portion of the City on the 1/2500 scale was produced, showing that within a radius of a quarter of a mile from the Lamb Inn there are 18 licensed premises, all fully licensed except for 2 On-beerhouses, a grocer's, and a wine merchant's premises. The plan is sent herewith. The distances of other licensed premises from the Lamb Inn were given as follows: -

"Star Hotel"	Practically Opposite
"King's Arms"	About 60 yards
"Plume of Feathers"	About 90 yards
"Bird in Hand"	About 110 yards
"Engineer's Arms"	About 120 yards
"Fisherton Brewery"	About 170 yards
"Railway Hotel"	About 185 yards
"Bull Hotel"	About 210 yards
"London Hotel"	About 230 yards
"Victoria Inn"	About 235 yards

'The nett rateable value of the Lamb Inn is £29 15s 0d.

'Evidence as to the sanitary arrangements, accommodation, and state of the premises was given by the Sanitary Inspector for the City, which on the whole was not unfavourable, but showed that the house was small, inconvenient, and poorly lighted and ventilated. A plan of the ground floor and first floor was put in, and accompanies this Report.

'There is no bedroom accommodation on the premises for visitors, nor are meals supplied.

'The stables at the rear are not used as such, but one has been converted into a licensed slaughter-house for pigs, some of which whilst awaiting slaughter are kept in other portions of the premises behind.

'Neither the yard and yard entrance nor the urinal are lighted at night, whilst the W.C. is kept locked, and the yard itself and the entrance are sometimes used as public conveniences.

'Evidence was given as to police observation of the premises from 26th January to 9th February, and the numbers of persons entering the house during that period were stated to be as follows: -

Tuesday, 26th Jan	58
Wednesday, 27th	47
Thursday, 28th	46
Friday, 29th	49
Saturday, 30th	131
Sunday, 31st	52
Monday, 1st Feb	61
Total week	444
Wednesday, 3rd Feb	42
Thursday, 4th	41
Friday, 5th	52
Saturday, 6th	131
Sunday, 7th	59
Monday, 8th	50
Tuesday, 9th	58
Total week	443

'The present licensee has been tenant of the premises since September, 1910. No convictions are recorded against the house in the Register of Licenses.

'On behalf of the Owners the following figures of trade done at the house were given in evidence:

a	b	c	d	e
31/12/1923	113	72	3	
31/12/1924	120	56¼	3	106
31/12/1925	117	60½	3	180.

[Note: a = year ending; b = Draught Beers and Stout (barrels); c = Spirits (galls); d = Wine (galls); e = Bottled Beers and Stout (doz) - 1924, 6 months only]

'And it was explained that previous to July, 1924 the house was free for bottled beers. It was contended that this was a very fair supply for a house of this size in Salisbury, and that the tenant would make a fair living from it. It was also stated that the owners were prepared to do what was necessary to meet the complaints as to lighting and ventilation.

'After careful consideration, we decided to refer to you, on the ground of redundancy, the question of the renewal of the licence, and provisionally renewed the same to the Tenant

'Observations on Premises

Public Bar - Small but clean, little or no ventilation

Private Bar - Very small, only one small window nearly six feet from floor.

Smoking Room - Larger room, window does not open; only a small ventilator in the wall. Public entrance only through Jug and Bottle Department. All drinks have to be supplied from Jug and Bottle Department or through private passage as it is shut right off from the servery. Most difficult to supervise. Room is very rarely used or lighted.

Servery- Clean, water supply and sink for washing up. Beer drawn from an engine the pipes of which are of considerable length having to reach cellar at rear of house.

Kitchen- Fair size but very dark.

Sitting Room- Very dark indeed and small

Scullery- Really a passage with only a tap and sink

Bedrooms - Three, in good repair and clean. There are two attics, not shown on plans they are not used.

Yard and Outbuildings - There are no lights in the Yard Entrance or Yard. The Public Urinal and W.C. have recently been put in order, but the urinal is not lighted and the W.C. is kept locked, hence the public are known to use the yard and even the yard entrance as a convenience. The stabling is not used as such, one of the two stables has been converted into a slaughter-house and the other is used as a sty for pigs awaiting slaughter. The yard is rarely, if ever, used for the garaging of vehicles, even on Market Day.'

Suffice it to say that the Lamb was recommended for closure and in June 1926, it was agreed that the license would not be renewed. The compensation to be paid to the landlord and the owner of the pub (Matthews Brewery of Gillingham) was set at £950. In December 1926, the Salisbury & District Temperance Society complained to the Council that the pub was still open but the Licensing Committee minutes of April 1927 make it clear that it was closed by that time.

145 Legge, High Street

The Legge was on the east side of High Street between the George Inn (Old George Mall) and New Street. It appears to have been an Inn as early as 1455 [469] and probably for some time before that date. In 1649 it was recorded in the minutes of the Tailor's Guild [470]: 'Memorandum. That upon payment to be made by John Green, Goldsmith, of the sum of £10 to the Wardens of the said corporation, a lease and grant shall be made to the said John Green of all that messuage or tenement or Inn commonly called and known by the name of The Legge and the garden thereto belonging in High Street alias Minster Street, within the City of New Sarum, and of all houses, edifices, buildings, shops, sellers, sollers, easements, profits, commodities and advantages whatsoever, to the said tenement or Inn belonging, or in any-wise appertaining, together with the back gate situate in New Street, in the said city ... '

By 1773 the premises were noted as being a 'messuage formerly called by the sign of the Leg' [471].

146 Leopard's Head, Salt Lane

The Leopard's Head was on the NE corner of the junction of St Edmond's Church Street and Salt Lane. A leopard's head features in the arms of the Weaver's Company and thus there seems to be some connection between this guild and the pub. It was originally an alehouse and the date at which it was licensed as a public house is in doubt. Gordon states it applied for a license in 1742 and had that application refused [15] while Haskins states it was licensed as an alehouse in 1766 [20]. But in January 1759, the Mayor and Justices of the City state that they will suppress "all such Houses and prosecute any Brewer selling Ale & Beer without being duly licensed thereto." – "The houses at present selling Ale without license are, the Leopard's Head, Valiant Soldier, Anchor and New Barley Mow." Whatever the actual situation, the Leopard's Head appears continuously in the licensing records from 1783 until 1822. In 1822, the lease of the Leopard's Head was put up for sale following the death of Mr Samuel Emly [472]. The lease was from the Corporation of the City of Salisbury. Since the pub does not appear in the licensing records after this date, it is assumed that the building was put to other purposes.

147 London Hotel, 135 Fisherton Street

The London Hotel came into being as a result of the railways reaching Salisbury and was conveniently situated opposite the London line entrance to Salisbury station on the north side of the railway. The Basingstoke and Salisbury Railway (later part of the London and South Western Railway) reached Salisbury in 1857 and the London Hotel appears to have opened in 1860.

In 1861, the pub was granted a spirit license [473]. And it was stated that the landlord was a tenant of Mr Thomas Trubridge who had built the premises (he became a partner in the King's Head Brewery at about this time). By 1869, Mr Brown applied for a license to sell beer off the premises for the property alongside the London Hotel in Windsor Road [474]. This would be the premises that were sold as the Brewery Tap in the same sale as that of the King's Head brewery and inn in 1887 by William Hicks & Co [475].

By August, 1891, an application was made to sell wines, spirits and beer for consumption both on and off the premises of the London Hotel, by which time it was owned by Eldridge-Pope of Dorchester [476]. They applied for a similar license for the adjoining premises (the old Brewery Tap) which it was intended to annex to the Hotel. These old premises were described as being 'in a most unsanitary condition, swarming with vermin and in every way unfit for habitation'. Unfortunately, it was shown that the landlord, Charles Southcliffe, was in fact a Mr Kerby who had been convicted of stealing forage and sentenced to six months imprisonment. As he was, thus, a felon he was illegible to hold a license and the application was refused and the London Hotel closed. Eldridge-Poe reapplied for the license in October, presumably after Mt Kerby left the pub, and the application was granted [477].

In 1907, Eldridge-Pope wished to move their retail bottle department from the Plume of Feathers in Fisherton Street to the London Hotel. This off-sales department was to be in a separate room from the bar of the hotel and no drinking would be allowed in it [478]. After much discussion, the Magistrates granted a license for the new off-license but emphasised that this should not be taken as a precedent for any future applications.

The Hotel had a prominent position on the acute corner between Windsor Road and Fisherton Street facing toward the Fisherton railway bridge. The site of the former Brewery Tap can be clearly seen as an adjoining building in Windsor Road that is now part of the hotel. It retained the London Hotel name until at least 1974 becoming for a short time the Dorchester Hotel before closing in about 1985. It has since been used as a restaurant under a variety of names.

148 London Inn, Bridge Street

The London Inn was originally called the Rose and was situated on the north side of Bridge Street next to the River Avon. The first mention of the pub was in 1625 when it was recorded that John Gifford of the Rose in Bridge Street attended a Council meeting where landlords were asked to take beer from the Common Brewhouse [18].

In 1780, a fire broke out at the Rose [479]: 'Wednesday night, about eleven o'clock, a fire broke out in the stables of the Rose alehouse, near Fisherton Bridge. Three fine horses belonging to the Dragoons were so much burnt, that one is since died, and the others, it is supposed, must do soon. The early Discovery of the fire, and ready assistance of the Dragoons quartered in the house, prevented the flames from getting to any height, or the consequences would have been dreadful. This misfortune arose from the carelessness of the Wimborne post-boy, who left a lighted candle in the stables, which fell among the straw; a practice too common and which is often the cause of many fatal accidents.'

In 1793, John White, the landlord of the Rose, was charged and convicted of an infringement of the licencing laws [3]: 'John White of the City of New Sarum, Victualler. Convicted in the penalty of £20 mitigated to £10 and to the payment of £1.5.0 Costs on the Oath of (?) of making use of an un-entered Room for laying Spirituous Liquors and the forfeiture of 4 Gallons & Three Quarts of foreign Brandy and one quart of foreign Geneva concealed in said un-entered Room.'

Things did not change as in 1815, his

widow, Jane White was charged with selling beer in an under-size measure [5].

In 1825, Jane's son John sold the pub to Thomas Rutter. The bill of sale gave an interesting description of the house [480]: '[The] Public House or Inn situate lying and being in a certain Street or Place called or known by the Name of Fisherton Street in the Parish of Saint Thomas in the City of New Sarum aforesaid and bearing the Name or Sign of the Rose with the Court Yard Brewhouse Cellars and Premises with the Appurtenances thereunto belonging and adjoining as the same now are and for some time past have been in the renting and Occupation of the said Thomas Rutter as tenant to the said John White And also, In the Cellar the several Casks numbered as follows No 1, 2 3, 4, 5, 8, 9, 10, 11, 14, 15, 16. and in the Brewhouse the Copper, Grate etc. as fixed – three Coolers – marked 1,2,3. Hop Strainer, Malt Bin, Lead Cistern, Hot Liquor Pump, Mash Tub and Underback and Force Pump.'

In 1829, a Mr D Ubsdell, who describes himself as having been the butler to the Rev D Price, announces that he has taken the Rose [481]. In his notice in the *Salisbury and Winchester Journal*, he states that although it had been found necessary to demolish the old inn, he expects to take possession of the rebuilt inn before mid-summer (this date for the new building matches the description in RCHM). However, it seems unlikely that Mr Ubsdell actually took possession of the inn as by February, 1830, Charles Welch announces a pigeon shoot at the Rose [482]. It is not clear where the shoot was to take place except that Mr Welch states that competitors should meet at the inn and at eleven o'clock they will adjourn to the place of shooting.

In 1838, Caleb Brunwin Caplin announces that he has taken the Rose and he intends to restore the beer trade of the inn to the quality for which it used to be known [483]. He states that he will supply families with Superior Ale and Strong Beer of the purest quality, in Small or Large Casks. However, Mr Caplin runs into trouble and his creditors are asked to send particulars of their debts to Mr Thomas Wolferstan [484]. By 1848, the owner of the Inn, Mr W B Brodie has been made bankrupt and the following year, the Rose is put up for sale along with several other licensed premises [485]. But in the notice of sale, the inn is now called the London Inn.

By 1851, Emma Higgins was shown as the Manager of the Inn but the Proprietor was Charles Higgins who was the brewer at the King's Head Brewery on the opposite side of Bridge Street. The inn must have been closed for a time as Charles Higgins announces in 1856 that the inn will re-open in June [486]. But Charles Higgins did not last much longer as in 1857, the furniture, stock-in-trade and effects of the inn were put up for sale as he had been made bankrupt [487]. The London Inn did not re-open and in 1858 it was announced that the Inland Revenue were to move all their offices scattered around Salisbury into the London Inn and additional offices added to that building [488]. From then on, the buildings were known as the Crown Chambers.

149 Maidenhead, Cheese Market

The Maidenhead was in the Cheese Market approximately where the current Library (in the building originally the Corn

Exchange) is now. It is believed to have been Deverell's Inn as early as 1442. It is said to have that name owing to it being owned by a dyer from Longbridge Deverill and this person sold it in 1423 to the wool merchant John a Port and his wife Juliana. By 1721 it was known as the Maidenhead with Mr Letel being granted a license for the Inn in that year [19]. It should be noted that the Queen's Arms was known as the Maidenhead at some time before 1624 and thus that is the latest date that Deverell's Inn could have become the Maidenhead).

In 1767, it was noted that a travelling show of animals and birds was exhibited at the Maidenhead [489].. It included 'that noble creature the Great He-Lion, which is thought to be larger than that in the Tower, and is the only one that travels in England that has a mane and periwig; and what is very remarkable, he is as tame as a lamb.'

In 1771, the learned English dog was on display [490]: 'This entertaining & sagacious animal reads, writes & casts accounts by means of typographical cards, in the same manner as a printer composes; & by the same method, answers various questions in Ovid's Metamorphoses, Geography, the Roman, English and Sacred History; knows the Greek alphabet; reckons the number of persons present; sets down any capital or surname; solves questions in the four rules of arithmetic; tells, by looking on any common watch in the Company, what is the hour & minute; knows the foreign and English coins; he likewise shews the impenetrable secret' or tells any persons thoughts in the company; and distinguishes all sorts of colours.'

In the same copy of the *Salisbury and Winchester Journal* in which the exhibition of the dog was advertised, a gentleman writes to ask if a lady who was dressed in black silk and red ribbons at the exhibition, was unmarried and that her affections were entirely disengaged. It appears that they got talking at the exhibition and the gentleman wished to develop the acquaintance. As he states that the strictest honour and secrecy will be observed, we unfortunately do not know the outcome of this affair.

By 1780, a number of coaches used the Maidenhead as a stopping place. These included the Gosport and Salisbury Diligence (which provided genteel and cheap travelling) [479] and the Old Exeter Stage Waggon which travelled from London to Exeter, Plymouth and Falmouth via Salisbury [492].

The Maidenhead continued to be a prosperous inn throughout the remainder of the 18th C. In 1799, a New Post Coach was announced travelling from Bristol to Portsmouth stopping at the Maidenhead [493]. It set out from the Talbot Inn in Bristol at 6 am on Mondays, Wednesdays and Fridays and returned on the following days. Coach travel was an expensive means of transport with the fare from Bristol to Salisbury being 12 shillings for a seat inside the coach and 7 shillings for a wet and cold seat on the outside. The fare from Bristol to Portsmouth was One Guinea for an inside seat, more than many workers would receive for a week's work

In 1820, Joachim Hibberd, the landlord died and the inn was put up for sale [494]. It was described as having 'two good sitting rooms (one with a bow window) opening into the Market-place, an excellent bar, two back parlours, large convenient kitchen, a very roomy and convenient market dining room, wherein is an ordinary provided on market days, and most numerously and respectably attended, with sleeping rooms to make up 30 beds; cellarage for 500 hogsheads of beer, wine cellar, etc. :stabling sufficient for 60 horses, and a large and commodious brew-house, opening to the River Avon, which runs by and bounds the back part thereof; together with a large yard and all necessary and convenient offices'. However, in October of this year, Joseph Hibberd, the brother of Joachim, announced that he would be running the Maidenhead in the future. Joseph died in 1827, and his widow, Jane, continued to run the Inn until 1830 [495].

In 1830, after John Baker took over the inn, it was advertised that a match of pigeon shooting would take place at the Maidenhead [496]. Unlike in modern times when clay pigeons would be shot, at this time, as was usual, live pigeons were used as the targets! Whether the shoot was actually held in the back yard of the inn or whether it was held elsewhere with transport from and back to the inn is not clear. Presumably, if the maltings behind the Maidenhead were just open water meadows at this time, the shoot could have been held at the inn, although there must still have been a danger to the public.

Despite the Maidenhead being a prosperous business during the time of the Hibberds, Eli Roberts, who bought the inn in 1835, announced in November, 1836 that he was putting the inn up to let, as he was embarking in a new line of business [497]. However, the truth was that he was insolvent and shortly after Christmas, 1836, his creditors were asked to send in details of his debts [499]. In the New Year, first his stock of wines, spirits and beer was put up for sale followed shortly after by a sale of the contents of the inn [500].

Later in the year, Jane Hibberd announces that she is returning to run the inn with her eldest son, Joseph [501]. But this venture also appears to have been unprofitable as in April, 1841, Joseph's library of over 4000 books was put up for sale [502]. Later in that year, Joseph assigns all his property to a banker for the benefit of his creditors [503]. The inn was put up for sale and an auction of its contents, including the stock of alcoholic beverages took place [504]. However, in September, 1841, Charles Hibberd advertises that the inn is not closing down and he will run it in the future [505].

Charles runs the Maidenhead until 1847, when he puts the inn up for sale owing to his illness [506]. His death is announced four weeks later, at the early age of 28. The Maidenhead never operated as an inn after this date. The building remained and presumably was used for various purposes until it was purchased to provide the site for the Market House and Corn Exchange. The inn was demolished in 1857-58 and the new Market House opened in 1859. This new building still exists as the Library.

It is said that part of the roof and a stone fireplace from the Maidenhead were incorporated in St Edmund's School in Bedwin Street when it was built in 1860. It is thought that the fireplace within St Edmunds Church Hall (the old school) is that from the Maidenhead.

150 Malmesbury Arms, 83 Wilton Road

Haskins states that this pub was licensed as the Lord Malmesbury's Arms in 1796 [21] but it may well have been an alehouse before this time. In September, 1799, it was put up for sale together with its stables, barns and other buildings and orchards, arable and meadow land amounting to 19 acres [507]. There was also a brick kiln with a copious supply of red and white brick clay available to be dug on the land. It becomes clear from a sale notice of 1814 that the meadows contained pens for use by drovers going to Salisbury Market [508].

By 1818, when the inn was advertised for sale, the land attached to the inn amounted to over 31 acres [509]. The advertisement implied that the meadow land could be used for building with bricks supplied from the brick kiln and clay available on the land.

From 1822 until at least 1828, pigeon shooting matches were held at the inn [510]. The first prize seems always to have been a fat pig. A dinner was provided after the completion of the shooting at 1 shilling and sixpence a head. The shooting was always on a weekday so it is unlikely that ordinary working folk could take part.

Malcom Magill took over the inn in 1831 [6] and preceded to make the most of the meadows attached to it. He was landlord until 1858 and at various times over this period, he advertised hay for sale in ricks or by the ton [511]. He also advertised six acres of turnips for sale which could be purchased by the ton after lifting or sold while still in the ground [512]. When Magill left in 1858, the inn was advertised for sale with the reason that he was leaving being he had amassed an ample fortune from his time at the inn and he now wished to have a comfortable retirement [513].

In 1842, a Coroner's Inquest took

Malmesbury Arms

place at the Lord Malmesbury's Arms concerning the death of James Lenton as a result of a bare fist fight against Joseph Coombs [514]. The two fighters were relatives and both of them were shoemakers. After over an hour's fighting, Lenton collapsed unconscious on the ground. He was taken to the Infirmary but died shortly after arriving. A verdict of Manslaughter by Coombs was the result of the Inquest and he was committed for trial. The strange part is that the Inquest was held at this inn whereas the fight took place off the London Road on the far side of Salisbury. The trial of Coombs did not take place until the following year and the Jury acquitted him, as much because Lenton picked the fight in the first place and was the larger and heavier man [515].

Charles Roberts occupied the Malmesbury Arms from 1860 until March, 1864, when he transferred the license to Samuel Naish. However, by the annual licensing day for inns and public houses in August, 1864, Samuel Naish was landlord of the West End Hotel. This pub had been an ale house up to this date but now appears in the licensing records as having a full public house license enabling sale of wines and spirits as well as beer and ale. Although it is not recorded in the licensing records, Samuel Naish must have transferred the license of the Malmesbury Arms to the West End Hotel leaving the former premises with a beerhouse license. Certainly, from 1871 until 1874 the inn is shown as having a Beerhouse Certificate until, in 1874, the Malmesbury Arms was granted a full license [8].

A photograph of about 1900 appears to show the pub to have only a small bar at the eastern end of the building with an entrance on the corner of Wilton Road and Longland. It is presumed that the remainder of the building was used as a lodging house. In 1903, a labourer by the name of Charles Maple was charged with being disorderly at the pub [516]. He had started singing and the landlord objected to this and asked him to stop. Maple refused to do so and thus the landlord refused to serve him and sent for a policeman. Constable Perry gave evidence that he had escorted Maple from the pub and that he went quietly and was not drunk. Consequently, the Magistrates dismissed the case but Maple was warned not to cause a disturbance again. The *Salisbury Journal* headed the report of the case as 'The Harmonious Labourer'.

Prior to it regaining its full license, it is clear that the inn was owned by the Hyde Brewery of Winchester as it applied to the court in 1869 to have its landlord, James Day, ejected from the premises [517]. The court refused to agree to the ejection over a technicality regarding the terms of the landlord's contract with the brewery.

Over the years, the pub lost most of its land to housing although it still retained a car park of noticeable size. The Hyde Brewery became Simonds & Co. which was eventually taken over by Marstons in 1923. But the Malmesbury Arms was at some time purchased by Gibbs Mew and was certainly in their ownership from at least 1932.

In about 1980, the pub was modernised by Gibbs Mew, the bars being opened out into one large room and the pub renamed the Hogshead. There was some confusion a little later as one bar of the King's Head, Fisherton Street, was renamed the Hogshead! This situation continued for a while but, in 2005, the pub reverted to its name of the Malmesbury Arms. By this time, Gibbs Mew had closed and the pub was operated by Enterprise Inns. However, in about 2012, the pub was closed and remains closed and for sale at the time of publication.

151 Market Inn, 16 Butcher Row

The name of this pub, which has entrances on Butcher Row and the Market Place, has changed between the Fat Ox, then the Mitre, the Butcher's Arms, the Market Tavern and the Market Inn at various times in its history. The original Mitre (qv) was situated between Silver Street and New Canal, giving its name to Mitre Chequer. That inn appears to have ceased trading as a public house in 1769.

The inn was called the Fat Ox from at least 1803 and probably for some years before that. Haskins gives a date of 1740 for the Fat Ox but he attributes this to what became the Dolphin in Fish Row [20]. Confusingly, the inn was often called the Ox but it should not be confused with the pub further to the east on the Market Square which in these years was still the Packhorse.

The Fat Ox was probably an alehouse up to 1809 when a meeting of the Mayor and Justices was called to consider the propriety of granting a license for the Ox [518]. This was probably to upgrade the inn to a fully licensed public house.

In May, 1813, Thomas Bullock announces that he is selling his household furniture and stock in trade at his premises in Silver Street as he is moving to the Fat Ox [519]. It is not clear what his profession was before taking the inn but his name does not appear in any records of licensed premises. His lack of experience in the licensed trade may explain his leaving in March, 1814, when Stephen Wilkins took over the inn.

A sale notice of 1817 describes the pub [520]: 'Mitre Tavern, Salisbury. For Sale by Auction, on the premises, by Wm. Gerrard, on Friday the 21st day of February, 1817, (unless previously disposed of by appraisement) – All the Household Goods, Stock, etc., the property of the proprietor, William Ray; consisting of two excellent Billiard Tables, one of them a very superior one, quite new, a better than which there is not in England; about three hogsheads of good cider, casks of various spirits, a quantity of bottles, excellent wardrobe and other bedsteads and beds, a Basilia or descending stove, quite new; a counter, large cupboard, tables of various kinds, swing and other glasses, crockery, etc., chests of drawers, kitchen requisites, grates of various kinds, etc. etc.'

William Ray had changed the name of the inn from the Fat Ox to the Mitre. He became the landlord of the Fat Ox on April 17, 1815, but clearly had changed the name by the time he sold the inn in 1817.

The inn remained as the Mitre until 1833 when James Kite names it the Butcher's Arms.

In August, 1840, Henry McSheen, a hawker, was drinking in the Butcher's Arms when he had to answer a call of nature [521]. He put the box containing his wares on the table while he was absent and on his returning, he found that the person he had been talking to had left and fifteen pairs of braces were missing from his box. He followed William Johnson to the King's Head where he found Johnson with three or four pairs of braces on his arm. McSheen asked Johnson for the other braces and received the reply 'I'll give ye more braces' as he was struck violently on the head. A woman, who apparently was Mrs Johnson, also flew at him. She had been carrying a bundle and subsequently, the remaining eleven pairs of braces were found in that bundle. William Johnson was sentenced to four months' hard labour.

An advertisement in the *Salisbury and Winchester Journal* of July, 1841 announced that the annual exhibition of Pinks (the flower!) was held at the Butcher's Arms [522]. No earlier or later notice of this apparently annual event has been found!

In February, 1853, William Gosney, the landlord, died and his wife, Sarah continued to run the pub [523]. Mr Gosney had been a porter at the Salisbury Infirmary for many years before taking the Butcher's Arms in 1851. It appears that the pub had a poor reputation. In April of 1854, John Sanger was charged with having stolen a half-crown and two shilling pieces from Henry Ware [524]. Mr Ware had slept the night at the Butcher's Arms in a room with five other persons. He had put his money in the pocket of his waistcoat and put that garment under his pillow. On awaking, he found that his money had gone. He threatened to call the police and Sanger 'bowled out of bed'. His bed was searched and nothing was found but a Sergeant of Police took Sanger into custody and searched him, finding the coins as described by Mr Ware. At the trial of Sanger, it was stated that the previous evening, somebody asked Sanger to stand him a drink but the request was refused as Sanger said he only had a shilling on his person. Sanger was found guilty and sentenced to six month's prison with hard labour.

Sarah Gosney had also appeared before the Magistrates on two occasions charged and fined for keeping an ill-conducted house. Consequently, at the annual licensing session in September, 1854, the Magistrates refused to renew her license [525].

There appears to have been some issues with Sarah Gosney leaving the Butcher's Arms and a new landlord entering the house. In 1856, Mr Rooke, a valuer, sued a Mr White for the costs of valuing the Butcher's Arms before Sarah Gosney left the premises [526]. Suffice it to say that Mr White lost the case and he never entered the house. But earlier in 1855, the pub was re-opened as the Market Tavern, with James King Norton as the landlord.

The pub remained under that name until March, 1867 when some of the household furniture was put up for sale as the landlord was leaving the premises [527]. In the same month, the brewing plant of the Butcher's Arms was put up for sale [528]. However, Joseph Arnold, who had taken the pub, continued to trade for two more years as the Market Tavern. When he left, George Cheverton used the name of the Butcher's Arms once again [529]. The pub continued as the Butcher's Arms to at least 1872 but by 1875, the pub was known as the Market Inn.

In 1886, a tightrope walker by the name of Signor Duvalli set up a slanting rope from the top of the Market Inn to the diagonal path that crosses the Market Place [530]. It was reported that the Signor 'balanced himself with a considerable amount of skill and received hearty plaudits from the immense crowd. When in the centre of the rope he suddenly stopped and discharged several fireworks which were arranged on his balancing pole'.

Throughout most of the 20th C., the pub was owned by Gibbs Mew. When that brewery closed, the Market Inn was unusual in that it did not become part of the Enterprise Inns group but became a free house in its own right.

On 31 March 2011, the pub was badly damaged by fire which spread to the restaurant next door and the fish & chip restaurant beyond that. It was rebuilt with a new interior that was modern style but in keeping with the age of the exterior. It re-opened in July, 2012 and continues in trade.

152 Mason's Arms, nk

There are licensing records for a pub of this name between 1800 and 1809 but no more is known about it.

153 Mermaid, Blue Boar Row

The Mermaid (or Meremayde) appears to have been in Blue Boar Row from at least 1624 until 1720 when it appears to have been granted a full license. Haskins states that Thomas Lawes from the Meremayde attended the meeting called by the Council in 1625 to discuss inns taking beer from the Common Brewhouse [18].

Haskins also states that Richard Sutton was granted a license for the Mermaid in 1703 [20]. But he also states it had a license as an alehouse in 1720. By 1787, it is referred to as a tenement in the Market Place but it does not appear in the licensing records after this date [531].

154 Mill, The Maltings

The Mill overlooks the River Avon next to the footbridge linking the Maltings with Bridge Street. This building was originally the Salisbury Power Station, supplying electricity from turbines powered by water from the River Avon. Parts of the building may be older than this as there have undoubtedly been mills on this site for as long as Salisbury has existed if not earlier. The refurbishment in 1989 created a large pub, called the Bishop's Mill, with the emphasis on all day opening with food and coffee. There was also a terrace alongside the river. In 2002, this pub was refurbished and renamed the Mill.

155 Mitre, Silver Street

The Mitre appears to have fronted onto Silver Street but ran right through to New Canal. It was to the west of the passage from the Poultry Cross to New Canal sometimes known as Mitre Passage. Of note is the fact that the chequer from Mitre passage through to Minster Street is still known as Mitre Chequer. This passage may have formed part of the premises as, after the Mitre was closed as an inn in 1759, a further note in a *Salisbury and Winchester Journal* of 1770 refers to the passage being re-opened.

There is a token of 1668 that was issued by Edmond Macks of Sarum [532]. This shows a mitre on its face and thus may well originate from this inn although Edmond Macks is described elsewhere as an apothecary. Until 1743, the inn appears to have been named the Mitre and Crown although this was often abbreviated to the Mitre.

In 1735, the Salisbury Lodge of the Freemasons moved from the Three Lions to the Mitre and Crown [533]. The landlord, Mr Davenport, was made a member of the Lodge.

By 1740, there is mention of the

Mitre Coffee House which operates as part of the Inn [534]. By 1755, Francis Collins, the landlord, is advertising that he 'has provided his Coffee Room with a collection of Maps, the Daily Advertiser, besides other Papers; and a good fire will be constantly found at Four o'clock in the afternoon during the Winter Season, and such other reasonable Accommodation as gentlemen may require' [535].

But by 1759, Francis Collins advertises that 'having determined to quit the Tavern Business [536], he wishes to acquaint his Friends & Customers that he can no longer retail Wines, Punch or other Liquors in his House, but will continue his Out of Door Trade & sell Wines abroad in any Quantity as usual; & hopes his customers will continue their Commands to the Mitre which shall be carefully observed. By 1769, the Mitre Tavern and Coffee Room is advertised to let by Mr Collins and he has moved his wholesale wine business to the corner of New Canal and High Street opposite the Assembly Rooms [537].

Mr Collins continued to let the Mitre but when he advertised it as being for sale in 1773, it is described as having been 'some time since the Mitre Tavern' [538]. It appears to have had multiple tenants at this time.

156 Moon, Woodside Road

This pub was built by the Mayor, Aldermen and Burgesses of the City of New Sarum in recognition of the need for a licensed premises on the expanding estate of Bemerton Heath. It was leased by Gibbs Mew and gained its licence on 7th July 1969 as the Conquered Moon, the year man first set foot on the moon. The name was chosen from suggestions put forward by local customers. It was later renamed the Moon (by 1994). Easy to drive past the building as in appearance it was similar to a large modern bungalow. It served real ales since their reintroduction by Gibbs in 1976. It closed in 2004.

157 Mortimer's Bar, 30 Fisherton Street

Although this had an address in Fisherton Street, the main entrance of this premises was in Malthouse Lane It opened in a building that was constructed as a department store. When first opened as a bar it was a Chicago Rock Café. At later date, it became Mortimer's Bar but then became known as Bar M although still trading as Mortimers. In 2010, it closed down and by late 2011 was boarded up and soon after became a large charity shop.

158 New Inn, 43 New Street

It is often said that this building is one of the oldest in Salisbury But the RCHM dates it to the late 15th C or early 16th C. and the rear of the building is dated to the 18th C. The adjoining Old House Restaurant, which now forms part of the New Inn, does date from the 14th C. but is in fact a separate building. It is not clear when the building was first used as an inn with the earliest mention found being a list of inns associated with the 1772 parliamentary elections.

In August, 1823, it was announced that the annual Carnation Feast had been revived after a long period after it had been discontinued [539]. The judging of the show of carnation flowers was followed by a dinner. The evening followed in an atmosphere of 'the utmost harmony and conviviality', no doubt helped by the consumption of alcohol. It seems that the annual show continued until John Patterson left the pub in 1832.

Over the years, there is little to record about the New Inn although in 1836, Edward Baker was summoned for unlawfully permitting tippling in his House called the New Inn on the 3rd May, but after hearing the evidence for his defence, the charge was dismissed with a caution [8]. Later in that year, the inn was initially advertised for sale and later available to rent. William Rogers is shown as the landlord in the licensing records of September 1836, and he appears to have sold off the furniture that he did not wish to retain [540].

In 1878, after the retirement of Sidney Henstridge, the landlord and owner, the pub was put up for sale [541]. It was purchased by Matthews Brewery of Gillingham. Shortly after this change in ownership, Matthews advertised the brewing plant of the pub for sale along with a portion of the household furniture [542].

The New Inn remained with Matthews until it became a Hall & Woodhouse pub in 1977 when this latter brewery merged with Matthews. In about 2000, the pub achieved minor headlines by banning smoking but, before smoking was banned in all pubs, the New Inn had reverted to the normal practice. In more recent years, the Old House restaurant that stood alongside the New Inn, was incorporated into the pub and the garden to the rear of the pub was opened to the public. The pub still trades as a Hall & Woodhouse house.

159 New Inn, Poultry Cross

Little is known about this inn other than a reference in 1475 to the New Inn near the Poultry (Polatria). It is also mentioned on the City Domesday of 1442. It is probably an early name for another inn, possibly a precursor to the Haunch of Venison.

160 New Inn, Winchester Street

This inn is mentioned in the City Domesday of 1442. It is almost certainly an early name of one of the other, known inns in Winchester Street but which one is not known.

161 NN Bar, Endless Street

This pub was on the east side of Endless Street between Salt Lane and Winchester Street It was originally called the Woolpack (and is still remembered by that name by many inhabitants of Salisbury). The original inn stood where the old bus station offices stood in Endless Street. In about 1939, at the time the bus station was built, it appears that the Woolpack moved into the building to the south and the old pub was demolished. If one looks high on the north wall of the current building, one can still see the mark left by the gable of the old pub.

The Woolpack existed by at least 1625 when Roger Holte attended the Council meeting that discussed whether pubs should take beer from the Common Brewhouse [18]. Various deeds exist covering the ownership of the Woolpack in the 17th C. These show Arthur Blinksworth purchasing the inn in 1647 and Mr Blinksworth letting the inn to Francis Fisher in 1649, to Alexander Williams in 1656 and finally selling the inn to Aramis Dove in 1661 [543].

Haskins states that the Woolpack received a licence as an inn in 1721 when William Nube was the landlord [19].

In 1783, John Loveless set up a trading hall for wool at the Woolpack [544]: 'Whereas the Dealers in Wool in the City of Salisbury, and the country adjacent, labour under many disadvantages, not having a Wool-Hall, as in other large trading towns; they are hereby respectfully informed, that, by particular desire of many, Mr John Loveless, at the Wool-Pack, near the Market Place, Salisbury, has fitted up a very large loft for that purpose (which is exceeding dry and healthy, and will contain upwards of 200 packs of wool) with which the public may be accommodated, and may be assured that the greatest attention will be always paid to the care of cloths, etc., committed to his charge. He also begs leave to inform them, that all orders respecting wool, or any other business relating thereto, (from the country gentlemen who trade in that article) will be duly observed and transacted by the said John Loveless; who returns thanks to his friends for past favours, and begs leave to assure them, that nothing shall be wanting on his part, to the utmost of his power, to ensure every accommodation at the said Inn agreeable.'

It is not clear how successful this sideline was but he had left the pub by 1786 and no mention is made of wool trading at the pub at later times.

In 1790, an unusual notice appeared in the *Salisbury and Winchester Journal* concerning Mr Sturgiss who had been the landlord of the Woolpack in 1780 [545]: 'A person, by name Sturgiss, who was some years past a waiter at the Three Lions, in this city, and afterwards kept the Woolpack, where he was unfortunate, was a few weeks since recommended by a person who thought him deserving, to an elderly gentleman in London, as butler; - he was hired at a salary of twenty guineas a year, with board and lodging. - Before he went to this place, he was destitute of everything, even provision; but, ere he had been there a month, he stole his Master's shirts, table-linen, and such other things as he could put his hands upon, and pledged them for money. - We state a plain authentic fact; and as the master's humanity to a rascal induced him merely to discharge him, and thereby outweighed the justice he owed to Society; we hold it our duty to tell what we know.'

In 1810, it was advertised that an Annual Pink Feast would be held at the pub [546]. This did not have the connotations that might be thought of in the 21st C. but was an exhibition of flowers grown by local enthusiasts with a prize for the best pot of pinks of twelve different varieties. The prize was a piece of silver plate valued at two guineas, a not inconsiderable sum in those days. The exhibition of flowers was rounded off by a dinner for the exhibitors in the afternoon. This feast was held annually until at least 1827.

In 1853, a tailor from Southampton, Mr Emanuel, advertised that he would be at the Woolpack, as usual, for his monthly visit [547]. He stated that 'an Inspection of the Stock is solicited, which, for variety in materials for Coats, Trousers, and Vests, suitable for the Autumn, being selected from the most Fashionable Markets, stands unequalled'. He also stated that the prices he charged were too well-known to require any comment.

In 1870, although many coaches and other horse-drawn waggons had disappeared owing to the development of the railways, Mr Tilley, the carrier, announced that he leaves the Woolpack on

Tuesdays and Thursdays. He stated that his was the only waggon that travelled from Salisbury through Bournemouth to Poole [548].

Walter Viney was the landlord in the last few years of the 19th C and the early part of the 20th up until the years of WW1. In 1906, Alfred Claus entered the Woolpack and, as he was drunk, Mr Viney refused to serve him [549]. Claus started shouting 'Toodle-oo, Toodle-oo', but refused to leave the pub. Mr Viney ejected him from the pub but once outside, Claus rushed at Mr Viney and kicked him in the groin. Unfortunately for Claus, a policeman was passing at the time, saw what had happened and arrested Claus. He was fined £2 in court with the option of ten days' imprisonment with hard labour. Since Claus was of no fixed abode, he decided to take the option of going to prison.

As stated earlier, in 1939, the pub moved to make way for the new bus station. It continued in trade through the 20th C. and in 1989 was rebuilt and renamed the Baron of Beef when it was a Gibbs Mew house. In 1994, further work was done on the pub and it was named the Tavern. In about 1991, the two shops adjoining the Tavern were converted into a nightclub called Churchills. After 1994, the pub became, in effect, an annex to the nightclub in Endless Street and became known as the NN Bar. The pub could no longer be considered to be separate premises. In 2008, the nightclub was closed and the pub was boarded up and by 2011 was for sale or rent as a bar, restaurant, nightclub or retail premises. In late 2015, it was announced that the building had been purchased by the developer of the bus station site and that it would become a restaurant to ensure there was not a noise nuisance to the new housing development.

162 Noah's Ark, Milford Street

Haskins states that this was licensed as an alehouse in 1735 when the landlord was Noah Hayter [20]. However, in late 1739, it was advertised for sale in the *Salisbury and Winchester Journal* together with its brewing utensils and household furniture [550]. This advertisement also stated that the house was previously known as the Black Boy. In 1742, a license was applied for and granted when it was known as the Ark but it is not clear whether this was as a public house or still as an alehouse. No later record under this name has been found and it is likely it continued in operation under another name. There is a possibility that this was the Royal Oak in Milford Street which was formerly called the Archangel. With a landlord whose name was Noah, it would be natural for the house to be colloquially called Noah's Ark!

163 Old Ale House, Crane Street.

The rear part of the Crown Hotel in High Street backed onto Crane Street and has at various times been a bar separate from the hotel. In 1624 it appears to be known as the Rose [229]. And in 1842 it was probably known as the Horse and Crown. But it probably was not used as a public house all the time as at least one old photo shows a sign stating Crown Hotel outside the premises.

In 1965, the ownership of the Crown Hotel in High Street was noted as changing from John Groves & Sons of Weymouth to Devenish Weymouth although the actual takeover of the brewery occurred in 1960. 1965 appears to be the year in which the Crown Hotel was closed and the rear part of the premises in Crane Street became the King and Bishop public house [14]. Brewing ceased at Weymouth in 1985 and moved to the Cornish Brewery Co Ltd of Redruth. At this time, the pub was renamed the Hard Rock Steam Café. By 1994, the pub had been sold becoming a free house known as the Old Ale House. It became owned by Star inns who advertised it as being available to rent in 2015 at an annual rent of £49,750. In 2016, the pub was closed for a while, re-furbished and re-opened while still retaining the name of the Old Ale House.

164 Old Castle, Old Castle Road

The RCHM estimate that the core of this house dated from the second half of the 16th C. The earliest reference to this inn found at the date of this publication is in 1781 when the *Salisbury and Winchester Journal* recorded that a past landlord, Thomas Dodd, had died at the age of 80. It also noted that he was the last male inhabitant of Old Sarum! [551] But suffice it to say, this record shows that the Old Castle was in existence at an earlier date.

In 1798, a Mr Ogden gave a dinner at the Old Castle House for forty members of the Volunteer District Assistants for Old Sarum and Stratford-sub-Castle, a society founded by Mr Ogden [552]. Its aim was 'to promote peace and unanimity in their neighbourhood, to cherish an affection for their native country, and to protect persons and property'. Interestingly, in 1849, members of the Old Castle Club met at the inn before proceeding to Stratford Church for a service [553]. They then returned to the inn for a dinner. It was stated that this was the 61st anniversary meeting of this society so, presumably, the two societies were one and the same.

In 1844, John Cusse, the landlord died, aged 37, after having been at the Old Castle for ten years [554]. His wife, Susannah, continued to run the inn until 1854, when it was advertised to let [555]. Applications for the inn were to be presented to Thomas Cusse, in Salisbury, so it is presumed that Susannah had died.

Richard Holloway took over the inn and it was noted in the *Salisbury and Winchester Journal* two years later, that Easter Monday was observed as usual at Old Sarum [556]. Mr Holloway organised rural sports and games and such were the numbers of people who attended, that many could not get into the inn. Despite this, it was declared that the day passed off to the satisfaction of all.

In 1858, William Phillips, a carter, was charged in the Magistrates Court with neglect of his duty while working for Charles Blake [557]. Mr Blake's son came across his father's waggon near Old Sarum with no driver. The young Mr Blake stopped and secured the waggon and went to the Old Castle Inn. There he found William Phillips who was very drunk. Mr Blake told the Court that he did not wish the defendant to be severely punished but that the defendant should be told what was his duty. Consequently, the Court did not apply the normal sentence of three months in gaol and, instead, gaoled him for seven days.

In 1867, the Bath and West Society held their annual agricultural show in the Butts off Castle Road in Salisbury. During the week of the show, some members of the Society visited Old Sarum Castle [558]. After this visit, they moved onto the Old Castle Inn for refreshments. It was noted that the landlord, Mr Pocock, had spent a lot of money renovating the inn, turning it from an 'ancient hostelrie' into a 'most pleasant suburban retreat'.

In 1889, there was a serious fire at the inn, not helped by the Fire Brigade being unable to obtain water for some hour and a half after arriving [559]. The fire caused several hundred pounds of damage but it was noted that the inn was fully insured by its owners, Lovibond's Brewery. It remained a Lovibond's house until that brewery was taken over by Courage, Barclay and Simonds in 1962.

This inn has continued under a variety of owners until the present day. It is worth recording that in 1938, it was described as being 'a quiet but up-to-date country inn retaining many interesting ancient features. It was described as being within easy reach of a golf course, an airport, an RAF aerodrome and Stonehenge. The airport would have been at High Post, later to become RAF High Post during the war. The RAF aerodrome would most probably have been Old Sarum airfield but could also have referred to Boscombe Down.

Later, in 1957, it was described as being fully licensed, with hot and cold water in all rooms and with a large caravan park. The inn came under Courage, Reading in 1977... Later, as Courage disposed of its pubs to Grand Metropolitan and concentrated on brewing, the ownership of the Old Castle changed many times until in 2016, it is described as a Harvester Restaurant, with Harvester being part of the Mitchell and Butler's Group.

165 Old George, 21 Winchester Street

The Old George sat on the west corner of Rollestone Street and Winchester Street. It appears that part of the buildings dates from about 1500 although the earliest record of it as an inn is in 1625 when the innkeepers and alehouse-keepers were summoned to attend the Council 'to be treated touching their taking some of their beer of the communal brewhouse' [18]. Widow Erliche of the George in Winchester Street attended.

In 1766, two Italian Artists advertised that they were to exhibit a grand collection of fireworks in the Market Place [560]. The fireworks were 'far superior to and more expensive than the former; consisting of Rockets full of Crackers, Stars, Snakes, Serpents etc., Wheels, Globes of Water etc, a capricious wheel will turn into a Soldier's Tent etc, with many other curious Devices too tedious to mention: Among which will be introduced a beautiful Representation of a Chinese Cypress Tree, with Illuminations attended with particular Variations, which will communicate fire to a large Tree displaying the Rays of the Moon; the Tree afterwards will change to a particular Red Fire, at the same Time representing a beautiful looking glass, or very large Sun, & a particular wheel which will redouble its splendour etc.etc. The whole to conclude with a complete Diamond Piece embellished with Jessemine & fine Illuminations, and a beautiful Inscription in honour of Queen Charlotte. A Pigeon upon a Cord, will communicate Fire to the grand Piece and then return back again'. The Italians lodged in the George Inn and had fireworks for sale at the Inn.

In April 1768 there was another spectacular associated with the George [561]: 'There is to be seen in a large commodious room in the George Inn, in Winchester St, a grand piece of Machinery being a most curious astronomical & musical spring clock, otherwise called the theatre of the muses, made by the famous Mr Pinchbeck. This wonderful machine gives general satisfaction, & equally surprises & delights all who ever hear & see it. It is most beautifully composed of music, architecture, painting & sculpture with such a diverting variety of moving figures in the front as renders it a very entertaining piece of art. Also the royal Wax-Works from Fleet Street, London, being a grand & curious collection of 28 figures, in such perfection & exactness that the royal & princely personages they represent seem to be really alive. They are esteemed the nearest human life of any collection ever seen in this kingdom. These effigies imitate life in such great perfection, that any person who sees these inimitable figures (it may almost be said) sees the illustrious Personages they represent. To the above collection have lately been added the lively representations of his present Majesty George III & his royal consort Queen Charlotte, dressed in the royal clothes which they themselves wear. These are excellent pieces of workmanship exceeding any of the kind ever exhibited, & are esteemed the richest curiosities ever shown in England. They may be seen by ½ a dozen persons at once as well as a large number, from 9 in the morning till 9 at night (Price 6d each).'

In July 1784, the landlord, Thomas Sellwood was reprimanded by the Magistrates for keeping a disorderly house [1]. Over the next few years, the George seems to have had a difficult time with one landlord being made bankrupt and the next quitting the trade after only a year at the inn.

In the early 19th C, congestion in the streets of Salisbury was as much of a concern as it is today. In September 1808 [562], 'A poor helpless woman, who came to Sarum by a stage waggon, from London, on her road to Exeter, alighted at the George Inn, in Winchester Street, to get some refreshment; and a loaded cart passing by, between the waggon and the opposite house, pushed her down and went over her foot and thigh, by which means she was rendered incapable of pursuing her journey. – The worshipful the Mayor being informed of the accident, humanely went to her assistance, and ordered her to be conveyed, in a sedan chair, to the Infirmary. – The accident happened in consequence of the aforementioned waggon being placed in a narrow part of the street, where the drivers, for a long period, have been in the practice of leaving it, and where it often remains for many hours at a time, to the great inconvenience of carriages, etc., in passing and repassing, as well as to the injury of the adjacent buildings.'

In 1815, James Blake takes over the pub and advertises that he is an importer of foreign wines and spirits, to be sold wholesale or retail [563]. Amongst other items, he advertises good, strong London Gin for sale at eleven shillings a gallon. In this advertisement, Mr Blake refers to the inn as the Old George and it was mostly known by this name until it closed. By 1832, while still selling wines and spirits, he states that he has just received a large supply of superior

Somerset and Devonshire Cider [564]. This advertisement refers to the inn as the George Inn but, by the time he considers leaving the pub in 1837, it was once more known as the Old George [565]. He finally leaves the pub in July, 1838, and recommends his successor, John Carly, who continues the wine and spirit trade.

John Carly runs the pub until July, 1849, when he dies [566]. His wife runs the pub for a further year, when John Folliott purchases the Old George [9]. Initially, the pub was also used as the brewery tap for Folliott's brewery in Rollestone Street. However, in 1871, Mr Folliott opens the Brewery Tap (originally known as the Old George Tap) in Rollestone Street. This separate house was unusual as it operated under the license for the Old George.

Folliott's brewery was taken over by Ushers of Trowbridge in 1919 and the inn continued under that ownership until its closure on 23rd January 1963. The Ushers Company Secretary held the license for the next few years as that of the Old George also covered the Brewery Tap in Rollestone Street as both pubs had been owned by John Folliott in the late 1800s. The license was allowed to lapse on 4th April 1973. In 1989, the building was extensively converted into offices and shops but it still retains the external appearance of a pub.

166 Old Mill, Town Path

The Old Mill at the Harnham end of the Town Path was for many centuries a mill but it never ground corn. As explained in the excellent monograph by Michael Cowan (Sarum Studies 2 – Harnham Mill), the mill was probably originally a fulling mill. The current mill building, probably built in about 1500, was most likely a paper mill and in later years, the building was used as a yarn factory and as a bone mill. The southern end of the building, which houses the public bar, did not exist in 1808 but is shown in an engraving dated 1834.

By 1938, the mill was in business as a restaurant and hotel, with the restaurant in the old mill building and the hotel rooms being in Mill House, the four-story building alongside the mill. This arrangement has continued to the present day.

In 1963, the restaurant was granted a restaurant liquor license. The license was granted to Joyce Winifred Sutherland with a provision that there was a door on the stairs between the restaurant and the club premises on the first floor. This license lapsed in 1969. In 1971, a full license was granted with club restrictions and it appears that the club, in the ground floor bar area was known as the Sutherland Club.

In about 1976, after a change in ownership, the ground floor of Mill House became the Miller's Club. This was in effect a public bar as the membership fee for the 'club' was very low. In about 1979, permission to renew the club licence was refused but a full pub on-licence was granted as the authorities believed they could by this means more easily control the drinking on the premises. Since that time, the bar has been known as the Old Mill and it continues as a public bar under the management of the proprietors of the hotel and restaurant.

167 One Bell, Fisherton

The earliest mention of the One Bell was in 1767 when Haskins states Benjamin Chant had been granted a licence for the Bell at

Fisherton [21]. There is some evidence of it operating as an alehouse at an earlier date with Jane Britten being the landlady in 1748. In about 1778, the pub became known as the One Bell. But by 1796, it was being offered for sale with the property being untenanted [567]. In the minutes of the 1797 annual licensing session, the license for the One Bell is shown as having been discontinued [3]. No further mention of it has yet been found so it must be assumed to have ceased to trade as a public house at this time.

168 Ox Inn, 4 Ox Row

Haskins states that that Thomas Freeman was granted a license, for a house known as the Packhorse, as an alehouse in 1743 [20]. William Kitchell was the landlord of the Pack horse in 1819-1820.

Something rather strange happens in the autumn of 1820. Richard Gibbons appears to take over the Packhorse while William Kitchell appears in the 1820 annual licensing session as the landlord of the Globe. But in a notice in the *Salisbury and Winchester Journal* advertising a meeting of the Mayor and Justices where they considered the propriety of assigning licenses, Richard Gibbons is assessed for taking the license of the Packhorse while William Kitchell is examined regarding the license of the Crown in High Street [568]. Whatever the outcome of this meeting, by the annual licensing session in September 1820, William Kitchell is the landlord of the Globe and Henry Swift, who was going to move to the Globe after passing his license for the Crown over to William Kitchell, is still in the Crown. The Packhorse is in the hands of Richard Gibbons [5].

By the 1821 annual licensing session, Richard Kitchell, the brother of William Kitchell, has taken over the Packhorse until September, 1822, when his application to have his license renewed was refused (for a reason not disclosed in the licensing records) [5]. The pub seems to have remained closed until June, 1823, when George Barrett, from Amesbury, announces that he will apply for the license at the next Annual Licensing Day. He does so with the name of the pub now given as the Bull. It is doubtful whether he actually moved into the Packhorse, and it certainly did not trade as the Bull, as the pub was pulled down on 18 September, 1823, to prevent the fire that had started in Mr Wheeler's premises from spreading further along Ox Row [569].

Mr Emly, who owned the Packhorse, was paid for the loss of the Packhorse, by the insurer of Mr Wheeler's premises [570]. The pub was rebuilt and William Grimes obtained the license for it as the Ox Inn in September, 1824 [6]. Mr Grimes ran the Ox until 1833 when the pub was advertised as being available to let [571]. The furniture and fittings were advertised to be auctioned in early June, 1834 [572], but by the end of the month, when Thomas Futcher was married, he is shown to be the landlord of the Ox [573].

In July, 1857, the Ox was put up for sale [574]. The advertisement described the pub as 'consisting of a bar-parlour, tap, and orivate room on the ground floor; a large dining-room, two good bedrooms, and water closet on the first floor; and three good bedrooms on the second floor; excellent underground cellars, with room for a small brewery, where one formerly was; and also all requisite conveniences'. In August of this year, the furniture, fixtures

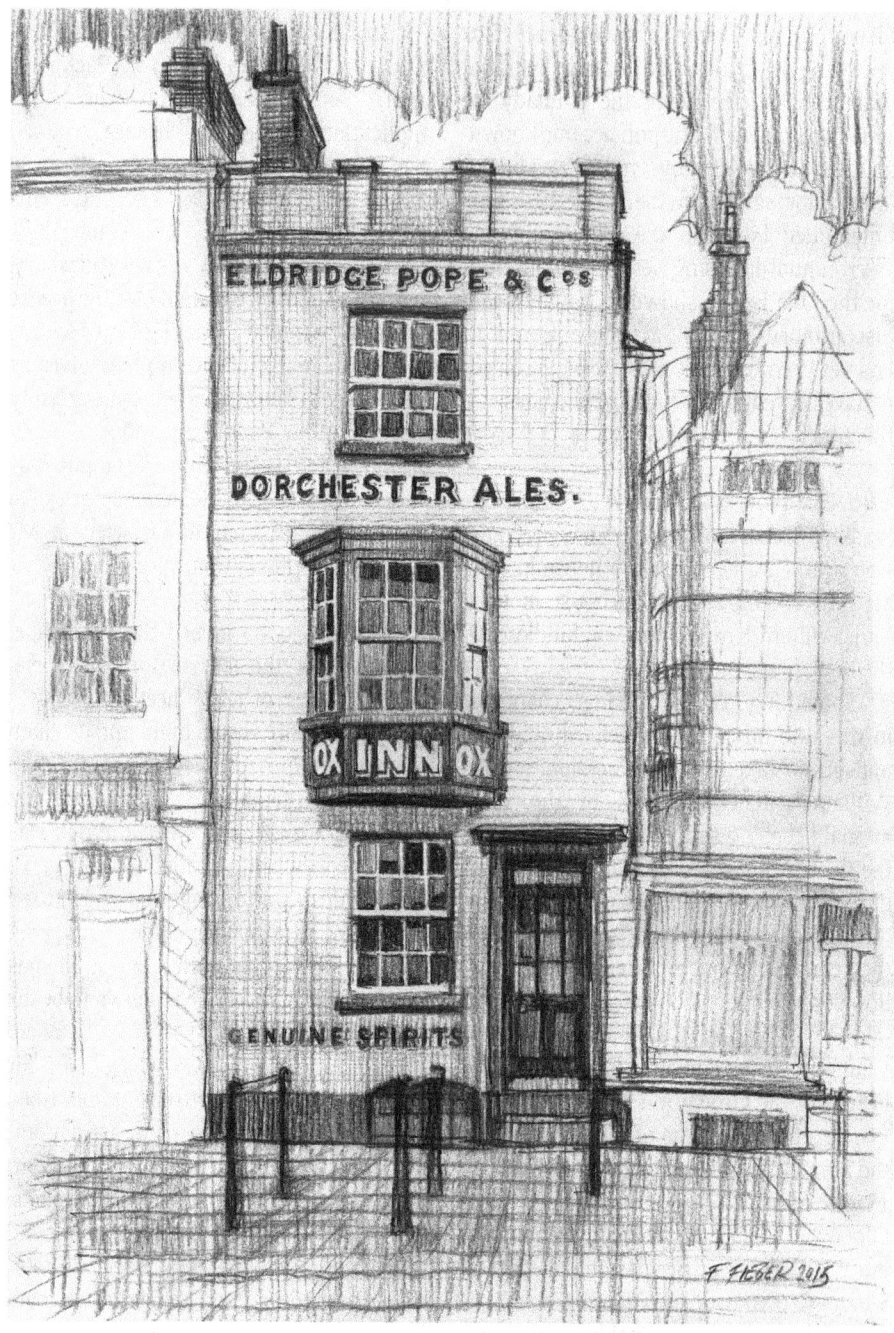

Ox Inn

and fittings of the pub were put up for sale [575].

The Ox seems to have been unoccupied from 1857 at the latest until some date approaching 1861. There is a reference to the Royal Marine Rendezvous in the 1861 Census at this address with the landlord, George Dixon, being described as a Sergeant of Marines! The landlord of the Elephant and Castle, next door to the Ox, was prosecuted in September, 1861, for removing the street name plate, 'Ox Row', from his pub. His main reason for this was that the Ox was used for recruiting and illiterate persons might mistake the sign saying Ox Row for that of the Ox Inn and enter his public house by mistake [276].

Later, in the same year, the Ox applied for renewal of the spirit license that had lapsed while the pub was unoccupied. This application was granted [576].

In 1924, the pub became the subject of a review by the Wiltshire County Licensing Authority under the provisions of the 1910 Licensing Act. This Act allowed the authorities to close a pub if it was considered that it was not required to provide for the needs of the public. A report was prepared [10]:

"The Ox" – On reading the report of the Renewal Authority as follows: -

'This house is also situated in one of the most congested districts as regards licensed properties.

'The plan of the district shows the position of the house in relation to other licensed premises. Fish Row and Butcher Row together only extend for 134 yards, and in this distance, there are six licensed houses, including the "Ox". In Minster Street, a very short distance from the end of Butcher Row, there is another fully licensed house, the "Haunch of Venison".

'The rateable value of "The Ox" for Poor Rate purposes is £21 5s 0d.

'A plan of the house accompanies this Report.

'The house is not well adapted for licensed premises. The interior is dark, and badly arranged as regards supervision by the licensee.

'The distances of the other licensed houses from "The Ox" were given as follows: -

"Duchess of Albany" Adjoining
"Roe Buck" Practically opposite in Butcher Row
"Market Inn" 16 yards
"City Arms" 33 yards
"Wheatsheaf" 41 yards
"Haunch of Venison" 97 yards

'Evidence from the sanitary point of view was given by the Sanitary Inspector for the City who stated that the public rooms were small, badly lighted and ventilated, and that the walls and ceilings were in a neglected and dirty state. There is no yard or open space whatever belonging to the premises, and the sanitary arrangements for customers are insufficient and offensive. The whole of the premises is in urgent need of repair both from a decorative and sanitary point of view.

'Evidence was also given of police observation from the 7th to 13th February, inclusive, from both Butcher Row and Ox Row sides; and showed that during the period only 80 persons entered the house, the daily totals being: -

7th	3
8th	3
9th, Saturday	35
10th	5

11th	4
12th, Market Day	29
13th	1
Total	80

'No evidence as to trade done at the house was offered on behalf of the licensee or owners, but it was argued on their behalf that the large number of licenses in this particular neighbourhood had been granted on account of the Market. It was explained moreover that the condition of the premises was due to the fact that this particular house was due for overhaul, and this would shortly have taken place.

'After careful consideration of all the evidence we decided to refer to you the question of the renewal of the licence on the ground of redundancy, and provisionally renewed the same to the tenant.

'And on hearing Mr C J Woodrow and Mr J W Clark on behalf of the Renewal Authority, it was resolved: That the Compensation Authority decides to proceed upon the report above mentioned.'

It is clear that the condition of the pub had deteriorated since it was advertised for sale in 1857.

In June 1924, the Compensation Authority resolved not to renew the license of the Ox Inn and in October of that year the total compensation paid to the owner and the landlord was set at £270.

169 Oxford Arms, 46/48 Catherine Street

This inn was about halfway along Catherine Street on the west side, almost opposite the Antelope Inn. It is probable it was the inn known as the Princes Arms in 1620. In 1625, Richard Friend at the Princes Arms took 18 barrels of beer and 7 couls of ale from the Common Brewhouse over the previous year [17]. Presumably, he either brewed his own beer or bought in additional stocks to satisfy the total demand of the inn! Richard Friend also attended the meeting called by the Council to consider inns taking beer and ale from the Common Brewhouse [18].

It appears that the inn was known as the Flying Horse for some period but in 1714, John Robbins, who had been at the inn for at least 34 years, was granted a licence for the Oxford Arms [19]. The change of name seems to be linked to the use of the inn by carriers to Oxford and, at a later date, by a stage coach service from the Oxford Arms to the Roe Buck in Oxford.

From 1762 until 1765, the *Salisbury and Winchester Journal* advertised that horses for the annual Races should be entered at the Oxford Arms [577]. In 1777, John Freemantell took over the inn and advertised that he had fitted up the inn and was supplying neat wines and good stabling [578]. But Mr Freemantell was obviously a sporting man and in 1777 and 1778, adverts were placed for cock fights at the inn [579]. But as a means of raising income, this seems to have been unsuccessful as Mr Freemantell's effects were sold in March 1779 [580] followed by a meeting of his creditors in the Three Lions [581[.

The inn never re-opened and later in 1779, E Stoddart announced that 'she has taken the late Oxford Inn, nearly opposite the Antelope, and is fitting up a handsome shop, where she will carry on her lace trade, removed from next the King's Arms in Catharine Street' [582]. However, in 1784, the Oxford Carrier was still advertising that he left Salisbury for Oxford from the Oxford Arms on Monday mornings – a little strange as the building was clearly no longer an inn! [583]

170 Ox Row Inn, 11 Ox Row

This well-known pub in the centre of the city is of 16th C. construction but has been much altered over the years. The first reference to it was when it was licensed as an alehouse named the Bull's Head, sometime between 1635 and 1685 [18].

Like many pubs, the Bull's Head often had displays given by travelling showmen. In 1742, it was advertised that: [584] 'To be seen without loss of time (from 9 in the morning till 8 at night) at the Bull's Head in the Market Place at 6d each person. The surprising little furniture of a Dining Room, consisting of a Looking Glass, a Card Table which opens with places for four candlesticks & a drawer in it; a Dining-Table with a cloth laid, a Gentleman & Lady seated as at dinner, with a footman waiting; a Sideboard & ½ a doz. dishes, 2 doz. of Plates, a doz. spoons, a doz. of silver-handled Knives & Forks, a Frame & Castors; 2 Salts & 12 complete Sheraton Back Chairs with Claw Feet, so beautifully finished in Miniature that a Cherry Stone contains them. Likewise, the curious little Four-wheel open Chaise with the figure of a Man in it drawn by a Flea, which performs all the offices of a large Chaise, as running of the wheels, locking etc, all together weighing but one grain. And a Flea chained by a Chain of 200 links with a Padlock & Key weighing but 1/3 of a Grain. Also a pair of Steel Scissors wrapped in the Wing of a Fly. Note the said scissors can cut.

In 1763, the formation of a Friendly Society at the Bull's Head was advertised [585]. 'As in divers Parts of the Kingdom Amicable Societies are held for the Relief of Persons afflicted with Sickness, there is now raising at the Bull's Head in this City, one to consist of 61 Members; in which any Person of Trade or Calling will be admitted, provided they do not exceed the age of 45 years. Further Particulars may be had by applying at the said Bull's Head ... N.B. No Landlords will be taken into the Society, but the Landlord of the said House.'

The practice of operating Friendly Societies from pubs for the benefit of their customers was quite common in the 18th C.

In 1780, John Webb, formerly of the Roebuck, became the landlord, renaming it the City Arms [586]. Mr Webb seems to have made great efforts to increase the trade of the pub. In the summer of 1780, he announces that the annual feast for Graziers and Butchers would be held at the pub [587]. And later in the next year, he announces the formation of a Musical Society. He states that 'a few Friends, Lovers of Harmony and Friendship, beg leave to inform those who love Music, and can enjoy a social Winter's Evening, that a Society is proposed to be established [588]'.

John Webb dies in 1792. His wife, Rachel, continued to run the pub until 1805 when it was taken over by William Cassey who was a relative of John Webb [4]. The Cassey family continued to run the pub until 1905 meaning that the pub stayed in the same family for 125 years! William Cassey dies in 1829 and his wife, Sophia, continues to run the pub [589]. Sophia marries William Potto, from the Wheatsheaf Inn, in 1831 [590]. This would have normally resulted in Mr Potto becoming the landlord but shortly after, her children, Rachel and William Edward Cassey, announce that they will take over the house [591].

In 1859, William Edward was summoned for keeping his house open for the sale of beer on a Sunday afternoon [592]. Mr Cassey apologised to the Court and explained that he had not realised the time was after three in the afternoon. As it was his first offence, the Court reduced his fine to ten shillings plus costs.

William Edward died in 1869 and his wife, Sarah, became the landlady [593]. She runs the house until 1875 when Harry Cassey (her son?) continues the dynasty. Harry dies in 1905 [594] and the City Arms was put up for sale. Interestingly, at the auction, the highest bid of £2,350 was considerably less than the reserve of £4,000 and the inn was not sold [595]. It appears that George William Waugh did purchase the City Arms and it continued in trade.

The pub, like several others in Salisbury, had a market license which enable it to keep open in the afternoons on market days. It retained this license until the advent of twelve hour opening in 1996.

During the early years of the 20th C., the pub remained as a free house until, in 1939, it was purchased by the Cross Keys Brewery from Rode in Somerset [12]. This brewery was acquired by Bass, Mitchell and Butlers in 1962. The City Arms remained a Bass pub until at least 1984.

In 1996, the pub was re-named the Ox Row Inn. While this reflects the fact that the pub is situated in Ox Row, with another entrance from Butcher Row, the Ox Row Inn is a different house from the Ox Inn and the Fat Ox of earlier days. In the spring of 2016, the premises to the east of the pub were purchased and renovated to become a part of the Ox Row Inn. The pub is now adjacent to the Market Inn.

171 Parade Tavern, 47 Blue Boar Row

The Parade Coffee House was opened in Blue Boar Row in 1778 by Mr Joseph Boyter, who was, until that time, the landlord of the Three Lions. From that year, it appears in the records of licensed premises and thus must have served alcoholic beverages as well as coffee. In February, 1784, the Parade Coffee House was advertised as available to rent [596]. The premises were described as having a spacious coffee room, a dining-room, two parlours, a billiard's room and with convenient out-buildings and an adjoining garden. Later, in May of that year, the advertisement was repeated with the addition of two notes which stated that there was an 'exceeding good billiard table and that the subscriptions to the Coffee Room had considerably exceeded the rent of the premises [597].

It appears that when it first reopened, it was purely as a coffee house [598]: 'Parade Coffee House, Blue Boar Row, Market Place, Salisbury. The public are respectfully informed, that the above Coffee House is continued under such regulations, as is presumed will make it quite to their satisfaction. The Room is supplied with the Gazettes, Morning and Evening Papers, and the *Salisbury and Winchester Journal*. Subscriptions of One Guinea per ann., are received at the Bar of the Coffee House.'

But by January, 1785, William Penney announced in the *Salisbury and Winchester*

Journal that the premises were now open as the Parade Coffee House and Tavern [599]: 'Parade Coffee House and Tavern, Blue Boar Row, Market Place, Salisbury. The Public are hereby most respectfully informed, that the Parade Coffee House is now opened as a Tavern and Coffee House, By William Penney, who solicits their favours and encouragement, which he will endeavour to merit by keeping the best of liquors, and paying the utmost attention to his business. There is an exceeding good Billiard Table in the house. N.B. Lodgings for Gentlemen.'

As was not uncommon with coffee houses, the Parade was host to activities other than providing refreshment. In 1786 and 1788, Mr Waltire advertises that he will give 'A Course of Experimental Philosophy and Chemistry, in the large commodious room, at the Parade Coffee House'. He also gives three lectures on Stonehenge [600].

It continued in this form until 1805 when it was advertised as being for sale [601]. Robert Heather bought the premises and then announced in January 1806 that he was opening 'a Warehouse in the Wholesale and Retail Wine and Spirit Trade, where he will sell the very best of goods, on the most liberal terms, for ready money' [602]. It remains as licensed premises until 1807 but does not appear in the records of licensing after that year.

172 Pelican, St Ann Street

The Pelican was situated near to the current 70-74 St Ann Street. It was licensed at some time in the 17th C to Joseph Jennings and appears in the licensing records of 1716 as being owned by Ambrose Perry. Haskins states that William Tapper was granted a license for the pub in 1722. If this is correct, it was, presumably, a full license for a public house and it was a beer only house before this date.

Throughout the remainder of the 18th C., there are several advertisements in the *Salisbury and Winchester Journal* related to the Pelican, almost all of which are related to the sale of dogs, horses and, in one case, 'two fine asses with foals'.

In 1813, John Webb, who had been the landlord of the Pelican, died. It appears that his son, also John Webb, continued to run the pub. However, in October, 1816, it is noted that John Webb was bankrupt. All the household furniture, goods, plate, linen and china was sold at auction [603]. Also for sale was the unexpired portion of the lease of the pub, which was seventeen years, with an annual rent of £20.

A Mr T Hobbs, from Gosport, finally takes over the pub a year after it was advertised [604]. He says that he has laid in a stock of the best spirits and has also started brewing. He intended to fill his cellars with good home-brewed Strong Beer, which, he assumes, will be of superior quality when it is ready for sale. The beer may not have been of the desired quality, as by late 1819, the pub is advertised to be let owing to the landlord, now Samuel Blake, being about to quit the pub trade.

The pub is still being advertised as available in the spring of the next year with Samuel Blake still in residence [605]. This time he states he is leaving the pub owing to the ill health of his wife. He is still there in October 1820, when he advertises that he will sell a pony if the owner does not collect it from his premises, and pays the expenses of its keep [606]. This may be the point at which Samuel Blake actually leaves the pub as the pony had been at the pub for only a week, a very short time in which to take this type of action.

Not long after in 1821, the new landlord, James Hibberd, had a complaint laid against him for allowing tippling in the Pelican [5]. Tippling was the offence of allowing alcoholic beverages to be consumed during the hours of church services (i.e. Sunday mornings). He was fined ten shillings and shortly after he appears to have left the pub. The Pelican disappears from the licensing records at about this time but is still advertised for sale in 1825 [607]. By 1830, it is advertised as being available to let and as being suitable for use as a pub, despite it being called 'late the Pelican' [608]. At about this time it was converted into cottages known as Pelican Place. In about 1886, these cottages were pulled down and three houses were built on the site.

173 Petersfinger Inn, Petersfinger

There are three different pub names given for premises at Petersfinger on the Southampton road out of Salisbury: The Elephant and Castle, the Anchor, and the Petersfinger Inn. Since it is unlikely that there was sufficient trade at Petersfinger to support more than one pub, and also since the dates associated with these three pub names do not conflict, it is assumed that they represent the same public house.

The Elephant and Castle at Petersfinger is known from a single advertisement in the *Salisbury and Winchester Journal* in 1762 [609]: 'To be sold on Monday Nov 10th at the Elephant & Castle, commonly known by the name of Peter's Finger, the underwood in Clarendon Park; in single lots, as it is now marked or bundled out.'

Similarly, in 1802, the Anchor is only known from the notice in the *Salisbury and Winchester Journal* stating that the landlord, Charles Wapshare, had died [610].

The Petersfinger Inn is known from a number of records between 1819 and 1825. In the first of these years, the pub is advertised as being available to rent together with between 4 and 5 acres of arable land [611].

Between 1821 and 1824, 'rustic sports' were held at the inn in June, on the anniversary of the Battle of Waterloo. These amusements included Single-Stick Playing for a Sovereign, Wrestling for a Beaver Hat, Jingling, and Boys eating treacled Loaves! Unusually, in 1821 it was proposed to have girls running for ribbons [612], the only mention of females taking part in the amusements. The amusements were followed in the evening by a dance.

The landlord between 1823 and 1825 was Robert Cole although he may have occupied the inn at an earlier date. In September, 1825, the inn was completely destroyed by fire [613]. It was said that most of the furniture was saved but that the stock of beer was destroyed. The *Journal* reported that the inn was insured but no further information has been found so it is not clear if it ever opened as a pub again.

174 Pheasant, 19 Salt Lane

The front of the Pheasant on Salt Lane is of 15th C origin and is said to have been built in 1435 when it was known as the Crispin Inn. In 1638, Philip Crew bequeathed his house on the corner of Salt Lane and Rollestone Street to the Shoemaker's Company recommending them to build a guild hall [614]. Since the building had been Phillip Crewe's house, it is believed that this is approximately the date when the Crispin Inn was founded. The Shoemaker's Hall is now part of the Pheasant and dates from about this time.

Haskins states that John Fort was granted a license for the Crispin, in Hog Lane, as an alehouse in 1743 [20]. Hog lane was the name given to the portion of Salt Lane between Endless Street and Rollestone Street. In 1784, F Gatehouse, advertises that he intends to take in all kinds of wearing apparel that requires cleaning [615]. He states that customers can be sure that due care will be taken of their property and that they will be speedily returned. A year later, a T Gatehouse, advertises that she is grateful for past favours and that she continues to take in garments and linen for cleaning [616]. Both these advertisers had some relationship with the landlord of this time, John Gatehouse.

In 1821, William Rogers takes the inn which was still known as the Crispin in June, 1821 [5] but which was now known as the Pheasant by the annual licensing session in September, 1821 [617]. He states that for many years before taking the inn he had been in the trade of bottling wine, porter and cider. It seems he would have visited houses to transfer these alcoholic beverages from casks into bottles. He intended to continue this trade while at the Pheasant but also to sell beer, wine and spirits off the premises. He also states that he is known for 'Beating the Tambourine'!

William Rogers stayed at the Pheasant until, in December, 1823, the stock of beer, the brewing equipment, some of the furniture and other items were put up for sale [618]. It seems that the pub may have stayed vacant until later in 1824, when James Wheatley became the landlord. He seems to have run the pub until 1826, when Thomas Wheatley, possibly his son, took it over. When Thomas died in 1830, his wife, Elizabeth, continued to run the Pheasant until 1840. When Elizabeth had been at the pub for six months after her husband's death, she advertises in the *Salisbury and Winchester Journal* that she has a good stock of Mild and Strong Beer that was of the superior quality [619]. She also states that the prices was as low as possible given that it was brewed from no other ingredients than malt, hops and water.

During this period, there was an annual exhibition of cucumbers at the pub with cash prizes for the best exhibits [620]. A dinner was for the participants after the exhibition. Similarly, in 1827 if not in other years, an exhibition of Pinks occurred as it did at two other pubs [621]. Again prizes were awarded for the best flowers and a feast held after the show of flowers.

In June 1829, the Ancient Druids held there meeting at the Pheasant [622]: 'On Monday the brethren of the Lodge of the Ancient Druids (39 in number) held their anniversary festival at the Pheasant Inn, in this city. The routine business of the lodge having been gone through, an excellent dinner was served up by brother Wheatley, whose exertions on the occasion procured him the thanks of the brethren. Brother Mason (as noble arch) presided, and did ample justice to the situation he filled, in promoting that spirit of harmony and conviviality which has always distinguished the institution of Ancient Druids. A number of loyal and patriotic toasts were drunk, and some excellent songs were sung. This lodge was established under the authority of the grand lodge of London; and is now in connexion with it.'

The pub changed hand several times after 1840 until in 1868, the complete contents of it were put up for sale when Mr Poulden left it [623]. Interestingly, in November of that year, the licensing records show the license being transferred from Mr Poulden to Mr Henry Smith [624]. Then a month later, the same records show the license being transferred from Mr Poulden to Mr Henry Sutton [625]. It is not clear whether the first notice was in error or whether Mr Smith failed to take up the license for some unknown reason.

The Pheasant was a Lovibond's house from at least 1876, as in that year the inn was advertised for rent with full particulars being available from St Anns Brewery [626]. The Pheasant remained under the ownership of Lovibond's Brewery until 1959, when that brewery was taken over by George's Brewery of Bristol. That brewery was in turn taken over by Courage in 1961 and the Pheasant remained a Courage house until at least 1975. More recently, the pub has been owned by Enterprise Inns. In 2015, it was closed for a while and advertised as being available to let by Enterprise inns at an annual rent of £28,000. In January, 2016, it was reopened after what was said to be a £230,000 revamp that included a new outdoor seating area described as a 'secret courtyard'.

175 Pilours, nk

A reference of 1455 mentions the Le Pilours that was next to the Colecorner Otherwise, nothing is known of this inn.

176 Plasterer's Arms, 94 Winchester Street

The Plasterer's Arms was known as the Ship before about 1870 and was situated on the south-east corner of Winchester Street with Pennyfarthing Street. Its license was transferred from R Beavis to Samuel Lovell in May, 1788, which suggests that it was in existence from before that year [2]. In 1772, a pub of this name was shown in a list of inns with known allegiances at the forthcoming Parliamentary Election.

In 1791, Samuel Lovell, the landlord, had twelve gallons of Rum confiscated as he had not notified the 'proper officer' of its purchase [3]. The implication was that this was smuggled rum but that the authorities could not prove its illegal origin. Samuel Lovell died in 1800.

In 1808, a soldier of the Somerset Militia, Joseph Smith, was convicted of stealing a dish containing a half-penny from the Ship [627]. Typically for this period, he was sentenced to two months in prison and also to be publicly flogged in the Market Square. How times have changed!

The Ship seems to have made a habit of falling foul of the law as in 1816, James Sims was fined £25 for selling wine without a license [628]. This also suggests that the Ship was still only an alehouse rather than being a public house or inn.

In 1830, the inn was offered for sale, with James Sims still being the landlord. Interestingly, the inn was said to have a cellar that could hold 170 hogsheads of beer (over 9000 gallons!) and stabling for 20 to 30 horses. Three months later, James Sims advertises that he was most grateful for the trade he had received during the 30 years that he had occupied the Ship, and recommends his successor, Owen Oliver, to his friends and customers [629]. He states that the inn will continue to supply the best home-brewed beer, wines and spirits. Since there was no indication of a change in the status of the inn since Mr Sims was fined for selling wine without a license, one wonders why he is now advertising wine for sale!

Owen Oliver only stays at the inn for two years and then James Sims appears to return to the Ship. He dies a short time afterwards. His niece, Mary Sandell, runs the inn for six months until Samuel Ricketts takes it over [630].

The Ship changes hands a few times over the coming years although from 1850 onwards, it does appear increasingly in magistrate's court records. Caleb Newman was convicted in 1853 for keeping the inn open on a Sunday morning [631]. There were six customers in the bar but three of them were said to be strangers and hence could drink at that time as they were deemed to be bona fide travellers. The other three were known to the police as local men and appeared not to have any beer until the police discovered a pint of beer under their seat. The landlord was fined £1 and costs. Three years later, Catherine Leadbetter was fined £1 for serving beer and wine after hours on Good Friday evening [632]. A little later, in 1858, a robbery took place in the inn and Catherine admitted witnessing the theft [633]. Later in this year, Catherine was in court again for selling beer on a Sunday morning [634]. She was again fined £1 and costs and, despite she saying that she was leaving the pub at Michaelmas (29 September), the magistrates suspended the renewal of her license as she had been convicted on three previous occasions.

Shortly afterwards, a strange matter arose. A basket was delivered that was addressed to Catherine Leadbetter at the Ship Inn [635]. But Catherine had left the inn two weeks earlier and so the basket was delivered to her house nearby. When she returned to her house, she looked in the basket and found it contained some straw, a black cape, and a dirty handkerchief, and underneath was the dead body of a young child. There was no indication as to whom had sent the basket to Catherine although the railway company were able to say that it had been put on the train at Waterloo station in London and the train fare had been paid but not the costs of delivering it to the Ship. The police were called but neither Catherine nor the new landlord of the Ship, Henry Rose, could throw any light on who might have sent the basket. A surgeon examined the body but could not determine what had caused the death of the child, but he was able to state that the child was already dead when it was put in the basket. The Coroner directed the jury to deliver an open verdict. The local police, with the aid of the Metropolitan Police, tried to discover who might have sent the basket to Salisbury but to no avail.

Henry Rose, the new landlord, was convicted twice in the new year for selling beer outside of legal opening hours [636 & 637]. He seems to have learned his lesson as he does not appear before the Magistrates again and in 1861, he advertises the contents of the inn for sale [638]. It is not clear what happens to the Ship after this date as it does not appear in the licensing records again apart from the years 1865 to 1867. It appears it may well have become an unlicensed lodging house.

However, in 1870, the household furniture of the Plasterer's Arms was advertised for sale [639]. From a later advertisement for the sale of property in Winchester Street, it is clear that the Plasterer's Arms and the Ship were one and the same building [640]. Thus, at some time between 1867 and 1870, the inn became known by the later name. However, the reputation of the pub does not seem to have improved and in August, 1872, the renewal of the license was opposed by the police on the grounds that disorderly conduct took place in the house [641].

A lengthy examination of the grounds of opposing the renewal of the license was held. This resulted in the Mayor and Magistrates determining that there was insufficient evidence to suspend the license but the landlord was warned to be very careful about how he ran the pub in the future. The representative of the owner of the pub, Simonds and Co of Winchester, stated that the landlord was only a monthly tenant and, if there were any further problems, he would be thrown out of the house. Despite this, there is no further information on the Plasterer's Arms, and since, in February, 1872, the pub and adjoining buildings were offered for sale, it is assumed that they were sold and the pub closed. It is certainly closed by July, 1876, as in a court case involving a runaway horse, a witness stated that he went to 'a building which belonged to Mr Cooper in Winchester Street, and which was formerly the Ship Inn' [642]. Wheeler, in his articles in the *Salisbury and Winchester Journal* in 1887, states that the inn had been pulled down a few years before. He also said that in its latter years, the inn did not have a very high reputation but that earlier in the 19th c it was a reputable house.

177 Plough, Brown Street

So far only a single article in the *Salisbury and Winchester Journal* of April 13, 1835 has been found that mentions this pub [643]. At that time, James Ingram was found guilty at the Quarter Sessions of being one of a gang of four who robbed a man of five guineas at the Plough Ingram was sentenced to fourteen years' transportation. The Plough was, presumably, a pub of another name in the street that took this name after the Plough in Chipper lane was closed in 1826.

178 Plough, Chipper Lane

This pub has been variously described as being on the corner of Castle Street and Scot's Lane or on the corner of Castle Street and Chipper Lane where the Post Office once stood. It is probable that the latter location is correct. It was known as the Grasshopper to at least 1813, when renewal of the license was refused [4], and then became the Duke of Wellington (or the Wellington) in 1814 [5], presumably as a result of the Battle of Toulouse and the abdication of Napoleon. It then became the Plough in about 1822.

Haskins states that the Grasshopper was licensed as an alehouse in 1774 [20], but it was advertised as being available to let in that same year when it was described as a 'good accustomed public house' [644]. Thus, it was most probably an alehouse before this year.

In 1781, Mary Pearce, the wife of the landlord, Daniel Pearce, eloped with Samuel Samuels, a barber, who had been lodging at the Grasshopper [645]. She took with her a sum of money, some linen,

Plume of Feathers, Fisherton Street

and some silver spoons. Her husband advertised that he would no longer by responsible for any debts she incurred.

In October, 1816, the Magistrates were summoned to decide whether to license 'the Public-House called the Wellington or Grasshopper' [5] and the license was granted. Six months later, the Duke of Wellington's Arms is advertised as being available to let [646], with one week later, the household furniture being put up for sale. This latter sale is shown as being the result of the execution of an order from the Sheriff of Wiltshire which would imply the landlord had an unsatisfied debt if not actual bankruptcy.

The pub seems to have been advertised to let every year until 1822 when it is named as the Plough. In September, 1823, the pub is once again advertised to let [647]. The advertisement states that the pub had recently undergone extensive repairs and had been fitted with a copper, coolers and other brewing equipment.

The pub is again advertised as being available in May,1825 [648], but when George Barrett applied for a license at the annual licensing session in September, 1826, the Magistrates refused to grant it [6]. Nothing more is heard of the Plough.

179 Plume of Feathers Inn, 105 Fisherton Street

This pub was on the east corner of Fisherton Street and Dews Road. The earliest license record for the pub is in 1865 when it was known as the Prince of Wales Arms. Shortly after in, 1867, it was called the Prince of Wales' Plumes and it retained this name until 1880 when it became the Plume of Feathers. In 1883, Mr Noyce requested that the Magistrates grant him a permanent license for the house, he having held a temporary license for over a month [649]. This was opposed by the police on the grounds that Noyce was not a fit person to hold a license, stating that they had found Noyce drunk in the pub and his wife also in an 'improper condition'. It was then stated to the court that the owners of the pub, Eldridge-Pope of Dorchester, had decided to get rid of Noyce, whether he was granted a license or not. The brewer was granted a temporary licence while a suitable tenant was found.

The pub at this time must have had an off-sales area, as in 1907, Eldridge Pope asked the Magistrates for permission to move their retail bottle department from the Plume of Feathers to the London Hotel (qv) [478]. This application was granted.

For many years it remained an Eldridge-Pope house but it was a small pub and could never have been very profitable. On 6th October 1975, the pub was closed although it retained its licence for a little time. It was then sold by the brewery and converted into flats.

180 Plume of Feathers, 15-18 Queen Street

This pub was roughly where the entrance to the Cross Keys Shopping Mall is nowadays. The walk way into the mall from Queen Street was originally known as Plume of Feathers Yard. This whole area has been significantly remodelled and it is very difficult to tell which buildings are original and which are modern reconstructions. The old stair case in the mall is shown in a 19th C photograph but it is not known if the present staircase is the original or a reconstruction. It is said that the lower part of this staircase was the entrance to the Plume of Feathers and that the pub itself lay immediately behind the gallery across the mall.

Haskins states that the pub was first licensed between 1635 and 1685 [18] but, otherwise, the earliest source so far found was a report in the *Salisbury and Winchester Journal* of March 26, 1737, which stated [650]: 'Yesterday Morning between one and two, the Bellman going his Rounds found the wicket of the Gate of the Plume of Feathers Inn in this City, open, upon which he went in and rais'd the Family which had been in Bed sometime, and in searching the House for Rogues, the Door belonging to a Room where the Carriers Packs were laid, (of which by Reason of the late Fair there were a considerable Number) appear'd to be broken open and several Goods stolen, but the Loss cannot be Computed, the Goods belonging to Dealers at the Fair, and the Rogues having also Carried away the Direction which was upon the Pack.'

In 1752, the Plume of Feathers is referred to as the Feathers Inn [651]. When in April,1769, Ransome Jeboult, takes over the Bull in Fisherton Street, the advertisement in the *Salisbury and Winchester Journal* states that he is the son of Mr Hugh Jeboult, who formerly kept the Feathers Inn in Sarum [139].

By 1752, the Exeter stagecoach stopped overnight at the pub [652]: 'The Exeter Stage-Coach sets out every Monday from the Saracen's Head in Friday St, and dines at Egham, and lies the same night at Murrel-Green; dines on Tuesday at Sutton, & lies the same night at the Plume of Feathers in Salisbury; on Wednesday dines at Blandford, and lies at the King's Arms in Dorchester; and gets into Exeter every Friday at One o'clock. Performed (if God permit) by James Precey & Isaac Merryweather. N.B. The Plume of Feathers is kept by the said Jas Precey; (removed thereto from the Oxford Arms) which is a commodious House, lately put into good Repair, & receives Coaches etc, where all Gentlemen & others may depend on the best usage.'

As was common in the past, rooms at the pub were let on occasion to travelling showmen as the following advertisement from the *Salisbury and Winchester Journal* of August 31, 1761, shows [653]: 'There is come to this City, & is now at the Plume of Feathers in the Market Place, the most amazing & astonishing Curiosity ever heard of in Human Nature. A Wonderful Man, who was born with two voices by which, as soon as the words are uttered by one, they are returned in the same Breath by another. To prove beyond dispute what here is mentioned, it will be sufficient to say, that he has been honoured with the Company of the Royal Family as well as the Royal Society, & principal Body of Nobility, from whom he received the greatest Applause. His stay is but till Thursday.'

The pub continued trading throughout the 18th C and clearly was a prosperous inn. It was quite common for inns at this time to run by women, often the widows of former landlords. One such was Mary Pearce who advertised in 1780 [654]: 'Plume of Feathers, Sarum – Mary Pearce, widow of Isaac Pearce, deceased, and who some years ago kept the Phoenix, at Romsey, returns her thanks to all her friends and customers of her late husband, and begs leave to inform them, and the public in general, that she intends carrying on business at the above Inn, where she hopes for the continuance of the favours of all her said husband's friends and customers; and at the same time acquaint them, and the public at large, that she will endeavour to merit their favours by moderate charges, civil usage and good entertainment. – Wine and Good Liquors of all kinds. Good stall stabling at the above Inn.'

Mary Pearce continued running the Plume until 1786 when it was taken by John Gatehouse who moved to it from the Crispin (the Pheasant) [2]. The pub continued to advertise the presence of travelling showmen and salesmen, one of the more noteworthy being the following from 1813 [655]: 'Arrived from London, and will be exhibited on this day, November 22nd, and following day, at the Feathers Inn, Market Place, Salisbury, from eleven in the morning till nine in the evening, that most wonderful Phenomena of Nature, the Hottentot Venus. In the contemplation of this amazingly wonderful Female the Public have a perfect specimen of that most extraordinary Tribe who inhabit the more southern parts of Africa; and considering their morose disposition, she is remarkably mild and pleasing in her manners. She has been honoured with the repeated visits of his Royal Highness the Prince Regent, and several branches of the Royal Family, also the principal nobility, and declared to be undisputedly the greatest curiosity of the human species in this kingdom, and well worth the attention of all the admirers of Natural History. N.B. She proposes being at Warminster on Wednesday, and at Frome on Friday next. Admission One Shilling each.'

But life in a 19th C pub was not always easy as this advertisement from 1816 shows [656]: 'A Case of Extreme Distress. Alicia Nichols, Widow of the late Mr Mark Nichols, of the Plume of Feathers, in this city, with a family of Seven Children, being reduced from a situation of relative comfort in life to one of extreme distress; who, after every effort of parental solicitude, toil, and industry, cannot procure the scanty means of base subsistence, much less the necessities of life, for herself and seven helpless children, even at their present happily depressed value, very humble and earnestly implores the sympathising exertions of the benevolent, for the relief of her own and her children's crying necessities. Some friends, whom are well acquainted with her deserts and distresses, and who have interested themselves in her behalf, return most grateful thanks to the nobility and gentry who have already subscribed. All benefactions, even those of the smallest kind, will be most thankfully received at the Printing Office, Canal; Mr Wilks, Market Place; Mr Guest's and Mr Fellow's, Catherine Street; and the sum raised will be very carefully applied for the purpose of settling the unfortunate Petitioner in some way of business, and thereby enabling her to support herself and rear her fatherless children.'

During the early part of the 19th C., the inn changes hands several times but appears to continue to be a prosperous concern. John Rumbold, the landlord in 1840, together with four other landlords, complains that the cost of having a booth at the Salisbury Races, to supply refreshments to the race goers, has become too high [657]. Consequently, they rent some ground off a Mr Gray that is adjacent to the race course.

In 1851, two American doctors lodge at the Plume of Feathers and advertise that they are available for consultation [658]. They claim that they can treat 'Nervous Debility, Epileptic and all other kinds of Fits, Dropsy, Piles, Gravel, Stones, Strictures, and all Diseases of the Urinary Passages; Asthmas, etc.; Rheumatism, Sciatica (or Hip Gout), King's Evil or Scrofula, Deafness and Singing Noises in the Head, and all Diseases of the Eye; Ulcerated Lungs and Pulmonary Consumption; Erysipelas, Dropsical Joints, White Swellings, etc'. But they also state that if a person cannot attend them at the inn, they should send the doctors a note describing their infirmity, enclosing ten shillings, and they will receive some advice and medicines that 'seldom or ever fail to perform a perfect cure'. Since they also say that they particularly wish to hear from persons who have been deemed incurable and turned out of hospital without receiving benefit. By modern standards, this all appears to be quack medicine!

The Plume of Feathers last appears in annual licensing records in 1855 when John Turner, the landlord, moves to the Catherine Wheel in Milford Street [659]. It is not known exactly when the pub closed but in 1860, an advertisement offering the inn and the other surrounding premises for sale describes it as being formerly known as the Plume of Feathers [660].

181 Punchbowl, Shady Bower

Haskins states that the Punchbowl was first licensed in 1710 [21]. It was on the site now occupied by Shady Bower Close on the north side of Shady Bower. For many years, this pub held a Pink Feast every summer [661]. This was not what might be thought in recent years but was an exhibition of the flowers called Pinks with a competition for the best display followed by a meal for the competitors! In 1791, this exhibition of flowers moved to the Star in Brown Street.

One of the Punchbowl's notable achievements was the launch of what must have been the first flying machine in Salisbury as noted in an advertisement of August 9 1784 [662]: 'An Air Balloon, or Grand Aerostatic Globe, sixteen feet in circumference, (an imitation of the great Montgolfier's, of Paris, which attracted the attention and rallied the admiration of thousands in this country) will be launched on Monday the 16th instant, at the Punch Bowl at Milford, by Robert Lampard; being a pleasant retreat from this city, and an agreeable situation for such an exhibition. The infusion of Inflammable Air, by a very compleat apparatus, will begin at one in the afternoon, and the cord will be cut at three.'

The success of this venture was recorded two weeks later in the *Salisbury and Winchester Journal* [663]: 'An air balloon, 15 feet in circumference, was launched from Milford, near this City, on Monday evening, by Robert Lampard, an ingenious young man there, to the entire satisfaction of a very large number of spectators − It continued visible nearly eight minutes, travelling almost due east, and was at length lost in the clouds. − The next morning, it was found in Farley Wood, near Winchester, by Capt. Ford, of the 7th Regiment, and carried to the Shakespeare's Head, St Cross, where a live cat was affixed to it, and a good market made of the credulity of the public, by shewing it and the animal as having made an aerial voyage together.'

This feat was repeated by Robert Lampard the following year [664]. On that occasion, the launch of the balloon was followed by a firework display in the evening, demonstrating that the young man was first and foremost a showman!

The pub continued to trade through the early part of the 19th C. until October, 1825 when the furniture and brewing equipment were put up for sale [665]. It was last licensed at the annual licensing session in September, 1826 [666], but this would seem to have been an action to encourage its sale as a public house. It seems to have been converted into a private house at about this time.

There seems to have been an attempt to re-open it in 1831-1832 as William Lawrence applied for a license in each of these years. It was described in the licensing records as being a new house and the license was refused in both years. This was most probably a different building.

182 Pynnok's Inn, High Street

Pynnok's Inn was one of a number of inns in High Street that catered for visitors to New Sarum and, particularly, for pilgrims to the Cathedral. The inn stood on the west side of High Street (known as Minster Street at that time) roughly where the old Woolworth's store stood.

The first known owner was William Pynnok who, on his death in 1270, bequeathed the building to his brother, Richard [667]. The Pynnoks owned the building until 1333 when it is recorded that they leased 'a tenement called 'Pynnokys Yn in Mynestrestret' to Alice, widow of John le Taverner [668]. It was at that point that we can be sure that the building had become an inn although it is highly likely, given the name of the inn, that the Pynnoks also operated an inn.

In 1428, the inn was demised to the Mayor and Commonalty of Salisbury at a rent of ten marks per year (the mark was about two thirds of a Pound) and thereafter appears in the city chamberlains rent rolls [669]. After 1432, it is described in the Corporation's records as "The Helme late Pynnokys Yn Mynstrestrete alias Hyghstrete" [670]. In 1438, the rent of Le Helme was set at £4 13s 4d per quarter when it was let to Stephen Hendy.

By 1485, Le Helme appeared to be in poor condition as Thomas Blakker rented the inn on the condition that he "bilde anew all the said ten'ts of the Helme" [670]. He obviously did not do this as he was released from his lease after a payment to the Corporation and Henry Horton took up the property. The struggle was lost and in 1491 the Corporation pulled down the inn and built four shops with dwelling houses [671].

183 Qudos, 38 Castle Street

Qudos was for many years known as the White Horse. A pub has been on the site for many years but the current building, on the corner of Scots Lane and Castle Street, is Victorian and built sometime after 1850.

In 1624, Edward Gillow took one barrel of beer from the Common Brewhouse for the White Horse [17]. He also attended the Council meeting in 1625 that considered whether local inns should take beer and ale from the Brewhouse [18].

The next we hear of the inn was in 1740 when a Sorrel Mare was left at the premises [672]. Thomas Webb advertised that if the mare was not reclaimed, he would sell her to offset his expenses.

In 1762, it was announced that the Marlborough Stage Coach had moved its Salisbury base from the Cart Wheel in Milford Street to the White Horse [673]. A special point was made in the advertisement that money could be conveyed to Marlborough at a cost of 2 pence per pound for one to five pounds of cash, two pence per pound for five to ten pounds and three halfpence per pound for ten pounds and upwards. It is not clear why transport of money was so specifically mentioned for this coach service when nothing similar was stated for other coaches.

John Footner took over the inn in 1771. In 1775, there were rumours that some person at the inn had smallpox [674]. He had to advertise that this rumour had had a very adverse effect on his business and he declared that nobody at the inn had smallpox and that there had not been a case on the premises for over three years!

In 1779, there was an auction at John Footner's house of 91 casks of spirits, including brandy, rum and gin, that had been seized by the Excise men. But despite this legal trade, rumours still followed Mr Footner in 1780 [675]: 'It has been maliciously reported that I have declined the business of a Cooper, I think it is incumbent of me to inform my friends and customers that I continue that trade in its different branches. At the same time I take the opportunity of acknowledging my most grateful thanks to those gentlemen and others who have been my customers, either in my business of a cooper, or innkeeper, and to assure them it has been and always shall be my utmost care and attention to convince them that I am their most obedient and obliged humble servant, John Footner.'

John Footner died in 1798 but his widow announced that she was continuing the business and that her son, John Footner Jnr, would be assisting her and also continuing his father's cooperage business [676]. They continued in that manner for a further year when John Jnr announced that he was leaving the inn and that it was being taken over by Isaac Petty [677]. But John Jnr was continuing work as a cooper next door to the White Horse.

In 1826, Isaac Petty retires from the White Horse and James West takes over. But Mr West stays at the inn for only one year and in October, 1827, the furniture, brewing equipment and other effects were put up for sale [678]. It is not clear if the contents of the pub actually belonged to Mr West or whether Isaac Petty had let the inn and contents to him. Suffice it to say that at the end of the month, Isaac Petty announces that he has retaken the inn and hopes that the trade will continue as well as when he was previously in it. He stays at the inn for a further year before he puts it up for sale [679]. Stephen Webb purchases the inn.

In 1837, a meeting of the Salisbury Reform Registration Society was held at the pub [680]. This society was formed to ensure that all residents eligible to vote following the 1832 Reform Act did register. Amongst other provisions, this Act abolished the rotten borough of Old Sarum and replaced it with the Borough of New Sarum. This meeting was called to discuss whether to petition parliament to ensure voting under the new Act should be by secret ballot rather than by a show of hands as had occurred previously. This did not occur in the UK until the Ballot Act of 1872 and thus for quite some period, votes could still be purchased and/or voters persuaded to vote for a particular candidate by means that would be considered illegal these days.

In 1853, James Corbin was summoned to the Magistrates Court for insulting Robert Andrews, the landlord of the White Horse, in the street [681]. It appeared that there had been a dispute between the two men that results in James Corbin being banned from entering the White Horse. Since that event, Mr Corbin had been repeatedly annoying Mr Andrews by calling him names in the street. This was corroborated by several witnesses. The Mayor and the Bench stated that they deemed it their duty to protect respectable tradesmen of the town from insult, and they should bind defendant over in his own recognizances of £10 to keep the peace for six months, and to pay 7s 6d the costs of the hearing.

In 1893, there was an interesting case came before the Magistrates when the landlord of the White Horse was charged with selling beer without a license [682]. The case was brought forward by the Inland Revenue. It appears that up to this time, the pub had a hotel license, which cost £20 per annum, but the Inland Revenue had decided that the pub no longer constituted a hotel and therefore a pub license was required which cost £25 per annum. The landlord had only paid £20 and therefore the Inland Revenue had not renewed the license. Thus, when an excise officer ordered and received half a pint of beer, the landlord was breaking the law. It appeared that the decision as to whether a house was an hotel or a pub was made by the Commissioners of the Inland Revenue and that there was no right of appeal against their decision. The Magistrates found the landlord guilty but demonstrated their opinion by fining him one shilling and with no costs ordered against him. Suffice it to say, the White Horse has been an hotel ever since this date!

By 1938, the White Horse Hotel was advertising that it had hot and cold running water in all its rooms and that it had parking spaces for fifteen cars. At this time, it had a large bar on the ground floor at the front but also had a small public bar leading off Scots Lane from the back yard of the Hotel.

For many years, it was a Hall & Woodhouse pub but by 1979, it was a free house selling a variety of real ales. In 2010, the pub was closed for a while but re-opened after refurbishment as Qudos.

184 Queen's Arms, 9 Ivy Street

The Queen's Arms is undoubtedly one of the oldest buildings in Salisbury that is in use as a public house. The eastern part of the pub was built in the 14th C and formed part of the house of John Caundel, clerk, who died in 1400 and left the property to the Dean and Chapter of Salisbury Cathedral. It was noted as being in the ownership of the Dean and Chapter in 1455 and records from 1637 clearly state that it is an inn.

It has been claimed that the Queen's Arms is the pub in Salisbury that has remained licensed under the same name for the longest period of any pub. This claim is demonstrably untrue as a lease of 1637 describes the pub as being 'heretofore called the Maydenhedd and nowe comonly called the Blewe Lyon' [683]. In the same lease, its location is described as 'lying and being in the City of New Sarum aforesaid in the streets there called New Street and

Brown Street between the lands belonging to Thomas Chaffin the Elder, Gentleman, now in the several tenances and occupation of the said George Mustin and Margarett Lawrence widow on the west and north parts and the King's highway on the east and south parts. It should be pointed out that Ivy Street was considered to be part of New Street at that time. Later leases use the same wording but refer to the pub as being the Queen's Arms and include a drawing of the site.

It is not clear when the inn changed its name from the Maidenhead to the Blue Lion. The Maidenhead in the Cheese Market had gained that name by at least 1721, and thus there appears to be no conflict with the Queen's Arms having been called the Maidenhead some time before 1624 (see below).

The Blue Lion became the Queen's Arms sometime between a lease of 1699 [684] stating it was the Blue Lion and another of 1715 stating it was the Queen's Arms [685]. Thus the claim that the pub was named after Queen Elizabeth I seems very unlikely as she died in 1603. If the pub's name can be attributed to any Queen, it would be related to Queen Anne who reigned from 1702 until 1714 and thus the name could have been given at Queen Anne's succession to the throne or at her death.

One of the earliest accounts of the Blue Lion is in the records of the Common Brewhouse (operated by the Mayor & Corporation of Salisbury) which show that between 10/5/1624 and 26/3/1625, George Mustiane at the Blue Lion took 100 barrels of beer and 17 cowles of ale from the Common Brewhouse [17].

In 1715. a lease of an inn from the Dean & Chapter of the Cathedral for forty years to Thomas Martin states that it was for 'All that their Corner Tenement Little Court and Stable rooms heretofore called the Maidenhead, lately called the Blew Lyon and now called the Queens Arms [685].

It is not clear when the Dean and Chapter disposed of the Queen's Arms but in 1804 a lease on the inn was offered for 7 or 14 years by Jasper Faulkner who is described as being the owner who has been in occupation of the inn for 28 years [686]. It is of note that the stock of the inn consisted of nearly ten thousand gallons of Strong Beer, and about two hundred and fifty quarters of malt which were valued at about £1000.

In 1852, Edward Purcell appeared in court where, as the *Salisbury and Winchester Journal* stated, he had often appeared on charges of drunkenness [687]. He was in the habit of drinking in the Queen's Arms and, on this occasion, he was taken into custody on a charge of drunkenness again. But when he was searched at the police station, a pewter spirit measure was found. Mr Moore, the landlord of the inn, identified the measure as being one of his and he stated that he had had several measures stolen in the previous weeks. Purcell was committed to stand trial at the Assizes.

In 1857, a theft occurred at the inn [688]. A carriage had been left there as there was not enough space at the White Hart. A young man saw John Jones take a shawl and a coat from the carriage and go off to a lodging house in Brown Street. There Jones sat with a man called Daniel Collins and very soon after, Jones put on Collins's coat and left the house. The young man saw a coachman and a policeman enter the lodging house and, realising that the theft had been discovered, rushed off after Jones. He found him in Gigant Street and persuaded a policeman to take Jones into custody. The shawl and coat were discovered under a bucket in the coal house of the lodgings. In Court, Jones pleaded guilty to the charge of theft but Collins denied any wrong, stating that all he had done was lend Jones his coat. The Clerk to the Court asked Collins if he pleaded guilty or not guilty. Again Collins said that all he was guilty of was lending Jones his coat. The Clerk explained that he could not accept this plea and told Collins that if he pleaded guilty, he would be sent to prison immediately, but if he pleaded not guilty, he would have to go to trial. Collins said he would do anything rather than go for trial and he pleaded guilty! Both men were sentenced to three month's imprisonment with hard labour.

In 1858, John Hibberd took the Queen's Arms. He died in early 1871. The 1871 Census shows Emily Deller as being in charge of the inn. But there was a Louisa Hibberd shown as a visitor to the inn but also as being the head of the household! It is presumed that she was the daughter of John Hibberd and had been bequeathed the inn in his will, but she was too young to hold the license.

In 1886, an application was made to transfer the license of the inn from Mrs Harriet Norton to George Gibbons [689]. George Gibbons began using the cottage, next door to the inn in Ivy Street, for the off sales of wines and spirits. Mr Gibbons did not have a Magistrate's certificate for this business. Mr Gibbons was also opening a door between the pub and the cottage but this would also be illegal as it would provide access to the pub out of normal opening hours. Gibbons could be fined £10 per day if the door remained open. He was advised to stop up the door immediately and apply for a certificate for the off-sales area. A year later, Gibbons was granted a license for an off-licence in the Market Place that replaced the previous one alongside the Queen's Arms [690].

At some later date, the pub came under the ownership of Ushers brewery of Trowbridge. It remained an Ushers house until 1974 when it became a Chef and Brewer house within the Watney Mann group. In 1986, it was an Usher's pub again and presumably became one after the management buy-out of that brewery. By 2016, it had become under private ownership and traded as a free house.

185 Queen's and Plasterer's Arms, Ivy Street

The Queen's and Plasterer's Arms was on the south side of Ivy Street, nearly opposite the Queen's Arms. It is not clear when the inn gained its unusual name and there is no record of how this name was derived.

A lease dated Sept 25 1817, describes the premises in Ivy Street as owned by Joachim Hibberd but an annotation on the lease states 'now of Ann Hibberd, Widow' [691]. As Joachim Hibberd died in 1820, this annotation must have been added at this later date. The building is stated to be opposite the Queen's Arms.

The pub in Ivy Street first appears in the licensing records as the Queen's and Plasterer's Arms in 1818 with the Landlord being Robert Samuel Hibberd. It seems very probable that Robert was Joachim and Ann's son, which explains why in the same sale as the Maidenhead in the Cheese

Market after Joachim dies, the Queen's and Plasterer's Arms is also for sale [692]. In the notice of sale, the pub is described as consisting of 'a good Dwelling-House, comprising a large and commodious kitchen, a convenient bar, two parlours and four bed rooms; excellent brewery, and wash-house, with ample cellarage, sufficient to contain 500 hogsheads of beer; a large court-yard with a good garden behind, and all convenient offices'. Associated with it was a malthouse capable of wetting 20 quarters of barley a week. Part of the overall site extended around the corner into Brown Street.

Charles Beale appears to have taken the pub immediately after the sale in 1820 and in 1822, he advertised a range of spirits for sale at what he described as very low prices for read money only [693]. By January, 1823, he was advertising the pub as being available to rent [694]. As was usual, the stock of beer was to be taken by the new tenant but, in this case, it amounted to 200 hogsheads of beer, a very large amount for what was a fairly small pub in a side street. Later in that year, Mr Beale's stock of spirits was put up for sale together with the casks and copper measures [695]. He also was selling several hundred gallons of spermaceti (derived from sperm whales) and other oils from a shop he owned opposite the Assembly Rooms in High Street. By May, 1824, the entire stock of the pub was put up for sale along with the furniture and brewing equipment [696]. The pub was also advertised as being available to rent. The whole of this sale was by order of the Sheriff of Wiltshire. This was explained when, in the following month, Charles Beale was described as being bankrupt [697]. However, in August of that year, a notice stated that the bankruptcy action against him had been superseded, which appears to have meant that the sale of his goods had raised sufficient money to pay off all his creditors.

At the annual licensing session in September, 1824, Mark Gillo was shown to be the landlord and the pub's name had changed to the White Lion [6]. This was somewhat confusing as the Cloisters, on the corner of Ivy Street used that name from 1772 until 1824 when it became the Bell & Crown. Thus, the licensing records show the White Lion continuing in trade after the pub that is well known to have had that name became the Bell & Crown! Even more confusing is the fact that the pub was put up for sale in December, 1843, when it was described as being 'late a public house, known by the name of the Queen's and Plasterer's Arms' and being in Trinity Street rather than Ivy Street [698]. Suffice it to say, despite a change in ownership, the pub continued trading as the White Lion. Note that this pub is listed as the Queen's and Plasterer's Arms in this book to save confusion with the earlier name of the Cloisters.

In 1845, the body of a woman was found in the River Bourne, midway between the Laverstock and Milford bridges [699]. The woman was identified as being the wife of George Woolford and that they had been lodging at the White Lion. George Woolford was described as being the exhibitor of a 'learned pig'. There was much circumstantial evidence that suggested that George Woolford had murdered his wife. Thus, at a Coroner's Court, the jury returned a verdict of 'wilful murder' against Woolford and he was committed for trial at the Assizes. This trial was reported as having lasted all day but its result was that Woolford was acquitted, presumably because there was insufficient evidence that he had killed his wife rather than her having an accident or perhaps committing suicide [700].

The last year in which the pub appears in the annual licensing records is September, 1849, and it is presumed it ceased trading sometime in the following year. Wheeler, writing in 1887, stated that it had been a private house for many years. There is a possibility that the building that became the Mayor Ivie restaurant in the 1970s was this public house.

186 Queen's Head, Ivy Street

There is a single record of this pub as being in St Thomas' parish in 1838 with the landlady being Mary Riddle. The association with Ivy Street may have been a clerical error but no other details have been found.

187 Radnor Arms, Queen's Road

This pub was on the north-west corner of the junction between Queen's Road and St Mark's Road. It was a beerhouse in 1895 (and for some time before) when Mr Folliott, the owner, asked the Magistrates if he could name it the Radnor Arms [701]. Thia application was granted. It seems to have received a license in 1897, probably at the time this area of Salisbury was developed. In the 1901 census it is shown as the Radnor Arms Beerhouse but in the 1911 Census it is shown as being an off-licence. In the New Sarum Register of Licenses for the years 1933 to 1954, the Radnor seems to have been listed as a public house owned by Usher's brewery although in 1937, the Register is annotated to say that a wine off-licence was added [12]. The 1955 to 1964 Register has Radnor Arms crossed out and Applegates Wine Merchant written in with a note to say that it was off-licence only [13]. It appears to have ceased to be a pub on 13th April, 1959.

188 Radnor Arms, 11 St Ann Street

The Radnor Arms was on the north side of St Ann Street, near to Brown Street, and appears to have had a boundary in common with the Cherry Tree (qv). Haskins states that it was licensed as an alehouse called the Northumberland Arms in 1770 [20] but if this is correct, it must have changed its name by 1803 as the Crown and Anchor in Exeter Street took this name in about that year.

In 1823, it was advertised as being available to rent [702]. The advertisement states that it was newly built and could be known as the Lord Radnor's Arms. The new tenant was required to take the stock of beer, which was brewed on the premises, and which was about 120 hogsheads of Strong Beer.

By 1825, the name of the pub was simplified to the Radnor Arms.

Over the next few years, it was advertised as available to let several times. In 1836, the annual, city, cucumber show was held at this pub [703]. The dinner held after the judging of the cucumbers was served by the landlord, John Sloane, in what was described as being in 'a very superior style'. The show was repeated in 1837 but may have been at different premises in other years.

The pub is last shown in the licensing records in 1847 [9]. By August, 1848, it was advertised for sale and described as 'lately called the Radnor Arms' [704].

189 Rai d'Or, 69 Brown Street

The Rai d'Or is on the north-east corner of Brown Street and Trinity Street and takes its name from an inn that was on the site in the 14th C. Sadly, the current building stems from the mid-16th C although it has been extensively rebuilt over the years and little, if any, remains of the ancient buildings. The name of the Rai d'Or can be roughly translated as the Golden Rays which is usually assumed to mean the rays of the sun and hence the more recent name of the Star shows some continuity through the years.

The oldest mention of this inn was in 1332 when John, son & heir of Clement atte Rydedore conveys to Alice his sister for her life his tenement in Brown Street between the street called New Street on the South & the tenement of William Brightwey on the North extending to the Watercourse on the East. The waterway mentioned is one of the old canals that ran through the streets of Salisbury, this particular one running south across Trinity Street as it returned the water from the canals to the River Avon.

In about 1400, John Chaundler passed the ownership of the inn to Trinity Hospital and, owing to this, there is considerable information regarding the leasehold of the inn although little about its development and re-building. Throughout its long history, it is very difficult to establish who the landlord of the inn was as it was common practice for the leaseholder to sub-let the inn to a professional innkeeper.

The earliest time at which the inn was known to be called the Star is in 1455 when William Swayne (a mayor of Salisbury and after whom Swayne's Chequer is named) paid rent for a house called Le Sterr. At a more recent date, the *Salisbury and Winchester Journal* in 1777 carried the following story [705]: 'Thursday evening a press gang headed by their Lieutenant attempted to press a young fellow at the Star in Brown Street, when with a true British spirit & the assistance of an iron poker, he valiantly repulsed those violators of liberty, and after breaking the heads of several, obliged them to decamp.

In 1791, it was announced that the Annual Pink Feast, previously held at the Punch Bowl, in Milford, would now be held at the Star [706].

Despite the complaint about a press gang in 1777, by 1796, it was advertised that recruits for the Army could receive a bounty of twenty guineas by applying to the Overseer, Mr Joseph Young, who was also the landlord, at the Star Inn [707]. The length of service that recruits were required to sign up for was the whole length of the war and one month afterwards. This would have been until at least 1802, the end of the war against Spain, but almost immediately, Britain declared war against France and, thus, the recruits of 1796 could have found themselves in the Army until 1815!

In the 19th C, there is some confusion as to who owned the Star. In 1807, the inn was put up for sale with the advertisement stating that it was held by the Corporation of New Sarum [706] while in 1830, it appears in a list of properties owned by Trinity Hospital.

In 1810, John Mitchell, who had been at the Star since 1806, moved to the Chough

Rai d'Or

[709]. As was the normal practice at this time, he advertised all the furniture of the inn for sale, but also included all the beer storage casks and all the brewing equipment in the sale. William Reeves took over the Star and he might have purchased all the furniture or may have provided his own.

In 1812, it appears that James Ainsworth held the lease of the Star. But in 1816, his wife, Sarah, died and ten months later, his son died. James decides to rent the pub to a sub-tenant and advertises it [709], but, whether he did actually let the pub is doubtful as he remains the licensee until 1820 [5]. In that year, the Mayor and Magistrates hold a meeting to decide whether to allow the license held by James to be transferred to James Absalom from Odstock. The license was transferred, but within five months, Mr Absalom had died [711]. He was only 29 years old and had had a short but very severe illness. In 1830, the Star is recorded as being in the ownership of the Trinity Hospital, with a lease being granted for 31 years with a fine being paid of £10 7s and an annual rent of £2 15s [712]. Also, to be paid annually was 1 shilling and sixpence flesh money which appears to be paid to Trinity Hospital in lieu of a piece of meat being given to the charity. It is presumed that this lease was granted to James Ainsworth. James Ainsworth continues to hold the license until 1833 [6]. But he still retains ownership of the lease of the Star, having renewed the lease in 1830 and then again in 1840.

It appears that James Ainsworth must have signed over the lease of the pub to Robert Tink, who was landlord of the George and Dragon in Castle Street, as Mr Tink advertises the pub as available to rent in 1843 [713]. The following year, the brewery plant of the Star is offered for sale by Mr Tink. Unusually, this equipment was moved to the George and Dragon for the sale [714]. It is presumed that from this year onwards, the pub was supplied from a brewery rather than brewing its own beer.

A young girl was brought before the court in 1868 charged with "having wilfully and maliciously injured various articles of wearing apparel, belonging to her master' [715]. She was a servant at the Star and the landlord, William henry Keene, produced the damaged clothes in court and they 'had certainly been cut in a most extraordinary manner, several of then being rendered utterly useless, large pieces being cut completely out of them'. However, there was no positive evidence that the girl had cut the clothes except that from a little girl, who the court judged was too young to be examined under oath. The court had no choice but to dismiss the charge. However, the Mayor, as Chairman of the Bench, said he believed there was little moral doubt of the guilt of the girl and she was given a caution before being released. On the same date that this case was reported in the *Salisbury and Winchester Journal*, Mr Keene advertised that he supplied every description of Coal, at the lowest, market prices!

In January, 1881, the sale of the Star was advertised although as the notice stated, the pub was leasehold so the sale was most probably that of the lease [716].

In the same sale, a malt house. dwelling house and shop that were adjacent to the pub in Brown Street were also offered for sale. It is not clear exactly where these premises were but their site is presumed to be where some modern dwellings have been built. However, in 1884, when the license of the Star was due to be renewed, the police objected on the grounds that there was a connecting door between the pub and the adjacent lodging house [717]. It seems that there was much drunkenness associated with the inhabitants of this lodgings. The landlord of the Star agreed to stop up the door. It is not clear if the lodging house was in Brown Street and could have been where the malt house and other premises had been or alternatively was in Trinity Street. The latter seems most likely as, in 1905, plans were approved for two new houses and a stable in Trinity Street [718]. Also in the plans were proposals to make alterations, additions and repairs to three cottages in Trinity Street and also to the Star. Looking at the site nowadays, there are clearly two houses and a smaller building between the Star and three terraced cottages

By the 20th C, the inn was just one of the small, local public houses in Salisbury. It is not clear if the pub still remains the property of Trinity Hospital or whether it has been sold by that institution at some time. From at least 1932 until 1957, it was a Lamb Brewery, Frome, house and then became an Usher's pub until 1974. It then became a Chef and Brewer house in the Watney Mann group. By the 1990s, it had a somewhat bad reputation as being a rather rough pub and at one time, a landlady surrendered her licence before the licensing authorities could confiscate it and close the pub. In 2003, the pub was sold and the incoming landlord applied for planning permission to convert the pub into three houses or flats. However, at the same time, the landlord changed the name from the Star back to the Rai d'Or and re-opened it as a pub that also specialised in Thai food. This was sufficiently successful for the pub to remain in business with a reputation for good, real ale and a Thai menu.

190 Railway Inn, 59 Tollgate Road

The Railway Inn is one of the few pubs in Britain that has two names. As well as being the Railway Inn, the pub is known as the Dusthole and the two names are shown on the two sides of the pub sign.

The pub gains its first name from being near to the original London & South Western Railway Station that opened in 1847. The name Dusthole comes from it being next to the coal depot of the railway. Coal was dropped from railway wagons into bunkers in what is now Blakey Road. At the level of the road were openings from which coal merchants loaded their lorries for coal deliveries in the area. The openings were colloquially known as dustholes.

The pub first appears in the licensing records in 1847 when John Rourke was the landlord and it is noted as being a new public house [719].

In 1861, a Coroner's inquest was held at the Railway Inn after John Sommerton was killed on the railway at Milford Station [720]. He was working with another man on the railway lines leading to Milford station. A goods train was entering the station and so they left their work and went to stand on the lines from Salisbury station. Unfortunately, a passenger train was coming down that line and the driver did not see the men until it was too late to stop. John Sommerton was knocked down and killed instantly. The jury returned a verdict of Accidental Death and the Coroner noted that there was no blame attached to the driver of the engine.

In 1868, Ann Wells Conway became landlady of her pub after her husband dies [721]. She herself dies in turn in 1874. Henry James Conway becomes her administrator and he holds the license for the pub for one day before it is transferred to William Burrough. This must be one of the shortest periods of time for a landlord on record.

A Slate Club was started at the pub in 1899 with its first annual dinner being held in November, 1900 [722]. It was said that full justice was done to the good things provided by the landlady, Mrs Whitlock. After a short list of toasts, the evening was pleasantly spent.

In later years, the pub was tied to Gibbs Mew until that brewery closed in 1997. Since 2013, the pub has been privately owned and operates as a free house.

191 Railway Tavern, 135 South Western Road

It has been said that the Railway Tavern is about 300 years old and developed from two cottages. An 1843 map shows two cottages at the site but one of them would have had to be demolished when South Western Road was built at the time the station was built.

The Railway Tavern first appears in the licensing records in 1859, when Henry Isaacs was the landlord, and is shown in the 1861 Census which is a little after the Great Western Railway station at Fisherton

Anger was opened in 1856 and the London & South Western Railway station opened in 1859.

In November, 1867, a soldier on a train from Southampton was found to be extremely ill and he was taken to the Railway Tavern [723]. A Doctor was called for but, by the time he arrived at the pub, the soldier had expired. The police arrived and took charge of the body and he was found to have had £3 5s 5d and a ticket from Portsmouth to Exeter. He also had discharge papers from the Army which gave his name as William Tea and stated that he had been discharged from the Royal Marine Artillery owing to a diseased heart. A Coroner's inquest was held at the pub with the resulting verdict stating that he had died owing to his heart condition.

In 1868, a sale was held at the Railway Tavern of surplus property of the South-Western Railway Company [724]. Lot 1 was the Railway Tavern itself. Since it had been owned by the railway company, this further supports the belief that the pub had opened in 1859, when the LSWR reached the Fisherton site and the LSWR station had been built.

In 1872, it appears that the landlord of the pub, George Hollick, had left his wife and the pub, taking £100 and saying that he was going to America. He had left the pub a few weeks earlier taking £50 with him but returned when that money was spent. On the second occasion, Mrs Mary Ann Hollick went to Court to obtain an order to protect her earnings from her husband [725]. Since George Hollick had signed a deed of separation leaving the pub and all his property to his wife, the Magistrates had no hesitation in granting the order and also transferring the license of the pub to Mrs Hollick. She ran the pub until the licensing session in September, 1875, but appears to have died in Marlborough later that year. As a consequence, George Hollick became the landlord again (presumably, having never gone to America) but with a new, younger wife, Caroline. He appears to have stayed at the pub until at least 1886.

The pub was known as the Railway Tavern until at least 1871 but by 1881 it was called the Railway Hotel. It retained that name for many years and was a Strong's of Romsey (later Whitbread) tied house. In about 1979, it was purchased by Gibbs Mew after being closed for a while. The pub's name was returned to the Railway Tavern at about this time and remained in the ownership of Gibbs Mew until the brewery closed in 1997. In the 1980s, Gibbs Mew used a horse drawn dray for delivering beer to pubs in the City. The two horses used, Danny and Dylan, were housed in stables to the rear of the pub.

192 Railway Tavern, St Ann Street.

This pub is known solely from an advertisement in the *Salisbury and Winchester Journal* dated January, 1854 [726]: 'Saint Ann Street, Salisbury. The Town Council of New Sarum, was prepared to Let by Tender, on Lease, for the Term of Seven Years - All that Messuage, or Tenement, Dwelling-House and Garden, situate in St Ann-street, Salisbury, known as the "Railway Tavern", late in the occupation of John Burnett, Beer-seller. The Lease (the form of which can be seen at my Office) will contain the usual covenants on the part of the Lease for payment of Rent and repairing the

Premises; also for the House not to be used as a Beerhouse, Common Lodging House, nor for the purpose of carrying on any offensive Trade or Business, and not to assign without licence of the Corporation. The Premises have within the last month, been thoroughly repaired, and put into good tenantable condition. The Tenders must be sealed, and contain the name and address of the party tendering, the amount of Rent for the term, and endorsed "Tender for Lease of Saint Ann Street Premises", and sent in to me on or before the 1st day of February next. Matt. Tho. Hodding, Town Clerk.'

This was clearly not the Railway Tavern in South-Western Road or the Railway Inn in Tollgate Road. There are two possible candidates if this pub was known by a different name at some time. The first is the Baker's Arms. This opened in 1854 but this inn does not equate with the statement in the advertisement that the refurbished building could not be used as a beerhouse. The second possibility is the Radnor Arms. This closed in about 1847. The Milford Railway Station opened in that same year so it is possible that the Radnor continued as a beerhouse known as the Railway Tavern for a little while. Of course, this Railway Tavern could have been another premises in St Ann Street that operated as a beer only house for a short while. Until this quandary can be resolved, this pub remains as a separate entry.

193 Red Lion, Fisherton Street

The Red Lion in Fisherton was on the north side of Fisherton Street approximately where the railway line crosses Fisherton Street and was demolished when the railway line from London reached the LSWR station in 1857.

Haskins states that the Red Lion was licensed in 1753 when Robert Turner was the landlord. In 1810, the lease of the Red Lion was offered for sale with the following, interesting details [727]: 'To be Sold by Auction, on Tuesday the 6th day of February 1810, at three o'clock in the afternoon, at the Maidenhead Inn, in the city of New Sarum, - All that Inn or Public House, called the Red Lion, conveniently situated in the street of Fisherton Anger, with a large Garden behind the same; also two Tenements adjoining – The whole of which (except one of the Tenements, which is unoccupied) are now in the occupation of Wm. Rutter. These premises will be sold for a term of 99 years determinable on three lives to be named by the purchasers, and possession may be had at Lady-day next. For particulars apply at the office of Messrs Tanner and Cooper, Salisbury.'

In 1829 and 1830, an exhibition of tulips was held at the pub with prizes for the best blooms [728]. In 1831, this show seems to have been displaced by an exhibition of Ranunculus [729]. In all three years, the landlord, John Norton, featured in the list of prize-winners.

In 1842, the landlady, Louisa Beale, applied to the Justices of Salisbury to transfer her licence to Joseph Scales who was described as being a Horse Dealer from Bristol. For whatever reason, the Justices refused the transfer after hearing from Mr Scales [8]. Louisa Beale succeeded in transferring the licence to Hugh Brine later in the same year.

The last landlord was a Mr Isaacs. In September, 1858, he asked the Magistrates to license a house adjoining the Red Lion, as the old premises, with the exception of the bar, had been taken down in order to construct the new railway [730]. The Mayor said that the application would be granted, as the Act gave the power of substituting other premises for any house which might be pulled down. However, the pub does not appear in the licensing records after this date. It is probably not a coincidence that a Mr Henry Isaacs became the landlord of the Railway Tavern in South Western Road the following year

194 Red Lion Hotel, 4 Milford Street

The author has followed the description of properties given in the RCHM by including the White Bear under the heading of the Red Lion. The reason for this is that there does not appear to be any mention of the Red Lion before 1752 when it was known as the Red Lion and Cross Keys. And yet the south wing of the hotel dates back to at least the 14th C. and is purported to have been built in 1220, probably as an inn or hostelry. The White Bear stood on the corner of Catherine Street and Milford Street and can be traced back to at least 1327 and its last mention was in 1749. Thus, it is most probable that the south wing of the Red Lion was part of the White Bear.

The name White Bear was certainly in use during the 17th C. but as early as the mid-15th C. the tenement at the corner of Catherine Street and Milford Street was known as Berecorner which name is almost certainly a corruption of Bear. Certainly, later deeds for Berecorner indicate that it was part of an inn.

Haskins states that in 1624, William Ray took three hogsheads and six barrels of beer from the Common Brewhouse for the White Bear [17]. He also attended the meeting in 1625 called by the Council to discuss inns taking beer and ale from the Common Brewhouse [18]. In 1671, the building that is now that on the south side of the Red Lion yard is referred to as the 'the great Hall of the White Bear'. By 1701, William Jones was granted a licence for the White Bear. In 1729, the corner of the street is referred to as White Bear Corner but by 1774, the property on the corner is described as the late inn called the White Bear. However, the latest mention of the White Bear in the licensing records in in 1749 when Mr Bricknell was the landlord.

By 1752, it is advertised that William King was running the Salisbury Waggons to and from London which set out from the Red Lion and Cross Keys every Wednesday and Saturday morning and returns from the King's Arms Inn, Holborn-bridge, on Wednesdays and Thursdays [731]. Further coaches and wagons were advertised as running from the inn over the next ten years

In 1764 we find an example of the summary manner that justice followed at that time [732]: 'On Monday the 11th inst about 4 o'clock in the afternoon the Landlord of the Red Lion & Cross Keys in this City, had a box broke into and upwards of £70 in notes and cash taken thereout. The most diligent search and enquiry were made on every suspected person; but all in vain; and the landlord gave it entirely up for lost. A Basil Francis, who had lodged in the said Inn about a month (a cripple and by trade a Silver Smith) having stolen a shirt from an exciseman who lodged in the same house, it gave great reason to suppose that he broke open the box, and stole the money also: accordingly he underwent a long and strict examination in which he persisted in his innocence to the last, but however was committed to gaol yesterday se'ennight for stealing the shirt, and on Saturday last he was again searched, when upwards of £7 were found concealed in one of his shoes, which proves beyond dispute, that he is the person who committed the robbery; for when he came first to the Inn he borrowed 5/- of the Landlord under pretence that he had a box of great value coming by the carrier; which was entirely false. He is a little miserable looking fellow, one leg shorter than the other, wears a brown coat, and hired a horse in London, which he sold at Basingstoke on his journey down here.'

In 1766, Daniel Safe took the Red Lion & Cross Keys and, as he was the Postmaster of the City, he moved the post office to the inn in April of that year [733]. In January 1769, Daniel Safe made the following announcement in the *Salisbury and Winchester Journal* [734]: 'I beg leave to inform my Friends & the Public in general that the Inn which I now keep, that for many years past has been known by the Name of the Red Lion & Cross Keys in Milford Street, will for the future, be the Red Lion only, being both Post & Excise Office; where I hope for the Continuance of my Friend's Favours, as well as all others who please to honour me with their Custom, and they may depend on good Accommodations, and the utmost Care being taken to oblige by their most obedient and humble Servant, D.P. Safe.'

This is one of the few cases in Salisbury when we can be certain of the date at which an inn or public house changed its name. Daniel Safe remained at the inn until 1772 but the house continued to be known as the Red Lion from 1769 until the present day.

Travel in the coaches of this time could be a risky business as highlighted in the *Salisbury and Winchester Journal* of February, 1797 [735]: 'Friday night a person who had just come to Salisbury, by the Taunton coach, died suddenly at Mr Young's, the Red Lion Inn, in this city; he had drank part of two pints of beer, and was going up stairs to bed, when leaning over the banisters he complained of extreme illness, and was taken down into the kitchen, where he died in a few minutes; he was ill when he got into the coach at London, occasioned, as he said, by having caught cold in going up on the outside in the late severe weather; he was apparently about seventy years old; and from letters in his pocket, his name appears to have been John Shore of Montacute, Somerset.'

From 1810, the inn was advertised for sale on many occasions by Isaac Young who had purchased the inn in 1796. His advertisements appear periodically in the *Salisbury and Winchester Journal* until well into 1812 with Isaac Young being described as a Bankrupt in the later versions. The advertisement of March 1812 describes the premises [736]: 'Capital Freehold Inn, Wilts. For sale by Auction, by order of the Assignees, on the Premises, by C. Norton, on Tuesday the 14th of April, 1812, at three o'clock; All that desirable, well-accustomed Inn (for Commercial and other Gentlemen), known by the name of the Red Lion, situate in the centre of the city of New Sarum, late the property of Mr Isaac Young, a Bankrupt, where the Portsmouth and Exeter Mails, Bath, Bristol, Gosport and Southampton Coaches stop daily; comprising a spacious, roomy House, containing three commodious dining-rooms and parlours, comfortable chambers and servant's apartments, large and convenient bar, kitchen, coach-office, brewhouse; beer, wine and spirit cellars; two yards, with stabling for fifty horses, and numerous other detached buildings. The Stock of Beer, Casks, Wines and Spirits, together with all the fixtures, to be taken at a fair valuation. The Mail Horses on the Exeter Road, with the whole or part of the Household Furniture, at the option of the purchaser.'

Thomas Harrington finally purchased the inn in October, 1812, and advertises that the house has 'undergone considerable additions and improvements' [737]. He also states that he has 'a New Apartment for them is nearly finished, in front of the House, with a suit of bedrooms over'. In 1814, John Beckingsale took over the inn and advertises it as the Red Lion Inn & Commercial House [738].

But all was not well with Mr Beckingsale. In 1821, the records of the Justices regarding licences for inns and public houses, contains the following note [5]: 'On granting the Licence to Mr John Beckingsale, The Mayor addressed him in the following terms — "Mr Brethren and Myself after considerable deliberation have come to a conclusion to grant your Certificate and that I may not deliver their Sentiments improperly or imperfectly, I have committed them to Paper and will not read them to you."'

Not much may be gathered from this comment although it is clear that Mr Beckingsale had upset the Justices by some means or another. A further note was found in the records, although it is not known if this is the letter to which the Mayor alluded: 'The Magistrates have taken into consideration the application from Mr Beckingsale to them to obtain their Licence for his continuing during the ensuing Year to keep a Public House within this City — The granting of such Licence depends altogether upon their pleasure in the exercise of sound discretion and they are bound upon such application whenever circumstances require it, to deliberate not only upon the fitness of the Individual but upon the Interests of the Public as connected with that proceeding — In your case they feel that it was not to be as an ordinary proceeding, but that deliberation was necessary on their part before they concluded in favour of your application — Feeling that it must be to you and your family a matter of great importance not merely as affecting property but also as involving reputation, they have determined to grant you the Licence, which you have solicited, but at the same time you are ever to bear in mind that in your situation it becomes your peculiar duty to show upon all occasions the most ready obedience to the Law and also the utmost respect to that Authority by which the Laws are administered, and you and the Public may be assured that the Magistrates in granting of Licences for Public Houses can never be indifferent to circumstances from which the want of such obedience or of such respect can be inferred.'

Whatever the problem, John Beckingsale stayed on in the Red Lion until 1835 so it is clear that he learned his lesson, even if we do not know the exact details of his original misdemeanour. During this period, the three storeyed part of the hotel fronting onto Milford Street, together with the archway into the yard was built. This is dated on the elaborate iron support for the inn sign

After the demise of John Beckingsale, George Slyfield took over the inn. He used the Red Lion as the office for his coaching enterprise and his advertisements refer to the inn as the Lion Commercial Hotel [739]. In late 1837, he advertised that seven different coaches either operated from the Red Lion or called at the inn with destinations of Bristol & Bath, Devizes & Melksham, Exeter & Plymouth, Gloucester & Birmingham, Southampton & Romsey and Yeovil & Sherborne [740]. Apart from these coaches, there were also coaches to and from London.

By 1838, one sees the first influence of the railways [741]. The Victoria Coach left the Pall Inn, Yeovil, every Monday, Wednesday and Friday morning, travelling through Sherborne, Wincanton, Gillingham and Shaftesbury to arrive at the Red Lion. It left this inn at one o'clock in the afternoon to travel through Andover, Whitchurch and Basingstoke to reach the Hartley Row railway station (near Hartley Wintney in Hampshire) in time to catch the 7pm train to London. The Coach returned to Yeovil on Tuesday, Thursday and Saturday mornings, again completing the journey in one day. It is of interest that the train journey was included in the cost of the coach and that the coach was carried on the train. By 1840, the London coaches were meeting the railway at Andover.

In 1843, Thomas Rogers became the innkeeper of the Red Lion. He died in 1859 but his widow, Sarah, continued to run the inn. The 1861 Census describes her as being the Hotel Keeper as it does again in 1871.

In 1868, Sarah Rogers was brought before the Magistrates for wasting water [742]. Water was kept running from a pipe in the cellar into a vessel where live eels were kept. It was stated that only six gallons of water a week were used in this way and this for only five months in the year. The bench decided that an offence had been committed but this was through ignorance rather than being a fraudulent act. Sarah was fined a nominal five shillings plus costs and told to cease the waste immediately.

By 1880, the hotel was owned by William Henry Matthews. But he became financially embarrassed and on 22nd July 1880, he voluntarily applied to the Court for liquidation. His creditors met and appointed a Committee of Inspection and two Trustees. On the 13th September the Trustees sold the whole of Mr Matthews interest in the Red Lion to Edward Waters who acted on behalf of several persons who established the Red Lion Hotel Company. A Miss B Pearse was appointed as the manager and license holder.

By 1881, we find Major Wilkins being described as the Hotel Manager. From 1885 until 1912, the proprietor of the Hotel was listed as George Wilkes Gawthorne although at some time in this period, Edward Wilkes Gawthorne appears to have been the Proprietor. The proprietors of the hotel did not live at the address and a manager or manageress was listed as being present on the premises.

The progress of the Hotel Company could not have been straightforward as in 1889, the authorised capital of the Company was reduced from £12,000 to £6,000 represented by 1,200 shares valued at £5 each [743]. Of these shares, 702 were fully paid up and 400 had not been issued. And the remaining 98 were described as being forfeit.

In 1912, George Thomas purchased the hotel. Although he died in 1959, his wife, Elsie, appears to have actually run the hotel until 1973, when her son Bill took over the reins. It is said that Elsie Thomas never drank alcohol or smoked for the whole time she was at the hotel! In 1977, Michael Maidment, Bill Thomas' nephew, appears as the owner and he continued until 2014.

195 Red Lyon, Castle Street

The Red Lyon was an alehouse in Castle Street but its exact whereabouts are unknown. Haskins states that it was granted a licence in 1742.

196 Red Rover, Barnard Street

In 1834, Robert Sworn informed the public that he was selling Good Home-Brewed Strong Beer, at 4 pennies a quart, as off sales from the Red Rover public house [744]. By October, 1841, a sale was announced of all the brewing plant, casks, strong beer and other effects which were the property of Robert Sworn, deceased, on the premises, late the Red Rover public house [745]. Nothing more is known of this pub. There is a possibility that this was a precursor of the Huntsman Tavern on the corner of Barnard Street and Gigant Street but no direct connection can be made.

197 Retreat Inn, 33 Milford Street

This pub was the Cart Wheel before 1793 and the Catherine Wheel until fairly recent times. The current building has elements of 15th C construction but it has been considerably altered over the years. There was a carriage entrance under the bow window until 1968 and this led into a back yard which had a second entrance from Pennyfarthing Street.

The pub was very old but the earliest reference to it is in the records of the Common Brewhouse where it is stated that William Strange at the Cart Wheel took 16 barrels of beer and 14 couls of ale between 1624 and 1625 [17]. He also attended the meeting in 1625 Called by the Council to discuss inns taking beer and ale from the Common Brewhouse [18].

During the Civil War Salisbury was occupied, in 1664-65, by a royalist force for some weeks under Goring. While he was here, something occurred which was deemed of sufficient importance to be reported to the Parliament. A party of Goring's men were carousing at the Cart Wheel Inn, and having drunk the usual toast of the King, the Queen, and Prince Rupert, one of the party proposed the health of the Devil [746]. To this a trooper objected, alleging, that he did not know whether there was a Devil or not; but if he could see him, he should have no objection to pledge his health. The room was instantly filled with the noisome fumes of sulphur, and an ugly creature rose up in the midst of the party, "which" adds the correspondent, "was the Devil no doubt". The phantom seized the sceptical trooper, and flew with him out of the window*. This fate was eagerly circulated, and contributed to increase the odium under which the followers of Goring had long laboured, in consequence of their licentiousness and profaneness

In about 1754, John Carter took the Cart Wheel. In 1755, mischievous rumours were spread that he had been arrested [747]. John Carter offered a reward of up to 10 Guineas to anybody who could tell him who started the rumour. By 1757,

John Carter had died and his widow had married George Willsheare [748]. By 1759, we find that John Baster had taken the inn and that in May of that year he had married Mrs Willsheare [749]. Finally, in 1761 there is an advertisement for the sale of salt at the Cart Wheel which is now under the care of Mrs Baster [750]! One guesses that at this point, the vigorous lady would have had difficulty in persuading another man to marry her!

In 1810, the ownership of the Catherine Wheel was offered for sale [742]. James Bolster was named as the landlord occupying the inn. In 1814, James Bolster died [752] but his son, also James, announced that he was carrying on the business of the inn for the benefit of himself and his infant brother [753]. The following year, James, the younger marries Miss Mary Chubb [754]. But in 1822, James dies [755] and his widow Mary carries on with the business until the following year when the inn is advertised as available to let and John Bannister Brown becomes the landlord [756].

In 1869, a young boy aged eight was charged with stealing two shillings and sixpence from the till of the Catherine Wheel [757]. A shoe-maker named Pearce from Pennyfarthing Street saw the boy steal the money and apprehended him. Unfortunately, the boy made such a fuss, claiming it was Pearce that had stolen the money, that Pearce was apprehended by the police and taken to the police station. There he managed to convince the Superintendent of Police that he was innocent. The boy was taken to the police station and, after he was locked up, he confessed to the crime and told the police where he had hidden the money. A police officer found the money thus corroborating the confession. The boy was found guilty in Court and taken to the police station where, after he was whipped, he was given six strokes with a birch. One of the Magistrates stated that he wished the punishment could have fallen on the boy's mother, as he thought the misconduct of the boy was the mother's fault.

In 1870, William Baiss, the landlord, was charged with "unlawfully and knowingly permitted and suffered divers persons of notoriously bad character to assemble and meet together in his house, contrary to the tenor of his license" [758]. The Sergeant of Police said he had entered the house and found, in an upstairs room, five or six prostitutes. The landlord claimed he did not know there were prostitutes and would have only known this if he had he had been improperly associated with the ladies. There was a fiddler playing music in the room and several men with the women. Two of these men gave evidence that although dancing had taken place, there was no improper conduct. The Magistrates thought there was insufficient evidence to warrant a conviction but they cautioned Mr Baiss about his future conduct.

In 1887, the pub was put up for sale as a part of the sale of the King's Head Brewery [759]. It is probable that the pub was purchased by Hall & Woodhouse of Blandford at this time. It continued under their ownership until in 1987, the brewery sold the pub without a licence. It re-opened in 1989 as the Trafalgar, a restaurant that had a bar attached. In 2003, it was re-branded as the Retreat Inn with the emphasis being shifted towards it being a public house again. However, in recent years, the Retreat was closed and the building converted to become the citylodge hotel and the pub was finally lost to the city.

198 Rifleman's Arms, London Road

The Rifleman's first appears in the licensing records in August, 1866, when it was recorded that this was a new license [760]. It may have been an unlicensed alehouse before this date. It appears to have been on the London Road out of the city, probably near the turning to Ford and the Winterbournes (the licensing records state it was near the Lobcombe Gate in the parish of Milford but I have been unable to find the location of this gate).

In 1871, a young man, who was a butcher's son, rode a pony to Laverstock to deliver some meat for his father [761]. As he returned, the pony took fright and the boy was thrown to the ground, near the Rifleman's Arms. At first, he was conscious and told Mary Lock, the landlady, that if he rested a while, he would be able to go home. She gave him some brandy and water but shortly after the boy became worse and eventually became unconscious. A man went to get a Doctor but not long after he arrived, the boy worsened and died. The doctor stated that there was no broken bones but he believed the boy died from a ruptured blood vessel in his head. The boy was buried in the London Road Cemetery with the *Salisbury and Winchester Journal* recording that five or six hundred persons attended the internment.

At the annual licensing session in August, 1878, nobody appeared to represent the Rifleman's Arms and the license lapsed [762].

199 Rising Sun Inn, 145 Castle Street

The Rising Sun was on the west side of Castle Street nearly opposite Wyndham Road. Records of this pub can be a little confusing as it was outside of the city boundary and was actually in the parish of Milford.

It appears that this pub was quite ancient but the earliest record found is from 1795 when William Smart was the landlord. It was most probably an alehouse before this date.

In November, 1811, the *Salisbury and Winchester Journal* reported a theft from the pub [763]: 'John Forty, alias John Broad, was on Wednesday committed to Fisherton Gaol, for trial at the Assizes, charged with having, on the preceding night, broken into the house of Mrs Alice Blake, the Rising Sun public-house, in the parish of Milford, adjacent to this city, and stolen therefrom four silver tea-spoons, and sundry other articles. – Broad is a cripple, who has frequently laboured under accusations of theft; and to these disadvantages he owes his present situation; the mark of a crutch on the ground, near the window which had been entered to affect the robbery, having excited the suspicion which led to his apprehension and commitment.'

In March of the following year, John Forty was sentenced to death for this robbery by the Wiltshire Assizes [764]. However, it was noted that the Judges reprieved him before they left the City. In May, 1812, he was sentenced to two years in the County Gaol [765].

In 1862, George Harris, the landlord, was summoned for six instances of selling beer on a Sunday before half-past twelve [766]. The Superintendent of Police stated that he had cautioned Mr Harris a month before the day in question and had been told that if he persisted in selling beer during illegal hours, his house would be watched in order to detect further offences. On the Sunday in question, the police noted 42 people had been served with beer before half-past twelve. Mr Harris denied the truth of this statement and the police said that if he questioned their accuracy, they would present evidence to support the statement. The Mayor, as Chairman of the Bench, said that Mr Harris had pleaded guilty to six charges and he was liable to a fine of £5 and costs for each case, or if he was in default of paying the fines, he would be liable to three month's imprisonment for each case. Since the landlord was quite young and had only recently been in the pub trade, the Bench fined him £2 plus costs for each of the six cases. Mr Harris asked for time to pay and was granted 14 days. At the annual licensing session, a month later, the police objected to the renewal of Mr Harris's license but the Magistrates granted the license as Mr Harris promised to conduct his house properly in the future [767].

During the middle part of the 20th C., the Rising Sun had the endearing habit of nailing a hot cross bun to the beams of the saloon bar each Easter. This bar was known as the Bass Bar as it had a beer engine for serving Bass beer even though it was an Usher's house. At this time, the pub was a busy social venue as it had a skittle alley in the public bar and several rooms for hire at the rear of the pub. Salisbury Folk Club met at the Rising Sun for many years. The pub was also popular in the summer as it had a back garden by the River Avon.

In 1986, the local trade of the pub was shocked to find the Rising Sun closed for a while and then re-opened as Sunny's, a one-bar theme pub for the younger customer that was all chrome and garish lighting. The new décor found a ready trade but, as other pubs in the City were updated, this trade reduced and by 1994, the pub was closed. Sadly, it was demolished in 1997 to increase the parking of the car dealer next door. More recently, that car dealer moved and the site was cleared to allow the construction of flats for the elderly that still occupy the site.

200 Roebuck, 21 Butcher Row (New Canal)

Haskins states that this house was known as the Old Roebuck when J Wansborough received a licence for it as an alehouse in 1742 [20]. But before these dates, there was no requirement to certify alehouses. It was only because the Mayor & Corporation made efforts to reduce the number of alehouses in the City to 40 earlier in the 18th C. that certificates were required.

It appears that the prefix 'Old' was used as the house had been in existence for some time. Certainly, the pub is variously described as the Roebuck and the Old Roebuck at different times right into the 19th C. But in the mid-18th C, the description of it being 'old' also distinguished it from the New Roebuck in Ox Row, a pub that later became the Duchess of Albany after a number of name changes.

The pub lay between Butcher Row and the New Canal in the area known as the Wood Market where taxis park these days.

In 1817, the household goods of the landlord, Richard Carter, were put up for sale by the order of the Sheriff of Wiltshire

[768]. This would indicate that Carter was severely in debt if not actually bankrupt.

In 1819, John Card became the landlord [5]. As well as running the pub, he also sold musical instruments and taught the playing of most woodwind instruments [769]. His obituary in the *Salisbury and Winchester Journal* when he died in 1825, showed he had had a colourful life [770]. During the American War of Independence, he had accompanied his father who was a sergeant in the Wiltshire Militia, to America and enrolled as a drummer. He was soon appointed to the band of the regiment and later became master of the band. He held this position for over thirty years. His widow, Elizabeth, took over the Roebuck and ran it for a further six months [771].

From 1827 until 1829, the landlord, James Kite, advertised his services as a veterinary surgeon as well as running the pub. In December, 1828, he gave instances of surgery on horses in the *Salisbury and Winchester Journal*, all of which were represented as having given a complete and permanent cure [772]. In September, 1829, he announced that he was leaving the Roebuck as his vet's business had grown so much he was concentrating on that trade [773]. He opened new premises in Culver Street.

In 1840, the annual Salisbury Cucumber Show was held at the Roebuck [774]. Messrs Trollope, Corp and Herod took the prizes and the assembled company enjoyed a good dinner afterwards. The report in the *Journal* also stated that the same three men had won the prizes in a

Roebuck

cucumber show at the Shoulder of Mutton the previous week.

In May, 1869, Isaac Dare, who had been landlord of the Roebuck for over thirty years, was robbed by three men who had been attending the Salisbury Races [775]. They took beds at the pub and the following day spent their time at the Races. When they returned, they ordered supper, and while waiting, one of the three went upstairs to their room. Mr Dare thought nothing of this nor the fact that the man stayed there for over half an hour. When the man returned, the three hurried their supper and seemed anxious to leave. Before their left, taking their luggage, they paid for the room for that night in case they decided to return. They did not return and when, the next morning, Mr Dare took his takings upstairs, he found he had been robbed of about £62 in gold, £2 in silver, three gold watches, two silver watches and six gold rings, representing a considerable value in those days. The police said that since the men had been gone for over twelve hours, they had got clean away and it was unlikely that Mr Dare's property would be recovered.

By 1886, the Roebuck was an Eldridge Pope house. In 1887, the brewery sold off the brewing equipment from the Roebuck as they intended to provide it with beer directly from the brewery [776]. It remained in their ownership until closed on 11th December 1958 [13].

201 Rose & Crown, 18 Harnham Road

The Rose & Crown is one of the earliest inns in Salisbury. The north wing, alongside the road, is of 14th C origin and is said to have been built in 1380. The west wing that runs back towards the river appears to be the same age but was altered in 1963. The south wing, is of later, 16th C construction.

The earliest record found is an indenture of 1680 which shows Bartholomew Haynes selling the property to John Minty [777]. The property is described as: 'All that Messuage or Tenement or Inn commonly called or known by the name of the Rose and Crown And the garden and Close of pasture thereunto adjoining belonging Situate and lying in East Harnham in the County aforesaid And also all that Tenement now converted into Two Tenements containing Four Rooms parcell of the said Messuage or Inn heretofore in the possession of John House & Richard Stanly their assignee or assignees Since in the tenure or occupation of one Lawrence Widdow and John Wilsheire their assignee or assignees And also one Cottage and little Close of pasture there unto adjoining now a garden in Harnham aforesaid

'And also one other Close of pasture ground lying in the Marsh of East Harnham aforesaid called the Marsh ground containing by estimation Two acres (be it more or less) which said Close upon the enclosure of the said Marsh was said to be held and enjoyed to and with the said Tenement or Inn in lieu or recompense of four Beast Lease which did thereunto anciently belong one acre of Meadow lying & being in the Common Meadow of East Harnham aforesaid And also Thirteen acres and one yard of arable Land lying dispersedly in the Common Fields of East Harnham aforesaid And Common of pastures & feedings for Five & Twenty sheep in & upon the Fields downs Commons and Commonable places of East

INVENTORY

Harnham aforesaid And also Common of pastures for Four Rother Beasts and Two house beasts in and upon the Common Fields of East Harnham aforesaid after the Corn thereon grown shall be yearly Cut Ridd and Carried away until the time Beasts leave of feeding in the Same Fields according as hath been heretofore held used and enjoyed to and with the said premises hereby intended to be granted & Conveyed And also Lease pasturage and feeding for one Gelding or Mare to go to pasture and feed in and upon the said ground called the Marsh ground from the Feast of St Michael the Archangel yearly until the last day of February then next following And also all houses outhouses desired buildings orchards gardens lands backsides passages ways paths easements waters watercourses profits Commodities & appurtenances whatsoever to the said Messuage or Tenement or Inn & premises or any or either of them belonging or in anywise appertaining or now or heretofore personally held occupied or enjoyed Leased reputed or taken to be part or parcell thereof.'

Similar documents dating to various years up to 1727 exist in the Wilts and Swindon History Centre.

In July 1755, the *Salisbury and Winchester Journal* reported [778]: 'A very successful Race Meeting. So crowded was the City in general upon this occasion, that our Inns could never have contained the Company if those of Rank and Distinction had not been in private lodgings. Many Gentlemen whose age and infirmities rendered them incapable of attending the Races, were at the Rose & Crown Inn at Harnham leading to the Course, in the highest spirits, expressing a general satisfaction at seeing the Company go by, and paying their respectful compliments, by taking a glass to every individual of any degree or distinction.'

In 1783 a strange occurrence of theft was reported [779]: 'One day last week, a man of Odstock called at the Rose and Crown, Harnham, to drink, and, during his stay there, the landlady had occasion to take her bacon from the rack to cut some for dinner; and soon after going out of the room, and leaving the bacon on the table, the man drew his knife to cut a piece, with an intention, as is supposed, to steal it, but the rind being hard, and his eye upon the door, he drew his knife across his fore finger, and cut it off at the first joint. The thief immediately took to his heels, leaving behind him his intended booty, and also his knife and finger, which may be seen any time, at the abovementioned Inn. So much for stealing bacon.'

An interesting point about this story is that despite the fact that it has not been repeated in any modern guide books on Salisbury, the staff at the Rose & Crown have often been asked by customers (particularly, American persons) if they could see the knife and finger. So the story has got into some publication – suffice it to say the knife and finger no longer exist.

In May, 1784, the inn was purchased by Francis Brown, who had a business as a Stonemason in West Harnham. He felt it necessary to advertise in the *Salisbury and Winchester Journal* that he had not stopped being a stonemason and that orders for stones could be placed at the inn [780]. It is sad to report that in 1790, the young daughter of Mr Brown fell into the river from the garden of the inn and was drowned [781].

The Rose & Crown, being outside of the City boundaries, could undertake activities that pubs within the City could not do. So in 1801, a cock fight was advertised to last three days [782]. It is clear that only the rich could indulge in this sport as the admittance was three shillings each day and the prizes for winning were up to fifty guineas. No doubt, there was a lot of gambling on the outcome of the fights!

In November, 1810, a sad story was reported in the *Salisbury and Winchester Journal* [783]: 'On Tuesday last, about four o'clock in the afternoon, a young woman, not more than twenty, of a very interesting appearance, stopped at the Rose and Crown Inn at East Harnham, in her way from this city, and called for half a pint of beer. The landlady, suspecting her condition, directed the maid servant to endeavour to make her quit the house without delay; the poor creature, probably from fear, left the house, and was seen by a shepherd on Harnham Hill, endeavouring to reach a rick of hay, in a contiguous field, near the road leading to Homington. A short time afterwards, there being a heavy fall of rain, the shepherd went to the same spot for shelter, and, to his great surprise, found that the young person had been delivered of a child, which she was endeavouring to wrap in a handkerchief or cloth; she incoherently said to him, "I am glad you are come, I wanted somebody with me". The shepherd left her with an assurance of returning again; and on his return to Harnham he procured the aid of a benevolent farmer, who, with much difficulty, provided a comfortable accommodation for her at the public house she had lately quitted; he also sent a cart and horse, with a man and two women, to convey her with safety to the place he had so kindly provided for her. To their great surprise and disappointment, neither the mother nor the infant were to be found, and no tidings have hitherto been given of the fate of either. – We shall be glad to be favoured with such information as may tend to unravel this distressful and mysterious affair.'

But the following week, a report showed that the story did not have a happy ending [784]: 'On Friday se'nnight the body of an infant was found in a field at Martin, wrapped in some flannel. The woman and child who disappeared from Harnham on the preceding Tuesday, as noted in our last, were of course brought to recollection by the incident, it being highly probable that this is the infant alluded to. An inquest was taken on the body by Mr Whitmarsh, one of the Coroners for the county; and there being no marks of violence, nor any evidence to show how the body of the infant came in the situation where it was found, the jury brought in a verdict of "Found dead".

'It is proper here to observe that the woman did not experience any harsh treatment at the public house at Harnham; but as she said her home was very near, it was merely considered advisable, on account of her situation, and the approach of evening, that she should not delay setting off.

'It being known that a woman, reported to be a stranger, had been several days ill at a public house at Thickthorn, on the road between this city and Blandford, suspicion was excited that she was the woman above-mentioned, and a gentleman, from motives of humanity, went to the house, in order to ascertain her identity, and relieve her distress. Her person and manner corresponded with the description received of the above woman, but her dress in every respect did not. The landlady asserted that she knew her well, and that she was not the person suspected. Her name is Sarah North, and her parish Poole; but as there are some mysterious circumstances attached to her tale and conduct, it is presumed the parish officers of Critchill will make a strict investigation thereof.'

This story is doubly interesting as it illustrates people's attitudes in these early days.

In the late 1830s, Miss Anne Naish, the daughter of the landlord, Samuel Naish, ran a school for local children at the Rose & Crown [785]. It is not clear exactly when she started this but it is known it was operating in 1837 and she is still unmarried and living at the inn in 1841. The 1841 Census gives her year of birth as 1826 which would suggest she was only 11 years old when she was teaching. But at a later date, after her marriage to John Dawkins, her year of birth is given as 1822 showing her to be 15 in 1837, still very young to be teaching small children but rather more realistic than the later date.

In 1866, Samuel Naish is described as being the owner of the Avon Brewery in Harnham [786]. Since he was also the landlord of the Rose & Crown at this time, it is believed he may have brewed beer in one of the outbuildings of the inn. By 1883, Frank J Naish, the son of Samuel Naish, of the Avon Brewery, advertises that he can supply families with ale in 4½ gallon casks at between ten pence and one shilling and threepence per gallon [787]. The same is advertised in 1884.

Later in 1884, a large part of the furniture and fitments of the inn were put up for sale [788]. This included the brewing plant which seems to mark the end of the Avon Brewery at the Rose & Crown. Also of note are the items from outside of the inn including 'a Capital Spring Van, a Brewers Float, a 4-wheel Phaeton, 4 Sets of Harness, a Bay Nag Mare, deal tables, tressels, stools, 15 Iron and Wood Garden Seats and a Pleasure Boat.

At some time in the 19th C, the ownership of the Rose & Crown came into the hands of the Earl of Radnor. Details of this are not clear but in March, 1888, the inn was leased by the Earl to Herbert Balfour Mew and Edward Aubrey Beverley Elers for 21 years at an annual rent of Fifty pounds per year [789]. During this period, there were a number of different landlords but it is not clear if they were appointed by the leaseholders or if they rented the property from them.

In 1894, there was severe flooding in all of the Avon and Wylye valleys [788] At the Rose & Crown the water was several feet deep. It was said that one old lady nearby, left her son's boots out to dry in the evening and woke the next morning to find them floating in the water in her cottage.

In 1903, the license of the inn was transferred from William Millard to George Charles Hills. There was some discussion in court regarding the license as it was said that the landlord of the inn had for some years hired out boats [791]. However, some of those who hired the boats could not handle them properly and caused a nuisance in the neighbourhood. The Superintendent of Police confirmed that he had received several complaints but that recently the situation had improved.

Continuing the inn's exploitation of its position on the river, in 1909 a one mile swimming race was held in the River Avon by the Sarum Open Air Swimming Club [792]. The contestants gathered at the inn and were then taken by boat up river to the starting point. The swim ended up at what was then known as the Lifeboat Field which is believed to have been in the vicinity of the current Sea Scouts building. Of the 33 contestants, 18 managed to complete the course in the stipulated time while 24 in total completed the course. Swimming was hampered by shallow parts of the river and water weeds. On completion of the activities, a substantial meat tea was held under the trees in the garden of the inn.

In November 1923, the inn was put up for sale and the inventory of the inn described it in the following terms: 'Front Bar with divider to Tap Room, containing full size billiard table and 42 feet of seating with a serving shelf on the partition; Smoking Room; Bay Window Sitting Room; Club Room with 14 foot stained counter; Small Room at end of Club Room; six bedrooms; Kitchen; Scullery, Loft over scullery and Cellar.'

A photo of the inn from about this time shows that it had its own petrol pump near to the carriageway between the north and south wings. Touring by car was becoming a popular way of discovering the countryside and a guide of 1937 describes the inn in the following terms [793]: 'Many a dingy roadside tavern has been restored to its original appearance as in Tudor or Jacobean times, and so becomes worthy of a note in a book on inns. There are many examples of this process: perhaps the best instance is the ancient "Rose and Crown" beside the bridge at Harnham, Salisbury. For forty years, I have known it as a humble roadside pub, scarcely better than a tavern, but a year ago the owners investigated the possibilities. They peeled off vast quantities of paper from the inside, and removed thick layers of plaster from the exterior, thereby exposing beautiful half-timber work nearly five centuries old. Today it is a beautiful old inn, whose charming gardens invite us to dally beside the silvery Avon, in whose waters is mirrored Britain's loveliest cathedral spire.'

A guide of 1952 states that the pre-war refurbishment had been undertaken by Ushers Brewery of Trowbridge. This guide also records that the new wing of the inn had every modern convenience and that some rooms even had their own bathrooms! In 1979, it was stated that the inn had one comfortable bar but it is not known if that referred to the Avon Bar or to the Oak Bar. It is believed that the Avon Bar was considered to be a local public bar whereas the Oak Bar was the hotel bar.

The inn was purchased by Grand Metropolitan who in turn sold it to Queen's Moat Hotels in 1983. It later became part of the Swallow Group of Hotels until the demise of that company in 2006. Swallow Hotels had the habit of selling their hotels to entrepreneurs and then renting them back. Thus, in late 2006, the owners of the property, Aube Properties of Birmingham, appointed Legacy Hotels to operate it on their behalf. In 2014, the Avon Bar was closed and converted into two bedrooms. The Oak Bar continued in use until a new bar was built at the end of the restaurant when the old bar was used as a hotel lounge.

202 Round of Beef, 19 Milford Street

The Round of Beef was on the northwest corner of Milford Street and Brown Street but it is not clear when the building became a public house. In the 1851 Census, Mrs Leah Clifton, a widow, is described as an eating house keeper. Previously, in 1849, she applied for a licence for the Round of Beef which was described as not having been an alehouse, inn or victualing house previously [9]. This application was refused. But a month after the annual licensing session in 1849, an advertisement for the General Steak and Chop House, run by Leah Clifton, states it has Genuine Home Brewed Strong Beer, Ales etc [794]! And, by the time that the premises were advertised as available to rent in 1853, it was described as 'the well-known public house, called the Round of Beef' [795]. But the advertisement stated that the public house was connected with 'the most noted Eating House and Refreshment Rooms in the City'.

John Kinsman took over the pub in 1859. He died in late 1871 and his brother, Levi Kinsman, took over the premises which were still being described as 'the Round of Beef Inn, Dining, Refreshment and Eating House'. Mr Kinsman states in 1872 that it has a large dining room with hot and cold joints of meat every day [796].

In 1878, a respectably dressed young man named Albert Macdonald was refused a drink by Levi Kinsman on the grounds that he was already drunk [797]. Macdonald refused to leave the pub. Mr Kinsman called for the police and Inspector Ainsworth arrived and put Macdonald out of the house. Mr Kinsman stated that Macdonald had been to his house on several occasions and he had never served a better-behaved gentleman in his life. Consequently, Inspector Ainsworth gave Macdonald every chance of going home quietly but, instead, MacDonald followed him back to the police station. Macdonald still behaved in a disorderly manner and the Inspector again gave him every chance to go home. But Macdonald refused to leave the police station and so he was locked up for the night. Owing to Mr Kinsman's testimony about Macdonald's previous character, the Court took a lenient view and fined him forty shillings.

By 1894, the nature of the house seems to have changed from being primarily an eating house to being a public house. A Royal Marines recruiting party is established at the pub [798], recruiting young men both for the Royal Navy and the Royal Marines. This recruiting party visits the pub again in 1895.

By 1903, the pub is owned by Styring's brewery of Tisbury and had probably been under this ownership for some time. The agent for the brewery applied to the Magistrates to put in a temporary manager to the pub as the landlord had left the premises [799]. The police objected to the application as it appeared that neither the manager nor Mr Styring's agent would live on the premises. Eventually, the Magistrates agreed to give Mr Styring a temporary license with him being responsible for the conduct of the premises. Four months later, Mr Styring applied for a license for a new tenant but there must have been various other temporary license holders between the two applications as Mr Styring was warned that this time the new tenant must be permanent. Styring's brewery was purchased by Eldridge-Pope of Dorchester in 1912 and the pub remained under that ownership until it closed.

But in 1928, the pub fell foul of the 1910 Licensing Act which allowed the local authorities to close a public house on the grounds that it was redundant, there being more than enough pubs in the locality to satisfy public demand. A lengthy report was prepared [10]: 'In further pursuance of their policy of reducing the number of licensed houses in the City, the City Justices, after a careful consideration of the matter at several meetings, and unsuccessful attempts to persuade the principal owners to make some suggestions as to reduction, decided that the premises specified above [the Round of Beef], which are situate in one of the areas of the City containing an excessive number of licensed houses, apparently might well be dispensed with. They accordingly instructed the Chief Constable to originate an objection to the renewal of the Licence on the ground of redundancy at the General Annual Licensing Meeting on the 6th February, 1928. This was done, and the question of renewing the Licence adjourned to the Adjourned General Annual Licensing Meeting on the 27th February, 1928. Formal notice of such objection was given and a copy accompanies this report. Evidence of service of the notice was given on the hearing of the objection to renewal.

'Prior to the General Annual Licensing Meeting a notice was received by the Clerk to the Licensing Justices from the Hon. Treasurer of the Salisbury and District Temperance Association giving notice of intention to oppose the renewal of the licence of the same premises "on the grounds that it is unnecessary for the supply of the reasonable requirements of the district in which it is situated." As a matter of fact, at the Adjourned Meeting service of the notice upon the Licensee could not be proved on behalf of the Association, and except for observations tending to show mainly a superfluity of licensed houses in the locality, their grounds of objection were not gone into and do not form part of the case for reference. Mr E J White of Trowbridge acted as the Solicitor for the Association.

'The owners [Eldridge Pope] and tenant [Henry George Few] were represented by Mr Lewis Williams, of the firm of Trethowan and Vincent, Solicitors, Salisbury.

'On the general question, evidence was given that the population of the City, since the recent extension of the borough boundaries, is estimated at 25,461 and that the Licences within the City are as follows:- 67 fully licensed Alehouses, 4 "on" Beerhouses, 3 "off" Beerhouses, 2 Refreshment Houses, and 12 off-Licences for the sale of Wines etc., a total of 88, or 1 in 289 of the population. Three fully licensed houses came into the City on its extension. A plan of a portion of the City on the 1/2500 scale was put in, showing that within a radius of a quarter of a mile from the "Round of Beef" there are 40 fully licensed houses, 2 Refreshment Houses, and 10 shops etc. with "off" licences. The plan accompanies this Report and shows that there are 8 fully licensed houses in Milford Street, including the one in question, and that all these are situated within short distance from each other and from the "Round of Beef". It also shows the close proximity of other licensed premises.

'The present tenant has held the Licence of the "Round of Beef" since February, 1914.

'With regard to the house itself, a plan of the ground floor was put in, and is sent herewith, giving the dimensions of the public rooms, height of ceilings, etc. The only large room is the smoking room, and supervision of this and the remainder of the public portions of the premises is difficult. It was stated that the licensee lives alone in the house, and that although there are five spare bedrooms on the first floor, there is no accommodation for travellers and no meals are served to customers. The sanitary arrangements, which are for men only, are primitive in character. The whole of the stabling has been sub-let.

'The rateable value of the premises is £25.

'Evidence was given by the Sanitary Inspector for the City, mainly as to the private portion of the premises, and on the whole his evidence is unfavourable.

'Observations have been kept upon the numbers of persons entering the premises from 1st to 14th February inclusive, and the result of such observations is shown in the following Schedule: -

Wednesday, 1st February	70
Thursday, 2nd	67
Friday, 3rd	85
Saturday, 4th	126
Sunday, 5th	76
Monday, 6th	72
Tuesday, 7th	122
Wednesday, 8th	67
Thursday, 9th	53
Friday, 10th	71
Saturday, 11th	140
Sunday, 12th	84
Monday, 13th	72
Tuesday, 14th	100
Total for the First week	618.
Total for the Second week	587
Daily average	86

'The figures were given in evidence, and it was also stated that the "Round of Beef" did less trade than any other licensed house in the locality with the exception of the "Catherine Wheel" and the witness (a Police sergeant) suggested it was desirable to retain that licence on account of the stabling and motor accommodation attached to and used with the house.

'No convictions are recorded against the house in the Register of Licences.

'The Tenant gave evidence, and stated that the house had a respectable working-class trade which had increased since he was tenant. He produced a statement of liquors supplied to the house for the three years to 31st December, 1927, a copy of which is as follows:

	a	b	c	d	e
1925	$124\frac{1}{8}$	147	$127\frac{1}{8}$	26	60
1926	$154\frac{3}{4}$	150	$157\frac{3}{4}$	27	$54\frac{1}{2}$
1927	$123\frac{3}{8}$	118	$126\frac{3}{8}$	16	$55\frac{1}{2}$

[Note: a = Malt Liquor (barrels); b = Malt Liquor (dozens ½ pints); c = Malt Liquor (total in barrels); d = Wines (gallons); e = Spirits (gallons)

'On behalf of the Owners an identical statement was produced, and it was stated that they were prepared to make any structural alterations to the house the Bench thought necessary.

'After careful consideration of all the evidence we decided to refer to you the question of the renewal of the Licence on the ground of redundancy, and provisionally renew the same to the Tenant.'

On June 20 1928, it was resolved by the Licensing Authority not to renew the licence and that the compensation to be paid to the owners and the landlord should total £1000. It closed shortly thereafter. However, it can be said that if a modern pub in Salisbury sold nearly 5 kilderkins of draught beer and over five gallons of spirits a week and had a daily average of 86 persons visiting it, they would be considered to be doing quite well!

The building remained unoccupied for a time but was said to have been demolished in 1930. A new building was constructed but it is clear that the roof line of the current structure is identical to that shown in earlier photos of the Round of Beef. This building was purchased by the local Conservative Association in 1931 and the Morrison Hall developed in memory of Mr Hugh Morrison. The front part of the building facing onto Milford Street became a gentlemen's outfitters.

203 Royal, High Street

It is not exactly clear where this inn was. The Salisbury First General Entry Book shows that in 1405, 5 shillings were spent for the repair of the bridge over the common ditch next to the Ryole [800]. There are also references in the Chamberlain's roll of 1453 to old timber sold from the bridge near le Ryall in High Street, for the making of the common trench in High Street opposite Le Ryol and for timber for the trench in High Street opposite Le Ryolle. In 1455 there is a rent of assize from le Robe in High Street when John ate Bergh was the landlord. It is possible that the later inn, the Fountain, which was either on or next to the Assembly Rooms on the corner of the Canal and High Street was on the site of the Royal.

204 Royal George, 17 Bedwin Street

The Royal George is of 15th C origin but there is little to see of an inn of this period. The front of the inn facing the road is of the 19th C.

The inn was originally called the Stone Bridge but it is not clear where this name originated from. It is possible that the name may have come from the fact that one of the streams that ran through Salisbury crossed Bedwin Street in the vicinity of the pub. The pub had that name until 1805 when it became the Crown. This name has not been associated with the pub before this publication. However, the dates on which the Crown in Bedwin Street appears in the licensing records exactly matches a gap between records of the Stone Bridge and that of the Royal George. It operated under that name until 1822 when the landlord, John Burden, renamed it the Royal George. It is most likely that pub was named after the Royal George, a 100-gun first-rate, launched in 1788 and the flagship of Admiral Sir John Duckworth during the Alexandria expedition of 1807. There is a possibility that the landlord at the time that the pub's name was changed served on this ship. This ship was broken up in 1822 which may or may not have been a coincidence.

It has often been said that some of the timbers of the pub came from the Royal George that sunk at Spithead in 1782. Although timbers were recovered from this ship, this does not appear to have happened until 1842 during the salvage operations commanded by Major-General Charles Pasley.

Haskins states that the Stone Bridge

was licensed as an alehouse to Peter Pearce in 1760 [20]. However, there is a list of alehouses licensed in 1743 that shows that Peter Pearce was the landlord at this time [15].

Pub life could be violent in earlier days (has it changed?). In 1775, the *Salisbury and Winchester Journal* reported [801]: 'On Tuesday last Jerry Lucas, a bricklayer, who was drinking at the Stone Bridge, began to lash the landlord Mr Hodges with his apron in a kind of a joke; however, continuing it too long & not leaving off when he was desired, Mr Hodges gave him a blow with a battledore, on which Lucas struck him with his fist, and knocked him down. Unhappily by the fall Mr Hodges' skull was fractured, & notwithstanding immediate assistance was procured from the Faculty, he survived only till Friday night at 11 o'clock, when he expired in great agonies. Jury's verdict, Manslaughter. Lucas absconded, but was caught and brought to justice. Mr Hodges left a wife and five small children.'

In 1776, it was noted that the validity of the title of the late Mr John Hodges to the inn formerly called the Stone Bridge but now called the Royal George was addressed [802]. Despite this reference, the inn continued to be called the Stone Bridge for another 30 years.

In the records of the September, 1804, annual licensing session the pub is shown as licensed to John Creaven at the Stone Bridge [4]. But there is a pencilled-in entry for the Crown licensed to William Cole. In November, 1805, the Mayor and Justices met to consider an application for a licence for the Stone Bridge [4]. It is probable that this application was for a full licence since it was noted in 1760 that it had been granted a licence as an alehouse. A week later, the licensing records show William Cole receiving the license for the Crown. Suffice it to say that at some time in 1805, William Cole took over the pub and renamed it the Crown.

In 1822, the landlord of the Crown, Henry Swift, applied for a renewal of his license but for some reason not given, the application was refused [5]. John Burden took over the pub on 30 Sept 1822 and by the 1823 annual licensing session it is shown as the Royal George with John Burden still the landlord. Perhaps he changed the name to emphasise that it was under new management after whatever difficulty had affected Henry Swift.

By 1841, the pub is advertised to let with immediate possession being available [803]. Particulars of the pub could be obtained from the tenant, Elizabeth Waters, or from Mr Pain's brewery in Castle Street. This suggests that the pub was owned by the Castle Street Brewery. But by 1875, the pub is clearly obtaining at least some of its beer from Bailey's brewery at Frome. A court case was heard relating to a dispute between the landlord of the pub and the Frome brewery as to whether a cask of beer had or had not been delivered [804]. The report on the case also suggests that Bailey's brewery actually owned the pub. But, in 1886, the pub is included as a separate lot in the sale of the Castle Street Brewery [805]. Up until that year, the Castle Street Brewery had been leased by Herbert Mew and he moved to Milford Street as the lease expired. So there is some doubt as to who owned the pub!

The pub was a Gibbs Mew house for most of the 20th C but this ceased when the brewery closed in 1997. In the mid-1970s, the public bar was used by the bikers of Salisbury. There were shelves along the side of the bar for crash helmets and when the requirement for motorcycles to have front number-plates was stopped in 1975, many of the bikers nailed their plates to the pub beams. Before the pub ceased to be a Gibbs Mew house, the pub had been updated by combining its three small bars into one bar while retaining much of its character.

205 Royal Oak, 59 Culver Street

This pub was on the east side of Culver Street roughly half way between Payne's Hill and Milford Hill. The site is now covered by the Culver Street car park.

The pub was quite distinct from the Royal Oak in Milford Street and opened (or was renamed) at about the time that the Milford Street premises closed. It is possible that this pub was known by a different name at earlier times (possibly the Nags Head) but there seems to be a large gap between the closing of these other pubs and the opening of the Royal Oak.

The pub seems to have opened around 1833 when Charles Sainsbury became the first landlord. Mr Sainsbury was fined 40 shillings in 1834 for allowing tippling in his house [6]. Later, an advertisement of December, 1836, states that the Royal Oak in Culver Street is available to let with applicants asked to apply to Charles Sainsbury to view the premises [806].

In 1854, the landlord, John Gray, was working in his Brewhouse when a man called Joseph Andrews entered the pub and immediately walked upstairs and stole a watch and one pound eight shillings in silver and copper coins [807]. Mrs Gray heard a noise and called her husband, but, being busy, he did not take much notice. But shortly after, he saw Andrews climb out of a window and drop from the roof into the garden. Mr Gray gave chase and saw Andrews throw the money away and drop the watch. He was arrested by the Police and committed for trial. By 1861, the Census returns show John Gray to be a retired publican and living in Milford Street.

In 1889, the landlord, Thomas Pavitt was charged with having permitted drunkenness in his premises [808]. Two policemen had entered the pub and they decided that a man named Finch, who was in the smoking room, was extremely drunk. They questioned Mr Pavitt about this but he stated that there was no person in his pub that was drunk. He gave evidence, supported by further evidence from his wife and a barman, that Finch had entered his pub in a sober manner and had ordered a pint of ale plus a pint of beer in a bottle to take home for his wife's supper. He later left the pub and walked home by himself. Despite the evidence, Mr Pavitt was found guilty but, as the Magistrates did not consider it to be a serious case, they fined him only ten shillings.

The pub continued in trade into the 20 C. and is mentioned in Arthur Maidment's book, 'I remember, I remember'. The pub was closed in early 1938 and its licence transferred to the new Royal Oak in Devizes Road on 7th February 1938.

206 Royal Oak, Devizes Road

The Royal Oak obtained its licence on 7th February 1938 when the Royal Oak in Culver Street was closed. The last landlord of the Culver Street premises, Herbert

Bailey, also moved to the new Royal Oak. It was built to serve the development of housing in Devizes Road and the surrounding area. The pub had two bars with the saloon bar offering a fine view across the Avon valley to Old Sarum. It was a Gibbs Mew house from the time of its opening until the pubs owned by the company were purchased by Enterprise Inns in 1998.

After minor changes to the pub, it was extensively refurbished in 2009.

It is of note that Strong's Brewery of Romsey applied for planning permission for a pub in Queen Alexandra Road in February, 1937 [809]. The site was just a short distance from the Royal Oak, opposite the entrance to Heath Road in Queen Alexandra Road. The plans submitted show that it was intended to have three bars: a public bar, a saloon bar and a private bar; and a jug and bottle off-sales area. It is not known if Gibbs Mew and Strong's were involved in a competition to provide a new public house to serve the Bemerton Heath area or whether Strong's just hoped to gain planning permission instead of Gibbs Mew. Perhaps the fact that Gibbs Mew were able to close a pub in the city centre as an offset to the new licensed premises swung any argument between the two proposed premises. (note in the cross-reference of pubs, this proposed pub is shown as the 'Romsey Arms')

207 Royal Oak, Milford Street

This pub was on the corner of Culver Street and Milford Street. It was known as the Angel or Archangel until sometime later than 1765 and became the Royal Oak by 1787. Haskins states that the Angel was licensed sometime in the period 1635 to 1685 [18]. There is a document at the WSHC dated 10 Feb 1669 which appears to lease land for 50 years to William Bishop and gives him permission to build a new messuage or tenement [810]. However, by 1679 William Bishop was informed upon for not declaring beer he had brewed and strong spirits he had distilled. No record of whether he was convicted or not has been found!

In 1746, a printed licence was produced granting Elizabeth Harrison the right to sell Beer, Ale and cider: [811]: 'To Wit, We His Majesty's Justices of the Peace for the said City at our General Meeting whose Names are hereunto subscribed (whereof One is of the Quorum) do Allow and License Elizabeth Harrison in the said city to keep a common Ale-House or Victualling-House, to utter and sell Bread and other Victuals, and to sell Beer, Ale, Cyder, by Retail, to be drank in the Same House, wherein he now dwelleth, as aforesaid, and not elsewhere, until the next General Licensing of Victuallers for the said City so as the true Assize in her Bread, Beer and Ale be duly kept; and no unlawful Games, Drunkenness or any other Disorder suffered in her House, Garden, or Backside, but that good Order and Rule be maintained therein, according to the Laws of the Realm, in that Behalf made and provided. For the due Observance whereof, the said Victualler is forthwith to enter into Recognizances, with Sureties, according to the Statute. Given under our Hands and Seals this Twenty Second Day of September in the twentieth Year of the Reign of our Sovereign Lord George the Second by the Grace of God of Great-Britain, France, and Ireland, King, Defender of the Faith, and in the Year of our Lord 1746.

'Signed Tho. Smith, Mayor; Tho.. Wentworth; Daniel Floyes.'

The name of the pub was hand written on the bottom of this licence.

In 1755, the pub is named as the Angel & Crown in an advertisement in the *Salisbury and Winchester Journal* [812]. This states that 'there is a person come to Salisbury from London, & is now at the sign of the Angel & Crown in Culver Street, where he rivets China-Ware of any sort in a very secure and neat manner ... with Brass Rivets'.

In 1787, the death of a young man at the Royal Oak provoked an editorial outburst from the *Salisbury and Winchester Journal* [813]: 'On Thursday last an inquest was taken before the Coroner of this City on the body of Richard Young, a shop-keeper, in Brown Street, who died almost suddenly on the preceding evening, at the Royal Oak, on Milford Hill; and it appearing by the evidence adduced to the Jury, that he died of an apoplectic fit, occasioned by excessive drinking, they gave their verdict accordingly – We are happy to find the attention of the Magistrates has lately been roused in most parts of the Kingdom, by his Majesty's late proclamation for the suppression of vice and immorality; and it is sincerely hoped that this laudable spirit of reform, thus happily excited, will become universal. Among the many objects that naturally present themselves to our observation as requiring regulation, it has been justly observed that no description of nuisances seem more to require the immediate and serious attention of the police than that of public ale-houses, and particularly those of the lower class; a rigorous reformation, or rather a total suppression of many of them, is now become necessary, and would probably be attended with the most salutary consequences amongst the lower ranks of the people, by whom alone such houses are frequented, and who there too often meet with incitements to drunkenness, lewdness, gambling, and every other species of debauchery, immorality, and profaneness. The untimely act of the above-mentioned unhappy young man, which happened in one of these houses, adds another to the many instances that daily occur of the necessity of such a reform.'

In 1799, the sale of a lease on the Royal Oak was advertised [814]: 'A Plot or Parcel of Ground, part of the Old Town Ditch, and the bank or mound on the west side thereof, with a Messuage or Public House, erected on part of the said ditch, bearing the sign of the Royal Oak, in Milford Street; the whole extending from Milford Street to St Anns Street aforesaid, part whereof is paled around, and used as a pleasure garden and shrubbery, facing the above dwelling, and other part as a kitchen garden and pleasure ground. These premises are also held on lease under the said Corporation for a term of 40 years from Michaelmas 1794, at a quit rent of £1 14 s.'

It is clear from this lease that the Royal Oak in Culver Street was built on part of the land belonging to the Royal Oak in Milford Street since the later Royal Oak was on the east side of Culver Street between Milford Street and St Anns Street. The Milford Street premises last appears in the licensing records in 1811 when William Trimby was the landlord [4].. In 1855, a continuation of this lease was surrendered to the Mayor and Corporation. It stated that the property that was formerly the

Royal Oak but had been converted into a private dwelling [810].

208 Running Horse, 41/43 Winchester Street

The Running Horse was on the north side of Winchester Street. Several publications state that it became the Coach and Horses but it can be said that by 1795, when it is clear that the Coach & Horses was in Winchester Street, the Running Horse was already well established. The Kingdom & Shearm map of Salisbury dated 1854 (that was used to plan Salisbury's sewage system!) clearly shows the Running Horse on the east side of the Coach and Horses. However, the Running Horse was known as the Hand & Flowers in the mid-18th C.

Suffice it to say, Haskins states that in 1759, James Scott was granted a licence as an inn for the Hand and Flower in Winchester Street [19].

In 1768, an unfortunate series of events was started at the Running Horse [815]: 'On Monday the 25th ult., the body of a person who had been most barbarously murdered was found thrown into a pit on the road's side near Coombe, about two miles from this City, supposed to have been done at the beginning of the fall of snow, as the legs and thighs were still covered with it ... the next day the Coroner's Inquest sat on it, and brought in their verdict Wilful Murder by some person or persons unknown ... Upon enquiry, he appears to be a travelling Jew, Woolfe by name between 30 and 40 years of age, who lodged on Sunday night the 27th of last month at the Running Horse in this city, where he also breakfasted the next morning, and went from thence about nine o'clock with his box at his back and enquired the way to Coombe ... It was presently concluded that John Curtis (as he called himself) a sailor (who came into town the very day, and a few hours after the Jew went out, and pretended he had been robbed and wounded on the Blandford road about 2 miles off, and was therefore had to our Infirmary to be cured as mentioned in this *Journal* of the 4th ult.) was the very man that committed the murder, and accordingly the Coroner immediately issued his warrant, and sent two persons with it to Gosport after him, where he was taken the same day aboard the Achilles man of war, and carried before Edward Bedford Esq, Justice of the Peace for the county of Hants, who committed him to the house of correction at Gosport, from whence he is to be moved this day to the city gaol.'

John Curtis made some half-hearted attempts at suicide in Winchester Gaol while on his way to Salisbury. He arrived at Fisherton Gaol on the 7th February, 1768, and was brought in front of the Justices on March 10 when he was sentenced to death. He was executed on March 14th and his body hung in chains near the scene of the murder [816]. Abraham Woolf, from Portsmouth distributed some copper pieces that had the motto on one side 'John Curtis hung in chains 14th March 1768' and on the other side 'For the murder of Woolf Myers; engraved by I Levi in Sarum'.

In 1775, another unfortunate event occurred at the Running Horse [817]: 'On Thursday evening a young man came into the Running Horse in Winchester St, and asked for a lodging for the night: after calling for three pints of beer, which he shared with the company then present, he desired to have ½ pint of small beer to carry to bed with him; but before he had been upstairs ten minutes an uncommon noise was heard, when the landlady going up to enquire the reason of, found her guest swelled to a great degree, and (as plain as he could speak) desiring a doctor. Mr Randal the apothecary was sent for, who imaging he had swallowed poison treated him accordingly, which in a few minutes had a very happy effect. He would confess nothing, but that he had bought a dose of salts at Portsmouth, which he took to ease him of an internal pain; but as he remains at present in a deep salivation, it is conjectured his intention was to destroy himself, as he confessed the dose he took was a white powder, & had not his body been in the most violent agitation it was in the power of medicine to accomplish he could not possibly have survived.'

The following week, the *Salisbury and Winchester Journal* reported that the young man had died but, as it was thought that he had been given the wrong powder by accident, the verdict of the Coroner was accidental death [818].

In 1813, the lease of the Running Horse was for sale and it was described as 'an old-established Free Public House, the sign of the Running Horse, Winchester Street, Salisbury, replete with every convenience for brewing, all the utensils and stores being quite perfect, and in excellent condition [819]. The Stock to be taken at a valuation, and will amount to from £200 to £300'.

A Polish man named Matthew Gally, who was a hawker, was robbed of his mahogany box, containing jewellery and his Hawker's license in December, 1822 [820]. It was believed he was robbed by a Russian man who he had been travelling with and who had also been staying at the Running Horse. This Russian went by the name of Herman but it was thought that he would use the name of Gally so that he could sell the jewellery legally. The Polish man who was robbed was said to be illiterate and left in great distress but insisted on offering a reward of four pounds.

Edmund Crouch, the landlord, died in January, 1840, at the age of 74 and was said to have been the oldest publican in the City at this time [821]. His son, William, left the King's Head in Westbury to take over the Running Horse [822]. But within three months, the stock of the pub, together with the furniture and brewing equipment were offered for sale [823]. This may have been because William Crouch brought such items with him from Westbury. Suffice it to say he stayed on at the Running Horse until he died after a protracted illness in October, 1841.

The last recorded landlord was Thomas Braxton in 1855 and, by 1857, the site of the pub was offered to the Council as one of a number of possible sites for a new Police station [824].

209 Salisbury Arms, 31/35 Endless Street

This is on the site of the Endless Street Brewery on the west side of Endless Street between Chipper Lane and Scot's Lane. It appears to have opened in February 1809 when Henry Macklin 'begs leave to inform his Friends and the Public, that he intends opening his Tap, in Endless Street, on Monday the 13th instant, for selling Good Home Brewed Beer, full measure, at a reasonable price' [825]. The premises became known as Macklin's

Tap. In 1819, William Crumley took over the premises [5] and it became, naturally, Crumley's Tap. He let the pub to Thomas Chamberlain (Chamberlain's Tap) but he kept the pub for only about a year before it was advertised again as available to rent as Chamberlain was leaving owing to ill health [826]. But in July, 1830, Thomas Chamberlain was declared bankrupt [827] and so this was probably the real reason for him leaving the Tap.. However, by September of that year, it was announced that the commission of bankruptcy was superseded, and that hence all his debts were to be paid [828].

William Crumley is shown in the licensing records as having taken the pub back into his ownership but this could have only been for a short time as in November, 1830, the pub is advertised to let or to be sold as William Crumley was deceased [829]. Thomas Wolferstan took over the premises which of course, became known as Wolferstan's Tap [6].

In 1838, William Fawcett purchased the Endless Street Brewery which included the Tap [830]. He rented the pub to George Bridger who remained the landlord until 1849 with it being known as Bridger's Tap [831]. In 1839, one of George Bridger's servants went down into the cellar of the Tap and found it to be knee-deep in beer and froth [832]! It was found that the cork at the bottom of a twenty-seven hogshead cask of strong beer had come out and something more than seventeen hogsheads of beer (more than 900 gallons) had flooded the cellar.

After George Bridger left the Tap, it became known as Fawcett's Tap. By 1901, it was known as the Endless Street Brewery Tap. Fawcett's Brewery was taken over by the Lamb Brewery of Frome in 1912 and it is probable that the pub was renamed the Salisbury Arms at that time. It is also probable that the present building dates from about 1912. Lamb Brewery was in turn taken over by Usher's of Trowbridge in 1957. In 1974, the pub became a Chef and Brewer house within the Watney Mann group. Now a free house that names itself as the Craft Bar at the Salisbury Arms selling bottled craft beers and a variety of food.

210 Saracen's Head, 44 Blue Boar Row

The Saracen's Head was in Blue Boar Row about one third of the Row from Endless Street (where there was a chemist's shop recently). Some records suggest that it was part of the Blue Boar Inn but it is clear from correspondence concerning the Common Brewhouse that in 1625, the two inns were different premises. Haskins states that John Sevyer, of the Saracen's Head, attended the meeting called by the Council to discuss inns taking beer and ale from the Common Brewhouse [18].

An indenture of 1636 describes the sale of a messuage or tenement 'between the lands of Robert Eyre Esquire wherein Thomas Batter now dwells called and known by the name of the Blue Boar on the west part And the lands of John Seviour called the Saracen's Head on the east and north parts and the market place of the said City of New Sarum on the south part [833].' This clearly indicates the existence of both the Blue Boar and the Saracen's Head in that year.

In May, 1771, the landlord of the Saracen's Head, James Linton, added some unusual information to his advertisement in the *Salisbury and Winchester Journal* [834]: 'Saracen's Head Sarum. I beg leave to return thanks to all my friends & customers for their past favours & hope for a continuance of the same; and as a mistaken report has been set about that the smallpox has been at the said house, I do now certify that it is not, nether has it been during my time, which has been ten years. In April last my children were inoculated by Messrs Tatum & Hick at their house at Laverstock and not brought home till they were well and clean. Neat Wines, Brandy, Rum etc etc by Their most humble servant James Linton.'

In 1780, evidence of smuggling that was rife at this time is provided by the sale at the Saracen's head of 51 casks of Spirituous Liquors, consisting of Brandies Rums & Hollands Gin, the same having been seized for unlawful importation [835].

In 1782, on the death of her husband, James, Judith Linton announced that she would continue running the inn [836]. But by 1783, the sale of the property of Judith is advertised on her death. The property consisted of bedheads, and furniture, feather-beds, blankets, quilts, chests of drawers, tables, chairs, looking glasses, and a variety of useful kitchen furniture, an eight-day clock, fowling piece, and a pony, warranted good and sound [837].

In 1841, the Salisbury Annual Cucumber show took place at the inn [838]. Three prizes were awarded for the best cucumbers and a dinner was held after the judging. After dinner, many observations were made on the science of horticulture and floriculture. The report in the *Salisbury and Winchester Journal* said that the company did not separate until a late hour.

In 1843, Lieutenant Hill, RN, summoned Mr Shuker, the landlord of the Saracen's Head Inn, before the city magistrates, charging him with breach of the law respecting conveyance of letters [839]. It appears that a letter was sent to the Lieutenant demanding payment of a debt, the letter being sent by the hands of a special messenger rather than through the post. It was proved that Mr Shuker knew nothing whatever of the matter, the letter in question having been written by his legal advisor. The case broke down against Mr Shuker, and the magistrates decided that sending a special messenger with a letter like the present was not an infraction of the law.

Joseph Rolls took over the inn after Mr Shuker was declared bankrupt. It was reopened in January, 1848, after undergoing repairs and alterations. Mr Rolls stated that care had been taken to arrange the Smoking-Room and Parlours in such a manner as to ensure the comfort of those who might honour him with their support [840].

In 1866, William Thomas was charged with having stolen a few shillings in copper and a large number of cigars from the inn [841]. Mrs Doughty, the landlady, found a window broken from the inside when she went downstairs in the morning and also found that the bar door had been unlocked from the inside. The landlord of the Green Dragon said that Thomas had paid for a room at his pub the previous night but had not slept there. Thomas came into the Green Dragon early in the morning and asked the landlord to look after a parcel for him. After Thomas was arrested, the parcel was opened and found to contain cigars of the same type as had been stolen from the Saracen's Head. Thomas claimed that they had been sold to him by 'Bristol Jack' Thomas was committed for trial at the next Assizes. There he was found guilty and sentenced to nine month's hard labour.

The Saracen's Head closed in 1876 [842] and was pulled down in 1882. The area was rebuilt by 1890 with the buildings that can be seen nowadays dating from then. Interestingly, an early photograph said to date from the 1850s, reproduced in Plate 14 of RCHM, clearly shows the Saracen's Head.

211 Sarasynhede, Catherine Street

This inn was described in 1455 in Bishop Beauchamp's Liber Niger as being a corner Tenement in Catherine Street and thus is probably not the Saracen's Head in Blue Boar Row.

212 Sawyer's Arms, Bugmore

The few records of the Sawyer's Arms describe it as being in Bugmore but it is believed that it was in St Ann Street. Haskins states that that it was granted a licence as an alehouse in 1772 [20] but by 1779, there was an auction of a house that was 'late the Sawyer's Arms in Bugmore' [843].

213 Shearmen's Arms, Fisherton

Nothing more is known of this pub except that Haskins states that John Bungay was granted a licence for it as an alehouse in 1741 [21].

214 Shipp, St Nicholas Road

Very little is known of this inn other than a reference in a marriage contract of 1740 between Martha Elderton and Ambrose Burch that describes the building and lands that will be changing hands and includes the following [844]: 'All that Messuage or Tenement lately called or known by the name of the Shipp with the appurtenances thereunto belonging situate in Harnham within the liberty of the Close of New Sarum part of the Capital Messuage & Site of the late dissolved College or Hospital of St Nicholas De Vaux near the City of New Sarum, And all that Garden now walled in and enjoyed with the said Messuage or Tenement.

The description seems to match de Vaux Lodge on the corner of de Vaux Place and St Nicholas Road but this attribution cannot be proved.

215 Shoulder of Mutton, Bridge Street

The Shoulder of Mutton was on the corner of Bridge Street and St Thomas's Square. It is stated in RCHM that it was of late 18th or early 19th C. construction but it had been in existence since at least the early 18th C. so it may have been rebuilt at some stage.

There is a reference to Widow Webb at the Shoulder of Mutton in 1721 but Haskins states that it was licensed as an alehouse to Austin Ledbury in 1743 [20]. In 1739 and 1740 it was advertised that horses to be entered in the annual Salisbury Races should be notified to Austin Ledbury at the Shoulder of Mutton [845].

In 1765, Joseph Haytor became the landlord but in later years (certainly by 1778) he was operating as a carrier between Salisbury and Southampton: this was described in an advertisement from 1780 [846]: 'Haytor, (late Judd) Salisbury,

Romsey and Southampton Carrier, removed from the Royal George to Mr Cox's, the Vine Inn, (the next door) near the Quay, Southampton, where parcels etc., are taken in – begs leave to inform his friends and the public, that a Waggon, will set out from his house at the Shoulder of Mutton, near Fisherton Bridge, Salisbury, every morning at six o'clock, and arrive at Southampton every evening, having entered into partnership with Samuel Barney, of Southampton, who will attend the arrival of the waggon, and see the goods are immediately and carefully delivered, and the Proprietors hope, by assiduity in their respective situations, to meet the future commands of an indulgent public, whose favours will ever be gratefully acknowledged by Their Humble Servants Jas. Haytor & Sam. Barney.'

Joseph Haytor later advertises in the *Salisbury and Winchester Journal* in 1783 [847]: 'Whereas a false report has been industriously propagated against Joseph Hayter, at the Shoulder of Mutton, in this city, That the Bailiffs were in possession of his effects in his house on an execution, and which report has been circulated to many of his friends and creditors; he therefore takes the liberty to acquaint the public, That he never, directly or indirectly, gave or confessed to any person any judgement, or executed any Bill of Sale, or other conveyance of his property whatsoever: And in contradiction to the said false, scandalous report, he desires all persons to whom he is indebted to send their bills immediately, and they shall be discharged, by their humble servant, J Hayter.'

But something strange happens at about this time. Joseph Hayter advertises the Shoulder of Mutton as being for sale in January, 1785 [848], and the licensing records clearly show that Ruth Wansborough was the licensee in the autumn of 1785 [2] followed by Samuel Loveden in 1787 until in 1789 when Joseph Haytor once more advertises the sale of the business [849]. What happened between 1785 and 1789 is not known except that he advertises in the *Salisbury and Winchester Journal* late in 1788 that he is still running the carrier service to Southampton from the Shoulder of Mutton. He also states that he still runs the inn 'notwithstanding the endeavours of a cruel party'! It seems that he may have retained ownership of the inn but concentrated on his carrying business with another person acting as landlord (or landlady!). Finally, John Highmore takes the inn in late 1789 [850].

In the meantime, an unusual event was reported in the *Salisbury and Winchester Journal* in August, 1785 [851]: 'The following extraordinary affair presented itself here on Tuesday evening: The son of Mr Joseph Hayter, landlord of the Shoulder of Mutton public-house, going into a lumber-room adjoining the dwelling-house for a besom, saw the legs of a man concealed, and immediately went and told his mother thereof; but she considering his tale merely a story, laughed at him and bid him go back. The lad at this burst into tears, and persisting on his account, search was made after the fellow. On examining the said premises, there was found knives, forks, dishes, the remainder of a gammon of bacon, etc etc but the villain had taken alarm, and made his escape. On searching further, a communication was discovered to an adjoining hay-loft, and there, concealed in the hay, was found a Negro Lad, about 18 years old, who was immediately secured,

Shoulder of Mutton

and on his examination, confessed, that he was ordered to lay there by "Richard", his accomplice; that they had been concealed in the house three nights; that he had been enticed by Richard, who had pulled him in at a window; that in the day-time they lay concealed, and at night, after the family were asleep, they provided themselves with apparel, provisions, liquor etc from below stairs. On Wednesday morning, he was re-examined before the Mayor, and fully committed for trial. On Thursday "Richard", his supposed accomplice, being one Richard Baish, of Wilton, was apprehended there, but for want of sufficient evidence was on Saturday discharged. – A quantity of gunpowder was found in the haunt of the negro and there is reason to suppose they intended to have made a general plunder of the house, and then to have set it on fire by the gunpowder, thereby preventing a discovery of the robbery.'

In 1790, George Soul took over the inn and announced that he was also opening an Eating House on the premises [852]. In 1792, George Soul had seven gallons of foreign gin confiscated as its presence had not been notified to the authorities [3]. Overall, George Soul does not appear to have been successful in his business endeavours as all his property at the Shoulder of Mutton was sold in February 1793 [853].

Thomas Heywood, who took over the inn in 1803, also described himself as a dealer in hay and corn. From 1805 through to 1811, he regularly advertised that he had Clover Hay, Meadow Hay, Sainfoin, Oats, Bran, Corn and Straw for sale [854]. It is doubtful that he kept these goods on the premises but he undoubtedly took orders at the Shoulder of Mutton. On his death in about 1820, his widow, continued to run the pub until 1829.

A lease of 1830 describes the site of the Shoulder of Mutton [855]: '...were bounded on the east by the road or way leading to the Town Mill, on the south by the public street or highway leading from Fisherton Bridge to the High Street in the said City of New Sarum, on the west by the Dwelling house and premises of William Dyer and the River Avon and on the north by waste lands leading to the said Mill... {855}'.

The *Salisbury and Winchester Journal* of 21st May, 1832, published a short conundrum: "Why is the Shoulder of Mutton Inn, Salisbury, like the Needles, in the Isle of Wight?" [856]. The answer was that they were both occupied by sea fowls! The landlord at the time was a certain Charles Fowles.

In 1833, the landlords of the Shoulder of Mutton and the New Inn advertised that they would have a stand at the Salisbury Races where refreshments of the best quality could be obtained [857]. An interesting comment on social values at the time is given by them stating that 'the upper Apartment of the Stand will be appropriated for Wines, Spirits, Bottled Porter, Beer, and Cider, and the lower Department for Draught Beer and Cider'.

In 1864, George Creed at the Shoulder of Mutton also described himself as a manufacturer of soda water, Lemonade and Ginger Beer [858]. Despite the fact that he states that he has run this business for several years, the only advertisements for these refreshments that have been found are from his time at the Shoulder of Mutton. In 1861, he had been landlord of the George & Dragon in Castle Street and by 1871, he is living at the Wheatsheaf in Wilton and described as a retired innkeeper and living with his daughter and son–in–law (the landlord). So one can only suppose that the soda water business was not completely successful!

Transcriptions of the 1881 Census show the pub as being the Bridge Inn with the licensee being William George Knight. However, if one looks at an image of the actual Census return, the words 'The Shoulder of Mutton' are written in pencil alongside the entry.

The inn continued in trade into the 20th C. when it was described as having two bars separated by a long corridor that ran alongside the Town Mill Yard. It was a Gibbs Mew house from at least 1932 until it closed on 27th November 1959 and was demolished in 1962 to make way for the current buildings.

216 Six Bells, Winchester Street

The Six Bells was on the corner of Winchester Street and Greencroft Street most probably on the western corner. It appears to have been known as the Rose & Crown in the 17th C. and became the Six Bells in about 1743. By 1767, it was known as the Coach and Six but when Joseph Rogers rebuilt the inn in 1779 it reverted to the name of the Six Bells.

Haskins states that it was licensed as the Rose and Crown between 1635 and 1685 [18]. He also states that by 1743 it was known as the Six Bells when John Gray was granted a license [19]. It was said that it was an important coaching inn and was said to have a frontage of 84 feet in Winchester Street but 164 feet in Greencroft Street where the entrance to its stabling and garden was.

In 1776, the inn was advertised as being for sale [859]. It is likely that it was bought by Joseph Rogers who later, in 1779, advertised the 'Six Bells (a new built Messuage or Inn) to Lett, enquire of Joseph Rogers' [860].. This attempt to let the inn was unsuccessful as later in the year the following advertisement was placed in the *Salisbury and Winchester Journal* [861]: 'Joseph Rogers from the Star has "rebuilt that ancient Inn called the Six Bells in Winchester St." and made very convenient with cellars, stabling, coach-house & garden, & every other conveniency for the public business.'

Finally, Joseph Rogers advertised it to let in 1780 [862] and it appears to have been taken by George Cave.

By 1798, there is the first advertisement in the *Salisbury and Winchester Journal* for a coach running from the Six Bells [863]: 'Six Bells Inn, Winchester Street, Salisbury. Richard Loder (from the Coach and Horses, Stockbridge), has taken and entered on the above House, has laid in a good assortment of Liquors, furnished it with good Beds and Beddings, with every accommodation for Travellers and others; and he has most excellent Stabling, he with confidence solicits the favours of those friends who visited him at Stockbridge, and of the Public at large, which he will endeavour to return by the most grateful attention to their comfort and accommodation in his house.

'He will continue to run the Telegraph or Royal Mail (with a Guard), from Salisbury to Portsmouth, which, after taking from the Plymouth and Exeter Coaches, sets out from the said Six Bells, Salisbury, every night at half past twelve o'clock, on its way to Portsmouth, passing through Stockbridge, Winchester, Waltham, Wickham, and Fareham, to the Crown Inn, High Street, Portsmouth, where it arrives every morning at half past nine o'clock.

'It leaves Portsmouth every afternoon at half past five o'clock, and at Cosham, not far from thence, it meets the Chichester, Brighthelmston and Lewes Coaches, from which it takes all the passengers and parcels for Salisbury and the West of England. It arrives at the Bell and Crown, Winchester, at ten, and reaches the Six Bells Inn, Salisbury every morning at two o'clock.

'The general utility of this Carriage must be obvious to every person, as by its means, a communication is effected between the ports of Portsmouth and Plymouth, and indeed a great part of the kingdom, with an expedition almost incredible, and with that attention to the safety of persons, and the care of property, which shall be exceeded by none.'

It is worth noting how well developed the network of coach routes was by this time. In 1799, the inn nearly met disaster when a fire broke out [864]: 'Yesterday morning, about half past four o'clock, a fire broke out in the Stables of the Six Bells Inn, in Winchester Street, which threatened devastation over a great part of the neighbourhood, as there was a considerable quantity of hay on the premises, and the surrounding buildings are in general very old. – Fortunately, however, the fire was extinguished without spreading farther; and for this the inhabitants of the city were again much indebted to the Officers and men of the 3rd Dragoon Guards.'

Wheeler, writing in the *Salisbury and Winchester Journal* in 1887, commented that there were seven troops of the Dragoon Guards stationed in Salisbury at that time (See Appendix 1). He says that it must have put great pressure on the inns and lodging houses to accommodate 578 horses and roughly the same number of men.

For the next 20 odd years, the inn seems to be continually being advertised for sale with the resultant change of landlord nearly every other year. Finally, in 1825, 'Henry Coombs conveys to Isaac Gray of the liberty of the Close, Carpenter, all that messuage and Inn heretofore called the 'Rose & Crown' but now and for some time past "The Six Bells" situate at the corner of Winchester Street & Greencroft St.'. Wheeler states that Henry Coombs was the last person to operate the Six Bells as an inn and it certainly disappears from the licensing records at this time.

217 Slug & Lettuce, Fisherton Street

The Maundrel Hall was built in 1880 on part of the site formerly occupied by the Sun Inn in Fisherton Street (qv) It was immediately to the west of Fisherton Bridge on the north side of the street. It seems that part of the inn was used as a builder's yard for some years. The Hamilton Hall was built on the site and in March, 1876, it was opened as the Royal Skating Rink by Mr B H Perman [865]. This was a roller skate rink and seems have been very successful.

Then in April, 1880, the skating rink was replaced by the Maundrel Hall [866]. This hall is undoubtedly the building we see today but it is not clear whether it was part of the Sun or a new building on the same site. The hall was named after John Maundrel who was one of three Protestants (the Salisbury Martyrs) who were burned at the stake in Salisbury in 1556 for not recanting their opposition to the reestablishment of the Roman Catholic Church in England during the reign of Queen Mary. The hall was intended for non-denominational Christian worship and discussion and was established by the Rev. Edgar Thwaites, the Rector of St Paul's church in Fisherton.

During the First World War, the hall became the Fellowship Hall designed as a meeting place for servicemen in the Salisbury area. Considering the background of the hall, it is thought that this was a temperance meeting place to give soldiers an alternative to the pubs of Salisbury.

It is thought that the hall was used as a printing works in later years and later became the outlet for Argos stores when they first opened in Salisbury. But in 1997, it was opened as a free house known as the Clock Tower. Considering the history of the hall, there must have been a few bodies spinning in graves around Salisbury at the thought of alcoholic beverages being served on the premises.

The old Spire Bar at the King's Head had been named the Hogshead Bar for a little time. When this closed as a separate bar in 2001, the Clock Tower was renamed the Hogshead, in keeping with the name of the chain of pubs run by Whitbread. This caused some consternation at Gibbs Mew Brewery as the Malmesbury Arms in Wilton Road was known as the Hogshead at that time. As Gibbs Mew ceased trading soon after, the matter was resolved by the renaming of the Malmesbury Arms. In

2007, the pub was renamed again to be the Slug and Lettuce, being again the name of a national chain of pubs.

218 Spread Eagle, 53/55 New Canal

This inn was on the south side of New Canal immediately next to the Assembly Rooms, that imposing building on the corner of New Canal and High Street and occupied by a bookshop. Before the existing building that was the Assembly Rooms, the Spread Eagle must have been adjacent to the Fountain Inn (qv). The RCHM categorically states that the Spread Eagle was demolished in 1966 when the Old George Mall was developed.

The earliest reference to the Spread Eagle is in the records of the Common Brewhouse in 1624 where it is stated that Abraham Collins of the Spread Eagle took one hogshead and five barrels of ale [17]. In 1625, the inn is described as the Splayed Eagle, with Abraham Collins still being the landlord [18].

By 1763, the establishment of mutual societies to provide support to members if they got into financial difficulties was coming into vogue. The *Salisbury and Winchester Journal* reported in May of that year [867]: 'A Society is now forming in this City, in order to raise a fund sufficient to allow the Widow of any Member, who has continued in it 3 years, an Annuity of Thirty Pounds per Annum, & that the first Meeting will be held at Mr Gibbons, the Spread Eagle, on the New Canal, on Wednesday Evening next, the 25th inst., at 8 o'clock, in order to discuss the Matter, & appoint a Committee to draw up such Articles as may be thought most conducive to answer so laudable an Undertaking. At which time all those who are desirous of encouraging a Scheme of such public utility are desired to favour them with their Company.'

The following week, the *Journal* reported that several persons had expressed an interest in forming the Society. Thus, in June the following announcement was made [868]: 'It is announced that an Annuity Society is formed. Sir Alexander Powell, Deputy Recorder, in Trust for the whole. Meetings at the Spread Eagle the first Monday in every month. "Any Person of good character in this City or Places adjacent, under the age of 45 willing to become a Member is desired to signify the same by Letter post paid, directed to the Stewards at the House of Meeting, setting forth his name, Age and Place of abode." The terms of admission were 2 guineas entrance & 4 shillings monthly to the Box. Those who exceeded the age of 45 paid £2 10 shillings for every year above, and no person over 50 was admitted.'

Notices of meetings of the Society continued to appear in the *Journal* until 1785 and it was still operating in 1839.

In 1787, the morality of the slave trade was being questioned and the Society for the Abolition of the Slave Trade was formed in London on 22 May 1787. Already, in 1772, a court case in England had determined that the condition of slavery did not exist in English Law and this had resulted in the freeing of some 10,000 slaves. In March 1788, a meeting was held at the Spread Eagle [869]: 'At a respectable meeting of the Quakers and other inhabitants of this city, held at the Spread Eagle last Thursday evening, for the purpose of considering on "the propriety of a petition to Parliament for redressing the grievances of the poor

African Slaves, or to affect a total abolition of that trade". The Rev Mr Rigby having taken the chair, the sentiments of the meeting were found to be unanimous in behalf of a reform in or total abolition of that inhuman and disgraceful branch of traffic. A petition to that effect was therefore resolved on, and a very able one being produced and read, was very highly approved, ordered to be engrossed, and handed round the city for the approbation and signatures of such other of the inhabitants as may be inclined to favour the good intentions of this meeting; after which it is to be presented to Parliament by the Hon. General Bathurst.'

In 1793, an unusual auction took place at the inn when the office of Porter of the Close of Salisbury was sold. The post included the use of a house and garden. It was advertised that an income of £33 a year could be expected from the post. It was not recorded what was the value of the resultant winning bid [870].

Health and Safety was a concept unknown in the 18th C. Thus in,1796, a young man who was working on repairs to the roof of the inn fell into the street. Remarkably, he only broke an arm and received a cut to his head and recovered from his fall. He had been warned to secure his ladders but ignored this advice resulting in his fall [871].

In July 1815, Samuel Gibbons died. He had been the landlord since 1783 although the advertisement in the *Salisbury and Winchester Journal* offering the inn for sale stated he had been the proprietor for 40 years [872]. However, other members of the Gibbons family had run the inn since at least 1734. For some reason, the sale of the inn was delayed several times and it was not until December, 1815, that William Elkins placed the following advertisement [873]: 'Spread Eagle and Commercial Inn, Salisbury. W Elkins, late Waiter at the above old established Inn, respectfully informs the Friends of the late Mr Gibbons, and the public in general, that he has taken and entered on the same, which will shortly be fitted up with every degree of comfort, where Travellers and others who may be pleased to favour him with their support, may depend upon the best accommodation, by being provided with well-aired beds, genuine Wines and Spirits, home-brewed Beer, good Stabling, and a lock-up Coach-house.'

It was common for sales to take place at inns which had the room to display the goods. In December, 1818, 'a large and elegant assortment of rich Cut and Plain Glass' was offered for sale at the Spread Eagle [874]. A year later, 'an Elegant and Beautiful Collection of Shells, Minerals and other Curiosities' was for sale [875]. They were the property of a gentleman who was leaving the Salisbury area and had been moved to the inn for the convenience of the sale. Also included were 'Oriental China, British China, chimney ornaments and figures and a handsome blue dinner set'.

A strange situation occurs in 1822. In February of that year, Vincent Wing applies for the license of the Spread Eagle in succession to William Elkins. The licensing records show that this application was refused [5]. However, a month later, Vincent Wing is advertising in the *Salisbury and Winchester Journal* giving thanks for the support he has received since moving into the inn [876]! He stays on at the inn until the annual licensing session in September with the inn being advertised from April to July, 1822, as being available to rent [877]. Eventually, John Hazell is shown as obtaining the license in late September [5]. Despite this situation, Vincent Wing does eventually become the landlord of the inn in 1835 without comment from the Magistrates.

In 1846, James Goddard, the landlord was involved in an accident [878]: 'On Wednesday afternoon last, as Mr James Goddard, of the Spread Eagle Inn, in this city, was proceeding in a gig through East Harnham, accompanied by another person, the horse, through unnecessary flogging, started at the bottom of Harnham-hill, and ran with great speed towards Salisbury. When the vehicle reached the Rose and Crown Inn, Mr Goddard was thrown from his seat with great violence, his head coming into contact with the wall of the new houses recently erected there, whereby he received a severe cut across his head, and was otherwise very much bruised. He was taken up insensible, and conveyed home, where, having received immediate medical aid, he is now in a fair way of recovery. The person accompanying Mr Goddard was shortly afterwards thrown from the gig, and escaped unhurt. The horse dashed furiously onwards, and came in contact with Harnham-bridge, where the gig was broken to pieces. A boy who was on the bridge, seeing the horse coming, had just time to escape by jumping over the bridge on to a faggot-pile below, from the very spot where the vehicle was dashed to atoms. The horse, being thus freed from the gig, proceeded towards Salisbury at full gallop. On nearing the turnpike gate, it met with a boy wheeling a barrow, whom it leaped over without injuring the boy further than by giving him a severe fright. The horse was eventually secured and taken home without doing further mischief.'

It seems likely that James Goddard remained the owner of the Spread Eagle until it finally closed in 1859. There were several other landlords between 1848 and 1855, but it is assumed that they were sub-tenants, as in the latter year, James Goddard returns as landlord. The household furniture and brewing equipment of the inn were put up for sale in June 1859 [879] and, a month later, James Goddard announces that he has moved to the Wheatsheaf Inn [880]. The Spread Eagle does not appear in licensing records after this year.

219 Squirrel, Guilder Lane

Haskins states that the Squirrel was licensed as an alehouse to Arthur Saunders sometime between 1635 and 1685 [18]. What is definitely known is that Saunders issued a farthing token in 1656 showing his name and an image of a squirrel on the obverse and his initials and the text 'OF SARUM 1656' on the reverse [881]. This appears to be the same Arthur Saunders who is recorded as being a retailer of tobacco in 1637 and who also gave a loan of £20 to support the Parliamentary Forces in 1646.

Interestingly, in a lease for a house in Guilder Lane in 1683, the street is named as Guilderland with an alternative name of Bellfounder Street [882].

No other records have been found of this alehouse although it is believed it changed its name to the Bear some time before 1780. However, a lease of 1780 has the name Squirrel written on its outside although the name is not mentioned in the lease itself [883].

An enclosure in a lease of the land associated with the Squirrel dated 1800 suggests that Mr S Emly had agreed to let Samuel Whitchurch use the house and orchard in Guilder Lane as a public house called the Black Bear. However, a condition of this agreement was that Mr Whitchurch obtained a license for the premises. Since this pub name does not appear in any records after this date, one must assume that Mr Whitchurch did not follow up on the agreement.

220 Stratford Inn, Stratford-sub-Castle

This pub is recorded as having received its first license in August of 1848 [884] but this must have been as a full public house license as William Gray, the landlord at this time, was convicted of selling beer outside of legal hours in 1846 [885]. The pub remained in trade until December 1897. In that month, Robert Marchment, the landlord, was brought to court for threatening his wife such that she was in danger of losing her life [886]. He was ordered to lodge £30 with the court such that he would lose this surety if he did not keep the peace for six months. He also had to find two other sureties from guarantors for his behaviour. Whether he paid this money is in doubt as he appears to have left the pub on this date and the pub remained closed.

The contents of the pub were sold in October, 1898 at the behest of Mr Marchment, who was described as leaving the pub although it is likely that he had left after the court case mentioned above [887]. No further mention of the inn has been found in the licensing records.

221 Sugar Loaf, Brown Street

This public house is only known from two announcements in the *Salisbury and Winchester Journal* in 1752 and 1756. In the first, Zachariah Talbot, the landlord states that he 'hath a very good and easy Post-Chaise & able Horses to Lett' and that 'he also sells Brandy & Rum, as Neat as imported; & all other Spirituous Liquors, in small Quantities, as cheap in proportion as by the Gallon' [888].

In 1756, his widow, Mary, announces that she is now the wife of Robert Hill and that those owing money to Zachariah should pay their debts to her at the Sugar Loaf [889].

This public house was probably known by another name at other times but no connection to other inns has been found.

222 Sun, Fisherton Street.

The Sun was in existence in 1716 and probably for many years earlier. It was on the northern side of Fisherton Street immediately next to the River Avon, the site now being partially occupied by the Slug and Lettuce (qv). Thomas Bungay was granted a licence for the inn in 1741. But as the Sun was in the village of Fisherton rather than the City of New Sarum, early records of the inn are very sparse.

Like many inns, the Sun provided a home for travelling exhibitions such as the following held in 1757 [890]. 'The Microcosm, now at the Sun over Fisherton Bridge will be exhibited, as usual to 5 or more any Time of the Day at 1/- each, & Children under 12 years of age at 6d, (the Prices quite inferior to the great Expenses & Merits of this Machine). But that none may be disappointed as to Time, it will be shown every Evening exactly at 7 o'clock, to more or less, during its stay here. And as there has been a far greater Number of Gentlemen & Ladies than could be expected in so short a Time, 'tis hoped the Remainder, who may be desirous of seeing a Piece so much superior to any Thing of its Kind (and so well worth the Notice of the most curious) will be as expeditious as convenient.'

Unfortunately, there are no details as to what the Microcosm was but a similarly named exhibition was displayed at the Grasshopper in Winchester Street in 1739.

Being across Fisherton Bridge from the city centre, the Sun was not within the city bounds and thus was not under the control of the Mayor and Corporation of Salisbury. Thus, it was able to have exhibitions and hold sales of goods without conforming to the restrictions on outside traders that were imposed to protect trade in the city. Thus in 1759, a sale of haberdashery and millinery was advertised with another advertisement in the same issue of the newspaper from the milliners of Salisbury showing their prices against the travelling salesman [891]. In 1760, a similar sale was held by Birt & Co from St James in London [892].

Not only exhibitions and sales were held at the Sun but travelling doctors also set up their stands (as in this case in 1762) [893]: 'Dr Stears, the famous operator for the Ears; who having had the Honour of 40 years' experience in his Majesty's Service, by Sea & Land, cures all manner of Deafness, if the Drum of the Ear is not burst; & cures most Species of Deafness in old & young, in a few Minutes without the least Pain, Trouble, or Danger of relapsing ... He cures Megrims, Dizziness of the Head etc. ... Those affected with the above Disorders being sure (through Divine Help) of a Cure, if he takes them in Hand ... He may be spoke with any Hour of the Day, at the Sign of the Sun at Fisherton ... John Swayne, Ostler at the Antelope, had been entirely deaf for near 7 years; but by applying to Mr Stears received the Blessing of Hearing in a short Time.'

A more salubrious entertainment was advertised in 1764 [894]: 'During the Race Week. In a commodious Room, (the best adapted for the purpose in or near this City) at the Sun in Fisherton. The celebrated Miss Heesom & her Brother, will perform several curious Pieces of Music, not only upon the Violins, but on the Angelic Harmony; or Surprising Musical Glasses; whose Performances have so often astonished the Curious & Learned in Music & Philosophy in London, and at the Assembly Rooms in Bath, Bristol and elsewhere. So great and so celestial is the Harmony performed by these Children when they play upon the so much admired Musical Glasses, accompanied with the Singing, that few, if any, believe their own Eyes & Ears, but insist upon it there are many other Instruments join them, which are concealed. Many favourite Songs will be sung by Miss Heesom, who is allowed by the best Judges to have the finest Voice of her Age, and is the best Performer on the Musical Glasses in England. After the above Performances, Mr Heeson, Philosophical Violin-Maker from London, will exhibit his curious new-invented Machine, that shews how to extinguish Fire, in half the Time of any Fire Engine now used; Likewise at the same Time how to preserve the Lives and Fortunes of Ladies & Gentlemen in such Distress. (Price

One Shilling). N.B. Any Hour of the Day, except from 12 to 1, or from 7 to 8 in the Evening, any Ten or More, may command a Performance at their own Houses at 1/- each, or as above at one Hour's Notice.'

In 1764, a theatre was established at the Sun and it opened on January 28, 1765, with a performance of 'Tragedy of Venice Preserved' which was patronised by the Earl of Pembroke amongst other noteworthy persons [895].

And so the Sun continues for many years with travelling exhibitions, sales of goods, performances in the theatre and less intellectual events such as cock-fighting. And the Sun was also the terminus for a variety of coaches and carrier's wagons.

By 1812, the inn was also advertising itself as a hotel in the more modern sense [896]: 'Sun Inn, Fisherton Bridge, Salisbury. B Stock begs leave to return his most sincere thanks for his numerous Friends for their liberal support during the short time he has lived at the above Inn, which he has fitted up in a style that he flatters himself will be found perfectly commodious, and earnestly solicits the favour and patronage of a generous public, which it will be his constant study to merit, and ever gratefully acknowledge. Every attention will be paid to the comforts of Commercial Gentlemen, the House being in a most convenient situation, on the Bath road, connected with the city by a bridge over the Avon, and within two minutes' walk of most of the principal streets; the bedrooms airy and pleasant; the yard and stabling spacious and commodious. Well-aired Beds, a good Larder, Stall Stabling, and a lock-up Coach House – Wines and Spirits of the best vintage and quality.'

In 1826, the yard of the Sun was used to house a circus [897]: 'New Olympic Circus, Sun Inn Yard, Fisherton. Monday Evening, January 30, 1826, and every other Evening during the ensuing week. Mr Ryan most respectfully begs leave to inform the Ladies and Gentlemen of Salisbury, and its vicinity, that he intends Opening his Circus, in Fisherton, on the above evening, and trusts that the merits of his Company of Equestrians and the sagacity of his excellent broken Stud of Horses will ensure him that public sanction which will always be his pride to deserve. – The Circus will be kept perfectly warm by constant Fires. - Boxes, 2s; Pit, 1s; Gallery, 6d. Places for Boxes may be taken every day at the Circus, from 11 to 2.'

In 1827, the inn was put up for sale [898]. It was described as being 'a substantially built Inn, with large dining parlours, and other sitting and bed rooms, brew-house and cellars, and a range of stall and other stabling, a very large yard, with convenient outbuildings, and a pleasant and extensive Garden. It also had a very convenient Dwelling-house adjoining, which was let to an under-tenant'.

In January, 1838, a sensation was caused by the death of Richard Nash, following a fight with Phineas Snow at the Sun [899]. Nash had gone to the Sun in the evening with two companions after spending the day on business in Salisbury. He had dined at the Pheasant and had obviously been drinking, At half past eight, Snow entered the Sun with a friend and they joined others, including Nash, in the smoking room. For some reason, Mr Nash took a dislike to Snow and 'singled out Snow as an object of insult and abuse, putting his thumb up to his mouth in token of derision, swearing at him, and even more than once putting his fist up to Snow's face, and daring him to fight'. Mr Biggs, the landlord, tried to prevent a fight from occurring and removed Nash from the room two or three times. But Nash managed to avoid Mr Biggs yet one more time and further irritated Snow by striking him such that Snow stood up to fight. Mr Biggs decided that he was unable to prevent the fight from taking place. Both men fell at various times and were helped back to their feet by other persons in the room. Nash was told several times to give up the fight as he was obviously less able than his opponent. This he refused to do and, eventually, he fell again and hit the back of his head against the projecting edge of a settle. He fell into a stupor but was helped up to sit on a chair in the corner of the room. When the inn closed, he was still apparently asleep and was helped up to a bedroom. It was said at the time that Nash showed little effects of the fight apart from a bruised lip while Snow bled from his ears, nose and mouth and was badly bruised. The next morning, Nash was still unconscious and a Doctor was called. The Doctor bled Nash and used some leeches on him. He called again several times during the day but, at seven o'clock in the evening, the Doctor found Nash to be dying and he expired shortly after. The Doctor examined the body but found only superficial bruising. The next morning, the Doctor performed an autopsy at the request of the Coroner. He found substantial bleeding under Nash's skull caused by a ruptured blood vessel. The Coroner's jury found that Nash had died from the ruptured blood vessel, caused by his fall against a settle during the fight with Snow. The Coroner stated that this amounted to manslaughter and Snow was apprehended for trial at the Assizes. When this trial took place in March, Snow pleaded guilty but the Court believed he had been severely provoked by Nash. Consequently, he was fined one shilling and was discharged!

In late 1843, Batty's Royal Circus was opened at the Sun [900]. With horses and acrobats, the circus could be viewed from boxes, a gallery and the pit and must have taken up the whole of the yard of the Sun. The circus continued into early 1844 but this seems to have been the last event of any consequence at the inn.

Later in 1844, the furniture and fittings of the inn were put up for sale [901]. Following this, the materials of the buildings were sold and the Sun Inn was no more [902].

223 Sun, Winchester Street

This alehouse is said to have been licensed between 1635 and 1685 [18]. However, all that can be definitely said is that Edward Lister issued a halfpenny token that had the design of a sun together with the words 'Edward Lister in Sarum' on the obverse while on the reverse it stated 'At Winchester Gate His Halfe Peny' [903]. It is probable that this alehouse was known by another name at other times but no connection has been made.

224 Sun & Lamb, 37 High Street

This is the building now known as Mitre House on the east corner of High Street and New Street. It was originally two houses of early 16th C. construction: 37 High Street and 79 New Street. They appear to be on the site of an earlier building that is mentioned in Bishop Beauchamp's 'Liber Niger' of 1455 which shows payment for a tenement in High Street named 'Le Lambe'.

In 1620, the two properties appear to have been combined and were an inn called the Holie Lamb. The landlord, Thomas Snook, attended the meeting called by the Council to discuss inns taking beer and ale from the Common Brewhouse [18]. By 1649 it was known as the Lamb. In 1747, it was offered to let as the Lamb Inn and Coffee House and was described as 'an old and good accustomed House in the High Street' [904].

A little later it was called the Sun & Lamb and in May 1756, the following advertisement was placed in the *Salisbury and Winchester Journal* [905]: 'The following Royal Grottoes and Shell-Rooms are to be seen at the Sun & Lamb Coffee House in High Street, Salisbury. First they are to be seen all by the naked eye, and afterwards through Convex Glasses, by which they appear as large as the Original. From Nine in the morning till Nine at Night, for 6d each Person. 1.The Royal Grotto at Marly in France. 2. A Shell-Room at the King of Portugal's. 3. A Shell-Room of the Emperor of Germany. 4. Mr Goldney the Quaker's Shell-Work at Bristol. 5. A Piece of Shell-Work that is in the Grand Segnior's Seraglio at Constantinople. 6. The Royal Shell-Room at Herrenhausen in Hanover. 7. Sir Nathaniel Curzon's Grotto in Derbyshire. The above are curiously intermixed with the most beautiful red and violet Coral and Shells that are to be found amidst all the Treasure of Nature's extensive Repository; adorned with Shell-Flowers, Paintings & Statues carved in Ivory and Pearl.'

By June 1760, the Salisbury Friendly Society met in the club room at the Sun & Lamb before processing to the Vine Inn and joined the members of another Friendly Society [906]. From there, they processed to the Cathedral for a service. They then returned to their respective inns for dinner.

But by October, 1760, the inn was offered to let [907] and by January 1761 it was offered to let as either a public house or as a private dwelling [908]. It does not appear to have traded as a public house after this date. A lease of 1807 from the Dean and Chapter of the Cathedral to Stephen Fulford describes the premises as 'formerly the Sun & Lamb' [909].

225 Swan, Winchester Street

This inn was described in Bishop Beauchamp's Liber Niger of 1455 as being a capital tenement or hospice in Wynmanstrete (an old name for Winchester Street). It is probable that this is a forerunner of one of the better known inns in this street but no connection has been made.

226 Tabard, nk

Sometime after the accession of Edward IV in 1471, there are notes in the city archives about Watch Keepers. One junction between Watches was the Tabard which appears to be in the High Street [910]. However, it had been described in 1430 as being opposite the Market and it has been suggested that this was the Plume of Feathers.

227 Tally Ho, nk

There is a single entry in the licencing records for 1795 which show the landlord of the Tally Ho was James Creed [3]. By 1803, James Creed was the landlord of the Vine in Bedwin Street but this inn had been known by this name for many years before 1795. So the identity of the Tally Ho remains a mystery.

228 Thissel, Market Ward

n 1721, Widow Web was licenced as a dealer in Brandy and was described as being at the Thissel [20]. Widow Web has also been named as Widow Burbidge in some archives. Nothing more is known of these premises.

229 Three Cranes, Milford Street

Haskins states that a licence for this alehouse was granted in 1734 but he also describes it as being in the Market Place! [20]. However, in September of that year, the licensee, George Stares surrendered his licence. The licence is held in the Swindon and Wiltshire History Centre in Chippenham but unfortunately is so faded that the reason for the surrender cannot be deciphered [911]. In 1747, the Three Cranes was offered to be let with a large malthouse attached but no further information has been found (see Old Inns of Salisbury Pt IV – Appendix 1).

230 Three Crowns, Brown Street

Haskins states that William Ellis was granted a licence for this house as an alehouse in 1779 [20]. But unless this record is in error it must have had a full licence as the licensee, William Ellis, was advertising in December of that year that he had the following spirits for sale: Jamaica full-proof Rum at 12/- per gallon; fine Wine Brandy at 7/- per gallon; best proof Geneva at 6/- and fine Cordial Peppermint at 6/- [912].

In 1794, Isaac Robbins took over the inn. The licencing records show that Mr Emly promised to be answerable for the taxes on the inn as Mr Robbins was not a local man [3]. Mr Emly was not doing this from a sense of philanthropy as he was a Salisbury brewer who was almost certainly supplying beer to Mr Robbins!

Problems seem to have been continually attached to this public house as when John Hunt applied for the licence of it in 1808, it was announced that the Justices were to meet to consider the considering 'the propriety of granting a Licence for a certain House in the parish of St. Thomas, in the said city, called the Three Crowns' [913]. The records of this meeting have not been found but, as John Hunt was recorded as being the licensee for a further six years, it must be assumed that the Justices found in his favour.

The last entry for the Three Crowns in the licencing records is in 1820 when William Lawrence was the licensee [5]. William Lawrence was refused a licence for the Nelson's Arms in 1819 and appears to be the landlord of other pubs in Salisbury in later years but none of these appear to be the same house as the Three Crowns.

231 Three Crowns, Town Path

This pub was on the Town Path near its junction with Middle Street, Harnham. It is said that parts of this pub date from the 13th C. but the RCHM dates the building to the late 18th C. This matches up with the earliest records of the pub from the *Salisbury and Winchester Journal*. In 1774, the landlady, Mary Stent, had a large damask tablecloth stolen along with some other items [914]. She offered a reward of five guineas but whether this produced results is not stated.

Three Crowns, Town Path

Again, in February, 1776, a robbery occurred at the Three Crowns [915]. Joseph Golding, Francis Gibson & Richard Narey were committed to Fisherton Gaol for breaking open a box at Mrs Stent's at the Three Crowns in West Harnham, and stealing 12 guineas, 2 pair of silver salts, 6 table spoons, one pepper box & one pepper castor. They were condemned to death. When they were apprehended, they had a pair of pistols, three large, broad, clasp knives, a set of picklock keys, a gag and a stone ring, with a contrivance in the nature of a syringe to put out eyes, by squirting pernicious liquor into them.

At various dates from 1811 through to 1819, Pigeon Shooting was advertised as being held at the Three Crowns [916]. Unlike clay pigeon shooting these days, these shoots involved live birds that were collected before the shoot and then released to be shot. Prize money of Ten Guineas in gold were to be awarded. Interestingly, this form of live pigeon shooting was not made illegal in the UK until 1921.

Also in 1811, William Drew, the landlord, advertised [917]: 'Three Crowns, West Harnham, Near Salisbury. W Drew, with grateful thanks to his friends for past favours, begs to inform them and the public in general, that he intends erecting a commodious Booth on the Down, near the Stand, at the ensuing Salisbury Races, and to have the same plentifully supplied with good old port and sherry wines, genuine spirits of all sorts, capital home-brewed strong beer, excellent Herefordshire and West Country bottled and draught cyder, prime London bottled porter, with well-cured hams, etc. etc.; and from the arrangements W.D. has made to give satisfaction to his customers, he flatters himself he shall meet with a liberal share of support on the above occasion.'

William Drew remained the landlord to at least 1821 but in that year, a notice was published in the *Salisbury and Winchester Journal* asking for all persons who were owed money by Drew to send details of the debt to Mr Cooper, a solicitor in Salisbury [918]. In September, William Drew assigned all his estate and effects over to trustees for the benefit of his creditors [919]. This indicated that he was broke but fell short of full bankruptcy. In the same issue of the *Salisbury and Winchester Journal*, the pub was advertised to let.

In 1830, robbers broke into the Three Crowns by making a hole in the cellar wall [920]. They proceeded to help themselves to drinks and then left with Strong Beer in 2-gallon jars, several bottles of spirits, a whole side of bacon, a pan of lard and various other articles. Presumably, the landlord was not present that night as it would have been difficult to escape quietly with such a haul.

In August, 1843, there was a fight between William Church and George Davidge at the inn [921]. They had been at the Salisbury Races during the day and met at the Three Crowns in the evening where a dance was taking place. They quarrelled during the evening, apparently about a parasol which had been lost by a young woman. Several people helped put a stop to the quarrel and Church left the inn with his lady friend, Louisa Hopkins. But they had only gone a short way back to Salisbury when Church, who was drunk, returned to the Three Crowns. A fight took place between Church and Davidge but, after a while, the landlord came into the room and stopped the fight by throwing

Davidge out of the inn. Church later left the inn with Louisa, but as he stopped to put on his clothes, he fell over unconscious. Louisa looked after him until the early morning when he woke up and the two of them set off back to Salisbury. But Church complained of a pain in his head and kept trying to lie down, but Louisa managed to get him to her lodgings in Scots Lane. He later threw up a large quantity of blood and a doctor was called for. There was little that medical attention could achieve and Church died during the night. A post mortem was held and several wounds were found that the surgeon attributed to the fight. The Coroner's Jury gave a verdict of Manslaughter against George Davidge but he had absconded. No evidence of a trial has been found.

During the mid-1800s, the pub was advertised to let several times [922]. The notices consistently described the pub as having a skittle alley and a large garden often described as a Tea Garden. The garden was available for parties to have picnics.

What in recent times was used as the lounge bar of the Three Crowns was decorated with a wide variety of plaster mouldings. It is thought that these pre-dated the inn. As the Three Crowns was outside of the City of Salisbury, there was more freedom for the landlord to open his inn to customers whenever he liked and allow pursuits that might be banned in City pubs. There is a possibility that this area of the inn was used for gaming and other nefarious pursuits.

In 2009, the pub was closed, supposedly after a leak of water caused some ceilings to collapse. Planning permission was received to convert the pub into a guest house. In November, 2015, the guest house eventually opened. It is good to know that the plaster mouldings have been fully restored to their former glory as part of the renovation of the building.

232 Three Cups Inn, 47 Winchester Street

This inn was on corner of St Edmond's Church Street & Winchester Street. The current, magnificent house was built on the site of the Three Cups in c.1673 by Gyles Naish. In recent years, it was completely restored after many years being empty and in use as a warehouse.

The history of the Three Cups goes back to at least 1431. In that year, the Corporation took over the property and let it to William Pette [923]. It is not clear whether it was an inn at that time or earlier as the first suggestion is in 1484 when it is recorded in the Chamberlain's accounts that "40 shillings for a quit rent out of the corner tenement called 'le III Cuppys in Wynmanstrete' late let to Thomas Hille of Abyngdon" [924]. In 1565 Thomas Burge paid the Mayor & Commonalty £4 per annum rent [925]. In 1625, Thomas Perricourt attended the meeting called by the Council to persuade landlords to take beer from the Common Brewhouse [18].

Giles Naish leased the property for 80 years in 1671 and he covenanted to pull the old buildings down and re-build them [926]. The current building appears to date from this period. In 1683, there is an entry in the city records "For the new house late the Three Cuppes". In 1748 a lease was granted to Richard Samborn, Wine Merchant, for 40 years whose tenancy started that year. In 1773 Richard Samborn assigned the lease to

Captain John Wyche who became mayor in 1783 [927]. He converted the premises to a private residence and it was during his tenancy that the new front made from mathematical tiles was added. He also retained a wine merchant's business in the adjoining cellar. In 1788, John Wyche was granted a lease for 40 years "of a corner tenement in Winchester Street, heretofore an Inne called the Three Cups". In 1804, we have Hezekiah Wyche, wine merchant, who married Frances Maria Tanner and hence, presumably, it passes to Josiah Tanner & others in 1805. By 1817 we find it owned by a business, Tanner, Cooper & Slade. This business continued into the 20th C. The name of the Three Cups lives on in the name of the Chequer and is perpetuated by the building development (1993-4) in the centre of the chequer.

233 Three Guns, Winchester Street

There is only one reference to this inn that has been found. In November, 1768, the following notice was placed in the *Salisbury and Winchester Journal* [928]: 'All persons indebted to the Estate & Effects of Mr Geo. Fox, late of the Three Guns, in Winchester Street, Salisbury, are desired, on or before the 16th of Dec: next, to pay the same unto Mr John Thresher, Auctioneer and Sworn Appraiser, in the Fish Market, Sarum.'

Nothing more has been found regarding this pub either before or after this date. It is possible that this was a printer's error and the notice should have read the Three Tuns! Alternatively, it is possible that the Three Tuns was known as the Three Guns for a short period.

234 Three Lions, Queen Street

The Three Lions stood on the corner of Queen Street and Winchester Street. In 1585, the landlord was Cuthbert Crooke. In 1625, John Barrow from the Three Lions attended the meeting called by the Council to persuade landlords to take beer from the Common Brewhouse [18]. It was noted that in the previous year, he had taken 15 barrels of beer and one cowle of ale from that source (it is not clear what volume of ale is contained in a cowle!) [17].

In 1671, King Charles II visited Salisbury and it was noted that the Mayor & Corporation met the Monarch at Three Lions Bridge (see Appendix 1 Old Inns of Salisbury Part 1). It is presumed that this bridge was one of the crossings of the many canals or ditches that threaded through Salisbury at that time (although in many accounts, these canals appear to have been little more than open sewers).

In July, 1730, Robert Hayter from Dinton ran into trouble with the law [929]: 'Robert Hayter, of Dinton in the county of Wilts, Shoemaker, having slandered Mr Andrew Waters, late of Harnham, in the same County, did on Tuesday the 23rd of June, at the 3 Lyons in Sarum, in the public Coffee Room, before several Gentlemen, acknowledge the Falsity of each Slander, asked the said Mr Waters Pardon, and promised not to give him Offence for the future, and gave a Note of Hand to pay Costs of Suite for the Action then depending; upon which, on the generous interpretation of a worthy gentlemen in Mr Hayter's neighbourhood, Mr Waters forgave him.'

This seemed a very gentlemanly approach to slander compared with today's use of civil law and the courts.

In 1739, a horse was stolen from the Three Lions resulting in the following detailed notice in the *Salisbury and Winchester Journal* [930]: 'This is to give Notice to all Gentlemen, Farmers and others, that on Tuesday the 9th of October 1739, was taken out of the stable of Edward Randell, at the Three Lions in the City of New Sarum; a black Nagg about 14 Hands high, betwixt 3 and 4 years old, white natural spot on his rear loin, about a Span from his hip-bone, and a rubb'd Flick Tail, a beautiful Carcass, with a genteel Carriage, a shortish Neck and a thickish Head. Whoever can bring Tidings of him to John Dennes of Greatley, or to Edward Randell, of New Sarum, so that he may be had again, shall be very well rewarded for their Trouble.'

In 1761, an ophthalmologist (known as an oculist in those days), by the name of the Chevalier Taylor lodged at the Three Lions where he offered to treat people with eye problems [931]. He visited Salisbury again in 1762 when it was stated that people should not be surprised by the short period of his stay at the Three Lions as his treatment was very quick and the results almost immediate. Since it was said that he treated 'distempered eyes', one wonders if he was actually removing cataracts.

It was at this time, under the management of John Gast, that the Three Lions seems to have reached its peak in trade. In October, 1765, the *Salisbury and Winchester Journal* reported that in quick succession, the Duke of Gloucester, the Earl of Halifax, the Earl of Sandwich and Lord Hinchinbrooke stayed at the Three Lions on their journeys through England [932].

Also in that month, Thomas Harmood was wrongly accused of theft [933]: 'Whereas I, Thomas Harmood, late Tapster at the Three Lions Inn, in Salisbury, now Waiter at the King's Arms, in the said city, was wrongfully charged with having got a certain Sum of Money, to the Amount of £70, and upwards, lately lost and stolen out of a Box belonging to William Selwood, Post-boy at the Three Lions Inn, whereupon I was taken up and examined before a Magistrate, and honourably acquitted of the same. To satisfy the Public, and to clear my Character from such a false and scandalous Accusation, I voluntarily make Oath and declare, that I ever saw, knew, or was in the least privy to the loss of the said Money, or to the Person taking the same. As witness my hand, Thomas Harmood, Sworn this 10th day of October, 1765, before me, John Davis. Thomas Harmood, in his Turn, now calls upon Mr J___ G___, for the further Satisfaction of the Public, to make a like Affidavit, with respect to his Ignorance of the above Fact.

It is not known if Mr JG ever made an affidavit or whether the person who stole the money was ever found. It is possible that the person referred to by Thomas Harmood was John Gast, the landlord of the Three Lions.'

On August 4, 1766, the inn had some unusual visitors that must have caused a sensation in Salisbury at the time [934]: 'On Thursday last arrived at the Three Lions in this City, three Sachems, or Chiefs, of the Mohecomack and Wappinger Tribes of Indians, together with another Indian attendant and 3 women; they were accompanied by three persons, one of whom was a Major, whose name we could not learn: they brought with them letters of recommendation from Gen

Johnson; and set out for London Saturday morning (after going to see Stonehenge and Wilton House) in order to wait on his Majesty with a complaint, that great part of their lands were taken possession of by persons belonging to New York. They sailed from Boston on Monday the 16th of June, and landed at Weymouth a few days since. According to their own account, they are Chiefs of two of the five Tribes of Iroquois Indians, situated between New York and Lake Ontario, the most considerate and best known of all the five Indian Nations in North America, as well as the stoutest and most desperate. The farthest of these five, and the nearest to the French Territories, are about one hundred leagues from our settlements; and are now in alliance with us, and serve as a barrier against the depredations of the French and their Indian allies. Though some of these nations they say, are not so firmly attached to the British interest as formerly. The Sachems are remarkably tall and stout, one of them 6 ft and an half high without shoes, which they don't wear, of a brown shining complexion and bold manly countenance, dressed in Indian manner.

'The women who are ladies of fashion, were of the same complexion with the men. They appeared very modest and decent in their behaviour, and seemed remarkably delighted with a few trinkets such as earrings, necklaces etc. that were presented to them by some ladies who went to pay their respects to them at their arrival. They all came here without scrip or purse having spent everything in the voyage; but were nevertheless very hospitably received and extremely well pleased, of which they seemed truly sensible, and desired the interpreter to return their most humble and grateful thanks and to signify that they should ever remember the goodness and generosity of the English nation, with whom they had long been in friendship, and held in the greatest esteem.'

Finally, in February, 1768, John Gast informed the public that he was leaving the Three Lions, after twelve years, to concentrate on selling wine [935]. He describes his successor, Joseph Boyter, as his tenant. Unusually, Joseph Boyter had previously been a Woollen Draper in Oatmeal Row, Salisbury, and sold the last of his stock of cloth in April of that year [936]. This seemed to be a strange choice for the proprietor of a successful inn but he remained at the inn for ten years. In 1772, he advertises that he has bought the house next to the inn and is going to add it to the premises. He also refers to the inn as the Three Golden Lions [937].

But the trade must have been slipping as in November, 1778, it was announced that the inn was to let but that John Gast was keeping it in trade until a new tenant could be found [938]. In December, it became clear that Joseph Boyter was bankrupt but that included in his assets was his interest in the Three Lions and also his interest in the Parade Coffee House in Blue Boar Row that he had only just opened [939]. Perhaps Joseph had over stretched himself financially. William Newman took over the tenancy in March 1779.

The inn seems to have continued to appear successful in business with many notices in the *Salisbury and Winchester Journal* of prominent persons who stayed at the inn. But by 1783, William Newman was bankrupt [940]. The inn was advertised as available to let, together with the Greyhound in Brown Street, with John

Gast still being the owner [941]. John Gast then opens a shop on the ground floor of the inn selling china and glassware, teas, coffee, cocoa, and chocolate (See Appendix 1 Old Inns of Salisbury Part 1). Of interest is that later in this year, the sign of the Three Golden Lions was put up for sale, complete with all its timber and iron work, and standing in the Market Place [942]. This is without doubt the sign of the Three Lions as the inn was referred to as the Three Golden Lions in 1777.

It appears that the remainder of the inn was not in business. But in 1790, the following advertisement appears in the *Journal* [943]. 'To be Lett and entered on at Lady-day next, the Three Lions Inn. The principal part of the house is completely furnished, twenty good beds, with silk darned needlework, and cotton furniture, eight parlours and dining-rooms, furnished with mahogany, oval, pier, and chimney glasses, marble slabs etc, three parts of which may be taken at a fair appraisement. If the house is not taken for an Inn before the 24th of this month, the Shop will be lett, with as much of the house as wanted, for a term of 7, 14 or 21 years. If anyone takes off the stock in the shop, they might have it considerably under prime cost. For further particulars, enquire of Mr Gast, on the premises, it will be advertised no more.'

This appears to be the end of the Three Lions as an Inn. By 1809, the premises are being advertised for sale and said to be formerly the Thee Lions [944].

It seems that the former inn was used for a variety of businesses over a number of years but in 1879, the inn was demolished and a new building constructed for Pinkney's Bank. In turn, that building was demolished in 1975 as part of the development of Cross Keys Chequer although the north and west fronts of the building were retained. It is the new building behind the 1879 walls that one sees on the site of the Three Lions today.

235 Three Mugs, Brown Street

This alehouse seems to have had a short career. Haskins states that it was granted a licence as an alehouse in 1775 [20]. But in 1776, an auction was held at the Three Lions of "A Public House now or late known by the name or sign of the Three Mugs" [945]. No more is heard of the Three Mugs although it may have continued under some other name.

236 Three Pigeons, Market Place

This is yet another pub that was on the south side of the Market Place but its exact whereabouts are not known. It is most probably a different name for some other pub but no connection has yet been made. Haskins states that the Three Pigeons was granted a licence as an alehouse in 1762 [20] but the landlord, George Woodford, may have operated the premises from as early as 1742. But in 1762, it was put up for sale whereas it was previously held on a lease from the Bishop of Salisbury [946]. But from this time on, the only times that the Three Pigeons is mentioned in the local newspapers and licensing records is when some crime or another was perpetrated on the premises and thus, one surmises, the pub was not of the highest standing.

In September, 1782, it was reported that a gentlemen's servant had his pocket picked by a 'lady of the town' while at the Three Pigeons. John Ingram, the landlord, quickly replied to this allegation [947]:

"Three Pigeons, Market Place, Salisbury. It having been reported that a Gentleman's servant was robbed by a Woman of light character in my house of two guineas and a half, I humbly beg leave to assure the Public, that the report is quite untrue, as the parties were not five minutes in my house, nor did they even sit down. Nothing will ever be wanting, that lies in my power, to maintain a fair character, and deserve the countenance of my friends, and the public, who are their most obliged humble servant – John Ingram".

In November, 1789, a similar event occurred in the pub. A butcher from Shaftesbury fell into the company of a girl of the town, whose name was Pateat, at the Three Pigeons, which was described as 'a house of general rendezvous'. He had his pocket picked of a purse containing three pounds in gold and silver, the result of selling some calves in the market that day. The following notice was posted in the Salisbury Journal [948]: "Whereas Hannah Pateat, otherwise Hannah Brown, did, on Tuesday last, privately steal from the pocket of a person standing in the kitchen of the Three Pigeons public house, in Salisbury, the sum of Three Pounds or upwards, and immediately absconded, and it is supposed is since gone to Portsmouth. Whoever will give information of the said Hannah Pateat, otherwise Brown, so that she may be apprehended and brought to justice, shall receive One Guinea reward by applying to Richard Oram, butcher, at Shaftesbury. The said Hannah Pateat is a stout jolly woman, about 5 feet 3 inches, with light hair, and very much marked with the smallpox".

Nothing more is heard about this event so one must suppose that Richard Oram's offer of a reward did not meet with success. Furthermore, nothing more appears in the licensing records regarding either the Three Pigeons or the landlord in 1789, Albinus Fleming. There is a possibility that the inn became the Packhorse which first appears in the licensing records in 1795. But this is pure conjecture.

237 Three Swans Hotel, 5 Winchester Street

The Three Swans was on the north side of Winchester Street close to the Market Square. The majority of the inn lay back from the road with a carriage entrance off Winchester Street. Many older inhabitants of Salisbury will still remember this entrance to the backyard behind the row of shops as it was only filled in with a new shop in the early 1980s.

As with many of the older inns in Salisbury, the oldest record of it is found in the council records of the Common Brewhouse in 1624/25 when Ferdinand Baynton took three humerkins of beer [17].

During the Commonwealth, the Country was divided into eleven military divisions by Cromwell. Salisbury came under the Western Division. Walter Bushnell, the Vicar of Box, was charged with profaning the Sabbath day; frequenting inns & alehouses, and drinking to excess. He was cited to appear on several occasions at various places before a commission appointed by the commander of the Western Division, Major General Destrowe, the seventh appearance being at the Three Swans in Salisbury on the 23rd of July, 1655, where he was going to hear his sentence. Not surprisingly in these puritanical years, he lost the benefice of Box.

During the next 100 years, the Three Swans became more prosperous and also became one of the coaching inns of Salisbury with coaches including the Gosport, Portsmouth and Salisbury Flying Caravan [949] and Avery & Russell's carrier service from London to Cornwall via Salisbury & Exeter [950].

It was common in these times for travelling shows to stay at prominent inns as they moved through the country and in June 1767, an advertisement appeared in the *Salisbury Journal* [951]: "The following very ingenious pieces of art in miniature just arrived here, and to be seen at the Three Swans in Winchester Street, are well worth the notice and observation of the curious, viz:- I. An ivory four-wheeled chaise complete with a person in it, all drawn by a flea, and scarce equal to a single grain in weight. II. A landau on traces, with 4 persons in it, 2 footmen behind, and a coachman on the box, with a dog between his legs, six horses and a postilion all drawn by a flea. III. A pair of steel scissors that weigh only the sixteenth part of a grain. IV. A common pepper-corn, containing 12 dozen of silver spoons, and the corn not above half full".

In 1772, William Ody announced that he had built a new front to the inn together with several new rooms facing on to the street [952]. This building can still be seen, being three stories high and with five bays of windows. The western four bays have straight sash windows whereas the eastern windows have arched tops. The carriageway to the remainder of the inn was under these arched windows.

Cock fighting was still a prominent sport (it did not become illegal in England until 1835) and the following match was advertised in 1775 [953]: "A main of cocks will be fought during the Races at the Three Swans between the gentlemen of Dorset & Wilts; to show 31 in the main & 10 for byes, & to fight for two guineas a battle & 40 the odd battle. Hurst & Northover, feeders".

An ordinary was also advertised as being available during the Races, this being a complete meal supplied at a fixed cost at lunchtime.

Despite the apparent prosperity of the inn, in 1780 William Ody, the landlord, was declared bankrupt [954]. The contents of the inn, including its brewing equipment, were put up for sale in March 1781 [955] and the inn itself advertised for sale in April 1782 [956] (although it is noted that the inn had been refurbished). But it was not until February, 1783, that the inn reopened [957]: "The Three Swans Inn was opened on Tuesday last by Mr Woodham, from the Sun, in Fisherton. – This industrious Landlord was honoured that day with the company of more than 120 Gentlemen Farmers to dinner; and our Correspondent adds, that the house has been remarkably full during the week with the friends of the Host and Hostess, who went to wish them success in their undertaking. It must give everyone pleasure to see an old established House again opened, after being shut up three years, and that it is in the management of people who are resolved to spare no pain or expense to deserve the public favours".

At the time of the re-opening of the Three Swans, the cultivation of flowers had become a prominent pastime. Along with other inns, the Three Swans held an Auricula Feast in April, 1783 [958], and a Carnation Feast in July of the same year [959] (Auricula being an ornamental form of Primula). At these feasts, gentlemen competed to exhibit their best plant and flowers for prizes and afterwards sat down to a celebratory dinner. These feasts became a regular feature at the Three Swans for a number of years.

But Mr Woodham also showed himself to be a philanthropist as demonstrated by the following correspondence in the *Salisbury Journal* of October, 1783 [960]: "A Card to the Printer of the Salisbury and Winchester *Journal*. A Gentleman who ranks philosophy and humanity high amongst the other amiable qualities of the cultivated mind, is extremely happy to notice those amiable virtues, and evince to the public that there are individuals hardy enough to stem the torrent of dissipation, and who possess goodness of heart sufficient to wipe off the tears of distress, and bind up the wound which error and folly had occasioned. Happening to be in the bar of the Three Swans Inn, the other evening, a note was delivered to Mr Woodham, which, after he had read, he offered to me for perusal. – Struck with the heart-felt gratitude it contained, I could not refrain begging a copy, and flatter myself, that everyone who abounds with the milk of human kindness, will join with me, in paying the humane donor that tribute of praise which so laudable a practice merits. The note alluded to contained as follows: "Mr & Mrs Woodham, We poor, unfortunate convicts, understanding we are to leave this place to-night or to-morrow morning early, think it is our duty to return to you our grateful and sincere thanks for your benevolence bestowed on us while in prison, and shall have cause to pray for you as long as we live, hoping God will reward you for the same. Fisherton Gaol, Sept 1783". On further enquiry I learned that Mr Woodham, on his taking the Three Swans, had a large tin vessel made to convey broth and offal meat to the prisoners confined in the above gaol, which contained eight gallons, and was three or four times a week regularly conveyed to them, which in great measure mitigated the horrors of their situation; and every meal was productive of grateful expressions to their worthy benefactors on whom they hourly bestowed every benediction which mind susceptible of gratitude are capable of feeling".

Perhaps Mr Woodham was too generous as in December, 1785, he was declared bankrupt! [961] Once again, the Three Swans remained unoccupied for a period until it reopened in September, 1787 under the management of John Loveless [962]. In his advertisement announcing that he had taken the Three Swans, it was stated that the inn had a carriageway onto Endless street as well as the entrance from Winchester Street.

To turn away from financial matters, a great storm hit Salisbury in late 1790, with high winds, thunder, lightning and heavy rain. Several chimneys were dislodged from the Three Swans and fell through the roof severely damaging two rooms and destroying the furniture within [963].

The inn changes hand several times over the next few years but it retained its prominence as one of the coaching inns of Salisbury. But it must not be thought that the coaching trade was well regulated and a gentlemanly business. The advertisements and letters resulting from a dispute between two coach operators may be found at Appendix 2.

In March, 1813, the proprietor of the Three Swans, George Matcham, was declared bankrupt [964]. This seems to follow a certain pattern involving the Three Swans! The contents of the inn were put up for sale in January, 1814, [965] and in February of that year, Charles Cusse enters the inn [966].

In early 1815, Mr Cusse announces that he has taken a house in front of the Three Swans and fitted it up to use as a hotel [967]. Mr Cusse ran the Three Swans successfully until 1828 with regular advertisements including the following from January 1819 [968]: "Three Swans Inn, Salisbury. C.Cusse, Importer of Foreign Wines and Spirits, Maltster and Retailer of Farnham and Country Hops, Home-brewed Strong and Table beer, etc. etc. with gratitude thanks his friends and the public for the flattering support he has experienced in the Wine, Spirit and Malting Trade, and to his customers in general since his residence at the above Inn, and hopes by assiduous attention to merit their future favours and support. – C.C. also begs the notice to his wholesale customers, that he can regularly supply them with genuine Wines and Spirits, as imported, on as reasonable terms as any house in the West of England. Prime Malt and Hops, London Bottled Porter, Home-brewed Strong and Table Beer, etc. etc. N.B. A good Ordinary every Tuesday".

In 1825, an unusual display was set up in the Three Swans [969]: "A Rattlesnake gorging a Rabbit, - This Rare and most interesting Exhibition will take place on Monday the 4th of July, 1825, in the Great Room of the Three Swans Inn, Salisbury, precisely at twelve o'clock at noon. The Reptile forms part of a Collection of Natural Curiosities that has for some time past been exhibited in High Street, and it will be removed to the above large Room in order to afford to a numerous assemblage the opportunity of witnessing a spectacle that will assuredly excite the most intense interest and astonishment. This venomous serpent is the only one that has been known to gorge in this kingdom, and is of the species called the Swamp or Green Rattlesnake. It has swallowed rabbits in the presence of numerous spectators at Bath, Oxford and Manchester, and it has now been six weeks without food. When the Rabbit is caged with the Snake the latter, erecting his head and neck, expands his dilatable jaws, erects his fangs, and with the quickness of lightning strikes the trembling animal; he will then encircle the rabbit in his folds, licking and smelling and occasionally gaping, as if to adapt his jaws for capacious swallow. During the act of gorging the neck of the Snake will be greatly distended, his colour changed, and his scales elevated, exhibiting the Reptile in a situation very rarely seen. Admission 2s".

Charles Cusse's widow, Mary, continued to run the Three Swans for four years after his death in 1828 [970]. The inn continued in trade throughout the 19th C. with the Figes family featuring as proprietors over many years.

In 1871, the inn was host to a demonstration of electricity [971]: "Short Visit. Mr J L Pulvermacher in Salisbury, at Three Swans Hotel, on Monday, April 10, Tuesday, April 11. Pamphlets, Gratis, at Office Bar of Hotel. Electricity is Life. Pulvermacher's Patent Galvanic Chain-Bands, Belt, and Pocket Batteries. These highly improved inventions render Electricity perfectly self-applicable, in a mild continuous form, and extremely efficacious, no shock or unpleasant sensation being experienced whereby it becomes a true fountain of health and vigour, speedily soothing agonising pains, reanimating torpid limbs, reviving the sluggish fountains of life, and imparting renewed energy and vitality to constitutions enfeebled by various influences. The daily increasing number of cures effected by Pulvermacher's Medico-Galvanic System is so extensive and varied, that it forcibly points to this invention as the embryo of a universal remedy".

The whole of one column of the *Salisbury Journal* was filled with testimonials of persons claiming to have been cured by Mr Pulvermacher.

But by 1894, the inn is described as being a Temperance Hotel [972]. Just before this, the inn is being run as a hotel with the Three Swans Bar being run by a separate innkeeper. By 1901, there is just the inn in business as a Temperance Hotel and there is no sign of a bar. By 1903, a separate business is being run from the Three Swans Yard [973] and thus it is supposed that the hotel only occupied the part that was built in 1772 fronting on to Winchester Street. It is not clear when the hotel ceased trading although this was certainly before 1969 and the inn does not feature in the licensing records after 1912.

238 Three Tuns, Winchester Street

It is not clear exactly where in Winchester Street the Three Tuns was situated but there is superficial evidence that it was on the corner of Winchester Street and Endless Street (still known as Pinder's Corner after the ironmongers that occupied the site for many years). Haskins states that this house was in existence in 1625 when the landlord, Henry Page, attended the meeting called by the Council to discuss inns taking beer from the Common Brewhouse [18].

It could not have been a large building as in 1750, the following advertisement was placed [974]: "Edward Reeves, who kept the Cooks Shop at the Haunch of Venison, is moved to the Three Tuns in the Blue Boar Row "where he keeps a Cooks Shop for Roasting or Boiling, and will dress all Sorts of Meat or Fowls for private families in the best manner and on reasonable Terms every Day in the Week. Likewise, Roast & Boiled Meat cut hot every day in any quantity with good entertainment for Man & Horse".

One is not sure how the Horse was to be entertained by meat being cut but it seems unlikely that a large pub would have supplied cooked meat to customers without offering meals to them.

In 1780, the Three Tuns is offered for sale, with the leaseholder being William Staples [975]. But it still continues under William Staples and is offered to Let in 1783 [976].

In 1789, a lease of the Three Tuns for 99 years was offered for sale by the executors of the estate of Benjamin Collins [977]. Mr Collins had been the proprietor of the Salisbury and Winchester *Journal*. This seems to have been the end of the Three Tuns as a public house.

239 Tollgate Inn, 2 Tollgate Road

The Tollgate Inn was at the end of St Martin's Church Street at its junction with Rampart Road. Before the Salisbury ring road was built, the inn was at the top end of St Anns Street. The oldest part of the inn

Tollgate

dated from the mid-18th C and this ties up with the earliest records so far found which date from 1774. At that time, the house was known as the New Inn. It is unusual for two pubs in Salisbury to have the same name (see the New Inn, New Street) but the inn that was to become the Tollgate was in the Parish of Milford and thus outside of the city boundaries.

The earliest record that can be definitely attached to this inn was in 1774 when William Potts was admitted to Salisbury Infirmary after having had his leg broken by a small cannon that ran back after being fired at the New Inn, near St Martin's Church [978]. It is not recorded why a small cannon was being fired at the inn.

The New Inn was within the Manor of Milford of which William Beckford was Lord in 1798. Records from this Manor are held at the Wiltshire & Swindon History Centre in Chippenham and give an insight to the powers of the Court Baron associated with the Manor [979]: "The Court Baron of William Beckford Esquire Lord or Farmer of the said Manor held in and for the said Manor the Fifteenth day of November in the year of our Lord One Thousand seven hundred and ninety-eight before James Charles Hill Gentleman Steward there. At this Court Licence is granted to Samuel Whitchurch of the City of New Sarum Gentleman to let or demise to any Tenant from the Twenty Ninth day of September last for a Term or Number of years Determinable upon the Deaths of him the said Samuel Whitchurch, John Whitchurch his Brother and Samuel Whitchurch his Nephew

All that Messuage or Tenement and Inn called the New Inn with a Stable on the other side of the Turnpike Road bounded on the East by a Mudwall belonging to Ambrose Wharton Gentleman On the North by Land of Henry Penruddocke Wyndham Esquire and the South and West by the Turnpike Road together with the six Tenements and a Barn situate and being between the said Inn called the New Inn and the Farmyard belonging to the Vicarage of Milford aforesaid All which said Premises were formerly part of the Estate of William Batt Esquire since of Ambrose Wharton but now of him the said Samuel Whitchurch and to which He is Admitted Tenant at a Court this day held Provided the Houses Buildings Hedges Ditches Fences and every other part of the said Premises be from time to time kept in good and sufficient Repair And the Rents Workes Burthens Customes Suits and Services therefore due to the Lord be well and truly rendered paid and performed otherwise this Licence to be void".

In 1824, ownership of the New Inn changed from the elder Samuel Whitchurch on his death to the nephew, Samuel Whitchurch, mentioned above [980]. On his death in 1835, his estate, including the New Inn, was put up for sale. Thomas Matthias Hodding purchased the inn resulting in further proceedings in the Court Baron [981]. Mr Hodding let the New Inn to Jane Turner. She was summoned in 1850 for having the inn open before 12:30 on a Sunday but was acquitted of the charge [9].

In 1847, the Court Leet of the Duke of Hamilton was held at the New Inn [982]. As part of their ceremonies, it was intended to walk the boundaries of the Manor of Milford. But they found a path that formed part of the boundary, near the Rising Sun in Castle Street, had been boarded up, blocking their progress. In the words of the report in the *Salisbury Journal*, "they effected an entrance and continued on their progress". Having returned to the New Inn for their dinner, they informed the Duke of Hamilton's Steward of what had happened. He insisted that there was a right of way on the path and so, having finished their dinner, the company went back to the site and removed the boarding at both ends of the path. The *Journal* stated that 'thus throwing open as before a pleasant walk to the citizens of Salisbury, and establishing a right of way which has existed for the last fifty years'.

By the early 1900s, it was quite common for pubs to sell brandy in a diluted form. But there had to be a notice clearly displayed stating the conditions under which brandy was sold. In 1906, Keziah Hillary was charged with selling brandy below proof at the New Inn [983]. When a policeman ordered half a pint of brandy, he swore that there was no notice displayed and hence the brandy should have been of full strength (though one wonders what the policemen was expecting when he ordered half a pint - presumably not full strength!). However, all those persons connected with the pub (including the agent of the owners, Matthews of Gillingham), gave evidence that the required notice was hanging in the bar in a position for everybody to see. The Magistrates felt that the notice was insufficiently visible but that the evidence was insufficient to convict Mr Hillary.

The inn continued as a minor public house with little news of it over the following years. The pub continued to be known as the New Inn until at least 1953 but by 1956, it was known as the Tollgate Inn. It was owned by Matthews Brewery of Gillingham for many years until that brewery was purchased by Hall & Woodhouse in 1963 and it traded under the latter brewery's name of a Badger Inn from 1977.

During the latter days of the 20th C, the pub was a popular haunt of students from Salisbury College. But times changed and by the early years of the 21st C, the trade of the pub was much diminished. It finally closed in 2008 and was eventually converted into private housing.

240 Traveller's Rest, Milford
Little information has been found about this pub except that it was put up for sale as a going concern in 1819 [984]. It was said to have a yard, stables, a garden and a skittle alley adjoining the pub. It appears to have become the Vicarage of Laverstock in 1858 although it is probable that it was extensively re-modelled or completely re-built as the current building, now Little Manor Nursing Home, is very grand for what would have been a rural pub.

241 Tucker's Shears, nk
This was an alehouse in the 17th and 18th C. but its whereabouts is not known. John Blathat from the Tucker's Shears attended the Council meeting in 1625 that discussed the supply of beer to pubs and inns from the Common Brewhouse [18]. Haskins states that it was granted a licence as an alehouse in 1775 [20]. Nothing more is known about this alehouse.

242 Two Sawyers, Brown Street
Where exactly the Two Sawyers was in Brown Street is not known. A licence was applied for as an alehouse and refused in 1742 [15]. Haskins states that in 1775, it was granted a licence as an alehouse but no more is heard of the house [20]. There is always the possibility that it was known by another name at a later date.

243 Valiant Soldier, nk
In 1759, the Town Clerk announced that the Mayor and Justices of Salisbury intended to suppress "all such Houses and prosecute any Brewer selling Ale & Beer without being duly licensed thereto." The Valiant Soldier was one of four houses that were noted as not being licensed to sell ale [985].

244 Vestry, 32 Milford Street
This house is on the south side of Milford Street and is of 15th C. construction although the front of the pub on the street is of a later date. John Wyse, a vintner, was granted a lease for the premises in 1475 and it is possible that it has been a pub ever since. In the earliest records, it is called the Rainbow.

In 1756, the pub was put up for sale and it was described as consisting of a Cook's Shop, a Kitchen, one large Parlour, and 2 lesser Rooms, a large Stable, very good Cellars, 4 Chambers & all other conveniences [986].

In 1824, an event occurred that gained the Rainbow some notoriety: Poet Rose was accused of libelling General Sir John Slade regarding his conduct at the Battle of Waterloo. He was followed by Marcus Slade, the General's son, and severely horse-whipped in Milford Street [987]. Rose took refuge in the Rainbow but was followed into the inn by Mr Slade. Rose was eventually locked in a room and rescued from further violence. The attack was the subject of an action at the following assizes which resulted in a verdict in favour of Rose of 40 shillings. Rose's story seems to be in error as General Slade was not present at Waterloo. But, in 1812, he was present at the Battle of Estremadura under Rowland Hill. He lost a cavalry action against the French and the Duke of Wellington wrote "I have never been more annoyed than by Slade's affair. Our officers of cavalry have acquired a trick of galloping at everything. They never consider the situation, never think of maneuvering before an enemy, and never keep back or provide for a reserve". One of Slade's officers stated that as a leader of cavalry he was deplorable. He was a byword for inefficiency throughout the army. Thus, Poet Rose's accusations seem to have been correct.

In 1831, on the death of King George IV, the landlord, James Goddard, renamed the pub as the William the Fourth after the new Monarch [988]. The new pub sign featured the King in the uniform of an Admiral on one side and on the other in his coronation robes. But later in this year, Goddard was so upset by the King's opposition to the reform of parliament that he took down the sign and hung it upside down (See Appendix 1 – Old Inns of Salisbury Part IV). When the Reform Act was passed into law in the following year, the sign was returned to its correct posture.

In the 20th C. the pub was owned by Usher's Brewery, but was sold in about 1990 and became Le Beq's, a one-bar, theme pub specialising in bottled, chilled lager. Unfortunately, many of the old partitions in the pub that gave it a special quality were removed at this time. In 1993, the pub closed until it was purchased by Wychwood Brewery and renamed the Hobgoblin after one of that brewery's beers. In that form, it became a noisy pub specialising in real ales. In 1998, it reverted to the name of the William the Fourth before, in 2002, it was purchased by the owner of the nearby Chapel nightclub. The pub was renamed yet again becoming the Vestry. The pub was open to entry from the street during the early evening but later in the evening, the front door was locked and a rear entrance linking it to the Chapel was opened. It then became an annex bar to the nightclub. Currently it remains as an annex to the Chapel and is not open to the public at any time.

245 Victoria Hotel, 76 Mill Road

The earliest mention of the Victoria in licencing records is in 1861 but in 1859, Edmund Gillo was summoned for keeping his beer-house open after eleven o'clock at night [989]. Later in that year, Mr Gillo applied for a spirit license of his beerhouse [990]. This was refused on the grounds that 'the time had hardly arrived for granting the application'. This was because it was believed that there was insufficient trade to warrant another fully licensed public house in Fisherton. However, Mr Gillo applied again in 1860 with the beerhouse now being called the Victoria Inn [991]. It was said that the pub had ten excellent bedrooms and four sitting rooms and was ideal for persons who had to wait for several hours for a train or who had to wait overnight. It was also stated that Mr Gillo intended to build extensive stabling once a spirit license was approved. The application was refused yet again with a suggestion that if Mr Gillo proceeded with building the stables, the Magistrates might take a different view. In consequence, in 1861, a spirit license was finally approved for the Victoria [992].

George Plank, the landlord of the inn in 1872, was summoned for keeping his house open during prohibited hours [993]. A Police Constable found the door of the pub open at twenty to five on a Sunday afternoon and, on entering, he found four men with beer in front of them. Mrs Plank told the policeman that she thought the times was just after five. Mr Plank said he was in his garden at the time and did not realise there were men in the bar. He said he had many travellers residing in his house and he kept the door unlocked to allow them free entry and exit. Mr Plank was found guilty and fined twenty shillings and costs.

To round off the century, there was a robbery at the house in 1899. An Army reservist who had stayed at the pub was charged with having stolen a cloth cap, a gun metal watch and a silver chain with a total value of eighteen shillings [994]. He was found guilty and sentenced to 21 days in prison.

The Victoria remained quietly in trade for the remainder of the 19th C. and it was not until 1915 that we hear of it again. In that year, the pub was referred to the Renewal Authority under the Licensing Act of 1904 and the Licensing (Consolidation) Act of 1911. This allowed authorities to refuse to renew a pub's licence if it was believed that there was insufficient local demand for the pub. Compensation was paid if the pub was closed. The report on the Victoria read [10]: 'Licensing District of the City of New Sarum. To the Compensation Authority for the area comprising the above District. At the Adjourned General Annual Licensing Meeting holden at the Council House in the said City on the Twenty-second day of February, 1915, for the above named Licensing District, We being the Renewal Authority for the said District decided to refer to you under Section 19 of the Licensing (Compensation) Act, 1910, the question of the Licence held in respect of the premises specified below:-

'Name and Situation of Premises: Victoria Inn, Church Street, Salisbury

Nature of Licence Spirit Retailer's (or Publican's)

Licensee: Horace Charles Wale

Registered Owners: Messrs. Bartlett & Co., Warminster, Wilts, Brewers.

'Report: In connection with the question so referred, we report as follows: -

'The present tenant has held the licence since the 24th April, 1911.

'We have inspected the premises, and find that the house has bedrooms in which 20 people can be accommodated. It has also stabling capable of holding 12 horses.

'The renewal of the licence was objected to by Mr Frank Shepherd of 69, Fisherton Street, Salisbury, represented by Mr E F Pye-Smith of Salisbury, Solicitor, on the grounds: -

1. That the said house has been conducted in such a manner as to constitute a breach of military orders.

2. That the said house is not required to supply the reasonable requirements of the district in which it is situated.

'We received evidence on oath from the objector and his witnesses to the following effect: -

'That the house is situate in Church Street, Salisbury, and within a radius of a quarter of a mile there are 16 other licensed houses, including the Refreshment Rooms at the Railway Station. That a great portion of the said area is occupied by water meadow and railway lines, and that the house is not required to supply the reasonable requirements of the district.

'We received evidence on oath from the licensee and his witnesses to the following effect: -

'That the trade done has been as follows: Trade for Year ending September 30th: -

	1914	1913	1912
Beer (barrels)	152	156	122
Spirits (gals.)	72	77	92
Total value	£369	£382	£330

Trade for the four months ending January, 1915:-

58½ barrels	value	£146 10s 0d
77 gals	value	£68 15s 3d

Equivalent to an annual trade of

175 barrels	value	£439 10s 0d
231 gallons	value	£206 5s 9d
		£645 15s 9d

'That the house is well used by members of the general public, and especially by railway employees. That there is a good demand for its sleeping accommodation and provision of meals. That during the three weeks ending 22nd February, 1915, 114 people were provided with beds, and 309 meals supplied.

'That the stabling is also used, and taxi-cabs put up. We further report as follows:

'The City of Salisbury comprises an area of 1720 acres, with a population of 21,217. There are in the City 71 fully-licensed houses, 4 on-Beerhouses, 3 off-Beerhouses, and 2 Refreshment houses, besides 15 other licences held by shopkeepers and others for sale by retail for consumption off the premises. One full licence, that of the Great Western Railway Refreshment Rooms, will lapse in April, no application having been made for its renewal this year. Upon such evidence and information we decided to refer to you the question of the renewal of the licence on the ground of redundancy, and provisionally renewed the same to the licensee.

'Resolved: That the Compensation Authority decides not to proceed upon the Report above mentioned.

As a result, the Victoria had its licence renewed and it continues until this day.

The Victoria continued as a Bartlett's of Warminster house until 1920, when that brewery was taken over by Ushers of Trowbridge. It remained an Usher's house until 1974 when it became a Chef and Brewer pub within the Watney Mann group. The Victoria did close for a period in 1986 but re-opened in 1989 with its two bars combined into a single area. .It is now known as the Victoria Hotel.

246 Village, Wilton Road

This pub opened in early 1865 and was called the Windsor Castle at that time. In the 1871 census, it is clearly shown as the Windsor Castle Inn with William Sheppard being the landlord. The 1861 Census shows the same William Sheppard living in Windsor Road and working as a Porter but the address is clearly not what became the pub.

The Oakhill Brewery, who owned the pub, applied for permission to make alterations to the inn in 1892 [995]. This was approved by he Magistrates who said that the alterations were better 'not only for better sanitary arrangements but for the convenience of those living in the house'.

In 1894, William Whitehorn, an outfitter from Minster Street, was charged with using obscene language to the police when they visited the pub [996]. It appears that he lost his temper when the police disturbed the customers while looking for a man. He apologised to the police and threw himself on the mercy of the Court. The Court responded by finding him guilty and fining him twenty shillings plus costs.

It continued throughout the remainder of the 19th C. and on through the 20th C. as a local pub without anything significant happening. It appears to have been owned by the Oakhill Brewery Company from Oak Hill, north of Shepton Mallet in 1892 but it was a Lovibond's house from at least 1932 until that brewery was purchased by Courage in 1962. It was sold by Courage in 1981 but continued on as the Windsor Castle. For a short while, an attempt was made to update it with the cellar opened as a bar with the emphasis on black paint and rock music. This approach was unsuccessful and the pub closed for a while. In 1988, Joe Morris refurbished and opened the pub as the Village free house.

It continued under the same landlord for much of the time since becoming the Village, gaining a reputation for the quality and variety of real ale. In 2011, the pub received a redecoration and a new landlord has taken the pub.

247 Vine, 97 Bedwin Street

This pub was in Bedwin Street at the west end of St Edmund's churchyard on the site that is now occupied by St Edmund's Church House. It was originally known as the Sun and Haskins states that it was licensed as an alehouse in 1741 [20].

By 1763, the house is described in an advertisement for a sale on the premises as 'the sign of the Sun situate near St Edmund's Church'. Later, in 1786, an unusual event occurred [997]: "Wednesday, Mrs George, wife of Mr George, of the Sun public house in this city, was delivered of two female children. – She is in the 50th year of her age, and firmly persisted that she was not with child till taken in Labour, nor did her husband or the family disbelieve her".

Sometime about 1796, when the Vine in the Cheese Market closed, the Sun was renamed the Vine. The Sun was put up for sale in 1796 [998] and it seems likely that when the new landlord entered the pub, he renamed it as the Vine.

Little more is heard of the Vine over the next forty years apart from a few advertisements for its sale as landlords changed. In 1839, the stock and furniture were put up for sale as John Clark was leaving the inn [999]. The sale advertised 'Forty Hogsheads of Old Strong Beer, several Store Casks, from five hogsheads to 25 ditto, a quantity of hops, building timber, and bricks; a range of pig-sties, with tiled roofs; sashes and frames; bedsteads and furniture; two feather beds and bedding; clock in mahogany case; ditto in oak case; handsome time-piece, in rosewood case; with numerous other articles.' James Clark advertised that he was taking the inn a week after the notice of sale.

By 1856, Thomas Leversuch was the landlord [1000]. He took a labourer from Winterbourne named Morris to court to recover the cost of 18 Gallons of beer which was sold to Morris's wife. She in turn sold the beer at an event in Winterbourne but she probably did not have a license to retail the beer. She claimed that Leversuch knew that she was going to sell the beer, and that she had offered him 10 shillings as an instalment for the cost as not all the beer had been sold and the remainder was being consumed by her family over a period of time. The Mayor, as Chairman of the Bench, stated that the reselling of the beer was a direct fraud on the Revenue and that Leversuch must have known about it. However, he ordered Morris to pay 10 shillings immediately to Leversuch and then pay 5 shillings a month until the cost was covered. It is not known if there was any further prosecution covering the loss of taxes by the Revenue.

Two years later, the police opposed the renewal of Leversuch's license because his house had been conducted in a disorderly manner and he had been convicted twice for keeping the inn open outside of legal hours [1001]. The Mayor considered that this was insufficient grounds to suspend the license, but warned Leversuch to run his inn n in a proper manner otherwise he would lose his license. However, Leversuch died a year later, at the age of 39, while still landlord of the Vine. His wife continued to run the inn until March, 1862.

By the annual licensing session in September, 1867, James Smith was the landlord. By the next summer, Smith had been found guilty of allowing persons of notoriously bad character to drink in the Vine and he was fined 40 shillings [1002]. Consequently, in September, 1868, the renewal of his license was opposed on the grounds that Smith had harboured women of loose character [1003] No application for renewal of the license was made and renewal was refused.

In 1869 and 1870, attempts were made to re-open the Vine, in the latter year by Symonds brewery of Winchester. In 1870, the paperwork was in a muddle, and the solicitor representing the brewery asked for an adjournment in order to correct the errors in the paperwork [1003]. This was granted. However, there is no record of the matter being discussed again and the Vine remained closed. In the 1871 Census, the house is noted as being 'late the Vine Inn'.

248 Vine, Cheese Market

The Vine was in the Cheese Market immediately to the north of St Thomas' churchyard and it extended back to the river. It appears to have become an inn in 1647 when William Joyce let the premises to William Vyner, a vintner (and the name of the inn probably derived from the vintner's surname) [18]. However, the site was that of a medieval courtyard house which was in existence by 1440. Over the years, the buildings must have been updated and rebuilt many times and the properties now on the site are largely from the mid-18th C. and the early 19th C.

In 1657, William Viner issued a farthing token which had a bunch of grapes in the obverse, together with his name and stated 'In Sarum 1657' on the reverse [1004].

In 1679, the premises were purchased by the Corporation of Salisbury from the estate of John Joyce and appears to have been let to landlords by the Corporation from that time until the inn closed.

In 1704, the house was known as the Vine Inn and Theatre and from this time until its closure, plays and other performances took place at the Vine. In addition, exhibitions were held at the inn as typified by the following display of sculpture that was staged at 1747 in the

Vine [1006]: "To be seen at the Vine in the Cheese-Cross, Four Hundred Fine Figures in Sculpture Found amongst the Great Treasure taken by the Prince Frederick and Duke Privatiers. These consist of 'Six Pieces in Relievo', designed as a Present for the French King. For this purpose, they were brought from Lima in the French South Sea Ships taken by the Prince Frederick and Duke Privatiers, and carried into Bristol, and are as follows: - 1. The Last Supper. 2. The Betrayal. 3. The Scourging. 4. The Bearing of the Cross. 5. Descent from the Cross. 6. Appearance to the Holy Women. "Price 1/-, 6d, and for servants 3rd.".

The theatre was described at this time as Salisbury's new Playhouse as shown in the following bill [1007]: "By Mr Hallam's Company from both Theatres in London (by particular desire) on Tuesday evening, January the seventh, 1752, at the New Playhouse in Salisbury, will be presented a Tragedy called Romeo and Juliet, wrote by William Shakespeare. At the end of the Play will be performed a new Dance called "Les Badinages Champetre." To which will be added a Pantomime Entertainment, called The Adventures of Harlequin, being the comic part of Perseus and Andromeda. Particular care has been taken to make the house warm. This company always begins exactly at six o'clock".

The theatre was supplemented by what would today be described as circus acts as shown by this example from 1755 "Matteaux Solomon, The famous Italian Artist & surprising Balance Master on the Slack Wire, Is just arrived in this City, from the New Theatre on the Haymarket, London (where he performed with universal Applause, before some of the Royal Family, and many of the first Nobility) & will Exhibit this Evening in the New Play House at the Vine, beginning precisely at Six o'clock. The Number of Performances shewn by this very curious & uncommon Artist is by far much too great for the Compass of an Advertisement, let suffice to mention only the few following, viz

1. On a single Wire, when in full Swing, he walks backward & forward, driving a wheelbarrow with a dog in it, & balances a large wheel at the same time.

2. He balances several Glasses filled with Liquor, walking on the Wire while in full Swing, without spilling a Drop.

3. On the Edge of a common drinking Glass, he balances a Sword on the Point, spinning round like a Top, and stands upright on the Wire, which is all the time in full Swing, and while in this position he balances Straw, standing upright on the edge of the Glass, tosses it thence to his Forehead, & from his Forehead on the Glass again, it still in the same Position, & the Wire all the while in full Swing.

4. He walks on the Wire when in full Swing with a Pole, & beats a Drum at the same time etc.

After the Equilibrium on the Wire, he performs many very curious & entertaining Italian Pieces of Art, & such as were never shewn in England by any but himself.

A Band of Music will play during the Performance. The Room has been well aired for several Days past, & the Doors will be opened half an hour after Five. He will perform during a short stay, every Monday, Tuesday, Wednesday * Saturday Nights. Front Seats 1/-, Back Seats 6d"

By 1762, the inn was considered to be sufficiently respectable for the Justices to meet there. In particular, in September of that year, the Justices met to licence the Inns and Alehouses in Salisbury. In the following year, a Friendly Society was set up at the inn [1009]: "At the Vine Inn in this City, a Society is established for allowing 10 guineas per annum to the Widows of such as shall deposit 10/6, and afterwards pay 1/6 per Month, which bears its proportion to the Society for allowing £30 per annum. Likewise, every sick Member shall have lent him, out of their Stock 5/- per week till such time as the Majority of Members shall, for certain good Reasons, think it necessary to withhold the same. If the said Member recovers his Health, he is obliged to pay back the Money lent him by the Society. And if he dies, his Widow shall not be entitled to or receive any part of her Annuity till such time as the said Society shall have first paid themselves the full money lent her late Husband, by withholding from her so much of her Annuity as shall discharge the same. This Society is to be governed nearly like the Thirty Pound Society in all Respects. N.B. Any Person of good Character may be admitted as a Member by paying as above, and from 45 years to 50 paying 12/- every year Entrance Money, & none above 50 to be admitted. The Society will meet at the Vine Inn Monday the 25th July inst. at 7 o'clock in the Evening, to receive the Names of such as shall offer themselves for Members".

Apart from entertainments, it is clear that other general meetings were held at the inn (as there were very few public buildings at that time) including a meeting in 1766 that resulted in the building of Salisbury Infirmary [1010]: "A Meeting of the Gentlemen and Inhabitants of the City & Close of Salisbury, and also of this and the neighbouring Counties is desired on Monday in the next Assize Week, at Five of the clock in the Afternoon, and again on the second Day of the Races at Eleven of the Clock in the Forenoon, at the Vine Inn, at the said City, to consider of a scheme for the erecting and establishing a General Hospital or Infirmary in or near the said City: At which time a Book will be opened for entering Benefactions & Subscriptions: And such Gentlemen as are disposed to encourage this Undertaking, and cannot attend in Person, are desired to signify their Intentions by a letter directed to Mr Robert Cooper, Linen-Draper, in Salisbury".

In May of 1766, it was noted that the Earl of Radnor had subscribed £500 toward the Infirmary and that by July, more than £1400 had been promised [1011]. In September, a Committee was set up to manage the Infirmary with the Earl of Pembroke nominated as the Visitor, the Earl of Radnor as President along with other worthies [1012]. Two physicians were appointed followed by two surgeons in October. The Infirmary was ready to accept patients by May of 1767 but this was in existing buildings and plans continued to be formed to construct the new building. The foundation stone was laid in September 1767 and the new Infirmary opened in 1771. Would it that public works could happen as quickly as this nowadays!

In 1770, an interesting display of new technology was shown at the Vine 1013: "To the Curious in Philosophy & Mechanics. Arrived from London & to be seen at the Vine Inn, The Self Moving Machine, that travels the turnpike road without horses at the rate of 6 miles an hour, it will ascend a hill with ease and descend no faster than the rider pleases; it is 500 weight, & set in motion & stopped with a finger, and turns about in a moment of time as the rider pleases, with several other Philosophical & Mechanical Experiments, - viz. – water works, engines, cranes, mills balance-table, mathematical doors etc. which are specified at large in the hand-bills, with a grand Electrical Machine that shows all the phenomena of thunder & lightning etc. on a new principle; palsys, rheumatics 7 other disorders cured – To be seen any hour of the day at 1/- each person from 10 to 8 at night. N.B. Electrical Machines made and sold on a new construction".

It has been said that the Self Moving Machine was Cugnot's steam tractor designed for towing artillery but there is no evidence that Cugnot ever left France. It is likely that what was demonstrated was a working model of a proposed steam carriage as there is no evidence of a working full size vehicle in Great Britain until Trevithick's of 1801.

In 1778, the last advertisements for plays at the Vine Theatre appear although various exhibitions continued to be shown at the Inn. A new Theatre had been opened at the Sun in Fisherton Street in 1765 and this appears to have taken the majority of performances in Salisbury. But the old theatre was still used for some purposes (September 1779) [1014]: "Monday Tuesday & Wednesday, a party of French prisoners passed through this city on their way to Winchester. They were accommodated whilst they remained here in the old theatre at the Vine, which answered the temporary purpose very well. Soon after the arrival of the party on Monday, which consisted of French and Spaniards, a violent quarrel ensued between them & the Spaniards, a great acrimony and vehemence, upbraided their fellow prisoners with being the cause of the war, & their present confinement. The dispute became serious & many blows were given on both sides; happily, the guard interposed and removed the Dons into another apartment".

And (March 1780) [1015]: "The Satyr, or Aetheopian Savage, who was shown before their Majesties at Kew, Nov 20 1879, and afterwards to the Duke of Cumberland at Windsor Lodge, & since that time to the Nobility & Gentry at Bath & Bristol, with the highest approbation, will arrive at his lodgings at the Vine on Tuesday next, where he will be exhibited for the satisfaction of the curious, who cannot fail of admiring such an extraordinary production of nature. He is of a different species from any other creature ever seen in Europe, and seems to be the link between rational and brute creatures. He is five feet high, sits in a chair like a human person, with a club in his hand, and from his remarkable beard has thence the appearance of an aged man. His arms are large & muscular, yet his hands and nails are extremely delicate. His make and shape in every other respect, & his beautiful colours are equally wonderful. Admission to Ladies & Gentlemen 1/- each".

In 1780, we see the first signs that the status of the Vine is beginning to slip. In that year, Joshua Gibbons takes over the inn. He was the Carrier between Salisbury and Oxford and immediately announces that his Caravan will run from the Vine every Tuesday [1016]. In July of that year, cock fighting is advertised at the Vine which represents quite a change from the theatrical productions of a few years earlier [1017]. In June, 1782, Joshua

Gibbons is made bankrupt {1018} but he dies in July of that year [1019]. and Thomas Gibbons moves the Winchester and Portsmouth Stagecoach from the Vine to the Maidenhead.

Over the next few years, the Vine seems to change hands every year or two. In 1785, the Justices move their court from the Vine to the Council Chamber in Salisbury [1020]. In 1786, part of the Vine is sold and it is noted that the old theatre is to be converted into a tennis court (this was probably Real Tennis as it is later described as a Fives Court and is obviously still inside the building [1021]). In January, 1788, the landlord, Moses Hurst, was found guilty of many misdemeanours and disturbances at the Vine and it was resolved that he would never be granted a license to keep a public house in Salisbury after his current license expired [2]. Consequently, the Vine is advertised to let after the annual licensing session of that year but it is noted that 'the useless part being taken for other business' [1022].

But still some entertainment takes place at the Vine. In 1790, an interesting display is held 1023: "The Amazing Pig of Knowledge. The Question at present among the polite and Curious is, Who has seen the Scientific Pig? And those who answer they have not, are looked on as persons that are blind to the most striking curiosity ever seen or heard of; for we know of no age or country that has, at any period, produced the like, and in all probability may never have an opportunity of seeing such another, ere the youngest of us shall be no more. Be wise then, and see it while you may. This very astonishing Animal is just arrived in this city and may be seen this day (Monday) at the Vine Inn, in the Market Place; on Tuesday, at a commodious Booth in the fair, and on Wednesday, and the following days, at Devizes Green fair. Admittance, Ladies and Gentlemen one shilling each; servants and children half price".

Over the next few years, the Vine seems to be almost continuously for sale or to let with a variety of proprietors coming and going. Some buildings to its south were already owned by the Dean and Chapter of Salisbury Cathedral and in 1795, the Corporation hand over the Vine to them in exchange for other property. 1796 sees the last appearance of the Vine in the licensing records and by 1804, George Short builds two shops on the site.

There is still some evidence of the Vine. The building at the southern end of the Cheese Market, occupied by an Estate Agents and a Kitchen shop in 2017, is the site of the Vine The carriage throughway leading from the Cheese Market to the yard of the inn has been enclosed becoming a shop (No.28). Inside is an 18th C. staircase which is probably the 'substantial staircase up to a room called the Vine' and a small notice can be found in the shop giving a brief history of the inn.

249 Volunteer's Arms Inn, 90 Winchester Street

This pub was at the top end of Winchester Street and any part of it that remained was probably demolished when the ring road was built.

It certainly had a license from 1876 when a Mr E Day was the licensee and may well have been a beerhouse before that date (see later in this description). In 1877, Flora Coles, the landlady, left the pub without giving notice and hence the owners, Bailey's brewery of Frome, asked for a temporary license to open the pub for sales until a new tenant could be found [1024]. This application was granted.

In 1891, the pub was advertised for sale as part of the auction associated with the King's Head brewery in Bridge Street [146]. It is possible this brewery had purchased the pub from Bailey's. It also seems probable that Bartlett's brewery of Warminster purchased the pub from this sale.

In 1913, the renewing of the licence of the pub was referred to the Renewal Authority under the provisions of the Licensing (Consolidation) Act of 1910. Their report read [10]: 'On reading the Report of the Renewal Authority for the City of New Sarum, as follows: -

'In connection with the question so referred, we report as follows with respect to the "Old Gate House" or "Volunteer Arms":-

'Ante 1869 Beerhouse. Poor Rate Assessment £21 10s gross. The present tenant has held the Licence since April, 1909.

'This house is situated in Winchester Street, Salisbury, at the following distances from other licensed premises in the same street: -

"Anchor and Hope" (Fully licensed) 93 yards

"Coach and Horses"ditto 186 yards

"Black Horse" ditto 220 yards

"London Inn", London Road 58 yards

'All the above houses (including the "Old Gate House") are contained in a distance of about 278 yards.

'The public rooms are small, and the accommodation is not good. There is no sleeping accommodation for travellers, and no stabling.

'All the other neighbouring houses referred to are larger, have better public accommodation, and all except the "Black Horse" have stabling.

'The assessment to Poor Rate of the "Old Gate House" is the lowest.

'A representative of the Owners attended before us, and stated that they assented to the question of the renewal of the Licence being referred to the Compensation Authority.

'No evidence was offered on behalf of the Licensee to show the amount of trade done at the "Old Gate House", but observations made upon the house showed that the number of people using the premises was small. The Licensee does not spend all his time in the business, but is employed by the Owners as a drayman.

'Evidence of the above statements having been given, we decided to refer to you the question of the renewal of the Licence, and provisionally renewed the same to the Tenant.

'The City of Salisbury comprises an area of 1720 acres, with a population of 21,217. There are in the City 72 fully Licensed Houses, 5 on Beerhouses, 3 off Beerhouses and 2 Refreshment Rooms; besides 14 other Licences held by shopkeepers and others for sale by retail for consumption off the premises.

'Resolved: That the Compensation Authority decides to proceed upon the Report above mentioned'.

The Compensation Authority refused to renew the licence and this decision was not opposed by the owners, Bartlett & Company of Warminster. The pub was closed and compensation of £671 4s 0d was paid.

It is a little strange that this report shows the owners of the pub as Bartletts as that brewery had been acquired by Ushers of Trowbridge in 1898!

250 Waggon & Horses, 32 Brown Street

This pub was on the west side of Brown Street and the building can still be seen immediately next to the north entrance of the Brown Street car park where it is used as staff accommodation by the Red Lion hotel.

It first appears in the licensing records in 1819 and was most probably known by a different name before this time [5]. It was owned by Samuel Whitchurch for a period before 1835 when it was sold as part of the sale of his estate [1025].

In 1842, the landlord, John Holdaway, was convicted of harbouring persons of a 'notoriously bad character' [8]. He was fined £1 with 8s 6d costs as it was his first offence. However, he was succeeded by John Parker later in that year. But his widow, Sarah Holdaway, became landlady in 1845 so one wonders if the change in late 1842 was a device to enable the family to continue running the pub despite the criminal charge.

But in 1854, when Jane Rutter applied to transfer the license of the pub from herself to John Burnett, the transfer was strongly opposed by the police [11]. It appeared that Mr Burnett had actually been running the pub for two or three months and during that period, the police had seen several local thieves and other notorious characters using the pub. After much discussion, the Magistrates decided that Mr Burnett had not been charged with any offence so the transfer was approved.

Mr Burnett was warned to be sure that he ran the pub with care or he might lose his license at the annual licensing session later in the year. He did retain his license at that session.

The Post Office Directory of 1859 shows a pub called the Coach & Horses in Brown Street where the Waggon & Horses stood. Since the pub in Winchester Street was known as the Coach & Horses at this date it is unlikely that the Waggon & Horses became known by this name at this time and thus it is believed that the entry in the Directory is in error. In 1861, John Stainton at the Waggon & Horses is described as an Upholsterer and Innkeeper which suggests that the pub did not command a great deal of trade.

During the late 1800s, the pub seems to have been involved in numerous occasions at the Magistrates court, often for drunkenness of customers but also for other disturbances. This resulted in the police twice objecting to the renewal of the license twice but on both occasions the Magistrates renewed the license.

By 1924, the pub was referred to the Renewal Authority [10]:

'The Waggon and Horses" – On reading the report of the Renewal Authority as follows: -

'This house is situated in Brown Street, within 53 yards of Milford Street, in the same congested district as "The Goat".

'The distances of the other licensed houses are:-

"Round of Beef"	70 yards
"Goat Inn"	78 yards
"Malt and Hop Tap"	85 yards
"Oddfellows Arms"	80 yards
"Red Lion Hotel"	95 yards
"William IV"	105 yards

"Cathedral Hotel"	106 yards
"Catherine Wheel"	118 yards
"Crystal Fountain"	182 yards
"Queen's Arms"	150 yards
"Star Inn"	150 yards

'The rateable value of the "Waggon and Horses" for Poor Rate purposes is £12 5s 0d.

'A plan of the ground floor of the premises was put in, and accompanies this Report. The only public room is a bar 13 feet 8 inches by 13 feet 6 inches, but occasionally the sitting room is used as a private bar; and there is no stabling or yard for vehicles.

'Evidence from a sanitary point of view was given by the Sanitary Inspector for the City, to the effect that the house is small, and the rooms public and private badly ventilated and lighted; while the sanitary conveniences provided for the use of customers are as regards situation and otherwise very imperfect.

'Evidence was also given of police observation from the 7th to the 13th February, both inclusive, and showed that during the period 383 persons entered the house, the daily totals being: -

7th	52
8th	43
9th, Saturday	75
10th	45
11th	44
12th, Market Day	83
13th	41
	383

'No evidence as to trade done at the house was offered on behalf of the licensee or the owners.

'After careful consideration, we decided to refer to you the question of the renewal of the license on the ground of redundancy, and provisionally renewed the same to the tenant.

'And on hearing Mr C J Woodrow and Mr J W Clark on behalf of the Renewal Authority, Resolved: That the Compensation Authority decides to proceed upon the report above mentioned'.

'It was decided not to renew the licence of the pub and it closed later in 1924. Compensation of £1200 was paid.

For a short period in about 1983, the building was opened by the Red Lion as the Churchill Rooms but this venture was unsuccessful and it closed again shortly afterwards.

251 Waggon & Horses, Fisherton Street

This pub was on the north side of Fisherton Street on the east side of Summerlock Bridge (the bridge at the Fisherton Street end of Water Lane). The pub and other contemporary buildings were demolished many years ago and so no trace remains.

Haskins states that it was licensed as an alehouse as early as 1769 [20]. It appears in an engraving in Peter Hall's 'Picturesque Memorials of Salisbury' that was published in 1834. It also featured in a picture in the Illustrated London News of December, 1852, which showed the floods in Fisherton Street.

In January, 1831, the landlord, Robert Welch, was fined £100 in court for having in his possession six quarts of molasses and 'a certain preparation, or ingredient, for the purpose of darkening the colour of Beer, and to be used as a substitute for malt and hops' [1026]. A sample of the latter preparation was produced in court and was described as 'a more detestable substance was never before seen'.

A very early photograph (probably from before 1858) also shows the pub. The last record of the pub is in 1867 and in July, 1868, the land occupied by the Waggon and Horses and seven adjoining cottages was put up for sale [1027]. Also on sale were the building materials of the pub and cottages. Not surprisingly, this was the last that was heard of the Waggon and Horses.

252 Weaver's Arms, Fisherton

There are several references to this pub dating from the 18th C. but its exact location in Fisherton is not known. The earliest date known is in 1756 when the landlord, Henry Russell, advertised a meadow in Dragon Street (Exeter Street) for sale [1028].

By 1796, it was advertised for sale with or without some adjoining meadow land [1029]. There are doubts whether the pub was still in trade at that time as the last recorded landlord was James Whatley in 1794.

In 1804, the 'Reversion of a Public House' called the Weaver's Arms in Fisherton Anger was advertised for sale together with some tenements and their gardens adjoining the pub [1030]. Nothing more is heard of the Weaver's Arms and it is supposed that it had ceased to be a public house.

253 Weaver's Arms, Milford Hill

It is not known exactly where this pub was in Milford Hill but in 1912 it was described as being near Mrs Pinckney's Lodge. Mrs Pinckney appeared to live at Milford Hill House at the top of Milford Hill.

This was an alehouse as early as 1766 if not before. In 1774, it was advertised for sale [1031]. By 1783 the landlord was Henry Derby. He was charged with 'suffering disorder and tippling in his house on Sunday' [1]. However, the Sergeant of the Dragoons who accused him failed to present himself at the court and the charge was dismissed. In 1787, the landlady is shown as being H Derby, Widow so presumably, Henry had died.

There is no further entry in the licensing records after 1787. By May 1808, a freehold house and garden in Milford Hill was advertised for sale and was described as having been formerly the Weaver's Arms [1032].

254 Weyhill Tap, Milford Street

There is a single reference to this pub in 1885 when William Norton was the landlord. It is probably a name for a pub most commonly known by some other title but no connection has been made.

255 Wheatsheaf, 7-9 Fish Row

The Wheatsheaf lay between Fish Row and New Canal. It consisted of two houses on Fish Row; No.9 being the western of the two and dated from the 14th C. and No. 7 dating from the 15th C. The extension of these two buildings to the south, facing on to New Canal dated from about 1800.

Considering the age of the buildings, it is rather surprising that the earliest mention of the Wheatsheaf comes from 1742 when it was licensed as an alehouse to Thomas Voise [20]. Presumably, the alehouse only occupied one of the two premises on Fish Row. It is not known when the later form of the Wheatsheaf as a substantial public house came about but it must have been contemporary with the southern extension as that formed the southern end of the main bar in later years.

Wheatsheaf

In May, 1768, a tragic occurrence is recorded in the *Salisbury Journal* [1033]: "Tuesday afternoon one John Parham, a journeyman tinman, who had lately worked in this city, went to the Wheat-Sheaf in the Fish Market, and complaining he was not very well, desired to lodge there that night; after drinking a cup of tea, he was shewn upstairs, where he went directly to bed. In the morning, the landlady going to call him to breakfast, was surprised to find the door tied with his garters, and on opening it found a great deal of blood on the floor and the man dead. Whereupon Mr Tanner the city coroner was sent for when, on examining the body, it appeared he had cut his throat ... a bloody razor was found in the bed, and near £17 in his pockets. The Coroner's Jury brought in the verdict Lunacy".

By 1795, Henry Smith was the landlord. He died in 1804 when it was noted in the *Salisbury Journal* that he had been a member of the Salisbury Troop of the Wiltshire Yeomanry Cavalry [1034]. His widow, Ann, ran the pub for another year but it seems likely that she married Thomas Richards who is named as the landlord from January, 1805. Thomas died in March, 1822. His widow, Ann, announced that she would continue to run the pub [1035] and she did until 1827 [1036] when William Potto, her son-in-law, became the landlord. In keeping with this continuing series of marriages, William Potto married Mrs Cassey, the widow of William Cassey who had been landlord of the City Arms [1037].

In July, 1832, a new coach called the Red Rover, which would run between Brighton and Salisbury was announced [1038]. It would leave the Wheatsheaf at 10:45 am and the Clarence Hotel in Brighton at 6:00 am. The two coaches would meet at 1:00 pm at the Red Rover Coach Office in Southampton. Presumably, they would continue their two journeys in the afternoon, so as to recommence the procedure the following day. This coach still appears to be running the following year although in an advertisement, it is referred to as the Rover coach and runs between Southampton and Salisbury with no travel to Brighton [1039].

Later in 1833, William Potto announced that he was opening a Wined and Spirit vault in Fish Row [1040]. This was, presumably, in the cellar of No. 7 Fish Row and it may be at this date that No. 7 was incorporated into the Wheatsheaf. If this was the case, it is also probable that the extension of the inn to provide an entrance from New Canal was also from this date.

William Potto stayed at the inn until the summer of 1834 when he moved to the Cross Keys in Queen Street [1041]. His successor at the Wheatsheaf was James Kite who moved to this inn from the Butcher's Arms in Butcher Row (now the Market Inn). James Kite describes himself as a Veterinary Surgeon. It is at this time that there is a mention of the Wheatsheaf Livery Stables in the New Canal. It seems that Mr Kite was more interested in the whole of the horse trade than in the business of an inn. He had in fact been at the Roebuck in New Canal from 1827 to 1829, premises in Culver street from 1829 to 1833, the Butcher's Arms, Butcher Row from 1833 to 1834, the Wheatsheaf from 1834 to 1836 and the Bell in Milford Hill from 1836 to 1846.

In 1835, the pub was sold as part of the late Samuel Whitchurch's estate. Then it was described as an inn and stable on New Canal but with an entrance on Fish Row [1042].

An unusual summons for theft took place in 1857. Elizabeth Penfold, a waitress at the Wheatsheaf, was charged with having stolen a sovereign from Joseph Cooper, a veterinary surgeon from Hampshire [1043]. He said that after he had gone to bed in the inn, the waitress had entered his room and taken the coin. However, there was plenty of evidence that Mr Cooper had consumed several glasses of ale before he retired to bed and that he was quite drunk. That, together with some discrepancies in his evidence led the Magistrates to dismiss the case.

In 1907, the owners of the Wheatsheaf, Matthews & Co of Gillingham, applied for permission to make some alterations to the inn [1044]. The main change was to the entrance from New Canal where some very steep steps were to be removed and replaced by a gentle rise.

The inn remained a Matthews Brewery of Gillingham house until that brewery was taken over by Hall & Woodhouse of Blandford Forum in 1963. The pub remained a Badger house until it was closed in about 1989.

256 White Hart, St John Street

The White Hart is certainly one of the older inns in Salisbury but exactly when it came into being is not known. In 1552, at a visitation held by Bishop Capon, it is complained (amongst other things) "that at the sign of the Whyte Hynde there is evil rule kept during divine service, and at other times also". The White Hynde is almost certainly the White Hart although this cannot be stated with certainty.

In 1618, Sir Walter Raleigh, who had just returned from his last and unsuccessful voyage to Guiana, lingered some time in Salisbury. Manourie, a French physician, helped him to feign illness. It was recorded that Manourie 'accordingly procured from the White Hart Inn a leg of mutton and some loaves which Raleigh devoured in secret and thus led his attendants to suppose that he took no kind of sustenance'. While he was in lodgings he prepared his 'Apology for the Voyage to Guiana'. This apology failed to appease the King who listened to complaints from the Spanish Ambassador about Raleigh's attack on a Spanish settlement. The King reinstated a death sentence for treason imposed on Raleigh in 1603 and he was duly beheaded in Westminster in October, 1618.

Haskins notes that in 1625, John Fryer of the White Hart took 4 barrels of beer and one barrel of ale from the Common Brewhouse over the previous year [17]. John Fryer also attended the meeting called by the Council to discuss inns taking beer from the Common Brewhouse [18].

In 1702, Haskins states that John Baker was granted a licence for the White Hart [19]. It is not clear if a license existed before this time as it is clear that the inn did exist before this date. But in 1707, John Baker was prosecuted for not honouring a billet of soldiers from the Earl of Ottery's Regiment of Foot that was issued by one of the High Constables of Salisbury [16]. At that time, a billet was a written notice allocating military persons to lodgings and only later became the name used for the lodgings themselves.

In 1765, a cock fight took place at the White Hart that was paid for by the noblemen and gentlemen of Wiltshire [1045]. The fights took place on the three mornings before the Salisbury Races.

Also in 1765, a Friendly Society was set up at the White Hart. The terms of membership were described as [1046]: "In order to allow each Member, who shall have continued in the Society Twelve Years, an Annuity of Twenty Pounds per ann. Clear of all Deductions. The present Terms of Admission are as follows: Every Person between the Age of twenty and thirty Years to pay three Guineas, Entrance, between thirty and thirty-five two Guineas and an Half, between thirty-five and forty two Guineas, between forty and forty-five one Guinea and an Half, between forty-five and fifty one Guinea, and after the age of fifty to pay no entrance Money, but each Member to subscribe six Shillings and six-pence monthly to the Chest; the sixpences of the present Members to be spent. Women may be Members of the Society".

As was common in those days, travelling doctors often set up in inns to treat member of the public. Thus we find the following advertisement from 1767 [1047]: "For the Good of the Public. This is to give notice, That there is arrived from London, the famous Physician and Oculist, Dr Fortunate Benvenuti, who during his long stay in the metropolis (London) has made himself renowned by his happy operations and many great cures ... as well of outward and inward diseases ... He Cures all disorders of the head and eyes, deafness and hard hearing, headache, weak memory, the vapours, epilepsy ... consumption, dropsy, rheumatism, gout .... Wounds, tumours, cancers ... He attends from eight to twelve in the forenoon, and from two till ten at night, at Mr Batt's the White Hart in Catherine St, where he cures the poor gratis, every day, from eleven to twelve in the forenoon".

One suspects that the cures of Dr Benvenuti were not an efficacious as the advert suggests but it might be too hard to describe him as a quack doctor.

Some stories regarding the White Hart are a little more unusual as exampled by this story from 1773 [1048]: "On Sunday morning the 5th inst about 9 o'clock the Hon Miss Cholmondelay, daughter of Lady Malpas set out from her Ladyship's house near Bath, in a post-chaise & four with Wm Clapcoat Lisle Esq, a young gentleman of Dorsetshire on a matrimonial expedition. The first stage was Devizes where they hired fresh horses for Marlborough, but as soon as they left the Inn the drivers were directed to take the Salisbury road. They came to the White Hart in this City about a quarter after 12 & gave out that they were going to Shaftesbury, but instead thereof drove to Thornley-Down, & arrived in the afternoon at Poole, where they immediately embarked on board a vessel for Guernsey. The pursuers passed through this city about 5 hours afterwards".

There were several coaches running from the White Hart in the late 18th C. but, as was normal at the time, coaches to London travelled overnight, presumably so that passengers on business would arrive for meetings in the morning and could travel back the following night. But in 1777, 'Genteel Travelling' was announced with a coach to London travelling during the day [1049]: "The conveyance between Salisbury and London having been found very inconvenient, on account of the carriages travelling all night, it is presumed that a well-conducted plan, free from such inconvenience, will be generally approved, The ladies and gentlemen of the City, Close, and neighbourhood of Salisbury, are therefore most respectfully informed, that a Salisbury Diligence will set out every morning at six o'clock, from the White Hart, at Salisbury, and the Angel, behind St Clement's, London, by way of Stockbridge, and will arrive at each of these inns early the same evening, as fresh horses will be taken at every stage, the same as with a post-chaise. To carry three passengers, at 3d per mile each, and 14lb baggage; all above 1d per lb. N.B The proprietors will not be accountable for anything above five pounds value. The carriages are quite new, elegant, and commodious; and as the proprietors are determined to make this conveyance as agreeable as any method of travelling can be, they humbly hope for the favours of the public".

This was the first mention of the Salisbury Light Coach that continued to run in this fashion until 1838, when the route was changed to meet the London and Southampton railway rather than go by road the whole way to London.

In 1780, the effects of the War of Independence in America impinged on the White Hart [1050]: "On Wednesday afternoon arrived at the White Hart inn in this City, on their way to London, Henry Laurens, Esq, late President of the American Congress. He was taken on the 5th September on board the Mercury packet, bound from Philadelphia to Holland, by the Vestal and Fairy ships of war, on the banks of Newfoundland, and was landed at Dartmouth on the 20th of the same month. He was attended only by Lieutenant Norris, of the Vestal frigate, who confirms the account of the dispatches being thrown overboard in a box, but not sinking immediately, a sailor jumped into the sea, and supported it till others came in a boat to his assistance, and took it up".

Henry Laurens was imprisoned in the Tower of London on suspicion of committing High Treason. But he was released in 1781 and later took part in the peace negotiations which led to the Treaty of Paris of 1783.

By 1780, the White Hart was becoming an important stopping place for coaches and in this year, it is clear that the coach networks were becoming very organised [1051]: "The Public are respectfully informed, that a Diligence will continue to set off every morning from the Crown Inn, Gosport, at four o'clock, and arrive at the White Hart, Salisbury, at half past eleven; where it meets the Exeter Post-Coach, which goes immediately for Exeter, and arrives at the London Inn by two o'clock the day following; from which Inn one Diligence sets out for Plymouth the same evening, and two more the next morning, at six o'clock; also meets the Bath Coach Monday and Thursday.

The above Diligence returns from the White Hart, Salisbury, for Gosport, every morning at five o'clock, where passengers (from all parts of the West) may depend on places for Gosport, as they will be regularly booked. Persons travelling from Plymouth and Exeter are informed that Diligences will set-off every morning from the Prince George, Plymouth, at six o'clock, and arrive the next evening at the White Hart Inn, Salisbury. Likewise, a Post-Coach sets out from the London Inn, Exeter, every night at eight o'clock (Saturdays excepted) and arrives the next afternoon at the White

Hart, Salisbury, where they meet the above Diligence to Gosport.

Performed by Weeks, White Hart Inn, Sarum
 Faithorn, Bell Inn, Romsey
 Fielder, Wheel Inn, Botley; and
 Crease, Crown Inn, Gosport

Fare Gosport to Sarum £0 11s 0d
From Sarum to Exon £1 4s 0d
From Exon to Plymouth £0 12s 6d
    £2 7s 6d"

By 1782, the White Hart was obviously becoming an hub for a network of coaches [1052]: "White Hart Inn, Salisbury. The Public are respectfully informed, that they may be accommodated with carriages from the above Inn to the following places:

A Post-Coach (with a guard) through Andover to London, every afternoon at four o'clock (Saturdays excepted).

A Diligence to London every night about twelve o'clock.

A Salisbury Diligence to London, through Stockbridge, every morning at five o'clock.

A Post-Coach to Exeter, through Blandford, Dorchester, Bridport etc every morning (Sunday excepted) at ten o'clock.

A Diligence to Exeter every night about eight o'clock.

A Post-Coach, through Romsey, Southampton, Botley and Titchfield, to Gosport and Portsmouth, every Monday, Wednesday, and Friday, at five, and Tuesday, Thursday and Saturday at seven in the morning.

A Post-Coach to Bath and Bristol, every Monday, Wednesday and Friday at seven in the morning.

Parcels regularly booked, and great care taken of their immediate delivery.

In February, 1785, the inn was advertised for sale but did not seem to find a purchaser as the advert was repeated a year later [1053]: "To be Sold by Private Contract. The commodious, well-known, and well-accustomed Inn, called the White Hart, situate in Catherine Street, in the direct road from London to the Land's End, now rented by Mr William Weeks, whose term expires at Saint Thomas day next (1786) together with Three Freehold and Four Leasehold Tenements, situate in Ivy Street, and a large Freehold stable in Brown Street, all which are immediately adjoining to and connected with the White Hart, by which means it might be rendered as large, and the most complete Inn in the west of England".

This advert was equally unsuccessful as William Weeks, was still proprietor of the inn in 1787. It is not known exactly when Mr Weeks left but it was certainly between 1791 and 1794, when Edward Keele was landlord.

In 1789, it was reported that a cask of rum which was being unloaded at the White Hart, was accidentally smashed, allowing the rum to escape into the gutter [1054]. It was said that the 'common people' managed to collect some of the rum from the gutter and became intoxicated. An enterprising soldier was passing the inn with a quart of beer in his hand and he quickly poured the beer away and filled his mug directly from the leaking cask.

At around this date, the shop belonging to John Fishlake, grocer, on the corner of Ivy Street and St John Street was pulled down along with the other houses in Ivy Street and the White Hart was rebuilt. At that time the front had only three windows either side of the portico. A further addition in St John Street was made at a later date as can be seen from the change in elevation on this frontage. When the large portico was added, the large effigy of a white hart was added, apparently in rivalry to the sign of the Antelope Inn! There once was a large first floor assembly room in the NE of the building that dated from c. 1840 but this is now divided into several bedrooms.

During his reign, King George III often spent time in Weymouth during the summer. On occasion, he stopped at the White Hart while horses were changed as on this occasion in 1804 [1055]: "On Friday night our beloved Monarch and his amiable consort, the Queen, with the Princesses Augusta, Elizabeth, and Mary, passed through this city on their way to Weymouth. They halted at the White Hart Inn, where they were received by Generals Ward and Mitchell, and Colonel Brereton, Officers of the Staff, and Colonel Boucher and his Guard of Sarum Volunteers; also by the Sarum Troop of Yeoman Cavalry; - The church bells ringing and bands playing. His Majesty looked remarkably well, and expressed himself much gratified by as handsome and numerous an appearance of our troops. His Majesty's words were "I am sorry for the trouble they have taken; I have long known the loyalty of Salisbury, and always have it in my recollections." Early on Saturday morning the Princesses Sophia and Amelia, accompanied by the Duke of Cambridge, arrived here on their way to join their Majesties; they were received in the like manner by our Military Staff, Cavalry, and Volunteers, and by a numerous and applauding people. All the Royal Family took refreshment and changed horses at Shergold's, the worthy landlord of the Woodyate's Inn. A party of the 10th Light Dragoons escorted the illustrious travellers on their journey".

In 1810, Samuel Jones, who was the proprietor of the Antelope in Catherine Street, took over the White Hart. But Jonathan Johnson who had been the proprietor of the White Hart took over the Antelope [4]. Since these two inns were great rivals for trade, it seems strange that the two landlords should apparently swap positions! Whatever, the reasons behind the moves, the Jones family came off better as they continued to run the White Hart until 1865 while Jonathan Johnson left the Antelope in 1833 and that inn closed in 1840.

In August, 1856, Queen Victoria, Prince Albert and the Royal Family passed through Salisbury [1056]. There journey was simply from the Great Western Railway Station at Fisherton to the South-Western Railway Station at Milford where they continued their journey to the Isle of Wight. They had lunch at the White Hart and the landlord, Mr Jones, also provided four carriages and an omnibus to convey the party between the two stations.

By at least 1870, the inn was owned by the White Hart Hotel Company [1057]. It later became a member of the Trust Houses group as early as 1938, later being a member of Trust House Forte. It became a Macdonald's Hotel before joining the Accor Group in 2007.

One final note regarding the White Hart. It has become the tradition for a newly elected Member of Parliament for Salisbury to appear before the public on the balcony above the entrance to the White Hart. Here, the new member sings 'The Fly be on the Turnip' in what purports to be Wiltshire dialect. It is said that the tradition has been upheld for 300 years. The traditional song was used as a marching song by the Wiltshire Regiment.

257. White Hart Tap, nk

It is not known if this was a name given to the bar of the White Hart or whether it was a separate bar somewhere else on the premises occupied by the White Hart. It is closely related as the first landlord of the Tap, recorded in February,1803, is Edward Keele [4], who is also shown as the landlord of the White Hart itself from 1793 [3]. It appears the White Hart Tap came into being when Jonathan Johnson became the landlord of the White Hart. Suffice it to say, the last mention of the White Hart Tap is in 1814.when it was again in the hands of Edward Keele. In between the two dates, the Tap appears continuously in the licensing records as does the White Hart but with different landlords.

258 White Horse, Fisherton Street

The White Horse was in Fisherton Street at about the place where the Infirmary was built. It is known to have been in existence by 1713 when Mr Woodward was the proprietor. The landlord in 1752 got into debt but friends tried to help him out [1058]: "Whereas the Sheriff of Wilts hath taken in Execution the Goods & Chattels of Wm Earle, Innholder, at the White Horse, in Fisherton Anger, at the Suit of John Street, on a Writ of Fieri Facias, in an action of Debt: We do hereby certify that at Mr Earle's request, and in friendship to him, We this day offered to purchase of the Sheriff's Officers, so much of the Goods & Chattels levied, as amount to the full Moneys claimed to be due to the Plaintiff on all accounts (including his Attorney's full Bill of Costs, Sheriff's Poundage & Fees of levying & keeping Possession). To which Sale the Defendant would have consented in writing; & that We did otherwise offer to indemnify the Sheriff for a years Rent, supposed to be due to the Landlord; but that the said Offers were rejected, to the great Detriment of Mr Earle, by whom the Plaintiff hath in our Opinion dealt very unkindly in causing the said Execution to be levied; but we desire the Printers of the *Salisbury Journal* to publish this Advertisement, that Mr Earle's Credit may not be prejudiced with his Acquaintance & Customers".

The efforts to help Mr Earle were to no avail as in March of that year, the pub was put up for rent and in April, the property of Mr Earle was sold [1059]. The pub was still being advertised for rent in October, 1752.

But the house did continue in trade and in 1765, a carriage left the White Horse every Saturday morning to travel to the George Inn in Snow Hill, London, arriving on Tuesday afternoon [1060]. This must have been a carriage carrying goods rather than a stagecoach carrying people.

In 1766, the pub was again put up for rent and it was described as 'being a large and commodious Inn; with good Stabling, Garden, Yard, Brewhouse and Back-Gate, all in good Repair' [1061]. William Corbin purchases the pub but the following year he moved to the Vine in the Cheese Market. It would appear that the pub was purchased by the Commissioners for the new Infirmary. The foundation of the Infirmary was in 1766 and it appears that in 1767, the buildings on the site, including the White Horse, were modified to accommodate the first patients. The foundation stone of the purpose-designed Infirmary was laid in

September, 1767 and it eventually opened in 1771 when the remaining original buildings on the site were removed.

259 White Horse, Milford Street

Haskins states that this was licensed to Richard Dickman as an alehouse in 1739 [20] but may well have been in existence before that time. Later in that year, Richard Dickman, the landlord, was prosecuted for not honouring a billet for a soldier issued by one of the High Constables of the City [1062]. What is unusual about this event is that the papers held at Wiltshire & Swindon History Centre not only contain affidavits from the soldier and the High Constable but also the actual billet [16]! The billet was a ticket issued by the High Constables ordering a landlord to house a soldier for an agreed sum of money per night. The term billet eventually became the name for soldier's lodgings.

Nothing more is heard of this particular White Horse but the White Horse in Castle Street was definitely in existence by 1740 and may have taken its name at this time.

260 White Horse, New Street

Another alehouse of which little is known including its position in New Street. Haskins states that John Fry was granted a license for it in 1732 [20]. However, this may well have been when the White Horse in Milford Street received its license assuming that there were not two pubs of the same name within the City at any one time. It was certainly in existence in 1744. It may well have still been in existence in 1774 when an auction of four houses in New Street was held at the pub [1063]. The dates of this White Horse seem to conflict with that of the White Horse in Castle Street and thus there seems to be a minor mystery.

261 White Horse Cellar, Rampart Road

This was on the London Road in the part now called Rampart Road (after the dual-carriageway Ring Road was built). It was on the east side of Rampart Road roughly half way between the Winchester Gate pub and Kelsey Hill.

Wheeler, writing in the *Salisbury Journal* in 1886, states 'it was principally a resting place for the drovers and others who were continually passing in those days, when all the cattle for the fairs and markets had to travel by road, and all the goods necessary for the trade of the city were brought here by means of stage waggons (See Appendix 1 – Old Inns of Salisbury Part IV). It stood some little way back from the road, and had a long horse trough in front, such as was at that time to be seen near the entrance to almost every town. Readers of Pickwick will remember a trough of this description in front of the Marquis of Granby, Dorking, which the Rev. Mr Stiggins became intimately acquainted with on the introduction of Mr Weller, Snr'

One of the earliest mention of this pub is in April, 1783, when it was reported that a dark-brown Mare had been stolen or strayed from a field belonging to the White Horse Cellar [1064]. Also, a lease of 1783, although not directly connected with the White Horse Cellar, refers to it as an adjoining property [1065]: "Lease from William Beckford of Fovant to Samuel Whitchurch, Brewer which states '... HATH Demised Leased Granted and to Farm letten and By These Presents DOTH

Promise Lease Grant and to Farm let unto the said Samuel Whitchurch his Executors Administrators and Assigns ALL those Ten Acres of Arable Land lying adjoining the Great Linchet in the Common Field of Milford bounded on the North by Lands heretofore in possession of John Robbins but now of Thomas Reading on the East by part of Stagg's Tenement heretofore in possession of George Evans but now of Thomas Coombs and on the South and West by parts of Milford Farm heretofore in possession of Bennet Swayne Esquire but now or late of William Westcott And Also One Close or half Acre of Land called Lobb's Close lying near Winchester Gate formerly in the occupation of Emanuel Gauntlett and abutting on the North with certain Lands heretofore in possession of Margaret Masters Widow afterwards of John Cotton and now of Thomas Reading and on the South with certain Lands heretofore in possession of John Rolfe Esquire afterwards of William Wheeler and now since of Samuel Case on the West by the Kings Highway and on the East by Lands heretofore in possession of Stephen Brownjohn but now of Thomas Burrough on part of which said Close called Lobb's Close some Buildings have been long since erected and now heretofore called or known by the name of the Red Lion afterwards the Rudder and since by the name of the Sack Carrier afterwards the Chequer Inn but now by the name of the New White Horse Cellar".

In 1788, it was advertised that the New White Horse Cellar was available to rent and that potential tenants should enquire with Samuel Whitchurch [1066].

In 1813, John Ireland, who ran a carrier service to Oxford from Salisbury via Andover, Hurstbourne Tarrant, Newbury, East Ilsley and Abingdon, took the pub [1067]. But by 1815, it was advertised as available to rent and to contact Mr Ireland for details [1068].

In 1822, John Lambert became the landlord. In 1825, he was involved in a scandal surrounding the theft of three horses from Worcestershire [1069]. The gatekeeper of the Petersfinger turnpike believed that three horses that had been taken through his gate matched the description of the stolen horses. Unable to leave his post, he told his story to a local butcher who was passing through his gate. This man chased up the road to Whaddon, and finding the horses and the young lad leading them, at the Sportman's Hall, he arranged for the horses to be detained and the young lad to be brought before a Magistrate in Alderbury. The whole matter was brought in front of the Clerk to the Magistrates in Salisbury. As a result, a man was detained at the White Horse Cellar and another man, who on realising that people had been detained, tried to escape from Salisbury but was himself detained. He was the man who had hired the young lad who was leading the horses out of Salisbury on the Southampton road. Late in the evening, it was realised that a third man was hiding in stables at Milford and he was detained as well as John Lambert of the White Horse Cellar who was found with the man. Thus, the three men and the young lad were committed for trial after two men from Worcestershire identified the horses as their property. The following week, John Lambert had a long letter published in the *Salisbury Journal*, in which he stated that despite rumours of his stabling stolen horses and harbouring horse thieves at the White Horse Cellar, he was entirely an innocent party in the events [1070]. He was certainly not charged with any offence. But by September, 1825, he had left the pub, so perhaps his reputation had been ruined but whether through good cause or malicious gossip cannot be determined.

In 1835, the lease of the house was offered for sale, as part of the Estate of Samuel Whitchurch, with a broad description [1071]: "All that Inn or Public House, known by the name of The New White Horse Cellar, with two Barns, Granary, three Stables, Coach House, Yards, Gardens, and Outbuildings, together with a Cottage adjoining, situate in the Parish of Milford, on the London Road, near Winchester Gate, containing 1 Rod, 11 Perches, more or less; and also all that piece of Arable Land, situate in the Parish of Milford, on the Western side of the London Road, containing 9 Acres 2 Rods and 19 Perches, more or less. This Lot is held by Lease, dated the 23rd of August, 1833, under the Duke of Hamilton and Brandon, and William Beckford, Esq, for a term of 99 years, determinable on the lives of the said William Beckford, Frances Julia Murray, and Jane Catherina Shaw Stewart, under the yearly rent of 10s, and 30s for apportioned redeemed Land-Tax, and the payment of 6s 8d as an Heriot on the death of each life".

The last entry of the White Horse Cellar in the licensing records is in 1861 when William Kaye was the landlord. It seems likely that the trade of the pub was significantly reduced by livestock being transported by railway, with the consequent reduction in movement of animals by drovers.

262 White Lyon, Fisherton

Nothing more is known of this pub except that Haskins states that it was granted a licence as an alehouse in 1736 [20].

263 White Rooms, 25 Milford Street

There is some doubt about the early years of what finally became the White Rooms. It has been suggested that this was the Queen's Head in Milford Street but this cannot be proved at the moment. But the history (what is known of it) of the Queen's Head has been included here.

Haskins states that Joseph White was granted a licence for the Queen's Head as an alehouse in 1740 [20]. He kept the alehouse until 1756 when he advertised that he was about to leave off business [1072]. Nothing more has been found of this house until 1834 when Thomas Maton announces that he has commenced brewing at the Malt and Hop Brewery in Milford Street [1073]. Thomas Maton is obviously selling beer and ale off the premises for consumption at home and this is evidence that he was operating an alehouse on the premises. There are old brewery buildings behind what became the White Rooms and it is believed that these were the Malt & Hop Brewery.

In September, 1838, it is described as having undergone considerable improvements and as having a new Brewhouse built [1074]: "Free Public-House. To be Let, with possession at Michaelmas, - The Queen's Head, Milford-street, Salisbury. The Premises have lately undergone considerable improvements, by having a brewhouse newly built, and most conveniently fitted up with the necessary brewing utensils, and a good cellar, with casks, etc. complete; the whole of which will be included in the rent. The coming-in will be very moderate, and affords a desirable opportunity for an industrious person. – N.B. Apply to J Beckingsale".

Seemingly, in anticipation of this new building, a week before the 1838 annual licensing session, John Smiles, a surgeon, wrote to the City Magistrates [8]: "Gentlemen, I understand that an application is going to be made this day for a Spirit Licence for the House in Milford Street known by the name of Maton's Tap. I earnestly entreat you Gentlemen not to grant it, for during the period of its being allowed to sell beer it has been a continued nuisance to myself and I can only add that had I not taken my house upon a fourteen year lease that knowing what I do of it I would not live in it rent free.

I am Gentlemen with respect

Your obedient Servant

John Smiles, Surgeon.

This letter also suggests that the pub had not been a retail outlet for beer for many years before this time (and it does not appear in the Licensing Records before this time although it may have been an unlicensed alehouse).

However, after 1839 the Queen's Head ceases to appear in the licensing records. The landlord in 1839 is recorded as being George Crook and it may be of note that the 1841 Census shows a George Crook of Milford as being a labourer.

In 1849, John Rolls applied for a license for the Malt and Hop Brewery, stating that it had not heretofore been an Inn, Alehouse or Victualling House [9]. This is clearly an erroneous statement as whether the premises had been the earlier Malt and Hop Brewery, the Queen's Head or Maton's Tap, it had certainly been an alehouse before this time. This application was refused as it was again when he applied in 1850 [9]. Confusingly, John Rolls applied in 1852 for a license for Maton's Tap, which was refused. But in 1853 he applied for a license for the Malt & Hop Brewery and this time it was granted. It is always possible that the Malt & Hop Brewery and Maton's Tap were different premises but this is extremely unlikely since all the failed applications were made by John Rolls and Thomas Maton clearly had earlier owned the Malt & Hop Brewery. It is more probable that the brewery sold beer off the premises and it may well have operated as an alehouse for many years.

In 1856, the license for the Malt and Hop Brewery passed from John Rolls to William Jameson [1075]. To further confuse the issue regarding the name of this establishment, when, in 1856, John Witt was accused of assaulting a policeman, he had been drinking in Mr Jameson's premises, the Milford Street Brewery [1076]! The policeman was assaulted while trying to remove Witt from the premises at the request of Mr Jameson.

Mr Jameson was still the landlord in 1870 when his house (still the Milford Street Brewery) was one of several pubs which had had complaints raised against them at the annual licensing session [1077]. The Mayor stated that, in all cases, the renewal of the licenses would be approved provided the landlords ran their pubs in an orderly manner in the future. But after the licenses had been granted, a grocer from Milford Street, Mr Gilbert, addressed the Magistrates with complaints against the Milford Street Brewery. Mr Gilbert stated he had lived near the pub for two years, and he had continually been affected by insulting and offensive language from the customers of the pub. This was sufficiently bad that it had adversely effected the trade of his shop and two lodgers had left his house because of the language. He also alleged that loose women from the pub had insulted his customers. The Mayor stated that it was a shame that Mr Gilbert had not lodged his complaints before the license of the pub was renewed. But if the disorderly conduct continued, it was probable that the license might be suspended in the future.

In 1886, Herbert Mew announced that he had moved his brewery from the Castle Street Premises to the Malt and Hop Brewery [1078]. In 1898, Herbert Mew and Bridger Gibbs merged their breweries to become Gibbs Mew. Brewing was centred on the Anchor brewery in Gigant Street and it is believed that brewing ceased at the Milford Street premises. The pub remained in Gibbs Mew hands until the closure of that brewery in 1997.

The 1901 Census shows the pub to be named as the Hop Brewery Bar. This is presumed to have been an error by the Census Enumerator. The pub became known as the Brewery Tap from about 1903 until 1927 when it became the Milford Arms. In about 1979, the name was changed to the Old Coach House when the pub was still owned by Gibbs Mew but traded as a Schooner Inn. After the demise of Gibbs Mew, the pub became a free house colloquially known as the Pound Shop owing to the price of a pint of beer in the premises. In 2004, the upper part of the pub became a pole dancing venue known as the Club Rouge while the remainder of the pub became known as the White Rooms, which was as much a night club as a pub. The premises closed in late 2014.

In August 2015, a plan was published to demolish the buildings on Milford Street and replace them with two shops and a walkway in between them. The walkway would lead to a development of flats centred on a refurbishment of the listed brewery buildings behind the pub – the whole development being known as the Old Brewery. This application was refused but a revised plan was submitted to the council and approved in 2016.

264 White Swan, Brown Street

The White Swan in Brown Street seems to have started trade immediately after the closure of the White Swan in Payne's Hill in 1778 and is presumed to be the premises to which the license was transferred that had not been licensed before, as mentioned in the records of the Payne's Hill establishment. However, Haskins states that the Swan in Brown Street received a licence as an alehouse in 1720 [20]. Among the same records, the White Swan in Payne's Hill is mentioned so it is not that pub. However, Haskins clearly added the names of the locations of pubs and alehouses himself and thus the record of the Swan in Brown Street in 1720 may be in error

Little is known of its earlier years until in 1781, the wife of the landlord, Mr Lake, was found drowned in a ditch behind the pub [1079]. The Coroner's verdict was lunacy! Then, a fire broke out in December, 1806 [1080]: "Yesterday (Sunday) morning, between two and three o'clock, a fire broke out in a malt house in Brown Street, in this city, at the back of the White Swan public house; but an alarm being immediately given, the city engines were procured, and effectually extinguished the fire before it could communicate in the adjoining dwelling houses, and with little loss beside the spoiling of a quantity of malt, the heating of which is supposed to have occasioned the fire".

From 1825 until 1827, the house seems to be offered for sale continuously. William Cole was the landlord from 1819 until October 2nd, 1826, when James Hibberd became the landlord. The licensing records for 1829 have the handwritten comment against the entry for James Hibberd at the White Swan of 'refused'. The White Swan no longer appears in the licensing records after this date.

However, in 1830, James Hibberd was bound over to appear before the Magistrates on the charge of keeping a disorderly house [6]. And in 1834, a Coroner's Inquest was held on the death of Mrs Hibberd from the White Swan public House [1081] (she collapsed and died while fastening her stays! – the verdict was 'Died by the Visitation of God'). Then further confusion arises as two years later, in 1836, the following note is found in the records [8]: "The following presentment of the Grand Jury for the Borough made at the General Quarter Sessions held on 27 June was laid before the Meeting by the Mayor: The Grand Jury do present that we consider in consequence of Information received that a certain House in the occupation of James Hibberd and known by the name of the White Swan situate in Brown Street in the City of New Sarum is a disorderly House and a receptacle for characters of the worst description and we strongly recommend the Court to give such directions as may tend to suppress the nuisance complained of. (signed by 18 citizens)"

Thereafter, nothing more is known about James Hibberd or the White Swan but quite what happened between 1829 and 1836 is not known.

265 Wig & Quill, New Street

The building which is now the Wig & Quill is of 16th C. origin and it was originally two cottages. It then became a single, private dwelling and at a later date became an antiques shop.

In 1977, it was converted to be a restaurant with a small bar adjacent to the road and known by the name of Burke's Bar. In 1987, the bar was enlarged and the restaurant area changed into further seating for the pub. It was renamed as the Wig & Quill at this time.

The pub changed hands three times in quick succession before being purchased by Wadworth's Brewery in Devizes under whose ownership it remains.

When the pub was changed to the Wig & Quill, the small bar at the front of the house was changed into a seating area and the bar moved further down the premises at the side. The cellar is on the ground floor next to the bar and features a window into the seating area. The pub also has a walled garden to the rear which backs on to the Cathedral Close.

266 Wilton Arms, 7, Wilton Road

The Wilton Arms was originally on the north side of Fisherton Street at approximately the site of the post sorting office. In deeds up to 1864, it is shown that it was originally called the Four Bells.

Haskins states that the Four Bells was granted a licence as an alehouse in 1767

[20] but was almost certainly in existence before this date. In 1796, an auction was held at the Four Bells, described as being the house of Joseph Sandell, of another pub, the One Bell, which was untenanted [1082]. It is next mentioned in 1799 when Joseph Sandell broke his arm by falling from his horse [1083].

It was still the Four Bells in 1810 [1084] but by 1816, when John Olding, the landlord at that time, announced that he had taken the Fives Court, it was known as the Wilton Arms [1085]: "Wilton Arms, Fisherton. John Olding begs leave to inform his friends and the public in general, that he has taken the Fives Court for the ensuing season, which he has put in complete repair. Gentlemen who will favour him with their company, may depend on being accommodated with Spirits of the best quality, good London Bottled Porter, Bottled Cyder, and good Strong Beer, on reasonable terms".

Presumably, the Fives Court was part of the public house or adjacent to it but this is not known.

At some time, the pub came under the ownership of John Rogers. But it appears that he never occupied the house as landlord but let the house to other licensees. After his death in 1830, his executors, Charles Browne and James Meatyard continued with this practice [1086]. It seems that Charles Browne came into ownership of the pub as he issued the following writ in 1841 (the lack of punctuation is the same as the original document!) [1087]: "As agent for and on behalf of your landlord Charles Browne of the Excise Office in the City of London Esquire I hereby give you notice to quit and deliver up to the said Charles Browne his heirs or Assignees or to his or their Agent or Agents on the eleventh day of September next ensuing the date hereof or at such other time as your present tenancy shall expire the peaceable and quiet possession of all that Messuage or Tenement and Public House called the Wilton Arms and the Messuage or Tenement thereto adjoining together with the Coachhouse Stable Yard Skittle Alley and other Appurtenances thereunto belonging situate and being in Fisherton Anger in the County of Wilts now in your occupation as Tenant of the said Charles Browne".

This writ to the landlord, Charles Barrett, must have been some form of legal requirement as in 1851, the bedroom of Mrs Barrett was broken into and two watches stolen [1088]. Charles Barrett was summoned in 1853 for keeping his house open during the hours of divine service on a Sunday [1089]. His defence was that the persons in the inn were travellers and hence he could serve them alcohol. But a policeman gave evidence that one of the men in the pub lived only 30 yards from the pub and another just 300 yards away. Barrett was found guilty and fined twenty shillings plus costs.

It appears that Charles Barrett died in 1854 and his widow, Mary, continued to run the pub. In 1855, she sued George Beckenham for the costs of beer supplied to railway workmen on Beckenham's order [1090]. The argument was complex and contradictory but after an adjournment to call more witnesses, Mrs Barrett won her case.

But, the 1871 Census shows no sign of the Wilton Arms, either in Fisherton Street or in Wilton Road. Since the London and South Western Railway opened a new railway station to the east of Fisherton Street at about this time, it is supposed that the original Wilton Arms disappeared to provide land for this development. However, in 1872, Mr Baker applied for a spirit license for his premises in Wilton Road [1091]. One of his reasons for the application was that he supplied refreshments to Salisbury Cricket Club who played on ground owned by him. If he was required to provide wines and spirits to the club he had to obtain them from a pub in Wilton. His application was approved.

In 1882, the Wilton Arms was put up for sale together with an adjoining shop and cottages [1092]. The pub was described as possessing a Front Smoking Room, a large Kitchen, a Scullery and other Offices, four Bedrooms, with spacious Landing and an underground Beer Cellar. It also had a greenhouse and a stable with a loft over it. The whole was purchased by Lovibond's brewery for £1,420 [1093]. Lovibond's pubs were purchased by George's brewery of Bristol in about 1959.

By 1969, it was known as the Wilton Road Hotel and by 1989 it had become the Wilton Hotel under Courage ownership. In 1994, it became an Usher's House after the shake-up of ownership of pubs by Grand Metropolitan and Courage. It remained as the Wilton Hotel until at least 2006 but by 2008 it had become the Wilton.

In 2012, the Wilton was closed for a short time but was refurbished and reopened as the Bacchus Hotel, a bistro and real ale bar. In 2015, the pub is shown as the Wilton Arms with the name of the Bacchus Hotel being retained for that part of the business having rooms to let. The pub was closed in 2016 and a planning application to convert the building into four apartments was granted [1094]. Thus, the Wilton Arms was finally closed.

267 Winchester Gate, Rampart Road

The Winchester Gate is on Rampart Road on what was the east side of the London Road before the dual-carriageway ring road was built. The pub is of early 16th C. construction although the east wing was added later in the 18th C.

The pub was originally known as the Green Dragon and Haskins states that it received a licence as an alehouse in 1732 when John Green was the landlord [20]. However, a note in the licencing records shows Joshua Groome as being prosecuted for selling beer without a licence at the Green Dragon in April 1732 [16]. It is presumed that Joshua lost his licence and John Green gained a new one for the Green Dragon!

In 1754, a violent episode occurred at the Green Dragon [1095]: "Saturday a Dispute happened at the Public-House above Winchester Gate, between the Landlady & a travelling Woman about three pence, in which a Soldier quartered there interfered, in Behalf of the Landlady; and carried his Resentment so far as to stab the Woman with his Sword, in so dangerous a manner that 'tis thought she cannot recover; for which he was immediately seized & secured in the Guard-House".

It shows that even in those days, one could be arrested for being over protective of one's own property.

The lease of the pub was put up for sale in 1817 when the premises was described as being 'very desirably and pleasantly situated fronting the London road at the entrance of Salisbury; with a very large garden, extensive yards, two skittle alleys, convenient brew house, stables, and all other necessary offices [1096]. The new Tenant was at liberty to brew his own beer, and was required to take the Stock (which was very small), brewing utensils, House hold Furniture, etc. at a valuation.

It was not uncommon for landlords of pubs to advertise that if the owner of a horse left at their inn was not collected and its keep paid for, they would sell the horse to defray the expense. But in 1829, William Cole advertised that if the owner of a waggon, that had a headboard labelled 'Samuel Hix, Ansford, Bristol and Poole' did not remove it from his yard, it would be sold. The waggon had been in the yard for over three years [1097]!

William Cole died at the end of August, 1832. His wife, Rebecca, continued to run the inn. But in late 1833, some villains broke into the Green Dragon by removing a window at the back of the inn [1098]. The burglars took many articles belonging to a traveller plus a large piece of salt beef and a lot of linen belonging to Mrs Cole. A bundle of cashmere cloth belonging to a waggoner was also stolen. In 1834, Mrs Cole married Matthew James Clark who, according to the law of the time, became the landlord of the inn. But later in the year, burglars once again entered the rear of the inn [1099]. This time they stole six chickens (presumably dead), a copper fountain and a pestle & mortar. One wonders if these were the same criminals as before, hoping to repeat their previous success?

Winchester Gate

Matthew Clark remained at the Green Dragon until 1856, when the inn was advertised as available to rent [1100]. And in June of that year, the inn having not been let, all the furniture, stock and brewing equipment was put up for sale [1101]. The pub is missing from the licensing records until 1859, when Isaac Chalk takes the license. He was followed as licensee by Henry Richardson. During his tenure at the Green Dragon, it is likely that the Cricketers public house (qv) was purchased and incorporated as an extension of the public bar of the inn.

The pub was still known as the Green Dragon at the time of the 1871 Census but in 1872, when Joshua Collins applied for a renewal of the license of the Green Dragon, his request was refused [1102]. A little later in the year, Mr Folliott, a brewer, applied for the renewal of the suspended license as the London Road Inn and this was granted [1103]. Folliott's brewery was purchased by Ushers of Trowbridge in 1919 and the London Road Inn remained in their ownership until 1974 when it became a Chef & Brewer pub within the Watney Mann group. At that time, the name was changed again to the Winchester Gate. At a later date, it was sold and became a free house under private ownership and remains a free house to this day.

268 World's End, St Martin's Church Street

Haskins states that this alehouse was licensed sometime between 1635 and 1685 [18]. A farthing token was issued in Salisbury in 1651. It had the initials EDM plus a skull on the obverse and the words 'If Thou Believest' and a heart on the reverse. C.M Rowe in his book on Salisbury's Local Coinage links the symbols on this token to the Resurrection and postulates that it was issued by the World's End tavern [1104]. Since most of these tokens were issued by innkeepers to give change to customers in the absence of official small coinage, this association seems probable. It is known that the World's End was in existence as a pub earlier in the 17th C.

Haskins also states that this the pub was granted a licence as an alehouse in 1713 when John Hall was the landlord [20]. Alexander Head succeeded John Hall and was at the World's End until at least 1722. But in 1742, it is noted that the pub applied for a licence but this was refused [15].

In 1776, a building was advertised for sale being described as 'a Messuage some time since a Public House, & late called or known by the name or sign of the World's End near St Martin's Church (See Appendix 1 – Old Inns of Salisbury Part VII).' Nothing more is heard of this public house although there remains a possibility that the World's End was an earlier name for the Tollgate as that does not appear in the licencing records until 1768.

269 Wyndham Arms, 27 Estcourt Road

The first record of the Wyndham Arms that has been found is in the 1881 Census where it is shown as the Wyndham Hotel. The hotel originally included the two houses to the north of it in Estcourt Road. This can be seen by the style of their construction and also by the back yard of the pub which extends behind these properties. The building is said to be constructed from concrete throughout.

By 1882, when the pub was advertised for sale, it was known as the Wyndham

Arms [1105]. The sale notice showed that it included the yard and stabling. The preliminary notice of sale two weeks earlier stated that it was 'situate in a populous and increasing locality, which offers an unusually favourable opportunity for a good Counter Trade, in addition to the other branches of the Public house business, there being no other licensed House on the College Property'. At some unknown later date, the name reverted to the Wyndham Hotel.

There was a fire at the pub in 1901 [1106]. It was said that a servant had been reading in bed but his candle burned down until it set the chair on which it stood on fire. The Fire Brigade attended and managed to confine the fire to the room in which it started. Undoubtedly, this was helped by the method of construction of the building as if the walls had been the more normal lath and plaster construction, there is no doubt the fire would have spread.

The name of the pub was changed from the Wyndham Hotel back to the Wyndham Arms in 1956 [13], It was probable that this was when the two wings of the pub were changed into separate private dwellings. The pub continued quietly in trade being an Usher's house up until 1974, when it became a Chef and Brewer house within the Watney Mann Group. However, in 1986, the pub was put on the market and was purchased by John Gilbert. It started a new life as a free house and the following year, a brewing plant was set up in the cellar of the pub. With the help of Roger McBride, John Gilbert started brewing Hopback beers at the Wyndham Arms, initially just for that pub but gradually growing their trade to other pubs.

The brewing of Hopback beers later moved from the Wyndham to a new site at Downton but the Wyndham Arms is still recognised to be the home of Hopback Brewery.

270 YOYO, Milford Street

This pub lies in Milford Street just to the east of the entrance to the Red Lion. The building dates from the 16th C but its first mention as a licensed premises is in 1833 when it was known as the Red Lion Tap [1107]. It is probable that the row of cottages of which it was one, was owned by the Red Lion and it was converted to a pub to provide a bar for other than hotel guests. It continued under this name until about 1840 when it became the Hope Inn

In 1856, The Hope Inn was advertised to let and was described as having [1108]: "A capital Front Bar, or Spirit Store, recently fitted up with every convenience in the London style, centrally situate in Milford-street, Salisbury, possessing a capital Brewhouse, with a most excellent Cellar, and every other convenience for carrying on a lucrative Beer and Spirit Business".

One wonders how a Brewhouse was fitted into what is a small pub! It changed its name to the Oddfellow's Arms sometime between 1861 and 1871 although there is a possibility it was called Chapman's Arms for a while during this period

The brewing equipment of the Oddfellow's Arms was put up for sale in 1872 [1109]. It seems possible that this was when Matthews Brewery of Gillingham acquired the pub. It remained with Matthews until that brewery was acquired by Hall & Woodhouse of Blandford Forum in 1963. It remained in the ownership of that brewery until at least the late 1980s.

The pub became the Frothblower's in 2000 when the Red Lion re-acquired ownership of the pub. The name of the Frothblower's originates from the fact that the father of the owner of the Red Lion was a member of the Ancient Order of Froth Blowers, a charitable organisation of the 1920s. The organisation stated it was: "A sociable and law abiding fraternity of absorbitive Britons who sedately consume and quietly enjoy with commendable regularity and frequention the truly British malted beverage as did their forbears and as Britons ever will, and be damned to all pussyfoot hornswogglers from overseas and including low brows, teetotalers and MP`s and not excluding nosey parkers, mock religious busy bodies and suburban fool hens all of which are structurally solid bone from the chin up".

In other words, it involved members in meeting to drink beer and collect money to help disadvantaged children. The Friends of the Froth Blowers is a modern group that research the activities of the original organisation and they have met regularly at the Frothblowers. During this time, there was a display of memorabilia from the Ancient Order in the pub, including the description of the organisation's aims shown above.

In 2010, the pub's name was changed once more to YOYO. This is an acronym for 'You're Only Young Once' and emphasises that the pub is now being aimed at the younger trade.

THE PUBLIC HOUSES AND INNS OF SALISBURY

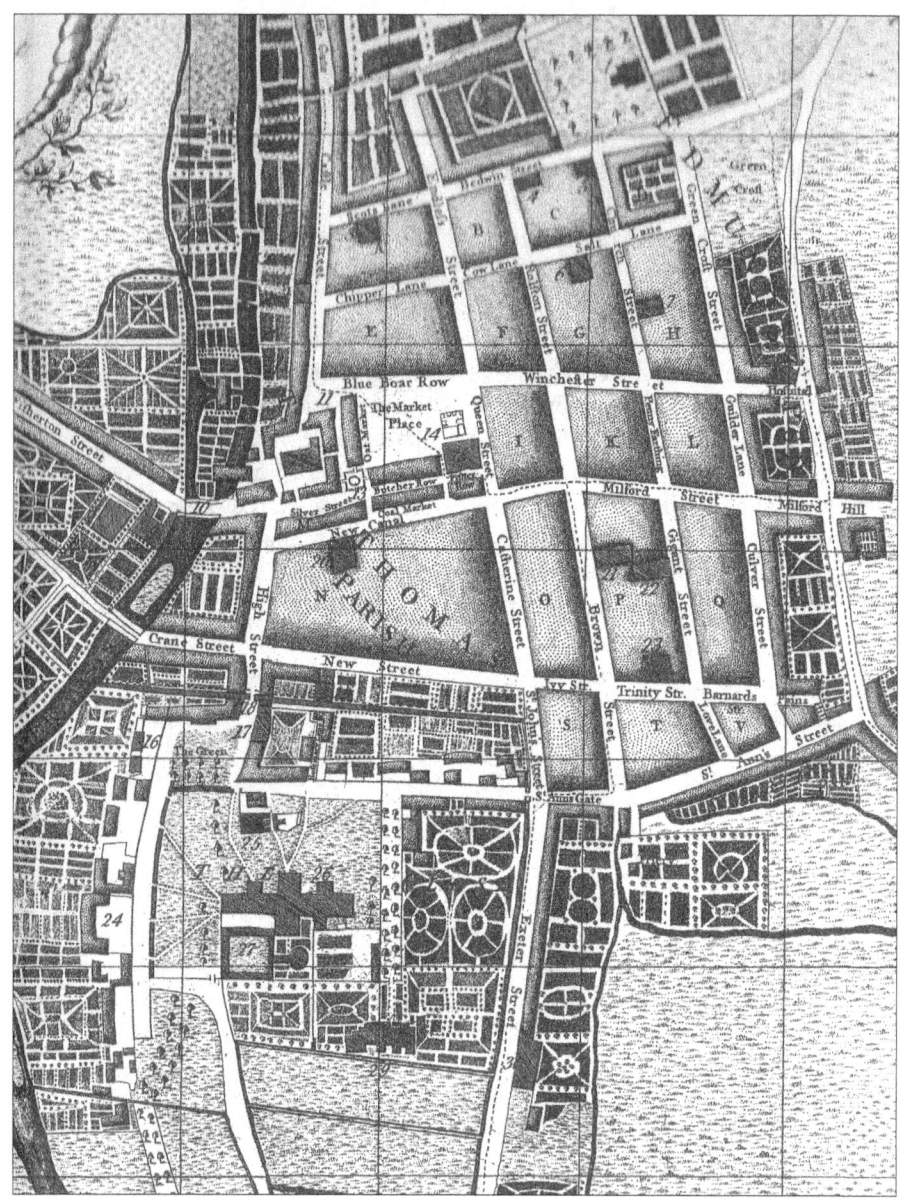

Detail from Benjamin Donn's Map of Salisbury, 1797 ed. (first pubished 1781)

Appendices

Appendix I
Old Inns of Salisbury

Introduction

The following is a transcript of a series of articles published in the Salisbury Journal in the late 19th century. They were written by W A Wheeler and were printed in the form of letters to the Editor. I have attempted to be as accurate as possible in my transcription but apologise for any mistakes that may have crept in. These articles are of some value to the local historian as Mr Wheeler was able to talk to the older inhabitants of the city and thus extend our first-hand knowledge of the inns of Salisbury back into the early 1800s. Thus, the situation of many inns and the changes in names of inns can be confirmed.

The only W A Wheeler that I have been able to find in the 1881 Census was a William A Wheeler who was a Printer's Overseer living at the Cricket Field, Britford with his wife and two children. It seems feasible that he was the author of the articles, as he would have had the opportunity to arrange with the Editor to obtain space for the long letters!

The original letters appeared in the Journal on July 24 1886, July 31 1886, August 21 1886, December 24 1886, March 26 1887, July 23 1887 and August 20 1887 with a further letter on September 29 1894.

E M Garman, Salisbury
February 2017.

Old Inns of Salisbury, No. I

To the Editor of the Salisbury and Winchester Journal

Sir, - At a time when a crusade is being waged against inns of all sorts and kinds, a glance at a few of those which existed in our city in bygone days may not be uninteresting. The Rev. Peter Hall in his "Picturesque Memorials" says that by statute of the last year of Edward VI (1553), the number of taverns in each town throughout England was limited to two, but Salisbury, with a few others, had a special license for three. When this Act was repealed I am unable to say, but I find that they had enormously increased by the beginning of the 18th century, having in 1709 reached the number of 60, when the Corporation resolved on reducing them to forty, which they considered would afford sufficient accommodation for the public. It has been recorded as somewhat singular that after laws for the better regulation of these houses had been passed, the first infraction should have been by the landlady of the Silent Woman, who was indicted for keeping a disorderly house. The Silent Woman was situated in Castle

Street, and still bore the same sign in 1822; when its name was changed, I cannot say, but I believe it to be the house now known as the George and Dragon.

Beginning with the Market Place, the principal inn about the middle of the last century was the Three Lions, which stood on the ground now occupied by Messrs. Pinckney's Bank: but even then this was an old inn, as a century previously, in 1671, Charles II was met and welcomed by the Corporation at the Three Lions Bridge, which was doubtless the bridge crossing the channel from Queen Street to the Market Place, in front of the hotel, and at that time not far from the front of the Council Chamber, where they had prepared a sumptuous entertainment, to which they invited the King, but which His Majesty, being anxious to continue his journey, most graciously declined. Mr Gast, who became the proprietor of the Three Lions about 1757, also carried on another large inn, the Greyhound, immediately behind the Three Lions, the premises now occupied by Mr Mullins, extending to Brown Street, which, as it had stabling for 70 or 80 horses, was no doubt a valuable adjunct to the Three Lions, which could have had little, if any, accommodation of that kind. Mr Gast would seem to have been a man of some enterprise, for in 1763 he announces that he has purchased a new hearse, "not inferior to anything in London, but superior to anything in the country." At this period, the Three Lions was the recognised resting place of any royal or other visitors of importance. In 1762 we find Lord Clive, the hero of Plassy, with his lady sleeping here *en route* from Bath to London. In 1764 it is recorded that Mr Gast, at the Three Lions, entertained the Corporation and clergy of the city in an elegant manner with a turtle presented to him by the Earl of Pembroke. In the same year, this hotel furnishes host and hostess for the neighbouring inn the Three Swans, William and Sarah Ody, late tapster and chambermaid to Mr Gast, announcing that they have taken that establishment. In 1765, on more than one occasion the Duke of Gloucester dined at the Three Lions, when visiting the Cathedral; and during the musical festival in September of that year, their Royal Highnesses the Dukes of York and Gloucester, accompanied by his Serene Highness the Prince of Brunswick, made it their quarters for three or four days, and on leaving "expressed their great satisfaction at the genteel furniture of their lodging, as well as the exceeding accommodation and very obliging and polite behaviour of Mr Gast, the landlord." The Duke of Kingston was also a visitor during this year. In September, 1766, three chiefs of the Mohecommick and Wappenger Indians, with three ladies and an attendant, who had come to England for the purpose of laying the complaints of the five tribes of Iroquois before the King, stayed at the Three Lions for two days, visiting Stonehenge and Wilton House before proceeding to London. In January, 1767, the Reigning Prince of Hainault Dessin made the Three Lions his headquarters for some time, for the purpose of visiting Stonehenge, Wilton House, the Roman Camp, near Dorchester, and other places of interest. In July, the Princess Amelia stopped there *en route* to Mount Edgecombe: and in August the Princess Poniatowski stayed there on returning from a visit to Mr Hoare's seat at Stourton, and the Earl of Pembroke's at Wilton. In 1768 John Gast announces that he is going into the wine trade, and requests the continuance of favours to his tenant, Joseph Boyter, woollen draper, of the Oatmeal Row; a large portion of the furniture was removed and sold in Endless Street, comprising "table china, dishes so large as not to be had in any shop in the country, and very seldom in London." In 1769 Earl Cornwallis, who was in command of the 33rd Foot, then stationed here, made it his headquarters. On the 22nd June the regiment was reviewed by General Clavering, who afterwards gave an elegant entertainment to the officers at the Three Lions. There were then staying at the hotel the Earls of Ilchester, Thomond, Buckinghamshire, Cornwallis, Suffolk, Guildford, Ancram and Upper Ossory; Lords Digby, Francis Seymour, and Robt. Spencer; the Hon Mr Conway, Generals Preston, Slade, and Rubens, and other nobility. In the evening Earl Cornwallis gave a ball at the Assembly Room to the nobility of the city and neighbourhood. In 1772 Mr Boyter calls it the Three Golden Lions, and announces that he has purchased the adjoining large house, and intends adding the principal part of it to the said inn. This house, which is now occupied by Mr Darke, was from 1836 for many years the residence of Dr Thomas, a physician practising in the city, author of "The Modern Practice of Physic" (published in 1821), and other works connected with his profession. It was moreover, I believe, the birthplace of Professor Fawcett. In 1774, the Duke of Gloucester again stayed here, having come to review several companies of Light Infantry then quartered on the Plain. From this time, the hotel seems to have gradually declined, as towards the end of the year 1778, Joseph Boyter becomes bankrupt, the stock and furniture being sold by order of the Sheriff of Wilts. In February, 1779, Wm Newman, from the Maidenhead, comes into possession, when it is again called the Three Lions, and the next house detached from it, Mr Gast announcing to let "an exceeding good house, inferior to none in this city, with two large shops." But the hotel did not prosper under Mr Newman's management, for he became bankrupt early in 1783, and retired to the King's Arms, Stockbridge, the whole of the fittings, etc., being again disposed of. In April Mr Gast offers to let the Three Lions, saying that "great encouragement would be given to a proper tenant, by reducing the rent £10 a year for the first three years and £20 a year after 7 or 14 years' lease." He describes the hotel as "well known to the nobility and gentry travelling the great western road to be the most pleasant and best situate between London and Land's End." The Greyhound he offered for sale. Neither appears to have been again opened as an inn, as in 1784 John Gast announces that he has removed from Endless Street to a large shop in the front of the late Three Lions Inn, where he has laid in a large assortment of china and glass ware, teas, coffees, cocoa, and chocolate; and in 1794 George Clarke opens a shop as druggist, chemist, and tea dealer, corner of Queen Street and Market Place, and called it "The Golden Head." The only mention of the Three Lions after this occurs in the record of the death of Mr Joseph Boyter, in 1807, which runs thus: - "April 7, died at his lodgings, on the Canal, Mr Joseph Boyter, formerly master of the Three Lions Inn (then the principal inn in this city), and more than half a century organist of the church of St Thomas." Mr Boyter was also for many years clerk of the course at Salisbury races.

Close by, in Queen Street, was the Plume of Feathers (now the Turkish Baths), an old house with a gallery on one side of the yard, the stairs leading from the yard to several of the chambers, after the style of the Old Tabard, of Southwark, part of which, I believe, is still in existence. It was formerly the house of call for the Jew pedlars, who, before the days of railways, travelled the country with their boxes of jewellery. It was also, like most inns, at a time when there were no halls for travelling exhibitions, provided with a large room, which was used for this purpose. In August, 1761, the following announcement of the exhibition of a wonderful man was published: -"This is to acquaint the Curious, that there is come to this City, and is now at the Plume of Feathers, in the Market Place, the most amazing and astonishing Curiosity ever heard of in Human Nature, a Wonderful Man, who was born with two voices, by which, as soon as the words are uttered by one, they are returned in the same breath by another. To prove beyond dispute what is here mentioned, it will be sufficient to say that he has been honoured with the company of the Royal Family, as well as the Royal Society, and principal Body of Nobility." In 1813, the celebrated "Hottentot Venus" was exhibited here; she was "declared to be indisputably the greatest curiosity of the human species in this kingdom, and well worthy the attention of all the admirers of natural history." Next door was another old inn, the Cross Keys, which was a well patronised market inn until the building of the new Market House took the farmers and dealers to the other side of the Market Place. The front is now occupied by Mr Gould, tailor and woollen draper, whilst the back portion is Herring's livery stables.

Yours etc W.A.W.
Salisbury, July, 1886.

Old Inns of Salisbury, No. II

To the Editor of the Salisbury and Winchester Journal.

Sir, - Passing to the south side of the Market Place, I find that early in the last century there was a somewhat important inn and tavern, called the Half Moon; but after many enquiries of old people for many years I have not found one who could recall having ever heard of such an inn. I am unable to give the dates of its establishment, but about 1788 Morris Bailey was the master (as the proprietors or landlords were then called) and it would seem to have been in some respects a rather formidable competitor with the Three Lions.

In 1761, the Race Ordinary was held here each day, in announcing which Mr Bailey thus calls attention to the capabilities of his establishment: -"Gentlemen may be supplied with the following neat wines, viz:- Champaign, Burgundy, Claret, Old Hock, Frontiniac, Rhenish, Moselle, Madeira, Florence, Port, Mountain and Lisbon. The public may depend on always meeting at this Tavern with the Genteelest Accommodations, a good Larder, and the best of wines, etc. And such as would prefer Lodging in the House may have their horses sent to stables just by, where they will be taken the best care of."

In 1764, on the occasion of the Duke of Richmond reviewing Lord Waldegrave's

Regiment of Dragoon Guards, he was afterwards entertained at a genteel dinner by the Field Officer and captains at the Half Moon. In 1766, Mr Bailey announced that at the Races he would have a commodious building called the Half Moon Tavern, with a stand to accommodate 200 persons, to view the races from start to finish, built in a very strong manner by Mr Luck, of the Close (who erected the curious scaffolding for repairing the spire).

About this time there must have been some negotiations for Morris Bailey taking the Three Lions, as in 1768 he announces that, by the advice of his friends, he declines leaving the Half Moon for the Three Lions, and states that he has added stabling to his former accommodation. He further says: - "For the information of those who know not my House, I beg leave to acquaint them that its situation is in the pleasantest Part of the Market Place, having ten Rooms which front the same; and, though but a few yards from the great Road (on which sign is lately erected for the direction of Strangers), is entirely free from the noise of carriages, etc., a circumstance which must be highly agreeable to many Travellers. A genteel Coffee Room in the front of the House is supplied with most of the Evening Papers, Votes of the House of Commons, etc, etc."

In 1772 Mr Bailey, becoming bankrupt, the lease was purchased by Daniel P Safe, of the Red Lion, who was also the postmaster. In announcing the change he says: - "The Post Office will be removed to the Half Moon after the 25th of April, where new printed lists of all the posts going out and coming into the city may be had." Mr Safe died in 1775, and was succeeded at the inn by John Ravenscroft; but James Gibbs became postmaster, and removed the office into Silver Street.

The new tenant of the Half Moon does not, however, seem to have prospered, for early in 1776 the furniture was disposed of, and George Fowles Benson, late in partnership with George Fort, advertises that he "will open the premises, late the Half Moon, under the firm of Benson and Son, where they will carry on the same business as previously carried on by Fort and Benson;" and in March, 1783, Wheeler and Dawson (successors to Benson and Son), hat makers and hosiers, announce their removal from Silver Street to the shop in the Market Place, formerly known by the name of the Half Moon. The name of Dawson subsequently disappears from the firm, and the business was known as Messrs Wheelers in 1823, when in the evening of the 18th of September, the premises were completely destroyed by fire in the space of three hours.

The house has become familiar to the present generation from the engraving in "Hall's Memorials" of the Old Council House, in which it forms a prominent feature, but the artist has taken a liberty in putting the name "Wheeler" over the door, as the Council House was destroyed by fire three years previously to Wheeler's occupation of the Half Moon premises. By another stretch of imagination he also shows the name of "Rhoades" on a sign next the Cross Keys to the left of the old Council House, when in fact Rhoades did not occupy those premises until Dec. 1814. In the engraving in Hatcher the Half Moon will be seen on the sign in front of the house, thus , and in Queen Street the sign erected for the direction of strangers, alluded to by Morris Bailey, may be seen attached to the house now occupied by Mr Webb, hatter, or the next to it.

It is somewhat strange that such a site should have remained so long without being built on, as it lay waste for nearly 30 years, when Pitcher, the photographer, put up a shed, or as it was designated "a studio" which has been added to until it has arrived at the present nondescript state – anything but ornamental to the centre of the city.

So many names of inns occur as being on the south side of the Market Place that I think, probably, when changing landlords, they must have frequently changed their signs. For instance, the Greyhound, which adjoined the Half Moon, and was much injured by the fire above-mentioned, had previously been the Black Dog and the Roebuck, and it is now the Elephant and Castle. The Pack Horse, which was pulled down to prevent the fire spreading, was in all probability, when rebuilt, called the Ox.

Then there were The Three Pigeons and The Fat Ox. Then came The Mitre Inn and Tavern, a name most likely adopted on the closing of The Mitre in Silver Street. This house in 1817 had two billiard tables. Some forty years since the sign was changed to The Butcher's Arms and it is now The Market Tavern. Not far from this was The Bull's Head, which in 1780 was taken by John Webb, of the Roebuck, who changed the sign to The City Arms, which name it still bears, and I believe has been conducted by his family ever since, Mr Cassey being a descendant of the above John Webb.

There does not appear to have been any inn in the Oatmeal Row, but in the last century there was an extensive concern in the Cheese Market known as the Vine: it occupied the whole space between what is now the Capital and Counties Bank and St Thomas' churchyard extending back to the river. The county justices held their meetings there for many years, till in 1786 they removed to the Parade Coffee House. In 1763 James Precey opened a Repository there for the sale of horses, an auction being held every three weeks. There was also a theatre on the premises, and, if we may judge from the following bill of the play, it was of no mean pretensions: -

'By Mr Hallam's Company from both Theatres in London (by particular desire) on Tuesday evening, January the seventh, 1752, at the New Playhouse in Salisbury, will be presented a Tragedy called *Romeo and Juliet*, wrote by William Shakespeare. At the end of the Play will be performed a new Dance called "Les Badinages Champetre." To which will be added a Pantomime Entertainment, called *The Adventures of Harlequin*, being the comic part of *Perseus and Andromeda*. Particular care has been taken to make the house warm. This company always begins exactly at six o'clock.'

On the 28th of March the same company performed *The Constant Couple*, Sir Harry Wildair, by Mr Hallam, with the farce of *The Stage Coach*. In 1761 was performed twice in a week "the play of *Henry VIII*, with the procession and coronation of Anne Bullen and the ceremony of the Champion in Westminster Hall. Great expense has been gone to in decorating the play of Henry VIII. Those who have not had an opportunity of seeing the late Coronation in London (that of George III) may have their curiosity in some measure satisfied, and a pleasing idea given them of that pompous and magnificent ceremony."

In October of this year the Duke of York attended the theatre for Concert and Ball and the play which followed. In 1763, we have *The Conscious Lovers* and *The Beggar's Wedding*, with an epilogue addressed to the ladies of Salisbury. In 1763, a morning performance was given, by command of their Royal Highnesses the Dukes of Gloucester and York. In 1767, the season was opened with *The Beggar's Opera* and *Marriage à la Mode*. In 1769, *Every Man in his Humour* was performed, under the patronage of Lady Juliana Dawkins, of Standlynch House (now Trafalgar): and in 1770, David Garrick was present at the performances with the Earl of Pembroke, and was pleased to compliment the comedians on their acting.

David Garrick, who was a favourite with the Earl of Pembroke, was a frequent visitor at Wilton, and doubtless during his visits made many friends at Salisbury, in illustration of which it may be stated that on one occasion he presented Mr James Wickins, a respected resident of the Close, with a valuable snuff-box, on the lid of which, to indicate the material of which it was composed, and the donor, the following was inscribed:- "Immortal Bard! This from thy sacred tree, thy Garrick rescued and reserved for me. J.W." In 1827, when John Vandenhoff had been playing a round of Shakespearian characters at our theatre, Mr Wickins presented this snuff-box to him, having caused the following inscription to be added:- "Presented by Mr Wickins, of Salisbury, to Mr Vandenhoff as a tribute to his transcendent merit as an actor, and to his steady attachment as a friend." Mr Wickins lived but a short time after, Mr Vandenhoff's last performance taking place on April 30, Mr Wickins dying on the 13th May, in his 82nd year.

Hatcher, in his remarks on Salisbury amusements, speaking of the theatre at the Sun in Fisherton, says "As the performances became more frequented, the Sun in Fisherton was soon exchanged for the Vine," whereas, in fact, the theatre at the Sun was started in opposition to that at the Vine, which I have shown was in existence in 1732, while the Sun theatre was not opened till 1763, on Jan 23, with *Richard III*, when "there was a goodly company, who expressed themselves much pleased with the elegance and commodiousness of the theatre."

The opening of the new theatre in New Street in 1777 (now Hamilton Hall) would seem to have interfered with the fortunes of the theatre at the Vine, the opposition being somewhat fierce, if we may judge from the following announcement which was advertised in the Salisbury Journal in January, 1778:-

'A Card. – It is humbly requested of such gentlemen who are at any time disposed to amuse the audience with Horse-laughing in the fifth Act of a fine Tragedy, as finely performed, that they would for the future indulge their friends at the Old Vine Pot-house, and not at the new theatre in Salisbury. – An Enemy of Tragi-Comedy.'

In 1786 the old playhouse was converted into a commodious tennis court, the inn premises being restricted to the left side of the gateway, the other side (now occupied by Mr Haskell and the Savings Bank) being let as a dwelling house and shop. But the Vine would seem to have had its day, for in 1796 it was offered for sale, and about 1804 Geo. Short and Son, grocers and tea men, built two shops on the site, themselves occupying the one nearest to St Thomas' Churchyard.

Almost adjoining the Vine premises was another good old-fashioned inn, the Maidenhead. The house stood some way behind, being approached through a long yard, and the premises extended to the river. In 1769, it was in great part rebuilt, and was said to be elegantly fitted up. A literary society was very early held here, which was, under certain restrictions, open to both sexes, but this arrangement does not seem to have answered, for in 1774 it was announced that a new society had been formed on the plan of the Robin Hood, in London. This was a debating society, at which, however, no subject having a religious or political tendency was allowed to be discussed. At the first meeting the following was the subject of debate: "Whether, considering the manners of the present age, a single or a married life may be deemed the most happy?" The question was decided in favour of matrimony by 47 to 4; but the next day the dissenting members entered a protest against the decision, supported by the following reasons: -

'1. Because they believe the question has been considered as an enquiry into the expediency of persons marrying, whereas its intention was, only to determine whether the married persons of the present age were not more unhappy, from an ill-judged choice, or other such cause, than the unmarried ones. 2 Because the persons who decided the question did not deny the principal arguments that were produced against them, viz 'That matrimonial connections were now in general formed upon the most sordid principles, being entered upon purely to supply an exigence, or to gratify a passion:- that a dissimulation, before marriage, was for that reason, too often met with, and it was easy to see that infelicity must follow from an union upon such weak principles. 3. Because it is evident that a majority of those who carried the question, were induced therein, against their own opinion, by the fear of being censored as enemies to matrimony, or dissatisfied with the partner they had chosen. And, lastly, because a decision carried by numbers, and not by argument, is totally repugnant to the meaning of a true Debating Society, and rather tends to establish erroneous opinions, then to investigate the truth of controverted matters.'

The forty seven advocates for matrimony were called upon at the next meeting to support their decision: after which the following question was debated:- "Whether mankind in general are more influenced by their own inclinations or by the prejudice of example." What the result of this protest and debate was I am unable to learn. A general idea of the scope of the society may be gleaned from the mention of a few of the subjects which were discussed: - "Whether music, poetry, or painting has the greatest influence upon the passions." "Whether the use of tobacco and snuff is a benefit to the community." "Whether civilisation has made mankind happier than they were in a state of nature." This latter proposition, we are informed, was carried in the affirmative by a large majority. The Maidenhead, and the houses on either side of it were, it will be remembered, pulled down to make room for the present Market House.

I am, sir, yours etc. W.A.W.
Salisbury, July 1886.

Old Inns of Salisbury, No. III

To the Editor of the Salisbury and Winchester Journal.

Sir, - In my last I omitted to mention that the Maidenhead was the scene of the exhibition of perhaps the earliest collection of wild animals that visited this city, as it must be remembered that it was not till much later that the famous Wombwell collections were formed. On September 28, 1767, we are told that there has "Just arrived in this city and to be seen on Tuesday next, at the Maidenhead Inn, in the Market Place, an elegant collection of Birds and Wild Beasts, consisting of rare and chosen animals from the great cabinet of nature: amongst which is that noble creature the Great He Lion, which is thought to be larger than that in the Tower, and is the only one that travels in England that has a mane and periwig, and what is very remarkable, he is as tame as a lamb."

The Parade, or, as it is now called, the Blue Boar Row, will complete the circle of the Market Place. At the time that the Corporation resolved on a reduction of the number of inns from 60 to 40, in 1700, it was stated that there were six on the Parade, the Blew Boar being the chief. I can only account for four – the Chough, the Blue Boar, the Saracen's Head, and the Parade Coffee House: this latter ought scarcely to be reckoned, as it did not become a tavern till 1785. Only one of these, the Chough, now remains, and of this there is not much history to recount. In 1762 Robert Fullforth, late gardener to the Earl of Londonderry, announcing that he had taken the inn, said, "Gentlemen, etc who please to favour him with their custom, may depend on the most civil Usage, and a grateful return for their favours." In 1809 it was announced that there was "to be seen at the Chough a wonderful and surprising Yorkshire youth, 17 years of age, 7ft 6in high, and weighing 24 stone."

When the name was altered to Blue Boar Row I do not know: but in 1799 the Chough was still described as being on the Parade, which must have been long after the Blue Boar had ceased to exist.

The Blue Boar Inn stood about the centre of the Parade, and must have been an extensive hostelry when at its prime; it had a large courtyard, extending to Chipper Lane, which I believe is still in existence. It is said to have been at the Blue Boar that in 1483 the Duke of Buckingham was beheaded by the order of Richard III, and a stone was formerly pointed out in the courtyard on which it was stated that the unfortunate nobleman suffered. It may be remembered that the duke was brother-in-law of the then Bishop of Salisbury, Lionel Woodville, who died the following year, his death being hastened, it was said, by the grief at the downfall of his family, occasioned by the tyranny of the King. It is a curious coincidence that this monarch, only two years after the execution of Buckingham, when on his way to the fatal field of Bosworth, should sleep at the Blue Boar Inn at Leicester (preferring it to the Castle which was then in a ruinous state), the next night being passed in a tent near the field of battle. A bedstead, brought there from Leicester, is still preserved in the hall of Rothley Temple, in Leicestershire, formerly a commandery of the Knights Templars, which is said to be the veritable four-poster upon which the crooked-backed tyrant passed the last night but one of his existence. Of the subsequent history of the

Blue Boar I can find no record – it was still an inn in 1730, Robert Read being then the master – and, as it was soon after this that the Three Lions became the chief inn of the city, it is probable that its custom gradually dwindled away till it was given up, as was the case with the latter some half century later. Almost at the beginning of the present century Dr Fowler built himself a house on a portion of the site of the Blue Boar, which he occupied till the latter part of 1819; shortly after which it was taken by the then newly-established "Salisbury and South Wiltshire Library and Reading Room," the lower part of the premises being converted into a shop – which was, I believe, not long after occupied by Mr Fawcett as a draper – and adjoining this was erected another house with shop which was occupied by Mr Charles Norton, cabinet maker and auctioneer. On his leaving Salisbury, in consequence of taking a hotel in Exeter, John Sparshatt, draper, removed thither from his shop next door to the Maidenhead. Both of these businesses having passed into the hands of Messrs Style and Gerrish, they are now the occupiers of the whole of the premises formerly the Blue Boar.

The Saracen's Head, which was pulled down some four years since, almost adjoined the Blue Boar, probably actually formed part of it originally. It was a curious old-fashioned inn. During some repairs, in the year 1838, beneath the floor of the tap room, was found a skeleton, minus the head and one arm, which was supposed to have been that of the unfortunate Buckingham. There was a considerable amount of letter writing about it at the time, both in the local and London papers. The site of this hostelry has recently been built upon, the shops being added to those of the firm previously mentioned.

The Parade Coffee House was not, as I have said, an inn but was supported mostly by subscribers of a guinea per annum, who met there to read the papers, discuss the affairs of the nation, the latest scandal, and other local gossip. It was conducted somewhat on the principles prevailing with the London coffee houses of the time of Addison, Steele, and Dr Johnson. It is highly probable that many of the citizens of that day may have there enjoyed the conversation of the great lexicographer, as he spent an agreeable fortnight with Mr Wm. Bowles, at Heale House, in September, 1783, during which he no doubt paid several visits to this city. That he not only inspected and admired our Cathedral, but also minutely examined that mystery of the plain, Stonehenge, is evidenced by the following letter, which he addressed to Mrs Thrale shortly after his return to town: -

London, October 9 1783

'To Mrs Thrale, - Two nights ago Mr Burke sat with me a long time: he seems much pleased with his journey. We had both seen Stonehenge this summer for the first time. I told him that the view had enabled me to refute two opinions which have been advanced about it. One, that the materials are not natural stones but an artificial composition hardened by time. This notion is as old as Camden's time; and has this strong argument to support it, that stone of that species is no where to be found. The other opinion advanced by Dr Charlton is, that it was erected by the Danes.

Mr Bowles made me observe, that the transverse stones were fixed on the perpendicular supporters by a knob formed on the top of the upright stone, which entered into a hollow cut in the crossing stone. This is a proof that the enormous edifice was raised by a people who had not yet the knowledge of mortar; which cannot be supposed of the Danes who came hither in ships, and were not ignorant certainly of the arts of life. This proves likewise that the stone are not to be factitious; for they that could mould such durable masses could do much more than make mortar, and could have continued the transverse from the upright part with the same paste.

You have doubtless seen Stonehenge, and if you have not, I should think it a hard task to make an adequate description. It is in my opinion, to be referred to the earliest habitation of the island, as a Druidical monument of at least two thousand years; probably the most ancient work of man upon the island.

Salisbury Cathedral, and its neighbour Stonehenge, are two eminent monuments of art and rudeness, and may show the first essay, and the last perfection of Architecture.'

The long room at the Parade Coffee House was sometimes used as a lecture hall and place for public meetings. In the autumn of 1792, an empiric, styling himself Dr Graham, gave lectures there on "Health, very Long Life, and Happiness," introducing his newly discovered system of earth bathing as a cure for all the ills that flesh is heir to. By way of illustration, he exhibited himself and some credulous people who had been his patients buried to the chin in the garden of the establishment for two hours at a time. The Doctor asserted that it was a "perfect cure for the palsy, gout, rheumatism, scurvy, leprosy, scrofula, bilious, nervous, and consumptive disorders; crooked back bones," etc. A proof of the innocency, if not the efficacy of the system was afforded by the fact that Dr Graham himself had been thus buried to the chin more than two hundred times.

But the Parade Coffee House had been for some time on the decline. In 1784 it was to let, and was kept open for nearly twelve months by the subscribers themselves as a sort of club. In 1785, it was taken by Wm. Penny and carried on as a tavern and coffee house. A good billiard table was added and gentlemen were lodged in the house; soups were to be had every morning, dinners were provided, in fact, this year the steward's ordinary at the races as held here, and the old coffee house seemed to have taken a new lease of prosperity; and in 1786, as I have before stated, the county magistrates made this their place for holding petty sessions instead of the Vine. Nothing worthy of notice occurs in connection with the Parade for the next few years, but in 1804 it is again to let, the occupier announcing that he is going into another concern. The next year it was offered for sale by auction, together with a large building in Endless Street, the whole being held on lease from the Corporation. It was not sold, but the furniture and fittings were disposed of a little later in that year, and the premises remained unoccupied till 1808, when I believe the lease was purchased by Mr Robert Squarey, chemist and druggist, who removed into these premises in July from the Oatmeal Row, whither he had migrated some three years previously from Silver Street, where he had first established himself in 1802. The Parade Coffee House will now readily be recognised in the shop of Messrs Read and Orchard.

Another house called Gauntlett's Coffee House was opened in the Market Place in 1775, but this I believe, was on the south side of the Square, near the Market Inn that is now; and Joseph Boyter, master of the Three Lions, in 1778 announced that he would open a Coffee Room in the Blue Boar Row at Lady Day in that year; but nothing more is heard of these houses, it is probable that they had but a short existence.

In Castle Street I have already mentioned the Silent Woman; I have since met two or three persons who tell me they well remember the Quiet Woman, and that it was, as I conjectured, the house now called the George and Dragon. This slight difference in idea of the name of the inn is easily understood when we learn that the only indication of its name was the pictorial representation of a decapitated woman carrying her head under her arm. There was at the upper end of Castle Street, in Milford in fact, an inn called the Bowling Green. I believe it was the house now occupied by Mr Richard Dear. In 1763, the following announcement appeared in the Salisbury Journal: -

'This is to acquaint the Curious that there is now at the Bowling Green, near this city, a person who, after spending many years with great expense and trouble, has collected the following ancient and valuable curiosities:- The original watch of Mary Queen of Scots, presented her by Francis the French king; the crucifix Her Majesty carried before her when she went to execution; two Egyptian Gods 4000 years old, one buried with King Pharaoh in the mummy shape; several curious manuscripts on vellum; an Egyptian sea-horse taken out of the Red Sea; a collection of putrefactions; upwards of 100 medals; a most curious piece of workmanship by a blind man; a scalp and scalping knife of an Indian chief, etc.'

This house was in great measure devoted to *al fresco* entertainments, and curiosity to see without paying for admission, would seem to have been rather prevalent in that day, as I find the proprietor, John Rogers, offering a reward of two guineas for the detection of offenders, his garden wall having been several times broken down. This house changed landlords rather frequently, for in 1776 Thomas Safe announces that "he has opened the Bowling Green at the upper end of Castle Street, and that he supplies Beer, Ale, Cyder, Coffee, and Tea at the shortest notice, the best of each kind." In 1778 we have Wm. Jackson, comedian, announcing that he is about to open the Bowling Green, having laid in a neat assortment of wines, etc. etc., and humbly hopes to receive the patronage and encouragement of the public."

In 1784, there was a great concourse of persons on the green and in the surrounding fields, to witness the ascent of an air balloon which a Mr Dinwiddie intended to launch as an illustration of some lectures he had been delivering for two or three days previously as the Assembly Rooms: a ticket was affixed to the balloon offering a reward of one guinea and expenses for bringing it to the proprietor at the White Hart, Winchester, which city he was about to visit. The ascent was most successfully accomplished; the balloon was visible for about ten minutes. It was found next day at Liphook, near Petersfield, having travelled about 50 miles.

In addition to the foregoing there

was in very early days an inn called the Squirrel, afterwards altered to the Black Bear, and was latterly the residence of Mr C M Lee; in 1776, the Grasshopper at the corner of Chipper Lane; this sign was at the beginning of this century changed to the Plough – of which in 1824 Mr George Barnett became the landlord – and was the last person, I believe, by whom it was occupied as an inn. Another, the date of establishment of which may be imagined by its name, was the Wellington Arms; but this was in want of a tenant in 1819, so, probably, had but a short career.

I regret I am unable to give Mr Pickford any information as to the name of the inn he believes to have been carried on on the premises he now occupies; but should imagine he would find a clue to it in his deeds, as I have found that to be the case with other older premises that were formerly inns. – Yours etc.

W.A.W
Salisbury, August, 1886.

Old Inns of Salisbury, No. IV

To the Editor of the Salisbury and Winchester Journal.

Sir, - Continuing the circuit of the city, I find that in 1778 there was in Endless Street the Golden Lion, the property of Messrs Whitchurch, the brewers, which was kept by John Brettel. With this exception there does not appear to have been in this street any inn besides the Woolpack, which was in existence about the middle of the last century. In 1809 Henry Macklin opened his tap for the sale of home brewed beer. This has always been called by the name of the proprietor for the time being; thus, it has been successively Macklin's, Crumley's, Chamberlain's, Wolferstan's, Bridger's, and it is now known as Fawcett's.

In Rollestone Street, in 1784, there was the Crispin, but this was I presume to have been but a small affair, as the landlord, F Gatehouse, also carried on the business of a calenderer and wearing apparel cleaner. In 1786 Mr Gatehouse announced his removal to the Plume of Feathers, where he intended still to carry on his business of a calenderer.

In 1775, I find the Stone Bridge in Bedwin Row, which name it still bore in 1805, but not long after the sign was changed to the Royal George. In 1796 there was the Sun near St Edmund's Church, probably altered to the Vine on the closing of the inn of that name in the Cheese Market; it is now St Edmund's Church House. This street must at one time have been called Church Street, for in 1779 I find a bake-house described as being "in Bednal Row or Church Street, facing Rollestone Street;" no doubt the same premises in which a baker's business is still carried on. So late as 1821, there was also in Bedwin Street an inn called the Crown. In Church Street in 1766, was the Leopard's Head, it was situated in the upper part of the street, and was the house next the corner opposite the Five Bells. It was the property of the Corporation, until a few years since it was sold by auction, I believe, when the money was required for re-building the Police Station on the Canal. Speaking of the Five Bells, reminds me that this house was at a very early date celebrated for its Carnation Feast. The following was the programme for 1791:-

'This is to acquaint all Gentlemen, Gardeners, and Florists, that on Wednesday, the 29th of this instant July there will be held at the Five Bells, at Salisbury a Florist

Feast. The persons that produceth the twelve best blossoms of whole blowing carnations, one of a sort, of his own blowing and propagating from layers, shall be intitled to a silver cup of one guinea and a half value. Secondly, the person that produceth ten of the best blossoms of his own blowing and propagating, but one of a sort, shall be intitled to a silver punch ladle of a guinea value. Thirdly, the person who produceth eight of the best blossoms of his own blowing and propagating, but one of a sort, shall be intitled to a silver spoon of fifteen shillings value. No person to win but one prize, but the person that does not win the first, has liberty to draw his Flowers, and show for second or third prize. No steward to Show. Dinner to be ready at, One o'clock; the ordinary one shilling.'

In the London Road, just outside the city, not far from where Winchester Gate formerly stood, was opened in 1813 the New White Horse Cellar: it was principally a resting place for the drovers and others who were continually passing in those days, when all the cattle for the fairs and markets had to travel by road, and all the goods necessary for the trade of the city were brought here by means of stage wagons. It stood back some little way from the road, and had a long horse trough in front, such as was at that time to be seen near the entrance to almost every town; readers of Pickwick will remember a trough of this description in front of the Marquis of Granby, Dorking, which the Rev. Mr Stiggins became intimately acquainted with on the introduction of Mr Weller, Sen. The establishment of railways and other circumstances having so changed the nature of the traffic, this house ceased to be required, and Elm Grove Terrace now occupies the site.

Returning into the city, I find, in 1767, the Coach and Six described as being near Winchester Gate; as I do not hear of this inn again, but some nine years later come across the Six Bells, also described as near Winchester Gate, I conclude it to be the same house newly named. It was rather an extensive place, situated at the corner of Greencroft Street, in which street it had a back entrance, its stabling and garden extending to a depth of 164 feet, whilst it had a frontage to Winchester Street of 84 feet. In 1779, Joseph Rogers, from the Star, announces "that he hath, at great expense, rebuilt that ancient inn called the Six Bells, in Winchester Street, which he hath now entered upon." In 1798 it was the starting place of the Royal Mail to Portsmouth. This inn had a narrow escape in 1799, a fire breaking out in the stables, where was a large quantity hay, but thanks to the energetic action of the officers and men of the 3rd (Prince of Wales's) Dragoon Guards, it was prevented from spreading to the old buildings adjoining. It is most probable that many of the soldiers were quartered in the house, as during the greater part of that year seven troops of that regiment were stationed in the city. It must have pressed rather hardly upon the innkeepers of that day, having to provide the cavalry with stabling for 578 horses, and lodging for nearly as many men, besides accommodating those of other regiments when changing quarters, many hundreds sometimes marching in and out of the city in the course of a week. About this time several of the numerous "Stages," as they were then called, which formed the means of communication between Salisbury and neighbouring towns, made this inn their starting point. In 1819, it was kept by a Mr Goodman, and in 1820 by Henry Coombs, who, I believe to have been the last person who carried it on as an inn. Winchester Street must at this time have been a thoroughfare of some importance, for John Sawkins, eating house keeper, announces his removal from Catherine Street to Winchester Street, opposite the Six Bells, "where may be had turtle and other soups." The vending of "real turtle soup" would scarcely be a lucrative occupation in the same locality at the present day. Although the Six Bells property has long since been divided and subdivided into tenements, yet the plan of the building may still be traced – the centre slightly projecting beyond the wings; there was a high gateway, through which probably the coaches drove into the spacious yard. In each wing there appears to have been a row of five windows on each floor; the window arches on one side are all still remaining.

At the corner of Brown Street was another large inn; this was the starting point for several of the coaches plying between this city and the Metropolis, it was at one time called the Star and Garter; Mr George Webb, who became the proprietor in 1775, announced that he had changed the sign to the Black Horse; but this would seem to have been only a restoration of its original name, as in November, 1763, we read that "the Salisbury Flying Machine, which has continued flying all the summer, will continue flying all the winter, in one day to London, from the Black Horse inn, in Winchester Street, to the Angel Inn, the Backside of St Clements, London, up one day and down the next." The Black Horse was a large concern, comprising all the premises now occupied by Messrs Harris and Son, coach builders, and extending a long way down Brown Street, where it had its tap, as was customary with most large inns in the early part of this century.

The Greyhound, which I have already mentioned in speaking of the Three Lions, immediately behind which hotel it was situated, was another large concern. It was closed as an inn by Mr Gast in 1783, when he offered to let the eight stables, capable of accommodating 70 or 80 horses, separately, and the remainder as a residence for a private family, as corn stores, etc. I believe the premises attached to this inn to have included all that now occupied by Mr Mullins and the corn store of Messrs Woodrow. Whilst speaking of Mr Gast, I will mention a somewhat curious scene which was enacted in the Three Lions, in 1730; in the Salisbury Journal for July 6 it is thus recorded:-

'Robert Hayter, of Dinton in the county of Wilts, Shoemaker, having slandered Mr Andrew Waters, late of Harnham, in the same County, did on Tuesday the 23rd of June, at the 3 Lyons in Sarum, in the public Coffee Room, before several Gentlemen, acknowledge the Falsity of each Slander, asked the said Mr Waters Pardon, and promised not to give him Offence for the future, and gave a Note of Hand to pay Costs of Suite for the Action then depending; upon which, on the generous interpretation of a worthy gentlemen in Mr Hayter's neighbourhood, Mr Waters forgave him.'

It may not be out of place to mention that, although several of the masters of inns I have alluded to became bankrupt, Mr Gast seems to have been an notable exception, for in 1766, the following account appears: - "On the first of February Mr James Davis, woollen draper of the Market Place, was married to Miss Gast, eldest daughter of Mr Gast, of the Three Lions, a very agreeable young lady, with a genteel fortune."

Yet another inn with very extensive premises, and substantially built, as may be seen at the present time, was the Three Cups at the corner of Church Street, now Mr Foreman's school. This belonged to the Corporation, and dates back to the 15th century. In the corporate accounts for 1484, credit is given for 40s as quit rent received for "the corner tenement le III Cuppes, in Wymanstrete, late let to Thomas Hille, of Abyngdon." From 1497 (in which year it cost the Corporation 54s 3d for repairs) to 1509 it was held by Robert Stacy at a quit rent of 60s. When it ceased to be an inn I cannot ascertain, but in the middle of the last century it was the residence and place of business of John Wyche, wine and spirit merchant, one of the city aldermen, and who served the office of Mayor in 1764. The property, I believe, continued to be held by his family for many years; a descendant, Hezekiah Wyche, who filled the civic chair in 1807, resided there and continued to do so up to 1817. Some ten or twelve years after this Mr John Finch carried on the same business, and held the lease till his death. The property was sold about the same time as the Leopard's Head. It must originally have occupied nearly one fourth of the chequer, which I believe was called the Three Cups Chequer. The vaults are still devoted to their original purpose, being occupied by Mr Richard Dear, wine and spirit merchant.

In 1767 there was in Winchester Street an inn called the Angel. In December of 1789 the stock of strong beer was sold by auction, and the house was to let. In 1805, the house itself was for sale, the proprietor leaving it to take a larger concern; whether the new purchaser changed its name I do not know, but I find no further mention of the Angel, and I believe it to be the same house as that now known as the Anchor and Hope. The description of the Angel fits in very well for the latter, which sign is first met with about 1820. In 1763 there was the Hand and Flower; and in 1767 the Running Horse, on the site of this house, which was pulled down by the late Mr J S Atkins, wine merchant, is now Mr Packer's dairy. Then there was the Lord Collingwood, a house started probably soon after the battle of Trafalgar, and possibly kept by some survivor who had been present with the gallant admiral in that and some of the subsequent battles in which he distinguished himself. Another house called The Ship will be remembered by many persons, having been pulled down not many years since, which, though latterly not bearing a very high reputation was at the beginning of the century, a respectable inn. In 1783 there was an inn in this street called the Three Tuns, of which William Staples was the master. I cannot ascertain its situation, but it was amongst the property disposed of by the executors of Mr Benjamin Collins, proprietor of the *Salisbury and Winchester Journal*, at his death in 1780, being held by him on a lease of 99 years granted by Mary Eyre, widow. Another inn, the exact locality of which I cannot trace, the Talbot, I have found mentioned more than once, even as lately as 1821: but in a note to No 30 of "Gleanings from the Archives of Salisbury," H.J.F.S. says "Mr Matcham informs me that among the MSS, at New House, there is a lease granted by his ancestor, Mr Eyre, in the 17th century, of a meadow attached to the Talbot, in Winchester Street."

In Winchester Street was another inn of very respectable antiquity, the George, by which name it was known till about 1826, when Mr Blake, who had been the landlord for some years, dubbed it "The Old George Wine and Spirit Vaults." In 1768 appeared the following announcement of what was, perhaps, at that time considered a very interesting exhibition: -

'This is to acquaint the curious, that there is to be seen and sold at the George Inn, in Winchester Street, Salisbury, a grand piece of machinery, being a most curious astronomical and musical spring clock, otherwise called the theatre of the muses, made by the famous Mr Pinchbeck. This wonderful machine gives general satisfaction, and equally surprises and delights all who ever hear and see it. It is most beautifully composed of music, architecture, painting, and sculpture, with such a diverting variety of moving figures in the front, as renders it a very entertaining piece of art.

Also the Royal Waxwork from Fleet Street, London, being a grand and curious collection of 28 figures, in such perfection and exactness, that the royal and princely persons they represent seem to be really alive. They are esteemed the nearest human life in any collection ever seen in this kingdom. These effigies imitate life in such great perfection that any person who sees these inimitable figures (it may almost be said) sees the illustrious personages they represent. To the above collection have lately been added the lively representations of his present Majesty George III and his royal consort Queen Charlotte, dressed in the royal clothes which they themselves wore. These are excellent pieces of workmanship, exceed any of the kind ever exhibited, and are esteemed the richest curiosities ever shown in England.'

In my account of the Three Lions I mentioned that in 1764 William and Sarah Ody, late tapster and chambermaid to Mr Gast, had become the host and hostess of the Three Swans; but we must go back a long way to arrive at the date of the first establishment of this inn. It will be remembered that Ludlow, the Parliamentary General, in his "Memoirs," in the course of his description of the skirmish with the Royalist troops in the Market Place in 1645, speaks of riding up by the Three Swans towards Winchester Gate. In 1730 I find Edward Williams, Sadler, announcing his removal from his late shop next the Blew Boar Inn in the Market Place, to the shop in Winchester Street, next door to the Three Swans. The entertainments at this house would seem to have been of a very diversified character, for in May, 1767, it was announced: -

'The following very ingenious piece of art in miniature, just arrived here, and to be seen at the Three Swans in Winchester Street, are well worth the notice and observation of the curious, viz: - 1. An ivory four-wheel chaise complete, with a person in it, all drawn by a flea, and scarce equal to a grain in weight. 2. A landau on traces, with four persons in it, two footmen behind, and a coachman on the box with a dog between his legs, six horses and a postillion, all drawn by a flea. 3. A pair of steel scissors that weigh only the sixteenth part of a grain. 4. A common peppercorn, containing twelve dozen of silver spoons and the corn not above half full.'

In 1776 appears the following: - "Cocking — A main of cocks will be fought at the Three Swans, in Salisbury, during the time of the Races — between the gentlemen of Wilts and Dorset. To show 45 of a side in the main, for four guineas a battle, and one hundred guineas the odd battle. Pike, Feeder for Wilts and Northover Feeder for Dorset." In this year the infirmary anniversary dinner was held here, Lord Radnor sending a fine buck. This house does not appear, however, always to have been a success, for in 1780 it was closed for want of a tenant. It was re-opened in 1783, and in the following year the London, Exeter and Plymouth coaches set out from the Three Swans every day, Sundays excepted. In October, 1822, Wm. Cobbett dined at the ordinary with the farmers, addressing them afterwards at considerable length. In 1825 the following highly intellectual entertainment was announced: -

'A Rattlesnake gorging a Rabbit, - This Rare and most interesting Exhibition will take place on on Monday the 4th of July, 1825, in the Great Room of the Three Swans Inn, Salisbury, precisely at twelve o'clock at noon. The Reptile forms part of a Collection of Natural Curiosities that has for some time past been exhibited in High Street, and it will be removed to the above large Room in order to afford to a numerous assemblage the opportunity of witnessing a spectacle that will assuredly excite the most intense interest and astonishment. This venomous serpent is the only one that has been known to gorge in this kingdom, and is of the species called the Swamp or Green Rattlesnake.

It has swallowed rabbits in the presence of numerous spectators at Bath, Oxford and Manchester, and it has now been six weeks without food. When the Rabbit is caged with the Snake the latter, erecting his head and neck, expands his dilatable jaws, erects his fangs, and with the quickness of lightning strikes the trembling animal; he will then encircle the rabbit in his folds, licking and smelling and occasionally gaping, as if to adapt his jaws for capacious swallow. During the act of gorging the neck of the Snake will be greatly distended, his colour changed, and his scales elevated, exhibiting the Reptile in a situation very rarely seen. Admission 2s.'

Nearly all the inns in Milford Street date back at least to the early part of the last century. It is scarcely possible to establish the time of their establishment. In 1761, we have the Red Lion and Cross Keys, from whence in 1765 it was announced that the Salisbury machine would commence flying in one day to London. It was stated to be genteely built, hung on steel springs, to carry four passengers only, and was to leave the Red Lion and Cross Keys every Monday, Wednesday, and Friday, returning from the Belle Savage on the alternate days. In the same year, Daniel P Safe, the postmaster, having taken this inn on the decease of R Musselwhite notifies that he will remove the post office there from the King's Arms. In 1769 Mr Safe announces that in future the sign would be the Red Lion only, the name it still bears, and which is known all over the kingdom as the principal home for commercial travellers visiting the city. Having passed through various vicissitudes, it recently became a Limited Liability Company, who have, however, now leased it to Mr Geo. Wilkes.

On Milford Hill, just without the city boundary, was the Bell; it may be recognised in the Shakespearian scene given at page 35 of "Hall's Picturesque Memorials;" and the Weaver's Arms, which in 1766 was described as a good accustomed house on Milford Hill, of which Francis Jones was the master, was, I believe, on the opposite side of the road, rather higher up the hill, in all probability the property recently pulled down. In 1764 the Cart Wheel is mentioned, the entries for the City Bowl at the races were to be made at this house – which seems sometimes to have been called the Cart Wheel and at others the Catherine Wheel: I find both names used in the same year. The sign which some 40 years ago was fixed on the back premises in Pennyfarthing Street, was unmistakably the wheel of St Catherine. There was also the Joiner's Arms in this street, but its exact situation I cannot ascertain: in 1747 the Three Cranes was announced to be let, having a large malthouse attached. In the middle of last century, too, there was the Archangel, which was the property of the Corporation, being built on the side of the Town Ditch; this subsequently became the Royal Oak, and the house, no longer an inn, is now occupied by a vendor of milk.

In 1767, we have the Rainbow; this house was the scene of a fracas which has now almost passed out of knowledge. Yet there may be a few readers who will remember a Salisbury character known as Poet Rose, who in 1824, being accused of having libelled General Sir John Slade as to his conduct at the battle of Waterloo, was followed by Marcus Slade, the General's son, and severely horse-whipped in Milford Street, and, taking refuge in the Rainbow, was followed by Mr Slade, but was eventually locked in a room and removed from further violence. This attack was the subject of an action at the following assizes, which resulted in a verdict of 40s for the plaintiff, Poet Rose. On the death of George the Fourth, Mr James Goddard, who was then the landlord, changed the sign to that which it now bears, the William the Fourth, and on the signboard the new monarch was represented on one side in his admiral's uniform, and on the other in his coronation robes. In 1831, Mr Goddard felt so indignant with His Majesty, who was believed to have prevented the passing of the Reform Bill, that he had the sign taken down and suspended upside down, and so it hung until in the following year that measure became law.

Another old inn still remains in this street, the Goat, which some sixty years ago was celebrated for its pink feasts; it was here that the late Mr John Keynes commenced his successful career as a florist, being a constant exhibitor, and seldom failing to obtain a prize. In 1826, and again in the following year we find Turner, of Wilton (I believe the father of the late Chas Turner, of Slough, who also made a name in the horticultural world), taking first prize, and John Keynes the second; the same thing occurred in the following year. The prizes, it will be seen, were somewhat handsome, for in 1829 Mr Turner received £3 for second prize, and Mr Keynes £1 4s for the fourth. In this year there was also a carnation feast, when melons also were shown, and we find the gardeners of Earl Nelson and Mr Wadham Wyndham taking prizes. Being called feasts, I suppose, accounts for their always winding up with a dinner; on one occasion as many as 70 are recorded as having dined and spent a convivial evening at the Goat Pink Feast. These friendly rivalries, in all probability, did much to stimulate that taste for floriculture which Mr John Keynes afterwards so successfully cultivated.

Although some distance from the city boundaries, it was so intimately connected with the city that I must mention the Punchbowl, where the citizens were wont to indulge in various *al fresco* amusements, and where also there were pink feasts occasionally held. This house was carried on till about 1824, when it was let as a private house, and has so continued; it was the residence of the late Mrs P. P. Cother. In 1775, there was also at Milford the Blue Post or Cheesecake House, and in 1819 the Traveller's Rest, but I cannot define the site of either of these houses.

A number of inns appear to have existed in the city in the last century, which have either disappeared, or now go by other names. From 1762 to 1800 we meet the Flower Pots, the Anchor, the Nag's Head, and the India Arms in Culver Street; this latter I think it probable was changed to the Royal Oak when the inn of that name on Milford Hill was closed. In Gigant Street there was the Flower-de-Luce, the Golden Fleece, the Nelson's Arms, and the Star and Garter — in connection with this latter the following announcement appears in March, 1765: "Robert Tuffin, Star and Garter in Jiggin Street, is possessed of a valuable Receipt of the late Dr Thompson, King's Physician, by which he has acquired the method of healing sore legs, be they of ever so long standing — no cure no pay. If any of the fair sex should object to his attendance, his Mother, who is perfectly acquainted with the Receipt, will wait on them." Nor was Mr Tuffin the only Boniface who was ready to administer to the ailments of his fellow citizens, as in 1810 Wm. West, of the Greyhound, in the Market Place, advertises "that he is possessed of a recipe which is an infallible cure for the ague — Fee 5s, if not cured in twenty-four hours, the money to be returned."

Salisbury
W.A.W.

Old Inns of Salisbury, No. V

To the Editor of the Salisbury and Winchester Journal.

Sir — Coming to Catherine Street, I find that at the beginning of the last century there were six inns in that street, five of which could even then boast of having existed upwards of a century, but three of them have now been extinct for many years. Catherine Street, it should be remembered, at that time extended from the Canal to the Close Gate. How the lower part obtained the name of St John Street I am at a loss to understand, the earliest date at which I have met with it is 1809. The principal inn was the Antelope, which was carried on by Mrs Lawrence early in the 17th century, and in 1760 it had for some time been conducted by Mr Best. At that time the London and Blandford Flying Machine, which left London every Monday and Thursday, stopped at the Antelope for dinner on Tuesday and Friday, and on the return journey stayed there for breakfast. On the death of Mr Best the house was carried on by his widow, Mrs Martha Best, who continued to be the mistress for nearly forty years, dying at the ripe age of seventy-five in 1798. On her decease, it was announced that the inn would be carried on by their daughter, who must, I suppose, have been succeeded by a brother as in 1805 it was again kept by Mr Best. On the 28th of June, 1770, the body of Wm Beckford, the Lord Mayor of London, who had died on the 21st, arrived at the Antelope, and lay in state for the night, being removed the next morning to Fonthill, escorted by forty-five of his tenants, where it was privately interred in the family vault. In 1786 the Archduke and Archduchess of Milan and Prince and Princess Albini and suite were at the Antelope, whence they paid a visit to Wilton House. In 1787 Prince Rezzonico, Senatore di Roma, stayed there on his way to Wardour Castle, on a visit to Lord Arundell. On the 2nd September, 1790, the Duke and Duchess of Cumberland slept at the Antelope, leaving next day for Windsor. In 1794, the meetings of the County Justices were removed here from the Parade Coffee House. On the 24th of August, 1797, the Prince of Orange, Stadtholder of Holland, arrived at the Antelope on his way to visit the Prince of Wales, who was then residing at Crichel; the Prince took refreshments at the Council Chamber with the Corporation, and afterwards visited the Cathedral. Later in the day the Corporation entertained his Serene Highness the Hereditary Prince of Wirtemberg. His Highness then visited the Cathedral, being escorted by the King's Dragoon Guards, and accompanied by the Corporation in State, and from the Cathedral to the Antelope, where he dined and slept, leaving next morning for Wilton House. On the 19th August, 1801, the Prince of Wales, on his way to Crichel, stopped there for refreshments. In 1805, the annual dinner of the Infirmary Governors was held there. From what cause I cannot ascertain, in February, 1806, the inn was to let, but in the course of the next month it was taken by Samuel Jones, from Luce's Hotel, Weymouth. In August of this year Count Woronzoff slept there on his return from visiting the Duke of Somerset. In March, 1810, Mr Jones left the Antelope for the White Hart, being succeeded at the Antelope by Samuel Johnson, who had until recently been the proprietor of the White Hart. George the Fourth, when Prince Regent, during the illness of his father, being in the habit of changing horses and taking refreshment at the Antelope on his frequent journeys to and from Weymouth, gave this inn a second name, and it was thenceforth called the Antelope Inn and Prince Regent's Hotel. In 1822 the Duke of Gloucester, having been on a visit to Fonthill Abbey and Wilton House, arrived there, and after visiting the Cathedral, dined, and left for Bagshot. On the 11th July, 1827, the Duchess of Clarence (afterwards Queen Adelaide) came to Salisbury, accompanied by the Princess Amelia, and slept at the Antelope; next day, their Royal Highnesses visited the Cathedral, and escorted by the Dean, ascended to the eight doors; shortly afterwards departing for Weymouth. They were met on coming into the city by the Salisbury Troop of Yeomanry, who also escorted the Royal party for two miles on their departure. The Duchess again slept at the Antelope on August 3rd, *en route* from Bath to join her husband, then Lord High Admiral, at Portsmouth. The Yeomanry acted as her Royal Highness' escort as before. In 1828 Don Miguel stayed at this hotel; on his departure, the Yeomanry acted as his escort. The last Royal visitor entertained at the Prince Regent's Hotel was, I believe, the Princess Augusta of Saxony, who slept there on 17th August, 1837. Her Royal Highness was attended by Baron Von Guersdorff and Reitzenstein and suite. Next morning the Royal party visited Stonehenge and Wilton House, where they lunched with the Countess of Pembroke; they afterwards paid a visit to the Cathedral, and left for Southampton, *en route* for Brighton, to take leave of the Queen, prior to embarking on their return to their own country. On the death of Mr Johnson, the premises were purchased by two brothers, John and George Mill, who carried on the inn for a time, the former eventually leaving the partnership, and after a few years, Mr George Mill closed the inn and commenced business as a chemist in the portion now the Salisbury Bazaar, the opposite side being a printing office and the centre a coachbuilder's shop and works. This inn was an extensive affair – its frontage in Catherine Street comprising all the premises from No 33 to No 37, then extending behind the other houses in Catherine Street to the right and left, the frontage in Brown Street reached from what is now No 38 to No 52.

Another of the extinct inns was the Lamb, now the residence of Mr Aubrey, veterinary surgeon. This inn dates a long way back, being kept by Philip Seymour about 1620. In 1752, I find the announcement that "the Salisbury Machine in two days to London sets out from the Lamb every Monday, Wednesday, and Friday, returning alternate days. N.B.: - For the greater satisfaction of passengers the Maker of the said Coach will drive it Himself." Some persons will, no doubt, remember this as the house at which the Magnet, London and Weymouth coach, changed horses. It was by this conveyance, which reached Salisbury about 3pm, that, until the introduction of the railway, the citizens were wont to receive their morning papers.

On the same side of the street was the Oxford Arms, which must have been an old inn: but it has now ceased to be used for that purpose for upwards of a century. The premises are now occupied by Mr Lindsey and Mr Highman. The gateway will be remembered by many, having been built into very recently. The Bath stage coach formerly started from this house: it did not run in the winter, but generally commenced with the month of April. In 1731, an opposition coach seems to have been started, for immediately on the announcement that on April 1st the coach would "start as usual from the Oxford Arms, being the old house the stage used to go from," it was also announced that "the Bath stage coach would begin on April 14th to set out from the Angel, in High Street, every Friday." In 1752, the Oxford Arms was kept by James Precey, who was, I believe, the auctioneer who in 1768 opened a horse depository at the Vine in the Cheese Market. In 1760, the house was offered for sale by Mr Earlsman, the owner, who lived opposite to it – his name will be remembered in connection with the Salisbury charities. In this year the entries for the King's Plate at the Salisbury Races were to be made there. The race for the plate was somewhat different to what it is at the present time, being decided by the best of three heats – each of four miles. This would seem to be the principal house from which started the various "stages" as they were called. It was doubtless from this inn that the Bath stage wagon started, which, with its valuable lading, was burnt on Salisbury Plain in 1756 from the wheels taking fire. In 1763, we find "Salisbury and Weymouth caravan from Oxford Arms every other day. Fare 6s; parcels at a halfpenny per pound. Performed, God permits, by William Hardyman." In 1762 and 1763 the entries for the City Bowl were to be made at the Oxford Arms. In 1776, the Oxford Coach left this inn every Tuesday morning, at 10 o'clock, getting to Oxford by one o'clock on Wednesday afternoon, returning on Thursdays. The Southampton carriage also started from the Oxford Arms every Monday and Thursday morning, going through Romsey – returning the same evening. Gibbons, the landlord at this time, was the Winchester and Shaftesbury carrier; but the business altogether does not seem to have prospered, for in this year he became bankrupt, as did also his successor, John Russell, a butcher, before the end of the year. A Mr Freemantle was next master of the Oxford Arms, but his was not a long career, for in 1779 he became bankrupt, his household goods, beer, casks etc. being sold by auction in February: and in April E Stoddart announces that "she has taken the late Oxford inn, nearly opposite the Antelope, and is fitting up a handsome shop, where she will carry on her lace trade, removed from next the King's Arms in Catherine Street." Notwithstanding this, the yard was, I believe, utilised as the starting place for various stages for several years afterwards. During the last few years cockfighting was occasionally indulged in at the Oxford, for in 1778 it was announced that a main of cocks between Wilts and Dorset would be fought there and another during the Races.

The principal cockfighting house, however, would seem to have been the King of Prussia on the opposite side of the street. The following advertisement for the year 1761 is, with little variation, the annual appendage to the announcement of Salisbury Races during the greater part of the latter half of the last century.

'To be fought a main of cocks (to show 31 each) at Mr James Imber's, at the sign of the King of Prussia, in Catherine Street, each day during the Races, for four guineas the battle, and forty guineas the odd. The cocks to be pitted each day at 10 o'clock. Turner and Hurst, feeders. N.B. A good ordinary will be provided at the King of Prussia aforesaid.'

I cannot be certain when exactly the alteration took place, but in 1789 the sign had changed to The White Lion. Nothing particular occurs in connection with this house for many succeeding years, but in 1824 the sign was again changed, and the house was called the Bell and Crown, the name it still bears. When the coaches were in full swing, the landlord, genial "Tommy West" as he was familiarly called, used to keep his house open for supplying refreshments to the passengers by the various coaches which passed through during the night – the London and Exeter Mail – the North Devon, London and Barnstaple coach, and some others whose names I cannot now remember. Many of the tradesmen of the city were wont to call there between six and seven in the morning to take a cup of tea or coffee and read the evening papers, the *Courier* and the *Globe*, which had arrived by the mail, and except by subscribers to the Salisbury and Wiltshire Library, were not to be seen elsewhere till some hours later. There was generally a good muster the morning after the Derby, as this was the first opportunity of obtaining reliable information as to the result. But all this came to an end when the railway drove the coaches off the road.

Shortly after the White Lion had become the Bell and Crown, the former sign was appropriated by the Queen and Plasterer's Arms, situated in Ivy Street, at the back of the White Hart, but this has long become a private house, the malthouse attached to it, however, being still devoted to its original purpose. The Queen and Plasterer's Arms must not be confounded with the Queen's Arms on the opposite side of the street, which dates from the time of Queen Elizabeth.

The White Hart next claims attention. About 1625 John Fryer was the master of this house. In 1765, an Annuity Society was established there. These societies sprang out of the life assurance system, which was then comparatively new. By a payment of about 25s quarterly the members secured an annuity of £30 to their widows. In 1768 is the announcement of a sale at the Old Post Office, Mr Batt's, the White Hart. In Feb, 1786, was advertised for sale by private contract "The commodious, well-known and well-accustomed Inn, called the White Hart, situate in Catherine Street, in the direct road from London to the Land's End, now rented by Mr Wm Weeks, together with three freehold and four leasehold tenements, situate in Ivy Street, and a large freehold stable in Brown Street, all of which are immediately adjoined to and connected with the White Hart, by which it might be rendered as large, and the most complete inn in the West of England." On the 27th of June of this year, the remains of Lady Margaret Beckford, the wife of Wm Beckford, Esq, who had died at the early age of 23, at the castle of La Tour, near Vevey, in Switzerland, arrived at the White Hart, where they lay in state that night, and the next morning passed through the city in great funereal pomp to Fonthill, preceded by a number of the principal tenants on horseback, and followed by the chief mourners and friends in coaches. At Chilmark, they were met by other tenants and friends, and the procession extended a full mile in length. The remains were that evening laid in the family vault at Stop, near Fonthill.

In June, 1788, the Duke and Duchess of Orleans slept at the White Hart, *en route* from Bath to Southampton. In 1789, the King, for the first time since his recovery from his serious illness, made an excursion on his journey to Weymouth, visiting Lyndhurst, where his son, the Duke of Gloucester, had then a residence, and then coming to Salisbury. Great preparations had been made for the reception of His Majesty, who was accompanied by the Queen and the three elder Princesses. A grand triumphal arch was erected near the White Hart, and the Woolcombers, Weavers, Tailors, and all other Companies of the city, characteristically dressed, with banners and bands, had assembled to welcome the Royal party. In the excessive loyalty which the citizens displayed, such a prodigious crowd pressed round the door of the White Hart, that it was impossible for their Majesties to alight and breakfast, as they had intended; they therefore changed horses and passed on to the Woodyates Inn, where they were genteely entertained and accommodated by Mrs Shergold, at very short notice. At this time the White Hart was but a small house, there being at the corner the shop of John Fishlake, grocer. This, with other houses in Ivy Street, as suggested in the advertisement above quoted, were pulled down and the White Hart rebuilt on the extended site indicated; but, as may be seen, it was then considerably smaller than now, the front having three windows on either side of the portico. When the rebuilding took place I cannot exactly say, but it used to be exactly reported that it was done out of the profits made at the time of the Fonthill sale. However, this may be, it is more than likely that the enormous number of persons requiring to be accommodated and conveyed to and from the sale may have convinced the proprietor of the necessity of extending his premises. A further addition in St John Street was made some years later, and will be noticed from its different elevation. On the 1st of August, 1798, the remains of Mrs Beckford, widow of the Right Hon. Wm. Beckford, Lord Mayor of London, who died during his year of office in 1770, were brought from Hampstead, and lay in state at the White Hart, and the next day were conveyed to Fonthill, in a hearse drawn by six horses, followed by six mourning coaches and six, and a long train of carriages. At the gate of the park the procession was met by 300 poor men, women, and children in deep mourning. The spectators in the park numbered nearly 10,000. After the funeral, refreshments were provided in the Grecian Hall for 300 of the gentlemen and tenants who attended the solemnity. In 1809, the Princesses Amelia and Mary stopped there for refreshments. In 1810, Mr Samuel Jones, on announcing his removal from the Antelope to the White Hart, said he "hoped by unremitting assiduity to enforce such order, regularity, and prompt attendance that his patrons should find the White Hart second only in comfort to their own mansions." In 1811 the Pilot coach from Salisbury to Cheltenham started from the White Hart at 6 am, and arrived at the Plough, Cheltenham, at 5 pm, returning alternate days. At this time, the Race Ordinaries used to be held on alternate days at the White Hart and the Antelope. In 1816, the Duke and Duchess of Orleans, with a numerous suite, stayed at the White Hart, and after having inspected the Cathedral, the royal party visited Stonehenge. On the 2nd of January, 1819, the Archduke Maximilian, brother of the Emperor of Austria, arrived at the White Hart. He visited the Cathedral, Old Sarum, Stonehenge, etc. attending the Roman Catholic Chapel next day, Sunday, and left on Monday morning. October 25th, 1830, the Duchess of Kent, the Princess Victoria, and suite arrived at the White Hart from Erlestoke, when the Salisbury troop of Yeomanry formed the guard of honour. Next morning the Royal party visited the Cathedral: they were attended by the Dean, Canon Bouverie, and the Rev W Fisher. They afterwards lunched, with Mr Wadham Wyndham at the College, and at 2:30 left for Southampton. From this time the White Hart was considered the royal house, and on the Princess's accession to the throne, I believe Mr S Jones was appointed posting-master to the Her Majesty. In October, 1834, the Lord Chancellor (Lord Brougham) was paying a visit to the Earl of Radnor, at Longford Castle, and a numerously-signed address had been prepared for presentation to him, complimenting him on the part he had taken with regard to the Reform Bill.

It was intended that the ceremony should have taken place at the Council House, but the Mayor refusing the use of the chamber, the presentation was made on the balcony of the White Hart, whence Lord Brougham addressed the people, who had assembled in large numbers. On Sept 4th Prince George of Cambridge slept there and visited the Cathedral and Wilton House next day. A day or two later the Duc de Nemours was there for the purpose of visiting the Cathedral. On June 29, 1844, the King of Saxony arrived at the White Hart from Oxford, having inspected Stonehenge *en route*. His Majesty visited the Cathedral, and at eight on Sunday morning attended the service at the Roman Catholic Chapel: he afterwards walked on the London Road, whence he made a hasty sketch of the city and Cathedral. The King then visited Wilton House, and on his return left for Weymouth. On August 15, 1856, the Queen, Prince Albert, the Royal Family and suite passed through the city *en route* from Plymouth to Osborne. Her Majesty was received at the station by the Mayor and Corporation, and was escorted to the White Hart by a detachment of the 11th Hussars, which had just arrived in the city. Having lunched, the Royal party visited the Cathedral, inspected the Chapter House, and retired to the Palace, which they left at 4:15. Whilst at the White Hart, Her Majesty recognised Picco, the blind Sardinian Minstrel, who was staying at the hotel, by the sound of his pipe. In October of this year, the Prince of Wales, accompanied by his tutor, arrived at the White Hart, having visited Wardour Castle and Wilton. After going through the Cloisters and Chapter House, His Royal Highness left for Osborne. In July, 1867, the Crown Prince and Princess of Prussia, Princess Helena and suite, lunched at this inn after having visited the Cathedral. September 27, 1882, Prince Edward of Saxe Weimar slept at the White Hart, and next morning, after inspecting the Cathedral, left for Longleat. Whilst conducted by Mr Samuel Jones this hostelry had the reputation of affording the best accommodation and supplying the best wines of any hotel in the West of England: after his death it was for some years carried on by his son, and on his retirement it became a Limited Liability Company, and appears to have lost none of the ancient reputation.

Though in no way connected with the White Hart, yet as referring to the house opposite, now occupied by Dr Coates, it may be interesting to note that this house was formerly the residence of Mr Goldwyr, surgeon, to whom in 1736, a man under sentence of death in Fisherton Gaol, sent the following letter:-

'To Mr Edward Goldwyr, at his house in the Close of Salisbury,

Sir, - Being informed that you are the only surgeon in this city (or county) that anatomises men, and I being under the unhappy circumstances, and in a very mean conditions, would gladly live as long as I can, but, by all appearances, I am to be executed next March, having no friends on earth that will speak a word to save my life, nor send me a morsel of bread to keep life and soul together until that fatal day, so, if you will vouchsafe to come hither, I will gladly sell you my body (being whole and sound), to be ordered at your discretion, knowing that it will rise again at the general resurrection, as well from your house as from the grave. Your answer, sir, will highly oblige yours, etc. James Brooke. Fisherton Anger Gaol, Oct 3rd 1736.'

I cannot say whether Mr Goldwyr had at any time resided in the Close, or whether it was a mistake on the part of the correspondent.

To complete the record of the area of Catherine Street I come to the King's Arms, which, although it has long fallen from its high position, was at an early date an important inn, and very possibly owed its name to the loyalty of the master. Early in the 17th century it was kept by Mr John Symons; and it is said to have been there that in 1651 the scheme for the King's escape was planned, and it is thought that his Majesty was for a short time concealed in a secret chamber in the house opposite, adjoining the Close Gate. In August, 1763, on the occasion of the Bishop (Dr John Thomas No 2) holding his primary visitation, the office for transacting all the business connected with the visitation as kept at the King's Arms Inn. In December of the same year the following announcement appeared: - "This is to acquaint the Public, that the Post Office, in this City, which is now at the White Hart Inn, in Catherine Street, will be removed on Monday, the 2nd of January next, to the King's Arms, in the same street, being a large and commodious Inn, and in the direct Post Road from London to the West of England." In 1764, the Prince of Mecklenburg-Strelitz (brother of the Queen), attended by the two Barons de Witz, dined there, after visiting the Cathedral. In 1765, the Dukes of York and Gloucester stayed there for refreshments. In 1801, the infirmary dinner was held there. In 1808 the Mayor's dinner was served by Ball, the proprietor of this house. In 1809, the Prince of Orange slept at the King's Arms. About this time, Ball appears to have become bankrupt, and the fortunes of the house materially declined, some portions of it being made separate buildings, and the house becoming a tap to the White Hart, the extensive stables being used for the post horses and coach horses in connection with the latter house, to which it still belongs.

Not far from the King's Arms, at the corner of Exeter Street, is the Bell, which has been an inn upwards of two centuries, Thomas Chaffinge being the master about 1624; but I am not aware of anything worth recording in connection with it.

Salisbury
W.A.W.

Old Inns of Salisbury, No. VI

To the Editor of the Salisbury and Winchester Journal.

Sir – I now come to High Street (originally called Minster Street), where were situated some of the oldest inns in the city, Pynnocks or Pynnokys Inn being undoubtedly the first established here. It must have been started by Wm. Pynnok at or soon after the foundation of the city, and Ricardus Pynnok, who was one of the first members of Parliament for Salisbury in 1264 carried it on for a time. By his will, dated Dec 6 1310, he bequeathed it to his wife, Lucy, at her death to his son John or his nearest heirs. John Pynnok let it to John le Taverner, whose widow, Alice, continued to hold it after his death, and in 1333 a lease was granted to her at £6 6s 6d sterling, paid quarterly. In 1385 John Pynnok leased it to John Fuystour and Edith his wife, for 100 years, at £8 3s quarterly. At their death, it was leased to

William Fyne, of Basingstoke, for his life, and he in 1438 sublet it to John Bromley and others. In 1361, this inn came into the hands of the Corporation, they holding themselves liable to a payment of 13s yearly for ever to the Vicars of the Cathedral. In the Corporation accounts for 1444, credit is given for £16 13s 4d, received of Stephen Hendy, as rent of Pynnocks Inn, viz, £4 13s 4d at the terms of Christmas, the Annunciation of the Blessed Virgin Mary, the Nativity of St John the Baptist, and of St Michael the Archangel. On the other side of the account credit is taken for the payment of the 15s to the Vicars as before specified. In 1449, Alice Hendy, presumably Stephen's widow, was paid 4s 4d for necessary repairs. She occupied it till 1454, when it was let to Wm. Boughton. In 1470, the inn was leased to John Heyford or Harford and Matilda his wife, for the term of twenty years, at £18 13s 4d; but in 1484 it is stated that John Herford's rent was reduced to half what it had been, viz, 46s 8d quarterly, instead of £4 13s 4d. In 1485, Pynnockes Inn had changed its name to the Helme, and a lease was granted to Thomas Blakker, on condition that he should 'newe bilde it afore strete with two storeys alofte after such patern as shall be agreed by the Mayor and Corporation;' but in the following March he was released from this agreement, and a lease was granted to Henry Horton. In 1491, the Corporation would seem to have undertaken the rebuilding themselves, but not as an inn, and two years later the accounts contain an item of 17s 4d allowed to John Sparynge for his labour in the daily oversight of carpenters, masons, helyars and daubers atte the new byldynge of the newe tenements lately called "Pynnokesyn." In 1498, £14 13s 4d is ordered to be paid to Richard Bartilmewe and Thomas Coke for an old debt due to them for the new building of the four tenements in High Street. In 1508-9, the city accounts contain the item of 15s quit rent paid to the Vicars of the Cathedral out of the new tenements in the High Street formerly called Pynnokkes-ynne.

I must here acknowledge my indebtedness to "H.J.F.S" for the foregoing particulars, as I presume, previous to the publication of his interesting "Gleanings from the Archives of Salisbury" few, if any, persons were aware that such an inn had ever existed. Even all his research has not enabled him to tell us precisely where this ancient hostelry stood. I think, however, that I have solved this question, and that further inquiry will show that it was nearly opposite the Assembly Rooms, and that of the four tenements, three of them, if not now, were until very recently still the property of the Corporation; the other, the most northerly of the four, and the one which abutted on the Canal stream, was exchanged with the Dean and Chapter at the same time as the Vine, in the Cheese Market, for their property in Guild Hall Chequer, required for the site of the new Council House. The three tenements remaining are now Nos. 28, 30, and 32 High Street.

The George or "Georges" Inn, although mention is made of it in the city archives as early as 1401, did not come into possession of the Corporation till 1414; the King, Henry IV, having just previously granted a license to the Mayor and Corporation of New Sarum to acquire, notwithstanding the statutes of mortmain, lands, tenements, and rents, within the said city, to the annual value of 100 marks, a somewhat similar license had been previously obtained from the Bishop (Hallam) and the Dean and Chapter. The property was subject to a payment of 19s 4d to the scholars of De Vaux, and, shortly after coming into possession, the Corporation appear to have expended a good amount upon it. In 1418 it was let on lease to John Burton at £20 per annum. In 1436, it was demised by John Noble, mayor, and the community to Thomas Allesley, osteler, "with the shops before, and with the solars, cellars, chambers, stables, houses, barns, etc., situate on the east side of Mynsterestrete, and with all the beds and other utensils appurtenant to the said inn, for the maintenance of the same." In 1444 Henry Smyth was the tenant, at the rent of £17 6s 8d; and in 1449 it was let to John Byshampton, his rent being £13 6s 8d. This year 3s 9d was paid to William Heliar with his man for five days at 9d per day and 16d for one quarter of quicklime, 6d for sand, 4d for tyle pynnes, 8d for 100 laths, 14d for lath nails, 3s 8d for 500 tiles, 7d for two boards for mending the gutter, 12d to a plumber, and for 'soudyr' for the same. In 1456, in the mayoralty of John Halle, there is an entry recording the letting of the Inn to Robert Cook for 16 years from Michaelmas at £16 per annum. There must about this time have been a fire at the inn, for on May 18th, 1457, John Wheler, Mayor, it was agreed that "the city Chamberlains should repair all the houses and chambers of Georgis Inne which had been lately burnt, at the cost of the city, and that when they should be so built the tenant should keep them in repair." In 1473 Edmond Ashley distrained upon the Georges Inn for 8s the rent of the Green Croft, which he had not been paid. In 1474 the George was demised to John Gryme, saddler, for six years from Lady Day, at £12 13s 4d, the former rent having been £17 6s 8d.

Some idea of the extent of the Inn may be formed from the particulars which were attached to John Gryme's lease: - 'The chambers for guests numbered thirteen,- viz:- The Principal Chamber, the Earl's Chamber, the Pantry adjoining, The Oxford Chamber, The Abingdon or Middle Chamber, The Squire's Chamber, The Lombards, The Garrett, The George Chamber, The Clarendon Chamber, The Understent Chamber, The Fitzwaryn Chamber, and the London Chamber. There were besides The Tavern or Wine Cellar, The Buttery, The Taphouse, The Parlour above the Buttery, The Kitchen, The Hostry, The Hostler's Chamber, and the parlour above the Warehouse." The furniture was of the most homely description. The beds, of which there were two or three in each chamber, were classed according to the number of planks, which supplied the place of modern sacking and amounted to from two to five in each bed. The dining tables were of oak or beech planks and supported on trestles with forms for seats. In 1484-5 John Gryme was tenant at will at the reduced rent of £12 13s 4d. In 1498 in the Corporation accounts credit is given for £14 6s 8d received as rent from William Thornell, whilst 21s 1d was paid for repairs, and 6s 4d was paid to Margaret Walsale for certain necessaries bought from her for the furnishing of the hostelry called "le George". In 1508-9 the rent had increased to £13 6s 8d. In 1579 the city was visited by the plague, and in consequence of this having kept visitors away the Corporation forgave the landlord of the George Inn the rent due at Lady Day, £22 10s. The Free School was held here till Feb 1623-4 when at a meeting of the Corporation it was resolved to remove it. At this same meeting, it was agreed that all players from henceforth shall make their plays at the George Inn. In 1625 George Bedbury was the master of the George Inn, and it is on record that from the 10th May, 1624, to the 20th March, 1625, he took 45 barrels of beer and 23 couls of ale from the new brewhouse which had recently been established by the Corporation – the profits of which were devoted to providing for the poor, who at that time were very numerous.

It was in 1668 that Pepys visited this inn; the entry in his diary has been so often quoted that I do not think it worth while repeating it but will merely remark that he found no fault with the accommodation, while he considered the charges rather high – a complaint that is sometimes heard even in modern times. When it ceased to be used as an inn I cannot ascertain; but it must have been considerably over a century ago, as will be seen from the following advertisement which appeared in the Salisbury Journal in March, 1769: -

'Sarum – to be Sold by Auction for a Term of 40 years, renewable every 14 years, on the 23rd day of March inst., at the Council Chambers in the City of New Sarum, between the hours of Eleven and Twelve of the Clock, a large Messuage or Tenement, situate in High Street, in the said city, formerly the George Inn, with several outhouses and buildings thereunto belonging; containing 30Feet in Front, 147 wide and 201 Feet deep, with Stabling sufficient for 50 Horses. The Conditions will be delivered at the time of the Sale. For further particulars enquire of Mr John Maton, Chamberlain of the city.'

When the corporation actually sold the property I am not aware, but it was in their hands in 1827. Many persons will remember the large yard called the Old George Yard with cottages on one side, and on the other the remains of a portion of the inn, with a large room in which concerts by the Salisbury Musical Society, conducted by Mr J T Biddlecombe, one of the lay vicars of the Cathedral, and religious and other meetings were held till some 40 years ago. Since then it has been much pulled about, the last alteration being the shop front of Mr Courtenay on the northernmost side, somewhat in character with the bay windows and gables above, which are almost the only features which now remain of what was probably in its day one of the best specimens of the old Shakespearian inns to be found in the provinces.

Next comes the Angel, of which, about 1624, John Hall was the master. No particular interest seems to have attached to this house. In 1751, as I have previously stated, the Bath stage, in opposition to that from the Oxford Arms, started from the Angel. I believe it to have been the premises a few years since occupied by Mr F R Fisher, the builder. The stock of the inn was sold off in 1762, and in 1768 the premises were offered for sale, described as "the dwelling house and timber yard of Mr Edward Whatmore, in High Street, formerly the Angel Inn."

Almost adjoining the Angel was the Rose and Crown, which in 1625 was held by John Morrys, who took from the Common Brewhouse 2 hogsheads and 1 barrel of beer and 6 couls of ale. The house was offered for sale in 1785, when it was stated to be held under the Vicars of the Church of Sarum. At this house was established in 1824, Lodge 102 of the Ancient Order of Druids, the members of which, it will be recollected, took part in the procession at the Reform Festival in 1832, and their doing so was commemorated by a print, after a drawing by Mr Wainwright, at that time master of the Salisbury National School, a copy of which is in the committee room of the municipal offices, having been presented to the Corporation in 1883 by Mr W I Wilkes. This house is now known as the Crown.

The Sun and Lamb was at the corner of New Street, the house now occupied by Mr Broadbere; it has been said to be the oldest house in this city, it is at any rate believed to be on the site on which the first house was built in Salisbury, and in which Bishop Poore lived during the building of the Cathedral. Probably this fact accounts for its having become customary for the Bishops of Salisbury to robe there previously to proceeding to the Cathedral to be enthroned. It would appear to have ceased for a time to be an inn. In 1760, it was to be let either as an inn or as a private residence; it was then the property of Walter Long, who was, I believe, a retired draper, living where Dr Roberts now does. On the occasion of Bishop Barrington's enthronisation, in 1782, it was stated that the Mayor and Corporation accompanied his lordship to the corner house in High Street, heretofore the Sun and Lamb. In 1791, on the entry of Bishop Douglas, it is again described as the Sun and Lamb; and in 1807 Bishop Fisher is stated to have robed at Mr Lacy's house, formerly the Sun and Lamb. With the exception of being opened for a short time as the Mitre Coffee and Refreshment Rooms; it has, I believe, remained a private house once again. It is now called, from its old associations, "Mitre House." The Rev Peter Hall says this house "appears to occupy the very first patch of ground on which a dwelling was constructed in the new city, and from the circumstance of Bishop Poore having resided there, while supervising the progress of the Cathedral, the custom has ever since continued for each succeeding prelate to be invested with the robes office on the same spot, and thence conducted by the clergy to his installation."

The only other inn in High Street that I can trace is the Fountain, which was attached to the Assembly Room, and there is every probability that the cellar now occupied by Messrs Large and Co. was originally that of the Fountain Tavern. It would appear to have been usual for the master or mistress to have an annual benefit concert. In 1760, it was announced that on Oct 28 there would be "a concert of Italian music, and the last act of the oratorio of Jeptha set to music by Mr Handel, for the benefit of William and Mary Tokett. After the concert a ball." It was customary at that time for the concerts always to be followed by a ball, and the announcements generally wound up as follows:- "Ladies and gentlemen accommodated with gloves at the bar of the Fountain Tavern." In June 1762, it was announced that a pair of diamond earrings were to be raffled for at the Assembly room by 60 members at 2 guineas each. In 1765, the ball after the concert in connection with the musical festival was opened by the Duke of York and the Countess of Pembroke, the Duke of Gloucester and the

Prince of Brunswick also taking part in the dance. These balls on the occasion of the musical festivals were generally not only numerously but fashionably attended. In 1767 the governors and subscribers of the Infirmary, after having accompanied the Duke of Queensberry to the laying of the foundation stone of the new Infirmary, continued the procession to Mr Tokett's at the Assembly Room, where 149, including the Duke of Queensberry, and the Earls of Pembroke and Radnor, sat down to dinner. On the 29th Feb, 1772, the death as announced, after a short illness, of Mrs Tokett, mistress of the Assembly Rooms. As nothing is said as to Mr Tokett, I presume he must have died previously, for in April, John Lavenu, late cook to the Hon Stephen Fox, announces that he has taken the assembly rooms in High Street, with the Fountain Tavern. Mr Lavenu's capabilities in the culinary art must have been well known to many of the citizens, as Stephen Fox, who was elected one of the members of Parliament for Salisbury in 1768, had been in the habit during his stay in the country of giving a general invitation to the Mayor and Corporation to dine with him at his residence in Winterslow every first Wednesday in the month after the full moon. Very considerate indeed of Mr Fox to thus guard against the possibility of the civic body losing their way in the dark. At this time the Fountain was much patronised by the members of the Bar and other persons having business at the assizes, mock turtle soup being ready every day from one till four. In September, 1789, the Earl of Radnor, as Recorder of the city, gave an elegant entertainment to the Mayor and Corporation and the members for the city at the Fountain Tavern. The Tavern business, I presume, must have fallen off, for in 1793 Messrs Walter and Philpot, leather breeches makers, announce that they have removed to the house facing High Street and New Canal, late the Fountain Coffee House. In 1797, the annual dinner of the governors and subscribers of the Infirmary was again held here, Lord Radnor sending a fat buck. In 1798, the following advertisement appeared: - "To be Sold by way of Tontine, in 13 shares of £100 each, all that messuage or tenement lately called the Fountain Tavern, including the Concert and Assembly rooms, and a small tenement adjoining in high Street." This scheme does not seem to have met with much success, as about three months later Richard Cooke announces that he has taken the whole premises of the Assembly Rooms, and intends carrying them on, with turnery and brush making business at the corner of Canal and High Street. In 1801, the premises were again offered for sale; but with no result. In the following year, however, a meeting was held, where it was resolved, on account of the decayed state of the Assembly Room, to enter into a subscription for the purpose of rebuilding on a more extensive scale. This resolution would appear to have been speedily acted upon, for in 1803 the concert and ball at the races were held in the Council Chamber, in consequence of the rebuilding of the Assembly Rooms not being completed. The legal forms of agreement, etc. were entered into early in 1804, and the Tontine was enrolled in Chancery in 1806. The concerts and balls in connection with the Musical Festival of 1804 were held in the new rooms, which were highly approved, and it was stated that "there never was a more lovely display of elegant and beautiful women than graced each ball night at the Rooms, which presented a *squeeze* not to be surpassed at the splendid routs of the most fashionable in the British Empire." These rooms have since served various useful purposes, among others they were on two occasions used by Madame Tussaud for the exhibition of her waxworks, staying there about a month on each visit.

Salisbury, July 18, 1887
W.A.W.

Old Inns of Salisbury, No. VII

To the Editor of the Salisbury and Winchester Journal.

Sir, - On the Canal, immediately adjoining the assembly rooms premises, was the Spread Eagle, or, as it was called in 1625, when it was kept by Abraham Collins, "The Splay'd Eagle," evidently from the heraldic term, as I recollect the sign being an eagle displayed, or, on a dark ground. This house was one of the earliest to establish an annuity society, on the principle which prevailed about the middle of the last century, one having been commenced there in 1763, and, at the annual festival held in Whitsun week, 1766, it could boast of a capital of £1500. This inn was a somewhat extensive affair, comprising the whole of the premises now occupies by Mr Naish, coachbuilder, and the adjoining Masonic hall. This latter was the large room at the inn, in which concerts were held, and which were used for exhibitions of various descriptions. In 1785, a somewhat important meeting was held there. The Mayor and Corporation, at their meeting on the 8th of August, having determined to levy toll upon all animals brought to Salisbury market, passed the following resolution:- "That upon, and from, and after Tuesday, the 23rd instant, the following tolls to be paid for all cattle exposed for sale in this market, viz, a toll of two-pence for every horse, mare, gilding, ox, bull, cow, 'with or without calf', heifer and steer; and for every calf without a cow, one penny; and four-pence per score for all sheep; and five-pence per score for sows, boars, and pigs. That Mr Thomas Brown, sergeant-at-arms, be appointed collector of the tolls." This met with so much opposition, that the following week it was announced that a free market would be held at Wilton on Wednesdays, with ordinaries at the Bell, the Greyhound, and the Pembroke Arms. Early in November, a free market was also opened at Downton; and a sale ground for fat cattle and sheep was opened in Fisherton, in the meadow immediately behind where Mrs Hayter's Almshouses now stand, opposite the Cross Keys, at which house an ordinary was held.

These various free markets seem to have somewhat alarmed the citizens, for in December the following invitation, to meet at the Spread Eagle was issued: -

Dec 13 1785 – To the Inhabitants of New Sarum, - Whereas the City of Salisbury appears, by the several charters, to have been a free city upwards of 500 years, and there is the greatest reason to apprehend that the cattle market of the said city will be irretrievably lost by the late imposition of toll on all cattle exposed to sale therein unless a free market is restored. A general meeting of the inhabitants of the said city is therefore earnestly requested at the Spread Eagle on Wednesday the 14th instant, at six o'clock in the evening to consider whether it will not be advisable to have the opinion of some eminent counsel to know in what manner to proceed in order to regain such free market.

As the result of this meeting a subscription was entered into to carry out the object, but it would seem without much effect, as I believe, except for a few modifications after the passing of the Municipal Corporations Act in 1836, the tolls have continued to be levied ever since.

In 1789 Mr John Goss announced that his benefit concert would take place at Gibbon's Concert Room at the Spread Eagle, after which there would be a ball as usual. Tickets 3s. In 1809, on the occasion of the celebration of the fiftieth anniversary of King George III's accession, Colonel Baker and the Salisbury Troop of Yeomanry, numbering 60, dined there, and the host Gibbons also supplied a dinner at the Assembly Rooms on the same occasion, at which the Mayor presided, and which was attended by the Earl of Pembroke and the Earl of Radnor. On the proclamation of peace, June 26 1814, the Mayor (Mr Wm. Andrews) invited a party of sixty to dine with him at the Spread Eagle. It has now ceased to be an inn for some years.

In 1761, the Mitre Tavern and Coffee House in Silver Street was kept by Francis Collins, who would seem to have continued the master till it ceased to be used as a tavern, as in January, 1769, the late Mitre Tavern and Coffee House was announced to be let, either together or in two tenements, being very roomy, a large shop to each tenement, all conveniences, and stabling for two horses, with back entrance from the Canal. It was, I believe, the premises now occupied by Mr David Stevens, and part of Mr Ely's. In the following March Mr F Collins acquaints his friends in the wine trade that he is removed from the Mitre in Silver Street to the new corner house opposite the Assembly Rooms on the Canal, in High Street, where he continues to sell wines, wholesale and retail. This would be the house now occupied by Mr Bingham. In 1773, the house in Silver Street was still described as having been some time since the Mitre Tavern.

In Bridge Street was an inn of considerable repute, called the Rose, which in 1624 was kept by John Gifford. It had stabling for 30 horses. In 1751 it was kept by Mark Goddin, who left it for the King's Head on the other side of the way. After many changes in the proprietorship it was between 20 and 30 years since bought by Mr Charles Higgins, the proprietor of the King's Head, who pulled it down and rebuilt it, taking in some adjoining properties, and he renamed it the London Inn. It has now for some time been occupied by Messrs. Wilson and the Inland Revenue authorities as offices.

The King's Head, on the other side of the way which I have alluded to, is a very ancient hostelry. It was formerly the property of the Corporation; it was originally called Le Ramme. The first mention of it in the Corporation accounts is in 1484-5, when it was let to John Brown as tenant-at-will, and 60s was received from him presumably for a quarter's rent. In 1487, it is stated that "Henry Horton paid 66s 9d for the hostelry at Fisherton Bridge called Le Ramme, and that the repairs cost 16s 10d." In 1508-9 the rent was still 60s 8d. Early in the 17th century the name would seem to have been changed to the King's Head, Richard Easton being the master in 1624. In 1623, John Taylor, the water poet, published a tract, "A Discovery by Sea from London to Salisbury," in which he describes the voyage made by him in a wherry, with a crew of five, round the North Foreland and along the southern coast to Christchurch Harbour, thence up the Avon to Salisbury – this latter stage being accomplished in one day. Taylor says: - "So on the same Friday at night wee came to Salisbury, where wee brought our Boate thorow Fisherton Bridge on the west side of the city, taking our lodging at the signe of the King's Head there, with mine host, Richard Eastman, whose brother was one of the watermen, which came in the Boate thither from London." In the Gleanings, No 53, it is recorded that Richard Eaton, no doubt the same person, was still the master of the King's Head in 1625, and that he took 90 barrels of beer and one coul of ale from the new brewhouse in the ten months ending in March of that year. I know of nothing further very remarkable in connection with this house, but it may be interesting to note that the last of the numerous coaches which at one time were on the road between Salisbury and London, "The Quicksilver," started from the King's Head, and that it made its last journey to town on the 2nd October, 1846.

From a document given in No 53 of "Gleanings from the Archives of Salisbury," H.J.F.S. gives the names of various inns, with their proprietors, which existed early in the 17th century, of which we now know nothing. Possibly some of them still exist, but under different names; most likely some of them disappeared at the time of the reduction of the number from 60 to 40 in 1709. Amongst these were the Horse Shoe, the Prinses Arms, the Tucker's Sheres, the Griffin, the Meremayde, the Dolphin, the Bugle, the Crown without Castle Gate, the Bush, the Blew Lyon, and the Glove. Of these the only two that I can throw any light upon are the Dolphin, which was still kept as an inn till some 20 years since, and was situated on Pain's Hill – in 1624 John Durneford was the master; the other the Griffin, which at that date was kept by John Scragge; it was in Draghall (Exeter) Street; and I find, from a mortgage deed dated May 17, 1792, that was at that date still called the Griffin, and was in the possession of Clement Miller. At what time the change was made I cannot ascertain, but it has been the Crown and Anchor as far back as my recollection goes. The White Beare, which in 1624 was kept by Mr William Kaye, who was about this time succeeded by Mrs Julian Perry, widow, was in all probability the same house as that at a later date known as the Black Bear, in Castle Street, merely the colour of the animal being changed.

A few other houses in different parts of the city I have found mentioned at different periods, of which the history is now almost, in some instances quite, lost in the lapse of time. In 1776, the following were offered for sale by auction, at the Three Lions, "a public house called the White Swan, on Pain's Hill, with a much esteemed vault or cellar under the same; an inn known by the name of the Pelican in St Ann Street; a public house now or lately known by the name of the Three Mugs, situate in Brown Street; a messuage some time since a public house, and late called or known by the name of the World's End, with a large garden, situate near St Martin's Church. These houses are looked upon as exceedingly valuable, being some of the oldest and best accustomed in Salisbury." Of none of these have I been able to glean any particulars, except the Pelican, which appears to have been a respectable inn, accommodating many persons attending the market, and having a well patronised ordinary on market days. It would also seem to have been an eminently loyal house, an annual dinner being held there to celebrate the King's birthday up to 1819, being the last his Majesty lived to see, and shortly after the Pelican ceased to be an inn, but was divided into cottages, its garden being let separately. The name was, however, kept alive as Pelican Place. This has now disappeared; the whole having been pulled down and three houses are being built on the site. In 1779 there was the Sawyer's arms in Bugmore, at the corner of Brown Street and St Ann Street was the Cherry Tree, and in the same year William Ellis, of the Three Crowns, Brown Street, announces that he "sells all sorts of spirits as cheap as wholesale dealers. A London newspaper three times a week." This house was still in existence in 1804. In 1805, we have the Swan in Brown Street, the Northumberland Arms, St Ann Street (afterwards changed to the Radnor Arms), and which has now for a long time been a private house. In 1782, a house called the Flower Pots, in Draghall Street, was for sale by order of the Executors of Alexander Minty.

I have met with several other signs, but have not mentioned them, as I believe they were signs adopted by other tradesmen, as was formerly customary. For instance, there was the Golden Gridiron, John Green and Co., ironmongers, in the Butter Market; the Golden Head was a chemist's sign in the Market Place; and in the High Street was the Cross Guns, James Grist, gunmaker, flying spring curtain maker, and bellhanger.

Crossing the bridge into Fisherton there was at an early date the Sun Inn, immediately opposite the County Gaol, occupying the site on which is now Maundrell Hall, the two adjoining houses and part of the Congregational Church. This house was much used for exhibitions of various kinds. In 1747 appeared the following announcement: - "This is to acquaint the curious, that at the Sun, near Fisherton Bridge, will be exhibited every hour for a few days longer (by Mr John Bennet, who is now recovered from his illness, which occasioned his longer stay) the most surprising phenomena of ELECTRICITY, as performed by Professor Mischenbroek, of Leyden, Le Monnier and De Buffon of France, with improvements by Mr Watson, Fellow of the Royal Society." In 1765, a new theatre was opened at the Sun in opposition to that at the Vine in the Cheese Market. The opening piece was *Richard III*, and it was stated that there was a good company, who expressed themselves much pleased with the commodiousness and elegance of the Theatre. On the 13th and 14th August, 1777, a main of cocks between Hants and Wilts was fought there. In April, 1787, Mr Everett, the master of the Sun Inn, died; he was by far the most corpulent man in the neighbourhood, and was familiarly known as "The Salisbury Baby." In 1823 Cooks and Bridges' Circus was at the Sun, and I have been informed by persons who were present at the performance on the 18th September, when the alarm of fire at Thos. Wheeler's, the hatter's, was given, that the building was speedily deserted for the more exciting scene in the Market Place. At this time the Sun was certainly the principal inn of Fisherton. For some time after it ceased to be an inn it was used as a building yard and workshops, till in March, 1876, it was opened by Mr B H Perman as the Royal Skating Rink, under the patronage of Prince Leopold; again, in April, 1880, it underwent another metamorphosis, being transformed into Maundrell Hall. On this spot formerly stood the monastery of the Dominicans or Black Friars; but on the dissolution of the monasteries in the reign of King Henry VIII the site was granted to John Pollard and William Byrte.

There were altogether a goodly number of inns in Fisherton, but many of them have disappeared and left no sign of their whereabouts. More than one, I have reason to believe, must have been demolished when the Infirmary was built. In 1746, there was a sale of timber at the Crown and Slipper; in 1752, I meet with the White Horse; in 1767, the Cross Keys. It was the enterprising landlord of this house, who, in 1765, when the Corporation first charged a toll for cattle, etc., opened a free market on the opposite side of the road, near where Mrs Hayter's almshouses now stand, and established an ordinary at his house. It was still called the Cross Keys as lately as 1823, but it is now the King's Arms. In 1776 there was the Bell, the landlord of which had a horse and chaise to let. In 1796, the One Bell was announced to be sold by auction at the Four Bells. In 1804, I meet with the Weaver's Arms and the Red Lion; this latter will be well remembered, as it only disappeared when the railway station was removed to Fisherton. The old Wagon and Horses will be preserved in our memories by the engraving of it with the old bridge in Hall's Memorials. Not far from this was the Angel which many will remember as a small public house, but which has now developed into a well-appointed family and commercial hotel. In 1805, we hear of the Bull, being informed that ten of the King's cream-coloured state horses and five others of His Majesty's favourites, rested for the night at the excellent stables of the Bull inn. In 1823 Fisherton was visited by what was said to be the greatest flood that could be remembered, and it was recorded that at the Bull Inn the water reached the uppermost part of the kitchen dresser, and floated an eight-hogshead cask in the cellar. In that year an inn called the Tap, with a tennis court attached, was to let, not improbably what is still known as the Bowling Green, the residence of Mr Lush.

In bringing these sketches of the old inns of Salisbury to a conclusion, I feel that had a little fiction been skilfully interwoven with the somewhat dry details they might have been more interesting to some, but my aim was to deliver "a round, unvarnished tale" of facts, which might give the citizens of the present day some idea of life in the old city in the generations that are gone, and this I have endeavoured to do in connection with the old inns.

The inns of England have always been celebrated: they have played no mean part in the history of our country, and they have received the meed of praise from poets and historians from the earliest times. Chaucer extolled them for the very excellent accommodation they afforded the pilgrims of the fourteenth century. In the reign of Elizabeth there were some in which two or three hundred people, with their horses, could, without difficulty, be lodged and fed. The Rev. William Harrison, the historian of that period, gave a glowing description of their Excellencies. The continent of

Europe, he said, could show nothing like them. In the seventeenth century England abounded with excellent inns of every rank. Sometimes, in a small village, the traveller lighted upon a public house such as Isaak Walton has described, where "the brick floor was swept clean, where the sheets smelt of lavender, and where a blazing fire, a cup of good ale, and a dish of trout from the neighbouring brook were to be procured at small charge." And who does not remember the concluding stanza of Shenstone's lines written at the Red Lion at Henley-on-Thames:-

> Who'er has travelled life's dull round,
> Where'er his stages may have been,
> May sigh to think he still has found
> The warmest welcome at an inn.

A former Bishop of Salisbury – Bishop Earle – thus expressed himself on the subject of taverns, "The tavern is the busy man's recreation, the idle man's business, the melancholy man's sanctuary, the stranger's welcome, the inns-of-court man's entertainment, the scholar's kindness, and the citizen's courtesy." Dr Johnson, in his friendly chat with Bosworth, said "There is nothing which has yet been contrived by man, by which so much happiness is produced as by a good tavern or inn." But times are changed, and it is now the fashion to regard all inns as the incarnation of evil. Doubtless there have always been inns of various qualities, good inns and bad inns; I would, however, commend to the minds of those who would ruthlessly sweep away every inn in the kingdom, the thoughtful utterances of the late Lord Iddesleigh. Speaking at Exeter in 1879, Sir Stafford Northcote said: - "If you were to imagine what the state of the country would be if we had no innkeepers and no persons employed in providing that which the licensed victualler provides for us, you would very soon see the importance of that calling. In point of fact, there is no position which is more honoured, in a certain sense, in early story, than the position of mine host, and you will find, if you turn to the pages of the Old Testament, or early history, or to Roman or Greek history, or the history of any civilised country, and the early pages of the history of England and its poets, that mine host is a person of great importance. He is one who not only administers to the physical wants of those who come to him, but exercises considerable influence and authority with regard to those who come under his hospitality, and I venture to assert that it is a position which is not altogether lost even in the present day. I say then that these men are men of great importance to society, and they are a profession which could not be taken out of society without inflicting a very heavy and serious loss. They are persons whom you could not dispense with."

Salisbury, Aug 19, 1887,
W.A.W.

Old Inns of Salisbury, No. VIII

To the Editor of the Salisbury and Winchester Journal.

When my Papers on the Old Inns were published in 1886 and 1887, I was unable to ascertain when the Blue Boar ceased to be an inn, the last trace I could find of it was that Robert Read was the master in 1730; and it seems that he was the last that acted in that capacity, as, on his decease in 1756, it was closed as an inn, and was pulled down, as will be seen from the annexed advertisements which appeared in the

Salisbury Journal of that year: -

"Sarum, February 28, 1756.

"This is to acquaint the Publick, that the Blue Boar Inn, in this City, is shut up, and the Excise Office removed to the Red Lion and Cross Keys, in Milford Street, within the said City; which is a very good Inn, having good Stall Stables, and all other proper Conveniencies: And where Gentlemen may depend on the best Usage, and their Favours gratefully acknowledged, By their most obedient humble servant'

"Ralph Musselwhite"

"Whereas the Tick Fair was kept in the Blue Boar Yard, and the House is now taken down, and not to be continued as an Inn; This is to acquaint the Buyers and Sellers of Ticks, that a Rank of Standings shall be set up opposite the Blue Boar, only for use of the Tick Trade, by me

"Walter Golding."

"The Fair will always be the Monday before Lady Day."

"To be Sold by Hand, on Wednesday, the 25th inst., February, at the Blue Boar Inn, in Salisbury, late Mr Robert Read, deceas'd, all the Household Goods, Beer, Hay, Cock Pens, etc. Also the 4th March will be sold, all the Linen, Plate etc."

The common opinion that the Saracen's Head was a part of the old Blue Boar must be given up, as I find they were both in existence in 1625, the Blew Boar being kept by Mr Gervas Ballar, and the Sarasin's Head by John Sevyer, the latter brewing his own beer. The Bugle, one of the missing inns of Blue Boar Row, was at that date kept by Thomas Elton. In 1756 it was in the possession of Mrs Sarah Baker, who advertised it to be let at Michaelmas in that year. Mrs Baker died in the following year, and the house long remained unlet.

The question has been asked, "When was the name changed from the Parade to Blue Boar Row?" As we find Blue Boar Row many years before anything is heard of the Parade, I think it probable it was not at any time the name of the Row, but that the person who established the Parade Coffee House gave it that name, from its being a favourite promenade for the citizens, and that it became customary for the sake of brevity to speak of going to the Parade, instead of to the Parade Coffee House. I am strongly inclined to believe that it was the same premises as were known as the Bugle Inn, as we do not hear of this inn after about 1760, and some few years after we get the Parade Coffee House, the exact date of the establishment of which I am unable to trace.

Sept, 1894
W. A. Wheeler

Appendix 2
A Dispute between Coach Masters

In 1808, a dispute occurred between the operator of the Old Salisbury Coach running from the Chough Inn and the Black Horse Inn in Salisbury to London and the operator of the New Commercial Coach running from the Three Swans Inn in Salisbury to London. The resulting advertisements and letters published in the Salisbury and Winchester Journal have been placed in this Appendix so that the flow of accusations and counter-accusations may be most easily followed.

The root cause of the dispute was the Old Salisbury Coach moving away from the Bell Savage Inn, Ludgate Hill, London, supposedly because the landlord of that inn was leaving: August 8 1807 - The Proprietors of the Old Salisbury Coach respectfully inform their friends and the public, that in consequence of Mr Grey being about to leave the Bell Savage inn, Ludgate Hill, the above Coach is Removed to the Saracen's Head Inn, Friday Street, and the Bell and Crown Inn, Holborn, from whence it will set off every afternoon, at a quarter before four o'clock.

However, the new owners of the Bell Savage eventually respond by starting a new coach from the Bell Savage in opposition to the Old Salisbury Coach: August 8 1808 - Salisbury and London New Commercial Coach, from the Three Swans Inn (afternoons at three o'clock) to the Bell Savage, Ludgate Hill, London. The gentry and Inhabitants of Salisbury and its Vicinity are informed this Coach is set up for their better accommodation, and to the House in London from whence the Old Salisbury went for such a number of years; and which, as it is newly furnished and fitted in a style of elegant neatness, combined with moderate charges, will, it is hoped, insure comfort to the Traveller and approbation to the Proprietors. N.B. This Coach is called THE COMMERCIAL, as it is the full determination of the Proprietors to give every encouragement to commerce by a moderate charge for the carriage of parcels, and as such all small parcels under one pound weight are charged sixpence only: it is therefore requested the friends of this concern will order their correspondents in London to send their parcels to the Bell Savage, Ludgate Hill, from whence the Commercial, for the present, sets out every Monday, Wednesday, and Saturday afternoons at three. Performed by Edward Prockter and Co. who will not be accountable for any package of plate, cash, etc. (however small the value) nor yet of any other parcel or luggage, above five pounds value, unless entered as such and paid for accordingly. It is the intent for this coach to run every afternoon (Sunday excepted) as soon as the carriages are ready.

By the following month, the Commercial is planning to run six days a week but, at the same time, undercutting the cost of travel via the Old Salisbury: September 5 1808 - Cheap Travelling. By the Commercial Salisbury and London Coach, from the Three Swans, Salisbury, to the Bell Savage, Ludgate Hill; afternoons at a quarter before four o'clock: performed by Edward Prockter and Co. Who inform the public it is their determination not only to convey their friends at a moderate price, but also with safety, and have given positive orders to the drivers on no account to attempt anything unpleasant to the traveller, by unnecessarily running the horses; and any complaints to that effect will be immediately attended to with thanks. The proprietors also beg to remark to the inhabitants of the towns of Honiton, Chard, Crewkerne, Yeovil, Sherborne, Shaftesbury, Wincanton, Sommerton, Taunton, etc. etc. in particular, that by forming a Party of Three in a Post Chaise to Salisbury, and then taking the Commercial Coach from the Three Swans Inn, they will save nearly one guinea in three each person, and be always certain of places on to London, N.B. – Good accommodation for Baggage and Parcels, and coverings to protect it from the weather. Carriage of Parcels under one pound weight Sixpence only, as usual.

Messrs Prockter and Co. also place this additional advertisement: September 5 1808 - Catherine Wheel Inn, Andover. A New and Cheap Elegant Commercial Expedition Coach, at Reduced Fares, to the Bell Savage, Ludgate Hill, London, performed by Edward Prockter and Co., who beg their Friends in and near Andover to be particular in ordering their Places and Parcels to be booked at the Catherine Wheel Inn, as the Proprietors of the Commercial Expedition Coach have no connection with any other Andover Coach whatever, and are fully determined their Friends in that part of the country shall travel cheap, and in safety.

In the same issue of the Journal, the proprietors of the Old Salisbury Coach, which has been operating between Salisbury and London for some years, respond with their own advertisement: September 5 1808 - Cheap Travelling. The Proprietors of the Old Salisbury and Andover Coaches, from the Black Horse Inn, Salisbury, to the Bell and Crown Inn, Holborn, and Saracen's Head Inn, Friday Street, Cheapside, respectively return thanks for past favours, and beg leave to assure their friends and the public, that they will be conveyed as cheap, in good carriages, with security and expedition, superior to any opposition coach. Whitmarsh, Brown, Fagg, and Penny. Proprietors.

A week later, Messrs Whitmarsh & Co retaliate further to the New Commercial Coach by launching a new service from the Chough Inn: September 12 1808 - Cheap, Safe, and Expeditious Travelling. The Proprietors of the Old Salisbury Coach, from the Black Horse Inn to the Bell and Crown, Holborn, and Saracen's Head, Friday Street, return their sincere thanks to their friends and the public for past favours; and inform them they have started A New Light Telegraph Coach, from the Chough Inn, Market Place, Salisbury, to the above Inns, London, afternoons at a quarter before four; and they are determined that their Coaches shall be conducted in a style superior, and cheaper, than any opposition. Whitmarsh, Penny, Fagg, and Co., Proprietors. Calls at Hatcher's and the Gloucester Coffee House, Piccadilly. Will not be accountable for any article exceeding £5 value, unless paid for accordingly.

These advertisements are repeated in the Sept 19th, Sept 26th and Oct 3rd editions of the Journal. But in the Oct 10th edition, a new round of advertisements appears: 10th October 1808 - Cheap Travelling. The Proprietors of the Old Salisbury Coaches, from the Black Horse and Chough Inns, Salisbury, the Bell and Crown Inn, Holborn, and Saracen's Head Inn, Friday Street, Cheapside, respectfully return thanks for past favours. – We have ever considered our Coaches truly Commercial; if Commerce is to be supported by fair pursuits we claim the priority; fair gains, with a regard to the public comfort, has been our utmost study; we do not profess to convey small parcels for a less price than the postage of letters; we hold out no such artefact, we have no such commercial views as our Opponent; we wish not to injure the revenue by pirating the Post-Office, nor other Coach Masters. That the Public may be in possession of the views of such a Speculator, we think it is our duty to explain them; - By injuring our trade, he presumes on getting our Coaches removed to his Inn, which he assures us is his only object for opposition; by reducing the carriage of parcels to 6d he calculates on the number he shall convey, and what the porterage and booking of them will amount to, - far more than the carriage. To counteract such pursuit, and to protect a trade we have a fair claim to, we pledge ourselves to the inhabitants of Salisbury and Andover, to convey the Public as cheap, in better carriages, and with more expedition, than our opponent, and will take in and book all parcels, etc. free from the charge of booking, and will safely deliver them in London free from the charge of porterage. Whitmarsh, Fagg, Penny and Brown.

10th October 1808 - The New Commercial Coach, from Three Swans, Salisbury, to the Bell Savage, Ludgate Hill. Edward Prockter and Co. respectfully return thanks to their friends of Salisbury, Wilton, Andover, etc. for the very liberal encouragement they have received; and beg to inform their friends, that for their better accommodation, the New Coach will commence from London and Salisbury every Night (Saturday excepted) on Sunday October 2. – Performed by Edward Prockter and George Matchem and Co. N.B Carriage of small Parcels, under one pound weight, 6d only, as usual. Prockter and Co also particularly request their friends in the country will be particular in ordering their correspondents to send their servants with the parcels to the Office in the Yard, as Fagg and Co. are endeavouring to establish an office under the Gateway in the Bell Savage entrance, to mislead Prockter and Co.'s friends. A Parcel Cart, for the accommodation of Prockter, Matchem and Co.'s friends resident at Wilton, will very shortly be ready to convey their Parcels, etc., to and from the London Coaches, free of any expense whatever, - as it is their full determination that their Salisbury and Wilton friends shall be accommodated upon much more liberal principles than before their concerns commenced.

It should be noted that George Matchem was the landlord of the Three Swans at this time. These two advertisements were repeated on the 17th October but a new level of dispute was reached with the following letters: 17th October 1808 - Cheap Commercial Opposition Coaches, from the Three Swans Inn, Salisbury, to the Bell Savage, Ludgate Hill. Prockter, Matchem and Co., with due deference to the public, beg leave to state to the inhabitants of Salisbury,

Wilton, Andover, etc., that the language of the Old Salisbury Coach Proprietors, as inserted in last Monday's Journal is false in toto. They tell the public, that nothing but fair gains and due regard to their comfort has been their study: compare their actions with their language, and see how they accord. In the first place, in must be fresh in every memory, that within the last twelve months they have advanced the inside fares only from 24s each passenger to the enormous price of 30s and, it is a well known fact, it was very shortly to have been 31s 6d and that upon a coach carrying eight insides, so that with the additional advance on the outside passenger, and the parcels, would absolutely have made an increase of at least from £5 to £6 per night, for six nights in each week, which comes to between £1500 and £1600 per annum; a very modest advance! And they have, in addition to that, the impudence to assert they had nothing but fair gains in view. The fact is, their language is neither more nor less than telling you, in a polite way, we do not wish you to imagine we have robbed you. What, then, has been their study of accommodation? Why, none; for it must be quite clear to the meanest capacity, that after allowing that, from the very unexampled high price of horse provender, it was necessary to advance the price of the fares, surely they ought to have been content with about half that sum, and waited, with other people, the regular course of the markets, as tradesmen; but no, they say, there is no one we have to fear but Prockter, and he dares not attack us; we have got it all our own way, and we will make the Salisbury people pay just what we please, in defiance of them. Answer, if they can, if they ever once consulted the public opinion upon it: - no, the public were beneath them, and not worth a thought; but when the Commercial started they became, all at once, the public's most obedient servants, and all at once very liberal, and, in good truth, from necessity; but after all it will avail them nothing, if the friends of the Commercial do but continue with their support as they have begun. Neither Whitmarsh, Fagg, Penny, or Brown, shall ever become the pilot of what they are pleased to term the piratical vessel, the Commercial, which has wrested, and will continue to prevent, extortions from the minds of such low cunning men, who act as they have done. The COMMERCIAL will therefore, for the future, set out from the Three Swans Inn, Salisbury, and the Bell Savage, Ludgate Hill, every afternoon (Saturday excepted) at half past three o'clock. *Observe*:- The Salisbury, etc. Coach Office is through the Second Gateway, on the left hand, at the bottom of the Bell Savage Yard; and the Golden Cross, Charing Cross; the White Bear, and Three Kings, Piccadilly. Mark:- The Office of the Old Proprietors is on the right hand, in the entrance from Ludgate Hill.

17th October 1808 - Cheap Travelling. The Proprietors of the Old Salisbury Coaches, from the Black Horse and Chough Inns, Salisbury, the Bell and Crown, Holborn, and Saracen's Head. Friday Street, Cheapside, respectfully return thanks for past favours. – We have ever considered our Coaches truly Commercial; if Commerce is to be supported by fair pursuits, we claim the priority; fair gains, with a regard to public comfort, has been our utmost study; we do not profess to convey small parcels for a less price than the postage of letters; we hold out no such artifice; we have no such commercial views as our Opponent; we wish not to injure the revenue by pirating the Post-Office, or other Coach Masters. That the public may be in possession of the views of such a Speculator, we think it is our duty to explain them. – By injuring our trade, he presumes on getting our Coaches removed to his Inn, which he assures us is his only object for opposition; by reducing the carriage of parcels to 6d, he calculates on the number he shall convey, and what the porterage and booking of them will amount to, - far more than the carriage. To counteract such pursuit, and to protect a trade we have a fair claim to, we pledge ourselves to the inhabitants of Salisbury and Andover, to convey the public as cheap, in better carriages, and with more expedition, than our opponent, and will take in and book all parcels, etc., free from the charge of booking, and will safely deliver them in London free from the charge of porterage.

These two advertisements were repeated on the 24th October but two letters appeared in the inside pages of the Journal: 24th October 1808 - Cheap Commercial Opposition Coaches from the Three Swans, Salisbury, to the Bell Savage, Ludgate Hill. Prockter, Matchem and Co. with due deference to the public, beg leave to state to the inhabitants of Salisbury, Wilton, Andover, etc. etc. that the language of the Old Salisbury Coach Proprietors, as inserted in last Monday's Journal, is false in toto. They tell the Public, that nothing but fair gains and due regard to their comfort has been their study; compare their actions with their language, and see how they accord. In the first place, it must be fresh in every memory, that within the last twelve months they advanced the inside fares only from 24s each passenger to the enormous price of 30s and, it is a well-known fact, it was very shortly to have been 31s 6d and that upon a coach carrying eight inside, so that with the additional advance on the outside passenger, and the parcels, would absolutely made an increase of at least from £5 to £6 per night, for six nights in each week, which comes to between £1500 and £1600 per annum; a very modest advance! And they have, in addition to that, the impudence to assert they had nothing but fair gains in view. The fact is, their language is neither more nor less than telling you, in a polite way, we do not wish you to imagine we have robbed you. What, then, has been their study of accommodation? Shy, none; for it must be quite clear to the meanest capacity, that after allowing that, from the very unexampled high price of horse provender, it was necessary to advance the price of the fares, surely they ought to have been content with about half that sum, and waited, with other people, the regular course of the markets, as tradesmen; but no, they say, there is no one we have to fear but Prockter, and he dares not attack us; we have got it all our own way, and we will make the Salisbury people pay just what we please, in defiance of them. Answer, if they can, if they have ever once consulted the public opinion upon it: - no, the public were beneath them, and not worth a thought; but when the Commercial started they became, all at once, the public's most obedient servant, and all at once very liberal, and, in good truth, from necessity: but after all it will avail them nothing, if the friends of the Commercial do but continue with their support as they have begun. Neither Whitmarsh, Fagg, Penny, or Brown, shall ever become the pilot of what they are pleased to term the piratical vessel, the Commercial, which has wrested, and will continue to prevent, extortions from the minds of such low-cunning men, who act as they have done. The Commercial will therefore, for the future, set out from the Three Swans Inn, Salisbury, and Bell Savage, Ludgate Hill, every afternoon (Saturdays excepted) at half past three o'clock. Observe: - The Salisbury, etc., Coach Office is through the Second Gateway, on the left hand, at the bottom of the Bell Savage Yard; and the Golden Cross, Charing Cross; the White Bear, and Three Keys, Piccadilly. Mark: - The Office of the Old Proprietors is on the right hand, in the entrance from Ludgate Hill.

24th October 1808 - Self Defence. Whitmarsh, Fagg, Penny and Co. request their Friends and the Public to read Edward Prockter's Letter to them, to read the Address signed by Whitmarsh, Fagg, and Co and the Violent Defamation of Prockter, Matchem and Co. – Judge then his motives, from his Letter, and say if he is entitled to your credit and support. Asserting our Address to be false in toto, is no reply to it: We answer Prockter and Matchem, by proving their Address to be false and salacious, inserted with no other view than to bring us and our concerns, by such disgraceful publication, into contempt. On the 17th of Jan 1808, in consequence of the enormous price of horse provender, we advanced the fare (which was of necessity general throughout the kingdom) from 24s to 28s, not to 30s and 31s 6d as they falsely assert. – We call on the Inhabitants of Salisbury to say, and on Mr Webb at the Black Horse to answer, if ever 30s was taken or demanded by us – Oats were then 46s per Quarter and Beans 68s per Quarter. We maintained a reasonable fare until Prockter's threats, contained in his letter to us, were put in force, by his reducing the fare to 21s. - We contend our fare was reasonable, and much less than such an unprecedented price on horse provender, and £800 per annum duty, demanded. – Let the public compare our fares with what was paid 20 years past, to the then Salisbury Coachmaster, when no duty was paid, whose business brought him down from affluence to ruin. – We looked for remuneration in a reduction of provender. The good sense of a liberal and discerning public will form their own opinion, from what is paid for similar distances, whether or not, we are the robbers, extortioners, and low cunning men, described. We never robbed our Creditors. – Prockter's letter is to be seen at the Printing Office., and the following is a Copy verbatim:

Sir,

Bell Savage, August 14, 1808

I once more think it is proper to address you on the subject of your Salisbury business. I presume I need not inform you my principal aim in the unpleasant business now pending is, to see the coach back to its old channel, not only to put the business at rest, but for the accommodation of the Salisbury people who frequent the house; and I beg to assure you, as I well know the fatigue and anxiety in getting a coach business to any satisfactory issue, I am equally tenacious of extent of injury, and which, from the nature of the trade, it being so very vulnerable, is easily accomplished;

and of course, the greater the extent of the trade, the greater the injury. – The fact is, both yourself and Mr Fagg have extensive concerns in the country, you in particular, and which I have no wish to interfere with, or injure, but rather the other way, provided an end can be put to the animosity between us, by suffering the coach to come back. I do not mean to infer that you, as having houses of your own in London, were not justifiable in removing the coach, but I contend it was not policy; for you might have been certain no opportunity would be lost to retaliate for it; and although pains have been taken to intimidate some of the post masters concerned, as fast as they think proper to retire, the ground will be covered; and you may also rest assured, there are speculative people now on the road who much wish us to become concerned, and, if admitted, and the concern should ultimately be unsuccessful, yet it will help to injure your trade. I have therefore only one mode left to inform you, that if the business cannot be compromised, and the coach brought to the Bell Savage again, it is the determination of the parties concerned to reduce the whole of the fares considerably, and that immediately. I am also desired to inform you, no compromise hereafter will be attended to, without the whole loss that may accrue being made good. I am also requested to ask you, if you will sell your Salisbury business, as far as you are concerned. – Waiting your answer, am respectfully, Your obedient servant, Edward Prockter. P.S. Shall wait your answer until Friday noon.

The Journal also printed a further letter from Mr Prockter which, although addressed to both Mr Whitmarsh and Mr Fagg, was inscribed 'To Mr Henry Whitmarsh, Friday Street':- To Messrs Whitmarsh and Fagg. I can only remark, if it is thought desirable to bring the coach back, your interests in it, as far as regards myself, shall be my study; and then most likely some future arrangement may also be made for adjusting Mr Fagg's and my difference about some other concerns.

It is clear from these two letters, originally sent before the Commercial started operations, that Edward Prockter's principal aim was to get the Old Salisbury Coach back to the Bell Savage, thus keeping the whole of the Salisbury coach trade via that inn while saving the cost of running another coach in opposition.

By November 28th, Edward Prockter is still advertising the New Commercial Coach as are Whitmarsh and Fagg for the Old Salisbury Coach. By the end of the year, Messrs Whitmarsh and Fagg are still complaining: December 19th 1808 - Cheap Travelling. The proprietors of the Old Salisbury Coaches, from the Black Horse and Chough Inns, Salisbury, the Bell and Crown Inn, Holborn, and Saracen's Head Inn, Friday Street, Cheapside,, respectfully return thanks for past favours. – We have ever considered our Coaches truly Commercial; if Commerce is to be supported by fair pursuits, we claim the priority; fair gains, with a regard to the public comfort, has been our utmost study; we do not profess to convey small parcels for a less price than the postage of letters; we hold out no such artifice; we have no such commercial views as our Opponent; we wish not to injure the revenue by pirating the Post Office, or other Coach Masters. That the public may be in possession of the views of such a Speculator, we think it our duty to explain them:- By injuring our trade, he presumes on getting our Coaches removed to his Inn, which he assures us is his only object for opposition; by reducing the carriage of parcels to 6d, he calculates on the number he shall convey, and what the porterage and booking of them will amount to, - far more than the carriage. To counter such pursuit, and to protect a trade we have a fair claim to, we pledge ourselves to the Inhabitants of Salisbury and Amesbury, to convey the Public cheaper, in better carriages, and with more expedition, than our opponents. Whitmarsh, Fagg, Penny, and Brown, Proprietors.

In defence of ourselves, and to prevent an artful speculator from acquiring our trade, many years established by us, as well as retaliating, (for in the first instance, taking a coach office contiguous to the Bell and Crown, and advertising all our Coaches from his Inn, thereby deceiving the public, and injuring us and our connections). We, for the convenience of our friends and the public, and to prevent, as much as in our power, such fraud, have opened a new Coach Office, under the first gateway of the Bell Savage, where passengers are regularly booked, parcels carefully and expeditiously forwarded, without any charges for booking, - Salisbury, Wilton, and Andover goods will be delivered in future without any charge for porterage. − Persons ordering their goods by Fagg, Whitmarsh, and Co.'s Coaches, and paying the carriage at Salisbury or Andover, their friends in London will punctually receive them free of every charge.

The two coaches continue to operate throughout the early months of 1809, with each advertising their fares. In June, 1809, both have fares of 16s for an inside seat and 10s 6d for an outside seat from Salisbury to London. However, the fare from Andover to London for the Old Salisbury Coach was 10s 6d inside and 7s outside whereas the Commercial 12s inside and 8s outside. This is perhaps the first sign that Edward Prockter was losing the financial battle with his Commercial Coach in his attempt to force the Old Salisbury Coach out of business or at least to return to the Bell Savage.

The last mention of the Commercial Coach in an advertisement in the Salisbury and Winchester Journal is on October 2nd 1809. There is no indication as to whether this coach just stopped running but there is an advertisement from Mr Matchem that he has started a waggon service to transport goods between Salisbury and London. So it is possible that Edward Prockter withdrew from the coach trade and left his partner, George Matchem, to operate the goods traffic.

Appendix 3
Street Names

Many streets in Salisbury have changed their names over the years. These changes are well documented in a variety of documents but it is thought worthwhile to summarise these changes here.

Old Name	Current Name
Beaden Row	Bedwin Street
Bellfounder Street	Guilder Lane
Blackbridge Street	Trinity Street
Carternstrete	Catherine Street
Culverstrete	Culver Street
Draghall Street	Exeter Street
Guilderland	Guilder Lane
Hog Lane	Salt Lane
(at least between Endless Street and Rollestone Street)	
Milford Way	Rampart Road up to Tollgate Inn
Tanner Street	St Ann Street
Wyneman Street	Winchester Street
Beaden Row	Bedwin Street

In addition, New Street extended to the east including what is now Ivy Street and, probably, Trinity Street as well. Catherine Street extended down to the junction of St Ann Street and Exeter Street and thus the name of St John's Street is fairly modern. And confusingly, the current High Street was originally named Minster Street and the current Minster Street was High Street!

Appendix 4
Measurements

Ale and beer was usually stored in wooden casks of various sizes. The smaller casks would be used in the bar of a pub for direct service of beer whereas the larger sizes were used to store beer in bulk. The most common sizes were:

Name	Size (Gallons)	Size (Litres)
Pin	4½	20.5
Firkin	9	41
Kilderkin	18	82
Barrel	36	164
Hogshead	54	245

Note that the gallons used here are the British Imperial Gallon, as the US Gallon is somewhat different.

There is some variation in the size of the Hogshead. The size of casks did not become standardised until about 1854. Before that, Hogsheads of Ale could contain 48 or 51 gallons, with the smaller sizes reduced proportionately. Beer seems have used a 54 gallon since at least 1454.

One rarely comes across a cask referred to as a Pipe. This, most commonly, contained 108 gallons or 2 Hogsheads and was sometimes referred to as a Butt. Similarly, a Puncheon contained 90 gallons or 1½ Hogsheads.

The Common Brewery in Salisbury supplied beer in Hogsheads but Ale in Couls. It is not certain how much ale a coul contained but it may refer to the ale hogshead of the period of 48 gallons.

When referring to the capacity of a brewery, this was usually measured in the number of quarters of malt that could be mashed to produce the fermentable wort. There is contradictory information as to what a quarter of malt weighed. Most commonly, a quarter is defined as being a quarter of a hundredweight, this being 28 pounds (12.7 kg). But elsewhere, a quarter is defined as having a volume of 64 gallons. Since a gallon of grain weighs about 4 pounds, this would equate a quarter of grain to 256 pounds. Another source states that Dark Malt is lighter than pale malt giving the weight of a quarter of malt being between 250 and 320 pounds (114 to 145 kg). It seems most likely that these latter definitions of the weight of a quarter of malt are those used in brewing.

Notes

1. Numbering of houses in a street started to be formalised by the Towns Improvement Act of 1847 but this still gave local authorities discretion regarding how numbers were allocated. However, it does mean that the numbers of houses before this time could take any form and it was quite common to number houses consecutively up a street on one side and then continue back down the other side of the street from the far end. It is later that it became common to number the left hand side of a street with odd numbers and the right hand side with even numbers, both series starting at the same end of a street. The discrepancies are apparent in census records and thus, according to the date of a Census, it does not follow that a higher numbered property will be further up a street than a lower numbered one.
2. Recognising that the metric system has been taught in our schools for many years, it is worth noting some of the imperial units used in the text of this book. First, the coins of the realm. Previous to the metric coinage, there were 12 pennies in a shilling and twenty shillings in a pound. A guinea was one pound and one shilling. Secondly length. There were three feet in a yard, which was slightly less than a metre in length (0.9144 meters to be precise). Lastly, volume. There were eight pints in a gallon, but also two pints in a quart. A gallon was 4.55 litres. Casks for storing beer came I n a variety of sizes: A pin contained 4½ gallons; a firkin, 9 gallons, a kilderkin, 18 gallons; and a barrel, 36 gallons. The size of a hogshead was a bit more variable depending on the contents of the cask, but in general a hogshead of beer contained 54 gallons.

Bibliography

Note that the abbreviation in brackets at the start of some documents is used in the References section to refer to the relevant documents.

1. (RCHM) Royal Commission on Historical Monuments (England) *Ancient and Historical Monuments in the City of Salisbury*, vol. 1 (HMSO 1980)
2. (Gordon) Gordon, Ronald Graham, *Inns of Salisbury*, (unpublished)
3. (Hoare) Hoare, Sir Richard Colt, History of Modern Wiltshire, Sir Richard Colt Hoare, *Old & New Sarum or Salisbury* by Robert Benson & Henry Hatcher (Bowyer Nichols, London, 1843)
4. (WAW) Wheeler. W A, Articles in the *Salisbury Journal* on 24/7/1886, 31/7/1886, 21/8/1886, 24/12/1886, 26/3/1887, 23/7/1887, 20/8/1887 plus letter on 29/9/1894. (reproduced as Appendix 1 above)
5. Saunders, Peter, *Salisbury in Old Photographs* (Alan Sutton 1987)
6. Daniels, Peter, *Salisbury in Old Photographs: A Second Selection* (Alan Sutton1988)
7. Godfrey, Alan, *North Salisbury & Fisherton 1900* (Alan Godfrey Maps 1990)
8. Godfrey, Alan, *City of Salisbury with West Harnham & East Harnham* (Alan Godfrey Maps 1990)
9. Chandler, John, *Endless Street, A History of Salisbury and its People* (Hobnob Press 1983)
10. (Rowe). Rowe, C M, *Salisbury's Local Coinage* (Tisbury Printing Works ,1966)
11. Kingdom & Shearm, *Salisbury Local Board of Health, Plan of District* (1854, known as the Sewer Map as it shows plans of proposed sewer system)
12. (Haskins) Haskins, Charles, *The Ancient Trade Guilds and Companies of Salisbury* (J P, Bennett, Salisbury 1912)
13. Chandler, John, *Salisbury History and Guide* (Alan Sutton 1992)
14. (Hall) Hall, Peter, *Picturesque Memorials of Salisbury* (W B Brodie 1834)
15. (SWJ) *Salisbury and Winchester Journal*.
16. (ST) *Salisbury Times*
17. Brewery History Society, *Century of British Brewers Plus* (2005)
18. Vaughan, David J, *Bloody British History – Salisbury*. (History Press, 2014)
19. (General Entry Book) Carr, David R (ed.) *The First General Entry Book of the City of Salisbury 1387-1452* (Wiltshire Record Society.2001)
20. (Small) Howells, Jane, and Newman, Ruth (eds.) *William Small's Cherished Memories and Associations* (Wiltshire Record Society, 2011)

References

The name after each reference is that of the inn or public house as given in the Inventory in this publication. Thus, the name given in the reference may be that of an earlier incarnation of the premises.

1. WSHC A3/161/1 Minutes of Justices Business in New Sarum 1783 - 1784 (All)
2. WSHC A3/161/2 Minutes of Justices Business in New Sarum 1785 - 1788 (All)
3. WSHC A3/161/3 Minutes of Justices Business in New Sarum 1791 – 1795 (All)
4. WSHC A3/161/4 Minutes of Justices Business in New Sarum 1802-1814 (All)
5. WSHC A3/161/6 Minutes of Justices Business in New Sarum 1814 – 1823 (All)
6. WSHC A3/161/7 Minutes of Justices Business in New Sarum 1823 – 1835 (All)
7. WSHC A3/161/8 Minutes of Justices Business in New Sarum 1823-1870 (All)
8. WSHC A3/161/9 Minutes of Justices Business in New Sarum 1836-1844 (All)
9. WSHC A3/161/10 Minutes of Justices Business in New Sarum 1845 – 1851 (All)
10. WSHC A1/615 County Licensing Committee Records (All)
11. WSHC B6/100/1 Petty Sessions - Salisbury City 1852-1854 (All)
12. WSHC B6/250/1 Register of Licenses New Sarum 1932-1954 (All)
13. WSHC B6/250/2 Register of Licenses New Sarum 1955-1964 (All)
14. WSHC B6/250/3 Register of Licenses New Sarum 1964-1975 (All)
15. WSHC A3/190/3 Alehouse Keepers 1701 (& other dates) (All)
16. WSHC A3/190/4 Recognizances 1690-1760 (All)
17. Haskins Brewers Guild pp326-327
18. Haskins Brewers Guild pp328-330
19. Haskins Brewers Guild Inns pp333-335
20. Haskins Brewers Guild Alehouses pp335-337
21. Haskins Brewers Guild Milford and Fisherton houses p338
22. SWJ Oct 2 1858 (Albert)
23. RCHM Salisbury Vol 1 p113 #235 (Anchor)
24. SWJ Sep 10 1859 (Anchor)
25. SWJ Sep 19 1781 (Anchor & Hope)
26. SWJ Dec 1 1794 (Anchor & Hope)
27. SWJ Nov 24 1794 (Anchor & Hope)
28. SWJ Nov 25 1805 (Anchor & Hope)
29. SWJ Dec 16 1816 (Anchor & Hope)
30. ST June 10 1898 (Anchor & Hope)
31. SWJ Sep2 1771 (Angel Fisherton Street)
32. SWJ Jun 5 1775 (Angel Fisherton Street)
33. SWJ May 24 1773 (Angel Fisherton Street)
34. WSHC CC/Chapter/116/9 Redemption of Land Tax (Angel Fisherton Street)
35. ST July 18 1891 (Angel Fisherton Street)
36. WSHC CC/VicarsChoral/29/3 Lease of 1815 (Angel High Street)
37. SWJ Dec 21 1761 (Angel High Street)
38. SWJ Jul 7 1766 (Angel High Street)
39. SWJ Jul 15 1751 (Angel High Street)
40. SWJ Jan 6 1752 (Angel High Street)
41. SWJ Nov 8 1756 (Angel High Street)

APPENDICES AND REFERENCES

42 Rowe Williamson Ref 205 (Antelope)
43 SWJ Aug 13 1798 (Antelope)
44 SWJ July 8 1805 (Antelope)
45 SWJ Mar 31 1806 (Antelope)
46 SWJ July 14 1806 (Antelope)
47 SWJ Feb 19 1816 (Antelope)
48 SWJ Sep 9 1839 (Antelope)
49 SWJ Oct 7 1839 (Antelope)
50 SWJ May 16 1840) (Antelope)
51 SWJ Dec 7 1840 (Antelope)
52 SWJ Feb 8 1841 (Antelope)
53 SWJ May 31 1841 (Antelope)
54 WSHC G23/50/3 lease of 1869 (Avon Brewery)
55 ST Sep 8 1877 (Avon Brewery)
56 ST Nov 16 1889 (Avon Brewery)
57 SWJ Sep 9 1854 (Baker's Arms)
58 SWJ Mar 5 1870 (Bar 44)
59 ST Jul 14 1883 (Bar 44)
60 ST Mar 29 1908 (Bar 44)
61 WSHC A3/190/3 Bundle of Licenses (Barley Mow)
62 SWJ Jan 1 1759 (Barley Mow)
63 SWJ Dec 13 1819 (Barley Mow)
64 SWJ Feb 9 1829 (Barley Mow)
65 SWJ Jul 23 1821 (Barley Mow)
66 SWJ Sep 25 1847 (Barley Mow)
67 SWJ Jun 18 1859 (Barley Mow)
68 SWJ Aug 2 1862 (Barley Mow)
69 Rowe Williamson Ref 182 (Bell Exeter Street)
70 WSHC CC/Chapter/54/1 Lease of 1696 (Bell Exeter Street
71 WSHC CC/Chapter/54/2 Lease of 1718 (Bell Exeter Street
72 WSHC CC/Chapter/54/3 Lease of 1737 (Bell Exeter Street)
73 SWJ May 21 1792 (Bell Exeter Street)
74 SWJ May 18 1812 (Bell Exeter Street)
75 ST Jan 30 1886 (Bell Exeter Street)
76 SWJ Jun 26 1780 (Bell Milford Street)
77 WSHC CC/Bishoprick/178 Lease of 1849 (Bell Milford Street
78 SWJ Mar 16 1772 (Bell Milford Hill)
79 WSHC CC/Bishoprick/181 Sale of Estate of Samuel Whitchurch (Bell Milford Hill)
80 SWJ Apr 6 1844 (Bell Milford Hill)
81 SWJ Aug 17 1844 (Bell Milford Hill)
82 SWJ Mar 11 1865 (Bird in Hand North Street)
83 SWJ Aug 26 1865 (Bird in Hand North Street)
84 SWJ Oct 2 1869 (Bird in Hand North Street)
85 ST Sep 4 1875 (Bird in Hand North Street)
86 ST Oct 12 1878 (Bird in Hand North Street)
87 ST Aug 20 1881 (Bird in Hand North Street)
88 ST Oct 13 1893 (Bird in Hand North Street)
89 ST Jun 17 1904 (Bird in Hand North Street)
90 Haskins Lease from Tailor's Guild 1691 (Bird in Hand Trinity Street)
91 Haskins Lease from Tailor's Guild 1715 (Bird in Hand Trinity Street)
92 SWJ Jan 17 1852 (Bird in Hand Trinity Street)
93 Haskins Tailor's Guild sale to John Clark (Bird in Hand Trinity Street)
94 SWJ Dec 2 179 3 (Bishop Blaze)
95 Hoare p459 (Bishop's Palace)
96 WSHC G23/150/14 Lease of 1667 (Black Bear)
97 WSHC G23/150/14 Lease of 1771 (Black Bear)
98 WSHC G23/150/14 Lease of 1797 (Black Bear)
99 SWJ Jul 11 1868 (Black Horse Castle Street)
100 ST Feb 8 1890 (Black Horse Castle Street)
101 ST Sep 1 1893 (Black Horse Castle Street)
102 ST Sep 2 1898 (Black Horse Castle

103 SWJ Mar 29 1762 (Black Horse Winchester Street)
104 SWJ Dec 21 1767 Black Horse Winchester Street)
105 SWJ Apr 17 1780 (Black Horse Winchester Street)
106 SWJ Nov 4 1782 (Black Horse Winchester Street)
107 SWJ May 4 1789 (Black Horse Winchester Street)
108 SWJ Jan 22 1781 (Black Horse Winchester Street
109 SWJ Oct 16 1797 (Black Horse Winchester Street)
110 SWJ May 24 1784 Black Horse Winchester Street)
111 SWJ Dec 4 1837 (Black Horse Winchester Street)
112 SWJ Oct 8 1838 (Black Horse Winchester Street)
113 SWJ Apr 13 1840 (Black Horse Winchester Street)
114 SWJ Jul 27 1840 (Black Horse Winchester Street)
115 SWJ Aug 10 1840 (Black Horse Winchester Street)
116 SWJ Aug 17 1840 (Black Horse Winchester Street)
117 SWJ Sep 21 1840 (Back Horse Winchester Street)
118 SWJ Aug 23 1841 (Black Horse Winchester Street)
119 SWJ Jun 20 1842 (Black Horse Winchester Street)
120 SWJ Oct 11 1845 (Black Horse Winchester Street)
121 SWJ May 29 1852 Black Horse Winchester Street)
122 SWJ Oct 2 1869 (Black Horse Winchester Street)
123 ST Jan 15 1881 (Black Horse Winchester Street)
124 ST Feb 7 1902 (Black Horse Winchester Street)
125 RCHM Salisbury Volume 1 Ref # 344. (Blue Boar)
126 WSHC 727/9/9/ Indenture of 1636 (Blue Boar)
127 SWJ Feb 23 1756 (Blue Boar)
128 SWJ Mar 1 1756 (Blue Boar)
129 SWJ Mar 27 1775 (Blue Post)
130 SWJ Dec 18 1786 (Blue Post)
131 SWJ Nov 1 1856 (Blue Post)
132 SWJ Feb 14 1763 (Bowling Green Castle Street)
133 SWJ Jan 19 1778 (Bowling Green Castle Street)
134 WAW Old Inns of Salisbury III (Bowling Green Castle Street
135 SWJ Jun 4 1764 (Bowling Green Crane Street)
136 SWJ Jul 28 1783 (Bowling Green Crane Street)
137 SWJ Dec 10 1870 Brewery Tap Rollestone Street)
138 WAW Old Inns of Salisbury VIII 1894 (Bugle)
139 SWJ Jan 2 1769 (Bull)
140 SWJ July 15 1805 (Bull)
141 SWJ Sep 4 1820 (Bull)
142 SWJ Nov 13 1820 (Bull)
143 SWJ Apr 2 1822 (Bull)
144 SWJ Jun 30 1828 (Bull}
145 ST Sep 17 1887 (Bull)
146 ST Mar 21 1891 (Bull)
147 ST Apr 18 1891 (Bull)
148 ST Nov 18 1892 (Bull)
149 Rowe Williamson Ref 166 (Bush)
150 SWJ Dec 14 1872 (Cat Tavern)
151 ST Oct 14 1876 (Cat Tavern)
152 ST Sep 8 1877 (Cat Tavern)
153 ST Nov 6 1891 (Cat Tavern)
154 ST Apr 15 1904 (Cat Tavern)
155 ST Dec 6 1879 (Cathedral Hotel)
156 ST Nov 19 1881 (Cathedral Hotel)
157 ST Oct 14 1892 (Cathedral Hotel)
158 ST Nov 16 1894 (Cathedral Hotel)

159 ST Mar 19 1909 (Cathedral Hotel)
160 WSHC CC/Chapter/45/1 Lease of 1569 (Chapter House)
161 WSHC CC/Chapter/45/2 Lease of 1638 (Chapter House)
162 SWJ Dec 4 1739 (Chapter House)
163 SWJ Oct 9 1752 (Chapter House)
164 SWJ Mar 31 1755 (Chapter House)
165 SWJ Nov 29 1756 (Chapter House)
166 SWJ Dec 19 1763 (Chapter House)
167 SWJ Oct 14 1765 (Chapter House)
168 SWJ Nov 15 1773 (Chapter House)
169 SWJ Dec 21 1795 (Chapter House)
170 SWJ Sep 9 1799 (Chapter House)
171 SWJ Feb 21 1852 (Chapter House)
172 SWJ Apr 17 1852 (Chapter House)
173 SWJ May 28 1853 (Chapter House)
174 SWJ Sep 25 1858 (Chapter House)
175 SWJ Jul 17 1869 (Chapter House)
176 SWJ Feb 26 1870 (Chapter Houee)
177 SWJ Mar 18 1822 (Cherry Tree)
178 WSHC 492/99 Lease of 1626 (Chough)
179 SWJ Feb 14 1780 (Chough)
180 SWJ Oct 22 1787 (Chough)
181 SWJ Jul 14 1788 (Chough)
182 SWJ Nov 16 1807 (Chough)
183 SWJ Oct 24 1808 (Chough)
184 SWJ Oct 16 1809 (Chough)
185 SWJ Oct 15 1810 (Chough)
186 WSHC G23/150/115 Deeds of 1878 (Chough)
187 ST Aug 18 1905 (Chough)
188 WSHC 3270/6/3 Lease of 1897 (Chough)
189 WSHC 3270/6/4 Lease of 1903 (Chough)
190 WSHC 3270/6/5 Sale of 1923 (Chough)
191 WSHC G23/760/258 Planning Application – Strong & Co (Chough)
192 SWJ Apr 29 1771 (Cloisters)
193 SWJ Jan 15 1821 (Cloisters)
194 SWJ Mar 5 1821 (Cloisters)
195 SWJ Jan 26 1824 (Cloisters)
196 SWJ Jan 1 1859 (Cloisters)
197 SWJ Dec 10 1859 (Cloisters)
198 ST Mar 13 1875 (Cloisters)
199 SWJ Aug 18 1760 (Coach & Horses Catherine Street)
200 SWJ Jan 28 1765 (Coach & Horses Winchester Street)
201 SWJ May 12 1783 (Coach & Horses Winchester Street)
202 SWJ Jan 15 1787 (Coach & Horses Winchester Street)
203 SWJ Nov 2 1795 (Coach & Horses Winchester Street)
204 ST May 17 1879 (Coach & Horses Winchester Street)
205 ST Jul 5 1884 (Coach & Horses Winchester Street)
206 SWJ Jan 29 1740 (Comb Pot)
207 Chandler, Salisbury History and Guide, Alan Sutton Publishing, 1992 (Crane)
208 Hall Plate XXVIII (Cross Keys Queen Street)
209 SWJ Jun 23 1755 (Cross keys Queen Street)
210 SWJ Apr 21 1788 (Cross Keys Queen Street)
211 SWJ Feb 22 1808 (Cross Keys Queen Street)
212 SWJ July 11 1808 (Cross Keys Queen Street)
213 SWJ Aug 22 1814 (Cross Keys Queen Street)
214 SWJ Feb 23 1793 (Cross Keys Queen Street)
215 SWJ Oct 18 1802 (Cross Keys Queen Street)
216 SWJ Apr 15 1811 (Cross Keys Queen Street)
217 SWJ Aug 22 1814 (Cross Keys Queen Street)
218 SWJ Dec 12 1814 (Cross Keys Queen Street)
219 SWJ May 13 1865 (Cross Keys Queen Street)

220 SWJ Mar 9 1867 (Cross Keys Queen Street)
221 SWJ Mar 16 1867 (Cross Keys Queen Street)
222 SWJ Aug 20 1853 (Cross Keys Tap)
223 SWJ Mar 25 1865 (Cross Keys Tap)
224 SWJ May 13 1865 (Cross Keys Tap)
225 SWJ Oct 6 1866 (Cross Keys Tap)
226 SWJ Nov 24 1866 (Cross Keys Tap)
227 Rowe Williamson Ref 226 (Crown Castle Street)
228 SWJ Aug 18 1788 (Crown Castle Street)
229 Haskins The Rose Inn p309 (Crown Hotel)
230 SWJ Dec 14 1772 (Crown Hotel)
231 SWJ Feb 28 1785 (Crown Hotel)
232 SWJ May 26 1834 (Crown Hotel)
233 SWJ Apr 8 1848 (Crown Hotel)
234 SWJ Aug 5 1848 (Crown Hotel)
235 SWJ Apr 28 1849 (Crown Hotel)
236 SWJ Feb 8 1862 (Crown Hotel)
237 SWJ Jan 2 1875 (Crown Hotel)
238 ST Sep 14 1878 (Crown Hotel)
239 ST May 27 1882 (Crown Hotel)
240 ST Jun 14 1884 (Crown Hotel)
241 ST Jul 26 1884 (Crown Hotel)
242 SWJ Sept 2 1782 (Crown & Anchor)
243 SWJ Aug 4 1817 (Crown & Anchor)
244 SWJ Jul 11 1757 (Dolphin Dolphin Street)
245 SWJ May 6 1776 (Dolphin Dolphin Street)
246 SWJ Dec 7 1801 (Dolphin Dolphin Street)
247 WSHC 776/830 Sale and Conveyance of the Dolphin 1849 (Dolphin Dolphin Street)
248 SWJ Dec 18 1797 (Dolphin Dolphin Street)
249 SWJ Apr 9 1832 (Dolphin Dolphin Street)
250 SWJ Aug 6 1832 (Dolphin Dolphin Street)
251 SWJ Jul 6 1840 (Dolphin Dolphin Street)
252 SWJ Oct 25 1841 (Dolphin Dolphin Street)
253 SWJ Dec 24 1842 (Dolphin Dolphin Street)
254 SWJ Mar 21 1846 (Dolphin Dolphin Street)
255 SWJ Dec 27 1851 (Dolphin Dolphin Street)
256 SWJ May 14 1853 (Dolphin Dolphin Street)
257 SWJ Mar 19 1859 (Dolphin Dolphin Street)
258 SWJ Feb 8 1862 (Dolphin Dolphin Street)
259 SWJ Oct 4 1862 (Dolphin Dolphin Street)
260 SWJ Feb 11 1788 (Dolphin Fish Row)
261 WSHC G23/150/65 Will of John Trowman 1648 (Dolphin New Street)
262 Rowe Williamson ref 219 (Dolphin New Street)
263 SWJ Feb 22 1762 (Duchess of Albany)
264 SWJ Jun 17 1782 (Duchess of Albany)
265 SWJ Oct 7 1782 (Duchess of Albany)
266 SWJ Jan 31 1785 (Duchess of Albany)
267 SWJ Oct 19 1795 (Duchess of Albany)
268 SWJ May 18 1801 (Duchess of Albany)
269 SWJ Sep 22 1823 (Duchess of Albany)
270 SWJ Dec 21 1835 (Duchess of Albany)
271 SWJ Feb 27 1837 (Duchess of Albany)
272 SWJ May 29 1837 (Duchess of Albany)
273 SWJ Mar 16 1840 (Duchess of Albany)
274 SWJ May 4 1840 (Duchess of Albany)
275 SWJ May 11 1840 (Duchess of Albany)
276 SWJ Sep 7 1861 (Duchess of Albany)
277 SWJ Jan 20 1872 (Duchess of Albany)
278 ST Aug 18 1877 (Duchess of Albany)
279 ST Jul 12 1879 (Duchess of Albany)
280 ST Jul 26 1879 (Duchess of Albany)
281 ST Aug 31 1889 (Duchess of Albany)
282 ST May 3 1890 (Duchess of Albany)
283 WSHC B18//100/56 Justices Minute Book 1862 – Salisbury and Amesbury

APPENDICES AND REFERENCES

Division   (Duck)
284 SWJ Jun 17 1871 (Duck)
285 ST Nov 30 1906 (Duck)
286 WSHC A1/615 (Duck)
287 ST Jan 10 1902 (Duke of York, York Road)
288 ST Sep 4 1875 (Eagle Fisherton Street)
289 ST Jun 2 1888 (Eagle Fisherton Street)
290 SWJ Dec 18 1837 (Elephant & Castle Brown Street)
291 SWJ Dec 26 1814 (England's Glory)
292 SWJ Jun 27 1846 (Falcon Brown Street)
293 SWJ Oct 18 1851 (Falcon Brown Street)
294 SWJ May 29 1852 (Falcon Brown Street)
295 SWJ Aug 29 1857 (Falcon Brown Street)
296 SWJ Dec 3 1859 (Falcon Brown Street)
297 WSHC A3/190/3 License application (Fiddle & Trumpet)
298 SWJ Jul 16 1759 (Five Bells Corn Market)
299 SWJ Jun 24 1799 (Five Bells Fisherton)
300 SWJ Jul 12 1762 (Five Bella Salt Lase)
301 SWJ Apr 12 1813 (Five Bells Salt Lase)
302 SWJ June 9 1817 (Five Bells Salt Lase)
303 SWJ Jun 30 1817 (Five Bells Salt Lase)
304 SWJ Aug 3 1840 (Five Bells Salt Lase)
305 SWJ Jul 21 1845 (Five Bells Salt Lase)
306 SWJ Jun 19 1858 (Five Bells Salt Lase)
307 WSHC B18/100/48 Justices Minute Book – Salisbury & Amesbury 1854 (Five Bells Salt Lase)
308 SWJ Aug 21 1858 (Five Bells Salt Lase)
309 SWJ Sep 18 1858 (Five Bells Salt Lase)
310 SWJ Feb 2 1861 (Five Bells Salt Lase)
311 SWJ Jan 20 1866 (Five Bells Salt Lase)
312 SWJ May 19 1866 (Five Bells Salt Lase)
313 SWJ Apr 27 1867 (Five Bells Salt Lase)
314 ST Feb 2 1906 (Five Bells Salt Lase)
315 WSHC A3/190/3 License for Flower Pots (Flower Pots)
316 SWJ Oct 27 1755 (Flower Pots)
317 SWJ May 26 1760 (Flower Pots)
318 SWJ Sep 15 1760 (Flower Pots)
319 SWJ Oct 28 1751 (Fountain)
320 SWJ Jan 27 1852 (Fountain)
321 SWJ Mar 2 1852 (Fountain)
322 SWJ Jul 14 1755 (Fountain)
323 SWJ Apr 13 1772 (Fountain)
324 SWJ Aug 6 1781 (Fountain)
325 SWJ Jun 20 1791 (Fountain)
326 SWJ Jan 21 1793 (Fountain)
327 SWJ Feb 12 1798 (Fountain)
328 SWJ Oct 12 1801 (Fountain)
329 SWJ Jan 18 1802 (Fountain)
330 Rowe Williamson Ref No 198 (Fox & Goose)
331 General Entry Book Folio7 (George High Street)
332 General Entry Book Folio 43 (George High Street)
333 General Entry Book Folio 87 (George High Street)
334 General Entry Book Folio 110 (George Hight Street)
335 WSHC CC/Chapter/71 Leases from 1661 until 1733(George High Street)
336 Rowe Williamson Ref No 165.(George High Street)
337 See, for example, www.pepysdiary.com (George High Street)
338 SWJ Feb 6 1769 (George High Street)
339 SWJ Nov 12 1864 (George High Street)
340 ST May 28 1887 (George High Street)
341 ST Mar 17 1899 (George High Street)
342 ST Apr 14 1905 (George High Street)
343 SWJ May 16 1846 (George & Dragon)
344 SWJ Apr 5 1856 (George & Dragon)
345 ST Mar 21 1891 (George & Dragon)
346 SWJ Mar 18 1765 (Globe)
347 SWJ May 30 1785 (Globe)
348 SWJ Sep 26 1803 (Globe)
349 SWJ Oct 5 1867 (Globe)
350 SWJ Oct 19 1867 (Globe)
351 SWJ May 18 1872 (Globe)
352 SWJ Jun 29 1872 (Globe)
353 ST Oct 16 1875 (Globe)
354 ST Dec 29 1877 (Globe)
355 ST Apr 20 1878 (Globe)

356 ST Feb 22 1879 (Globe)
357 SWJ Jul 7 1783 (Goat)
358 SWJ Apr 1 1803 (Goat)
359 SWJ June 27 1814 (Goat)
360 SWJ Sep 8 1817 (Goat)
361 SWJ Jul 23 1832 (Goat)
362 SWJ Feb 26 1853 (Goat)
363 SWJ Sep 12 1857 (Goat)
364 SWJ Feb 27 1858 (Goat)
365 SWJ Jan 4 1779 (Golden Lion)
366 SWJ Aug 21 1780 (Golden Lion)
367 SWJ Oct 15 1810 (Golden Lion)
368 SWJ Oct 8 1739 (Grasshopper Winchester Street)
369 SWJ Jul 19 1865 (Great Western Tavern)
370 SWJ Oct 14 1865 (Great Western Tavern)
371 ST Mar 18 1898 (Green Dragon Fish)
372 SWJ Sep 22 1741 (Green Dragon Fisherton)
373 Rowe Williamson Ref No 206 (Green Man)
374 SWJ Jun 21 1762 (Grey Fisher)
375 SWJ Apr 30 1821 (Grey Fisher)
376 SWJ Mar 17 1828 (Grey Fisher)
377 WSHC B18/100/45 Justices Minute Book – Salisbury & Amesbury 1851(Grey Fisher)
378 ST Jun 9 1877 (Grey Fisher)
379 SWJ Apr 14 1849 (Grey Fisher)
380 Hoare p 355 (Greyhound Brown)
381 SWJ Nov 29 1790 (Greyhound Brown Street)
382 Hall Plate XXVIII (Half Moon)
383 SWJ May 8 1739 (Half Moon)
384 SWJ Apr 6 1761 (Half Moon)
385 SWJ Jul 5 1762 (Half Moon)
386 SWJ Nov 6 1762 (Half Moon)
387 SWJ Aug 15 1763 (Half Moon)
388 SWJ Jan 9 1764 (Half Moon)
389 SWJ Jun 29 1767 (Half Moon)
390 SWJ Feb 8 1768 (Half Moon)
391 SWJ Jul 29 1771 (Half Moon)
392 SWJ Dec 23 1771 (Half Moon)
393 SWJ Mar 16 1772 (Half Moon)
394 SWJ Apr 20 1772 (Half Moon)
395 SWJ Jul 18 1774 (Half Moon)
396 SWJ Mar 27 1775 (Half Moon)
397 SWJ Jul 19 1775 (Half Moon)
398 SWJ Feb 19 1776 (Half Moon)
399 SWJ Jun 1 1761 (Halfway House)
400 SWJ Nov 17 1781 (Halfway House)
401 SWJ Jul 15 1833 (Halfway House)
402 SWJ Oct 2 1837 (Halfway House)
403 SWJ Apr 1 1839 (Halfway House)
404 SWJ Jul 22 1839 (Halfway House)
405 SWJ Aug 5 1839 (Halfway House)
406 SWJ Dec 7 1840 (Halfway House)
407 SWJ Aug 29 1868 (Halfway House)
408 SWJ Nov 1 1784 (Haunch of Venison)
409 SWJ Jul 15 1833 (Haunch of Venison)
410 SWJ May 23 1868 (Horse & Groom)
411 SWJ Apr 16 1870 (Horse & Groom)
412 SWJ Sep 21 1872 (Horse & Groom)
413 ST Apr 20 1889 (Horse & Groom)
414 ST Aug 22 1902 (Horse & Groom)
415 WSHC CC/Chapter/66/1 Lease of 1609 (Horseshoe High Street)
416 WSHC CC/Chapter/66/4 Lease of 1682 (Horseshoe High Street)
417 WSHC CC/Chapter/66/8 Lease of 1751 (Horseshoe High Street)
418 SWJ Jun 18 1780 (Horseshoes Britford)
419 Haskins Brewers Guild p338 (Horseshoes Fisherton)
420 SWJ Jun 29 1850 (Huntsman)
421 SWJ Jan 14 1860 (Huntsman)
422 ST Jul 16 1887 (Huntsman)
423 SWJ Feb 18 1799 (India Arms)
424 SWJ Apr 8 1822 (India Arms)
425 SWJ Sept 18 1780 (Joiners)
426 SWJ May 31 1824 (Kings Arms Fisherton Street)
427 SWJ May 23 1857 (Kings Arms Fisherton Street)
428 ST Dec 11 1890 (Kings Arms Fisherton Street)
429 ST Feb 16 1906 (Kings Arms Fisherton

430 ST Jun 8 1906 (Kings Arms Fisherton Street)
431 Haskins Brewers Guild p299 (Kings Head)
432 Haskins Brewers Guild p301 (Kings Head)
433 SWJ Jun 16 1783 (Kings Head)
434 SWJ Nov 26 1804 (Kings Head)
435 SWJ Oct 2 1846 (Kings Head)
436 SWJ Aug 22 1868 (Kings Head)
437 ST Oct 9 1891 (Kings Head)
438 ST May 31 1895 (Kings Head)
439 WSHC G23/150/151 Lease of 1823 (King & Queen)
440 SWJ Sep 11 1858 (King & Queen)
441 SWJ Jun 17 1871 (King & Queen)
442 WSHC B18/100/10 Justices Minute Book – Salisbury & Amesbury 1813 (King of Prussia Milford Hill)
443 SWJ Oct 23 1815 (King of Prussia Milford Hill)
444 Haskins Tailors Guild p 202 (Labour in Vain)
445 Rowe Williamson Ref No 228 (Lamb Catherine Street)
446 SWJ April 2 1750 (Lamb Catherine Street)
447 SWJ Sep 23 1799 (Lamb Catherine Street)
448 SWJ Apr 6 1801 (Lamb Catherine Street)
449 SWJ Dec 27 1802 (Lamb Catherine Street)
450 SWJ June 20 1803 (Lamb Catherine Street)
451 SWJ July 4 1803 (Lamb Catherine Street)
452 SWJ May 21 1804 (Lamb Catherine Street)
453 SWJ Aug 6 1804 (Lamb Catherine Street)
454 SWJ Jan 12 1824 (Lamb Catherine Street
455 SWJ May 14 1831 (Lamb Catherine Street)
456 SWJ Jul 16 1832 (Lamb Catherine Street)
457 SWJ May 25 1835 (Lamb Catherine Street)
458 SWJ Jun 12 1837 (Lamb Catherine Street)
459 SWJ Oct 17 1842 (Lamb Catherine Street)
460 SWJ Jul 10 1847 (Lamb Catherine Street)
461 SWJ Aug 21 1847 (Lamb Catherine Street)
462 SWJ Aug 10 1850 (Lamb Catherine Street)
463 SWJ Feb 18 1854 (Lamb Catherine Street)
464 SWJ Feb 9 1856 (Lamb Catherine Street)
465 SWJ Dec 25 189 (Lamb Catherine Street)
466 SWJ Sep 20 1819 (Lamb Fisherton Street)
467 SWJ Sep 18 1820 (Lamb Fisherton Street)
468 WSHC 776/429 Draft Indenture of 1828 (Lamb Fisherton Street)
469 Haskins Brewers Guild p316 (Legge)
470 Haskins Tailor's Guild p168 Lease of 1649 (Legge)
471 Haskins Tailor's Guild p207 Lease of 1773 (Legge)
472 SWJ May 18 1822 (Leopards Head)
473 SWJ Sep 7 1861 (London Hotel Fisherton Street)
474 SWJ Oct 2 1869 (London Hotel Fisherton Street)
475 ST Sep 17 1887 (London Hotel Fisherton Street)
476 ST Aug 29 1891 (London Hotel Fisherton Street)
477 ST Oct 2 1891 (London Hotel Fisherton Street)
478 ST Nov 1 1907 (London Hotel Fisherton

	Street)		Market)
479	SWJ Oct 16 1780 (London Inn Bridge Street)	501	SWJ Jun 19 1837 (Maidenhead Cheese Market)
480	WSHC 451/469 Lease of 1825 (London Inn Bridge Street)	502	SWJ Apr 12 1841 (Maidenhead Cheese Market)
481	SWJ Jun 8 1829 (London Inn Bridge Street)	503	SWJ Aug 9 1841 (Maidenhead Cheese Market)
482	SWJ Feb 8 1830 (London Inn Bridge Street)	504	SWJ Aug 23 1841 (Maidenhead Cheese Market)
483	SWJ Dec 10 1838 (London Inn Bridge Street)	505	SWJ Sep 27 1841 (Maidenhead Cheese Market)
484	SWJ Sep 13 1845 (London Inn Bridge Street)	506	SWJ Oct 2 1847 (Maidenhead Cheese Market
485	SWJ Apr 29 1849 (London Inn Bridge Street)	507	SWJ Sep 30 1799 (Malmesbury)
		508	SWJ Feb 28 1814 (Malmesbury)
486	SWJ May 31 1856 (London Inn Bridge Street)	509	SWJ Aug 24 1818 (Malmesbury)
		510	SWJ Dec 30 1822 (Malmesbury)
487	SWJ Aug 15 1857 (London Inn Bridge Street)	511	SWJ Feb 17 1844 (Malmesbury)
		512	SWJ Feb 21 1848 (Malmesbury)
488	SWJ May 29 1858 (London Inn Bridge Street)	513	SWJ Jun 5 1858 (Malmesbury)
		514	SWJ Sep 26 1842 (Malmesbury)
489	SWJ Sep 29 1767 (Maidenhead Cheese Market)	515	SWJ Mar 11 1843 (Malmesbury)
		516	ST Feb 13 1903 (Malmesbury)
490	SWJ Jun 10 1771 (Maidenhead Cheese Market)	517	SWJ Dec 18 1869 (Malmesbury)
		518	SWJ Nov 27 1809 (Market Inn)
491	SWJ Jan 17 1780 (Maidenhead Cheese Market)	519	SWJ May 17 1813 (Market Inn)
		520	SWJ Feb 17 1817 (Market Inn)
492	SWJ July 10 1780 (Maidenhead Cheese Market)	521	SWJ Aug 24 1840 (Market Inn)
		522	SWJ Jul 12 1841 (Market Inn
493	SWJ Aug 26 1799 (Maidenhead Cheese Market)	523	SWJ Feb 5 1853 (Market Inn)
		524	SWJ Apr 8 1854 (Market Inn)
494	SWJ Aug 21 1820 (Maidenhead Cheese Market)	525	SWJ Sep 9 1854 (Market Inn)
		526	SWJ Nov 22 1856 (Market Inn)
495	SWJ Jun 29 1830 (Maidenhead Cheese Market)	527	SWJ Mar 2 1867 (Market Inn)
		528	SWJ Mar 30 1867 (Market Inn)
496	SWJ Oct 13 1830 (Maidenhead Cheese Market)	529	SWJ Dec 11 1869 (Market Inn)
		530	ST May 20 1886 (Market Inn)
497	SWJ Nov 14 1836 (Maidenhead Cheese Market)	531	SWJ Jul 16 1787 (Mermaid)
		532	Rowe Williamson Ref No 203 (Mitre Silver Street)
498	SWJ Dec 26 1836 (Maidenhead Cheese Market)	533	SWJ May 21 1735 (Mitre Silver Street)
499	SWJ Jan 16 1837 (Maidenhead Cheese Market)	534	SWJ Nov 11 1740 (Mitre Silver Street)
		535	SWJ Oct 20 1755 (Mitre Silver Street)
500	SWJ Mar 20 1837 (Maidenhead Cheese	536	SWJ Nov 12 1750 (Mitre Silver Street)

APPENDICES AND REFERENCES

537 SWJ May 27 1769 (Mitre Silver Street)
538 SWJ May 24 1773 (Mitre Silver Street)
539 SWJ Aug 13 1823 (New Inn New Street)
540 SWJ Sep 12 1836 (New Inn New Street)
541 ST Jun 8 1878 (New Inn New Street)
542 ST Jul 20 1878 (New Inn New Street)
543 WSHC 776/1059 Deeds of the Woolpack (NN Bar)
544 SWJ Oct 13 1783 (NN Bar)
545 SWJ Apr 5 1790 (NN Bar)
546 SWJ June 11 1810 (NN Bar)
547 SWJ Oct 22 1853 (NN Bar)
548 SWJ Apr 16 1870 (NN Bar)
549 ST Dec 5 1902 (NN Bar)
550 SWJ Nov 13 1739 (Noah's Ark)
551 SWJ Dec 17 1781 (Old Castle)
552 SWJ Feb 1 1798 (Old Castle)
553 SWJ Jun 2 1849 (Old Castle)
554 SWJ Jun 1 1844 (Old Castle)
555 SWJ Jul 22 1854 (Old Castle)
556 SWJ Mar 29 1856 (Old Castle)
557 SWJ May 8 1858 (Old Castle)
558 SWJ Jun 15 1867 (Old Castle)
559 ST Oct 26 1889 (Old Castle)
560 SWJ Jan 13 1766 (Old George Winchester Street)
561 SWJ Apr 4 1768 (Old George Winchester Street)
562 SWJ Sep 5 1808 (Old George Winchester Street)
563 SWJ Dec 11 1815 (Old George Winchester Street)
564 SWJ May 14 1832 (Old George Winchester Street)
565 SWJ Aug 7 1837 (Old George Winchester Street)
566 SWJ Jul 28 1849 (Old George Winchester Street)
567 SWJ Feb 15 1796 (One Bell)
568 SWJ Jun 26 1820 (Ox)
569 SWJ Sep 22 1823 (Ox)
570 SWJ Oct 6 1823 (Ox)
571 SWJ Dec 30 1833 (Ox)
572 SWJ Jun 2 1834 (Ox)
573 SWJ Jun 30 1834 (Ox)
574 SWJ Jul 25 1857 (Ox)
575 SWJ Aug 22 1857 (Ox)
576 SWJ Sep 7 1861 (Ox)
577 SWJ Jun 14 1762 (Oxford Arms)
578 SWJ Jun 2 1777 (Oxford Arms)
579 SWJ Jun 23 1777 (Oxford Arms)
580 SWJ Mar 15 1779 (Oxford Arms)
581 SWJ Mar 29 1779 (Oxford Arms)
582 WAW Part V (See Appendix 2) (Oxford Arms)
583 Mar 29 1794 (Oxford Arms)
584 SWJ Feb 22 1742 (Ox Row Inn)
585 SWJ Jan 31 1763 (Ox Row Inn)
586 SWJ March 6 1780 (Ox Row Inn)
587 SWJ July 1 1780 (Ox Row Inn)
588 SWJ Oct 1 1781 (Ox Row Inn)
589 SWJ Sep 29 1829 (Ox Row Inn)
590 SWJ Feb 7 1831 (Ox Row Inn)
591 SWJ Apr 25 1831 (Ox Row Inn)
592 SWJ Feb 26 1859 (Ox Row Inn)
593 SWJ Jan 9 1869 (Ox Row Inn)
594 ST Jan 6 1905 Ox Row Inn)
595 ST May 31 1905 (Ox Row Inn)
596 SWJ Feb 2 1784 (Parade Tavern)
597 SWJ May 10 1784   (Parade Tavern)
598 SWJ Oct 4 1784 (Parade Tavern)
599 SWJ Jan 10 1785 (Parade Tavern)
600 SWJ Aug 25 1788 (Parade Tavern)
601 SWJ Mar 18 1805 (Parade Tavern)
602 SWJ Jan 27 1806 (Parade Tavern)
603 SWJ Oct 14 1816 (Pelican)
604 SWJ Oct 27 1817 (Pelican)
605 SWJ Apr 17 1820 (Pelican)
606 SWJ Oct 23 1820 (Pelican)
607 SWJ May 30 1825 (Pelican)
608 SWJ Oct 18 1830 (Pelican)
609 SWJ Nov 8 1762 (Petersfinger Inn)
610 SWJ 25 Jan 1802 (Petersfinger Inn)
611 SWJ Jun 14 1819 (Petersfinger Inn)
612 SWJ Jun 11 1821 (Petersfinger Inn)
613 SWJ Sep 26 1825 (Petersfinger Inn)
614 Haskins Shoemakers Guild p229 (Pheasant)

615 SWJ Apr 16 1784 (Pheasant)
616 SWJ Apr 18 1785 (Pheasant)
617 SWJ Jun 25 1821 (Pheasant)
618 SWJ Dec 1 1823 (Pheasant)
619 SWJ Dec 27 1830 (Pheasant)
620 SWJ Apr 3 1826 (Pheasant)
621 SWJ Jul 2 1827 (Pheasant)
622 SWJ Jun 1 1829 (Pheasant)
623 SWJ Sep 5 1868 (Pheasant)
624 SWJ Nov 28 1868 (Pheasant)
625 SWJ Dec 5 1868 (Pheasant)
626 ST Apr 29 1876 (Pheasant)
627 SWJ May 2 1808 (Plasterers Arms)
628 SWJ Dec 16 1816 (Plasterers Arms)
629 SWJ Aug 2 1830 (Plasterers Arms)
630 SWJ Mar 3 1834 (Plasterers Arms)
631 SWJ Aug 13 1853 (Plasterers Arms)
632 SWJ Apr 5 1856 (Plasterers Arms)
633 SWJ May 1 1858 (Plasterers Arms)
634 SWJ Sep 11 1858 (Plasterers Arms)
635 SWJ Nov 6 1858 (Plasterers Arms)
636 SWJ Jan 8 1859 (Plasterers Arms)
637 SWJ Feb 26 1859 (Plasterers Arms)
638 SWJ Jul 6 1861 (Plasterers Arms)
639 SWJ Aug 20 1870 (Plasterers Arms)
640 SWJ Feb 24 1872 (Plasterers Arms)
641 SWJ Aug 31 1872 (Plasterers Arms)
642 SWJ Jul 22 1876 (Plasterers Arms)
643 SWJ Apr 13 1835 (Plough Brown Street)
644 SWJ May 9 1774 (Plough Chipper Lane)
645 SWJ Dec 29 1781 (Plough Chipper Lane)
646 SWJ Mar 10 1817 (Plough Chipper Lane)
647 SWJ Sep 22 1823 (Plough Chipper Lane)
648 SWJ May 30 1825 (Plough Chipper Lane)
649 SWJ Nov 17 1883 (Plume of Feathers Fisherton Street)
650 SWJ Mar 26 1737 (Plume of Feathers Queen Street)
651 SWJ May 25 1752 (Plume of Feathers Queen Street)
652 SWJ Jan 13 1752 (Plume of Feathers Queen Street)
653 SWJ Aug 31 1761 (Plume of Feathers Queen Street)
654 SWJ Jan 17 1780 (Plume of Feathers Queen Street)
655 SWJ Nov 22 1813 (Plume of Feathers Queen Street)
656 SWJ June 3 1816 (Plume of Feathers Queen Street)
657 SWJ Aug 3 1840 (Plume of Feathers Queen Street)
658 SWJ Feb 15 1851 (Plume of Feathers Queen Street)
659 SWJ Jul 7 1855 (Plume of Feathers Queen Street)
660 SWJ Apr 14 1860 (Plume of Feathers Queen Street)
661 SWJ Jun 1 1780 (Punchbowl)
662 SWJ Aug 9 1784 (Punchbowl)
663 SWJ Aug 23 1784 (Punchbowl)
664 SWJ Jun 13 1785 (Punchbowl)
665 SWJ Oct 10 1825 (Punchbowl)
666 WSHC B18/250/20 Justices Minute Book – Salisbury & Amesbury Division 1826 (Punchbowl)
667 RCHM Salisbury Vol 1 p67 (Pynnoks Inn)
668 Haskins Brewers Guild p296 (Pynnoks Inn)
669 Haskins Brewers Guild p 297 (Pynnoks Inn)
670 Haskins Brewers Guild p298 (Pynnoks Inn)
671 RCHM Salisbury Vol 1 p68 (Pynnoks Inn)
672 SWJ Jun 10 1740 (Qudos)
673 SWJ Dec 27 1762 (Qudos)
674 SWJ Jun 5 1775 (Qudos)
675 SWJ Dec 30 1780 (Qudos)
676 SWJ Mar 5 1798 (Qudos)
677 SWJ Dec 30 1799 (Qudos)
678 SWJ Oct 8 1827 (Qudos)
679 SWJ Jul 7 1828 (Qudos)

680 SWJ Jan 16 1837 (Qudos)
681 SWJ Jun 18 1853 (Qudos)
682 ST Jan 27 1893 (Qudos)
683 WSHC CC/Chapter/55/1 Lease of 1637 (Queen's Arms)
684 WSHC CC/Chapter/55/3 Lease of 1699 (Queen's Arms)
685 WSHC CC/Chapter/55/4 Lease of 1715 (Queen's Arms)
686 SWJ May 14 1804 (Queen's Arms)
687 SWJ May 22 1852 (Queen's Arms)
688 SWJ Aug 1 1857 (Queen's Arms)
689 ST Aug 12 1886 (Queen's Arms)
690 ST Sep 3 1887 (Queen's Arms)
691 WSHC G23/150/65 Lease of property in Ivy Street 1817 (Queen's & Plasterer's Arms)
692 SWJ Aug 21 1820 (Queen's and Plasterer's Arms)
693 SWJ Jul 15 1822 (Queens's & Plasterer's Arms)
694 SWJ Jan 13 1823 (Queens's & Plasterer's Arms)
695 SWJ Oct 27 1823 (Queens's & Plasterer's Arms)
696 SWJ May 24 1824 (Queens's & Plasterer's Arms)
697 SWJ Jun 14 1824 (Queens's & Plasterer's Arms)
698 SWJ Dec 30 1843 (Queens's & Plasterer's Arms)
699 SWJ Apr 12 1845 (Queens's & Plasterer's Arms)
700 SWJ Aug 15 1845 (Queens's & Plasterer's Arms)
701 ST Aug 30 1896 (Radnor Queens Road)
702 SWJ Aug 18 1823 (Radnor St Ann Street)
703 SWJ Apr 11 1836 Radnor St Ann Street)
704 SWJ Aug 5 1848 (Radnor St Ann Street)
705 SWJ Jan 20 1777 (Rai D'Or)
706 SWJ Jun 13 1791 (Rai D'Or)
707 SWJ Dec 19 1796 (Rai D'Or)
708 SWJ July 27 1807 (Rai D'Or)
709 SWJ Apr 30 1810 (Rai D'Or)
710 SWJ Mar 4 1816 (Rai D'Or)
711 SWJ May 29 1820 (Rai D'Or)
712 Hoare p824 (Rai D'Or)
713 SWJ Nov 18 1843 (Rai D'Or)
714 SWJ Oct 12 1844 (Rai D'Or)
715 SWJ Aug 22 1868 (Rai D'Or)
716 ST Feb 5 1881 (Rai D'Or)
717 ST Aug 30 1884 (Rai D'Or)
718 ST Dec 1 1905 (Rai D'Or)
719 SWHC B18/100/41 Justices Minute Book – Salisbury & Amesbury Division 1847 (Railway Inn Tollgate Road)
720 SWJ Sep 28 1861 (Railway Inn Tollgate Road)
721 SWHC B18/100/62 Justices Minute Book – Salisbury & Amesbury Division 1868 (Railway Inn Tollgate Road)
722 ST Nov 23 1900 (Railway Inn Tollgate Road)
723 SWJ Nov 23 1867 (Railway Tavern SW Road)
724 SWJ Jul 18 1868 (Railway Tavern SW Road)
725 SWJ Feb 24 1872 (Railway Tavern SW Road)
726 SWJ Jan 7 1854 (Railway Tavern St Ann Street)
727 SWJ Jan 22 1810 (Red Lion Fisherton Street)
728 SWJ May 25 1829 (Red Lion Fisherton Street)
729 SWJ Jun 21 1831 (Red Lion Fisherton Street)
730 SWJ Sep 11 1858 (Red Lion Fisherton Street)
731 SWJ Feb 10 1752 (Red Lion Milford St)
732 SWJ Jun 25 1764 (Red Lion Milford St}
733 SWJ Apr 7 1766 ((Red Lion Milford St)
734 SWJ Jan 30 1769 (Red Lion Milford St)
735 SWJ Feb 27 1797 ((Red Lion Milford St)
736 SWJ Mar 30 1812 ((Red Lion Milford St)
737 SWJ Oct 26 1812 (Red Lion Milford St)

738 SWJ May 2 1814 (Red Lion Milford St)
739 SWJ Oct 23 1837 (Red Lion Milford St)
740 SWJ Dec 11 1837 (Red Lion Milford St)
741 SWJ Oct 29 1838 (Red Lion Milford St)
742 SWJ Aug 1 1868 (Red Lion Milford St)
743 ST May 23 1889 (Red Lion Milford St)
744 SWJ Jun 16 1834 (Red Rover)
745 SWJ Oct 25 1841 (Red Rover)
746 Hoare p400 (Retreat Inn)
747 SWJ Feb 24 1755 (Retreat Inn)
748 SWJ Jul 18 1757 (Retreat Inn)
749 SWJ May 21 1759 (Retreat Inn)
750 SWJ Aug 24 1761 (Retreat Inn)
751 SWJ Oct 1 1810 (Retreat Inn)
752 SWJ May 2 1814 (Retreat Inn)
753 SWJ May 9 1814 (Retreat Inn)
754 SWJ Jan 39 1815 (Retreat Inn)
755 SWJ Dec 2 1822 (Retreat Inn)
756 SWJ Aug 18 1823 (Retreat Inn)
757 SWJ Aug 21 1869 (Retreat Inn)
758 SWJ Jan 15 1870 (Retreat Inn)
759 ST Sep 17 1887 (Retreat Inn)
760 WSHC B18/100/60 Justices Minute Book 1866 – Salisbury & Amesbury Division (Rifleman's Arms)
761 SWJ May 20 1871 (Rifleman's Arms)
762 WSHC B18/100/72 Justices Minute Book 1878 – Salisbury & Amesbury Division (Rifleman's Arms)
763 SWJ Nov 25 1811 (Rising Sun)
764 SWJ Mar 16 1812 (Rising Sun)
765 SWJ May 4 1812 (Rising Sun)
766 SWJ Aug 16 1862 (Rising Sun)
767 SWJ Sep 13 1862 (Rising Sun)
768 SWJ Mar 17 1817 (Roebuck Butcher Row)
769 SWJ Feb 5 1821 (Roebuck Butcher Row)
770 SWJ Feb 21 1825 (Roebuck Butcher Row)
771 SWJ Feb 28 1825 (Roebuck Butcher Row)
772 SWJ Dec 22 1828 (Roebuck Butcher Row)
773 SWJ Sep 29 1829 (Roebuck Butcher Row)
774 SWJ May 30 1840 (Roebuck Butcher Row)
775 SWJ May 15 1869 (Roebuck Butcher Row)
776 ST Jul 16 1887 (Roebuck Butcher Row)
777 WSHC 490/370 Lease of 1680 (Rose & Crown Harnham Road)
778 SWJ Jul 7 1755 (Rose & Crown Harnham Road)
779 SWJ Nov 17 1783 (Rose & Crown Harnham Road)
780 SWJ May 17 1784 (Rose & Crown Harnham Road)
781 SWJ Jul 19 1790 (Rose & Crown Harnham Road)
782 SWJ Aug 31 1801 (Rose & Crown Harnham Road)
783 SWJ Nov 26 1810 (Rose & Crown Harnham Road)
784 SWJ Dec 3 1810 (Rose & Crown Harnham Road)
785 Small p xxii (Rose & Crown Harnham Road)
786 SWJ Jan 13 1866 (Rose & Crown Harnham Road)
787 ST Jan 13 1883 (Rose & Crown Harnham Road)
788 ST Nov 8 1884 (Rose & Crown Harnham Road)
789 WSHC 1946/2/2A/118 Lease of 1888 (Rose & Crown Harnham Road)
790 ST Nov 16 1894 (Rose & Crown Harnham Road)
791 ST Mar 13 1903 (Rose & Crown Harnham Road)
792 ST Aug 13 1909 (Rose & Crown Harnham Road)
793 English Inns & Road Houses, George Long, T Werner Laurie Ltd, 1937 (Rose & Crown Harnham Road)
794 SWJ Oct 13 1849 (Round of Beef)
795 SWJ Apr 9 1853 (Round of Beef)

APPENDICES AND REFERENCES

796 SWJ Mar 16 1872 (Round of Beef)
797 ST Jan 19 1878 (Round of Beef)
798 ST Dec 28 1894 (Round of Beef)
799 ST Jan 9 1903 (Round of Beef)
800 General Entry Book p.21 (Royal High Street)
801 SWJ Apr 24 1775 (Royal George)
802 WSHC 529/150 Analysis of Title of John Rogers (Royal George)
803 SWJ Oct 4 1841 (Royal George)
804 ST Apr 17 1875 (Royal George)
805 ST Aug 5 1886 (Royal George)
806 SWJ Dec 5 1836 (Royal Oak Culver Street)
807 SWJ Apr 22 1854 (Royal Oak Culver Street)
808 ST Oct 5 1889 (Royal Oak Culver Street)
809 WSHC G23/760/1097 Planning application from Strongs of Romsey (Royal Oak Devizes road)
810 WSHC G23/150/39 Leases of Royal Oak, Milford Street (Royal Oak Milford Street)
811 WSHC A3/190/3 Bundle of Licenses (Royal Oak Milford Street)
812 SWJ Jun 9 1755 (Royal Oak Milford Street)
813 SWJ Aug 27 1787 (Royal Oak Milford Street)
814 SWJ Jan 28 1799 (Royal Oak Milford Street)
815 SWJ Feb 1 1768 (Running Horse)
816 SWJ May 21 1768 (Running Horse)
817 SWJ Dec 4 1775 (Running Horse)
818 SWJ Dec 11 1775 (Running Horse)
819 SWJ Oct 11 1813 (Running Horse)
820 SWJ Dec 9 1822 (Running Horse)
821 SWJ Jan 27 1840 (Running Horse)
822 SWJ Mar 2 1840 (Running Horse)
823 SWJ Apr 13 1840 (Running Horse)
824 SWJ Nov 14 1857 (Running Horse)
825 SWJ Feb 13 1809 (Salisbury Arms)
826 SWJ Feb 1 1830 (Salisbury Arms)
827 SWJ Jul 19 1830 (Salisbury Arms)
828 SWJ Sep 20 1830 (Salisbury Arms)
829 SWJ Nov 25 1830 (Salisbury Arms)
830 SWJ Jul 2 1838 (Salisbury Arms)
831 SWJ Jan 14 1839 (Salisbury Arms)
832 SWJ Apr 8 1839 (Salisbury Arms)
833 WSHC 727/9/9 Deed of 1636 (Saracen's Head)
834 SWJ May 20 1771 (Saracen's Head)
835 SWJ May 15 1780 (Saracen's Head)
836 SWJ Aug 19 1782 (Saracen's Head)
837 SWJ Jan 27 1783 (Saracen's Head)
838 SWJ Mar 19 1841 (Saracen's Head)
839 SWJ Mar 23 1843 (Saracen's Head)
840 SWJ Jun 29 1848 Saracen's Head)
841 SWJ Jun 16 1866 (Saracen's Head)
842 ST Sep 16 1876 (Saracen's Head)
843 SWJ Nov 1 1779 (Sawyer's Arms)
844 WSHC 727/8/5 (Shipp)
845 SWJ May 22 1739 (Shoulder of Mutton)
846 SWJ Oct 23 1780 (Shoulder of Mutton)
847 SWJ Nov 10 1783 (Shoulder of Mutton)
848 SWJ Jan 17 1785 (Shoulder of Mutton)
849 SWJ Feb 9 1789 (Shoulder of Mutton)
850 SWJ Nov 2 1789 (Shoulder of Mutton)
851 SWJ Aug 8 1785 (Shoulder of Mutton)
852 SWJ Mr 29 1790 (Shoulder of Mutton)
853 SWJ Feb 4 1793 (Shoulder of Mutton)
854 SWJ Dec 16 1805 (Shoulder of Mutton)
855 WSHC G23/150/4 Lease of 1830 (Shoulder of Mutton)
856 SWJ May 21 1832 (Shoulder of Mutton)
857 SWJ Aug 5 1833 (Shoulder of Mutton)
858 SWJ Apr 30 1864 (Shoulder of Mutton)
859 SWJ Jun 24 1776 (Six Bells)
860 SWJ Jan 11 1779 (Six Bells)
861 SWJ Mar 29 1779 (Six Bells)
862 SWJ Apr 24 1780 (Six Bells)
863 SWJ May 7 1798 (Six Bells)
864 SWJ Mar 4 1799 (Six Bells)
865 ST Mar 11 1876 (Slug & Lettuce)
866 ST April 24 1880 (Slug & Lettuce)
867 SWJ May 23 1763 (Spread Eagle)
868 SWJ Jun 20 1763 (Spread Eagle)

869 SWJ Mar 10 1788 (Spread Eagle)
870 SWJ Nov 25 1793 (Spread Eagle)
871 SWJ Feb 1 1796 (Spread Eagle)
872 SWJ July 17 1815 (Spread Eagle)
873 SWJ Dec 25 1815 (Spread Eagle)
874 SWJ Dec 21 1818 (Spread Eagle)
875 SWJ Nov 29 1819 (Spread Eagle)
876 SWJ Mar 4 1822 (Spread Eagle)
877 SWJ Apr 1 1822 (Spread Eagle)
878 SWJ Sep 19 1846 (Spread Eagle)
879 SWJ Jun 25 1859 (Spread Eagle)
880 SWJ Jul 16 1859 (Spread Eagle)
881 Rowe Williamson Ref 223 (Squirrel)
882 WSHC G23/150/20 Lease of 1683 (Squirrel)
883 WSHC G23/150/20 Lease of 1780 (Squirrel)
884 WSHC B18/100/42 Justices Minute Book – Salisbury & Amesbury 1848 (Stratford Inn)
885 WSHC B18/100/40 Justices Minute Book – Salisbury & Amesbury 1846 (Stratford Inn)
886 WSHC B18/100/91 Justices Minute Book – Salisbury & Amesbury 1897 (Stratford Inn)
887 ST Oct 21 1898 (Stratford Inn)
888 SWJ Apr 27 1752 (Sugar Loaf)
889 SWJ Jan 12 1756 (Sugar Loaf)
890 SWJ Jul 11 1757 (Sun Fisherton Street)
891 SWJ Oct 1 1759 (Sun Fisherton Street)
892 SWJ Jul 7 1760 (Sun Fisherton Street)
893 SWJ Feb 22 1762 (Sun Fisherton Street)
894 SWJ Jun 25 1764 (Sun Fisherton Street)
895 Hoare p 526 (Sun Fisherton Street)
896 SWJ Aug 17 1812 (Sun Fisherton Street)
897 SWJ Jan 30 1826 (Sun Fisherton Street)
898 SWJ May 7 1827 (Sun Fisherton Street)
899 SWJ Jan 15 1838 (Sun Fisherton Street)
900 SWJ Dec 16 1843 (Sun Fisherton Street)
901 SWJ Sep 21 1844 (Sun Fisherton Street)
902 SWJ Oct 12 1844 (Sun Fisherton Street)
903 Rowe Williamson ref no 201 (Sun Winchester Street)
904 SWJ Aug 10 1747 (Sun & Lamb)
905 SWJ May 24 1756 (Sun & Lamb)
906 SWJ Jun 2 1760 (Sun & Lamb)
907 SWJ Oct 13 1760 (Sun & Lamb)
908 SWJ Jan 19 1761 (Sum & Lamb)
909 WSHC CC/Chapter/82/2 Lease of 1807 (Sun & Lamb)
910 Hoare p156 (Tabard)
911 WSHC A3/90/4 License of Three Cranes (Three Cranes)
912 SWJ Dec 6 1779 (Three Crowns Brown Street)
913 SWJ Oct 31 1808 (Three Crowns Brown Street)
914 SWJ Feb 14 1774 (Three Crowns Town Path)
915 SWJ Feb 26 1776 (Three Crowns Town Path)
916 SWJ Jan 7 1811 (Three Crowns Town Path)
917 SWJ July 15 1811 (Three Crowns Town Path)
918 SWJ Aug 27 1821 (Three Crowns Town Path)
919 SWJ Sep 3 1821 (Three Crowns Town Path)
920 SWJ May 29 1830 (Three Crowns Town Path)
921 SWJ Aug 12 1843 (Three Crowns Town Path)
922 SWJ May 15 1847 (Three Crowns Town Path)
923 Haskins Brewers Guild p303 (Three Cups)
924 Haskins Butcher's Guild p265 (Three Cups)
925 Haskins Brewers Guild p 304 (Tree Cups)
926 Haskins Brewers Guild p304-305 (Three Cups)
927 Haskins Brewers Guild p305 (Three Cups)
928 SWJ Nov 21 1768 (Three Guns)
929 SWJ Jul 6 1730 (Three Lions)

930 SWJ Oct 16 1739 (Three Lions)
931 SWJ Sep 14 1761 (Three Lions)
932 SWJ Sep 30 1765 (Three Lions)
933 SWJ Oct 14 1765 (Three Lions)
934 SWJ Aug 4 1766 (Three Lions)
935 SWJ Feb 8 1768 (Three Lions)
936 SWJ Apr 18 1768 (Three Lions)
937 SWJ Apr 13 1772 (Three Lions)
938 SWJ Nov 16 1778 (Three Lions)
939 SWJ Dec 14 1778 (Three Lions)
940 SWJ Jan 6 1783 (Three Lions)
941 SWJ Jan 20 1783 (Three Lions)
942 SWJ Jul 28 1783 (Three Lions)
943 SWJ Jun 7 1790 (Three Lions)
944 SWJ May 1 1809 (Three Lions)
945 SWJ May 6 1776 (Three Mugs)
946 SWJ Jul 5 1762 (Three Pigeons)
947 SWJ Sept 30 1782   (Three Pigeons)
948 SWJ Nov 9 1789 (Three Pigeons)
949 SWJ Sep 24 1759 (Three Swans)
950 SWJ Feb 24 1766 (Three Swans)
951 SWJ May 11 1767 (Three Swans)
952 SWJ Jan 27 1772 (Three Swans)
953 SWJ Jul 10 1775 (Three Swans)
954 SWJ July 8 1780 (Three Swans)
955 SWJ Mar 12 1781 (Three Swans)
956 SWJ Apr 1 1782 (Three Swans)
957 SWJ Feb 24 1783 (Three Swans)
958 SWJ Apr 21 1783 (Three Swans)
959 SWJ Jul 14 1783 (Three Swans)
960 SWJ Oct 13 1783 (Three Swans)
961 SWJ Dec 19 1785 (Three Swans)
962 SWJ Sep 24 1787 (Three Swans)
963 SWJ Nov 29 1790 (Three Swans)
964 SWJ May 10 1813 (Three Swans)
965 SWJ Jan 10 1814 (Three Swans)
966 SWJ Feb 28 1814 (Three Swans)
967 SWJ Feb 20 1815 (Three Swans)
968 SWJ Jan 11 1819 (Three Swans)
969 SWJ Jul 4 1825 (Three Swans)
970 SWJ Nov 9 1829 (three Swans)
971 SWJ Apr 8 1871 (Three Swans)
972 ST Oct 12 1894 (Three Swans)
973 ST Feb 13 1903 (Three Swans)
974 SWJ Apr 2 1750 (Three Tuns)
975 SWJ Jun 18 1780 (Three Tuns)
976 SWJ Mar 17 1783 (Three Tuns)
977 SWJ Aug 10 1789 (Three Tuns)
978 SWJ Nov 14 1774 (Tollgate)
979 WSHC CC/Bishoprick/185/1 Court Roll of 1798 (Tollgate)
980 WSHC CC/Bishoprick/185/3 Court Roll of 1824 (Tollgate)
981 WSHC CC/Bishoprick/185/4 Court Roll of 1835 (Tollgate)
982 SWJ Nov 20 1847 (Tollgate)
983 ST Jan 19 1906 (Tollgate)
984 SWJ Jan 11 1819 (Traveller's Rest)
985 SWJ Jan 1 1759 (Valiant Soldier)
986 SWJ Mar 22 1756 (Vestry Milford Street)
987 SWJ Mar 22 1824 (Vestry Milford Street)
988 SWJ Jul 18 1831 (Vestry Milford Street)
989 SWJ Jun 18 1859 (Victoria Hotel)
990 SWJ Sep 10 1859 (Victoria Hotel)
991 SWJ Sep 29 1860 (Victoria Hotel)
992 SWJ Sep 7 1861 (Victoria Hotel)
993 SWJ May 11 1872 (Victoria Hotel)
994 ST Jun 16 1899 (Victoria Hotel)
995 ST Jan 29 1892 (Village)
996 ST Sep 14 1894 (Village)
997 SWJ Apr 3 1786 (Vine Bedwin Street)
998 SWJ Apr 18 1796 (Vine Bedwin Street)
999 Jul 1 1839 (Vine Bedwin Street)
1000 SWJ Aug 23 1856 (Vine Bedwin Street)
1001 SWJ Sep 11 1858 (Vine Bedwin Street)
1002 SWJ Aug 29 1868 (Vine Bedwin Street)
1003 SWJ Sep 12 1868 (Vine Bedwin Street)
1004 SWJ Sep 10 1870 (Vine Bedwin Street)
1005 Rowe Williamson ref 227 (Vine Cheese Market)
1006 SWJ Aug 3 1747 (Vine Cheese Market)
1007 SWJ Jan 6 1752 (Vine Cheese Market)
1008 SWJ Feb 10 1755 (Vine Cheese Market)
1009 SWJ Jul 25 1763 (Vine Cheese Market)
1010 SWJ May 26 1766 (Vine Cheese Market)
1011 SWJ Jul 21 1766 (Vine Cheese Market)

1012 SWJ Sep 29 1766 (Vine Cheese Market)
1013 SWJ Sep 24 1770 (Vine Cheese Market)
1014 SWJ Sep 13 1779 (Vine Cheese Market)
1015 SWJ March 20 1780 (Vine Cheese Market).
1016 SWJ May 8 1780 (Vine Cheese Market)
1017 SWJ July 1 1780 (Vine Cheese Market)
1018 SWJ June 17 1782 (Vine Cheese Market)
1019 SWJ July 1 1782 (Vine Cheese Market)
1020 SWJ July 4 1785 (Vine Cheese Market)
1021 SWJ Dec 31 1787 (Vine Cheese Market)
1022 SWJ Sep 29 1788 (Vine Cheese Market)
1023 SWJ Oct 18 1790 (Vine Cheese Market)
1024 ST Sep 8 1877 (Volunteer's Arms)
1025 WSHC CC/Bishoprick/181/3 Estate of Samuel Whitchurch (Waggon & Horses Brown Street)
1026 SWJ Jan 17 1831 (Waggon & Horses Fisherton Street)
1027 SWJ Jul 4 1868 (Waggon & Horses Fisherton Street)
1028 SWJ Oct 4 1756 (Weaver's Fisherton)
1029 SWJ Dec 19 1796 (Weaver's Fisherton)
1030 SWJ Oct 27 1804 (Weaver's Fisherton)
1031 SWJ May 16 1774 (Weaver's Milford Street)
1032 SWJ May 30 1808 (Weavers Milford Street)
1033 SWJ May 30 1768 (Wheatsheaf)
1034 SWJ Mar 19 1804 (Wheatsheaf)
1035 SWJ Jan 14 1822 (Wheatsheaf)
1036 SWJ Apr 9 1827 (Wheatsheaf)
1037 SWJ Feb 7 1831 (Wheatsheaf)
1038 SWJ Dec 24 1832 (Wheatsheaf)
1039 SWJ Aug 5 1833 (Wheatsheaf)
1040 SWJ Jan 28 1833 (Wheatsheaf)
1041 SWJ Jun 30 1834 (Wheatsheaf)
1042 WSHC CC/Bishoprick/181/3 Estate of Samuel Whitchurch (Wheatsheaf)
1043 SWJ Jul 11 1857 (Wheatsheaf)
1044 ST May 10 1907 (Wheatsheaf)
1045 SWJ Jul 1 1765 (White Hart)
1046 SWJ Nov 25 1765 (White Hart)
1047 SWJ Aug 17 1767 (White Hart)
1048 SWJ Sep 13 1773 (White Hart)
1049 SWJ Jun 2 1777 (White Hart)
1050 SWJ Oct 9 1780 (White Hart)
1051 SWJ Oct 23 1780 (White Hart)
1052 SWJ Nov 4 1782 (White Hart)
1053 SWJ Feb 28 1785 (White Hart)
1054 SWJ May 25 1789 (White Hart)
1055 SWJ Aug 27 1804 (White Hart)
1056 SWJ Aug 16 1856 (White Hart)
1057 SWJ Feb 12 1870 (White Hart)
1058 SWJ Mar 16 1752 (White Horse Fisherton Street)
1059 SWJ Apr 27 1852 (White Horse Fisherton Street)
1060 SWJ Dec 30 1765 (White Horse Fisherton Street)
1061 SWJ Mar 10 1766 (White Horse Fisherton Street)
1062 SWJ Dec 13 1739 (White Horse Milford Street)
1063 SWJ Apr 18 1774 (White Horse New Street)
1064 SWJ Apr 28 1783 (White Horse Cellar)
1065 WSHC CC/Bishoprick/175/1 Lease of 1783 (White Horse Cellar)
1066 SWJ Feb 11 1788 (White Horse Cellar)
1067 SWJ Oct 18 1813 (White Horse Cellar)
1068 SWJ Mar 27 1815 (White Horse Cellar)
1069 SWJ Jul 18 1825 (White Horse Cellar)
1070 SWJ Jul 25 1825 (White Horse Cellar)
1071 WSHC CC/Bishoprick/181/1 Estate of Samuel Whitchurch (White Horse Cellar)
1072 SWJ Aug 30 1756 (White Rooms)
1073 SWJ May 12 1834 (White Rooms)
1074 SWJ Sep 17 1838 (White Rooms)
1075 SWJ Mar 10 1856 (White Rooms)
1076 SWJ May 24 1856 (White Rooms)
1077 SWJ Sep 10 1870 (White Rooms)
1078 ST May 13 1886 (White Rooms)
1079 SWJ Jan 29 1781 (White Swan Brown Street)
1080 SWJ Dec 29 1806 (White Swan Brown Street)

1081 SWJ Nov 17 1834 (White Swan Brown Street)
1082 SWJ Feb 15 1796 (Wilton Arms)
1083 SWJ Sep 23 1799 (Wilton Arms)
1084 SWJ July 2 1810   (Wilton Arms)
1085 SWJ Apr 15 1816 (Wilton Arms)
1086 SWJ Mar 6 1830 (Wilton Arms)
1087 WSHC 529/150 (Wilton Arms)
1088 SWJ Nov 22 1851 (Wilton Arms)
1089 SWJ May 7 1853 (Wilton Arms)
1090 SWJ Aug 25 1855 (Wilton Arms)
1091 ST Jul 31 1872 (Wilton Arms)
1092 SWJ Mar 4 1882 (Wilton Arms)
1093 ST Mar 25 1882 (Wilton Arms)
1094 SWJ Oct 27 2016 (Wilton Arms)
1095 SWJ Oct 7 1754 (Winchester Gate)
1096 SWJ Oct 27 1817 (Winchester Gate)
1097 SWJ Nov 9 1829 (Winchester Gate)
1098 SWJ Dec 16 1833 (Winchester Gate)
1099 SWJ Jun 30 1834 (Winchester Gate)
1100 SWJ May 17 1856 (Winchester Gate)
1101 SWJ Jun 7 1856 (Winchester Gate)
1102 SWJ Aug 31 1872 (Winchester Gate)
1103 SWJ Oct 5 1872 (Winchester Gate)
1104 Rowe Williamson Ref No 202 (World's End)
1105 ST Oct 14 1882 (Wyndham Arms)
1106 ST Jun 29 1901 (Wyndham Arms)
1107 SWJ Oct 14 1833 (YOYO)
1108 SWJ Feb 9 1856 (YOYO)
1109 SWJ Mar 16 1872 (YOYO)

Cross-Reference of Pubs

Pub Name	Street	See
Abbey	nk	Le Abbey (1)
Afon	Millstream Approach	Boathouse (30)
Albert	nk	Albert (2)
Albion	St Ann Street	Baker's Arms (30)
Alchemy	Blue Boar Row	Chough (49)
Ale & Cider Press	Fisherton Street	Bar 44 (11)
Anchor	Culver Street	Anchor (3)
Anchor	Gigant Street	Anchor (4)
Anchor	Petersfinger	Petersfinger Inn (173)
Anchor & Hope	Winchester Street	Anchor & Hope (5)
Angel	Fisherton Street	Angel (6)
Angel	High Street	Angel (7)
Angel	Milford Street	Royal Oak (207)
Angel	Winchester Street	Anchor & Hope (5)
Antelope	Catherine Street	Antelope (8)
Archangel	Milford Street	Royal Oak (207)
Ark	Milford Street	Noah's Ark (162)
Avon Brewery	Castle Street	Avon Brewery (9)
Avon Brewery	Harnham Road	Rose & Crown (201)
Bacchus Hotel	Wilton Road	Wilton Arms (266)
Baker's Arms	St Ann Street	Baker's Arms (10)
Bar 44	Fisherton Street	Bar 44 (11)
Bar M	Fisherton Street	Mortimer's Bar (157)
Barley Mow	Greencroft Street	Barley Mow (12)
Baron of Beef	Endless Street	NN Bar (161)
Bear	Guilder Lane	Squirrel (219)
Belfry	Cathedral Close	Belfry (13)
Bell	Exeter Street	Bell (14)
Bell	Fisherton	One Bell (167)
Bell	Milford	Bell (15)
Bell	Milford Hill	Bell (16)
Bell & Crown	Brown Street (?)	Cherry Tree (48)
Bell & Crown	Catherine Street	Cloisters (51)

CROSS-REFERENCE OF PUBS

Pub Name	Street	See
Bird in Hand	North Street	Bird in Hand (17)
Bird in Hand	Trinity Street	Bird in Hand (18)
Bishop Blaze	Milford Street	Bishop Blaze (19)
Bishopdown	Pearce Way	Hampton Inn (122)
Bishop's Mill	The Maltings	Mill (154)
Bishop's Palace	Cathedral Close	Bishop's Palace (20)
Black Bear	Castle Street	Black Bear (21)
Black Bear	Guilder Lane	Squirrel (219)
Blackbird	Churchfields Road	Blackbird (22)
Black Boar	Market Ward	Black Boar (23)
Black Boy	Milford Street	Noah's Ark (162)
Black Dog	Ox Row	Duchess of Albany (80)
Black Horse	Castle Street	Black Horse (24)
Black Horse	Winchester Street	Black Horse (25)
Black Horse Tap	Brown Street	Falcon (88)
Black Lion	Market Ward	Black Lion (26)
Black Swan	Ox Row	Duchess of Albany (80)
Black Swan	St Martin's Parish	Black Swan (27)
Blue Boar	Blue Boar Row	Blue Boar (28)
Blue Lion	Ivy Street	Queen's Arms (184)
Blue Post	Milford Hollow	Blue Post (29)
Boathouse	Millstream Approach	Boathouse (30)
Bover's Place	Bridge Street	King's Head (139)
Bowling Green	Castle Street	Bowling Green (31)
Bowling Green	Crane Bridge Street	Bowling Green (32)
Brewery Tap	Fisherton Street	London Hotel (147)
Brewery Tap	Milford Street	White Rooms (263)
Brewery Tap	Rollestone Street	Brewery Tap (33)
Bricklayer's Arms	nk	Bricklayer's Arms (34)
Bridge	nk	Bridge (35)
Bridger's Tap	Endless Street	Salisbury Arms (209)
Brown Bear	Castle Street	Brown Bear (36)
Bugle	Blue Boar Row	Bugle (37)
Bull	Fisherton Street	Bull (38)
Bull	Ox Row	Ox Inn (168)
Bull's Head	Ox Row	Ox Row Inn (170)
Burke's Bar	New Street	Wig & Quill (265)
Bush	Market Ward	Bush (39)
Butcher's Arms	Butcher Row	Market Inn (151)

– 303 –

THE PUBLIC HOUSES AND INNS OF SALISBURY

Pub Name	Street	See
Butt of Ale	Sunnyhill Road	Butt of Ale (40)
Cactus Jack's	Water Lane	Cactus Jack's (41)
Café Bar Circolo	Fisherton Street	City Hall (50)
Café Prague	Salt Lane	Danny's Craft Bar (73)
Café Pride	Salt Lane	Danny's Craft Bar (73)
Carpenter's Arms	Market Ward	Bricklayer's Arms (34)
Cartwells	Minster Street	Cartwells (42)
Cartwell's Inn	High Street	Countewell's (60)
Cart Wheel	Milford Street	Retreat Inn (197)
Cat Tavern	South Western Road	Cat Tavern (43)
Cathedral Hotel	Milford Street	Cathedral (44)
Catherine Wheel	Milford Street	Retreat Inn (197)
Chamberlain's Tap	Endless Street	Salisbury Arms (209)
Chapman's Arms	Milford Street	YOYO (270)
Chapter House	St John's Street	Chapter House (45)
Checkers	Endless Street	Checkers (46)
Chequer	Rampart Road	White Horse Cellar (261)
Chequers	nk	Chequers (47)
Cheesecake House	Milford Hollow	Blue Post (29)
Cherry Tree	Brown Street	Cherry Tree (48)
Chicago Rock Cafe	Fisherton Street	Mortimer's Bar (157)
Chough	Blue Boar Row	Chough (49)
Churchfields Beerhouse	Churchfields Road	Blackbird (22)
Churchill Rooms	Brown Street	Waggon & Horses (250)
Churchills	Endless Street	NN Bar (161)
City Arms	Ox Row	Ox Row Inn (170)
City Hall	Fisherton Street	City Hall (50)
Clock Tower	Fisherton Street	Slug & Lettuce (217)
Cloisters	Catherine Street	Cloisters (51)
Coach & Horses	Brown Street	Waggon & Horses (250)
Coach & Horses	Castle Street	Coach & Horses (52)
Coach & Horses	Catherine Street	Coach & Horses (53)
Coach & Horses	Exeter Street	Bell (14)
Coach & Horses	Winchester Street	Coach & Horses (54)
Coach & Six	Winchester Street	Six Bells (216)
Cock	nk	Cock (55)
Cokk	Winchester Street	Coach & Horses (54)
Comb Pot	Milford Street	Comb Pot (56)
Commercials	South Western Road	Commercials (57)

– 304 –

CROSS-REFERENCE OF PUBS

Pub Name	Street	See
Conran's Bar	Salt Lane	Danny's Craft Bar (73)
Conquered Moon	Woodside Road	Moon (156)
Cope	High Street	Cope (58)
Cornish Choffe	Blue Boar Row	Chough (49)
Cornmarket	Cheese Market	Cornmarket (59)
Countewell's	High Street	Countewell's (60)
County Hotel	Bridge Street	King's Head (139)
Crane	Crane Street	Crane (61)
Cricketers	Rampart Road	Cricketers (62)
Crispin	Salt Lane	Pheasant (174)
Cross Guns	Market Place	Crown & Guns (69)
Cross Keys	Fisherton Street	King's Arms (138)
Cross Keys	Queen Street	Cross Keys (63)
Cross Keys Tap	Brown Street	Cross Keys Tap (64)
Crown	Bedwin Street	Royal George (204)
Crown	Castle Street	Crown (65)
Crown	Fisherton	Crown (66)
Crown Hotel	High Street	Crown (67)
Crown & Anchor	Exeter Street	Crown & Anchor (68)
Crown & Guns	Market Place	Crown & Guns (69)
Crown & Slipper	Fisherton	Crown & Slipper (70)
Crumley's Tap	Endless Street	Salisbury Arms (209)
Crystal Fountain	Milford Street	Crystal Fountain (71)
Cup Inn	High Street	Countewell's (60)
Cups	South Western Road	Cups (72)
Danny's Craft Bar	Salt Lane	Danny's Craft Bar (73)
Deacons	Fisherton Street	Deacons (74)
Deacon's Alms	Fisherton Street	Deacons (74)
Deverell's Inn	Cheese Market	Maidenhead (149)
Devizes Inn	Devizes Road	Devizes (75)
Dolphin	Dolphin Street	Dolphin (76)
Dolphin	Fish Row	Dolphin (77)
Dolphin	New Street	Dolphin (78)
Dorchester Hotel	Fisherton Street	London Hotel (147)
Dorchester Inn	Sunnyhill Road	Butt of Ale (40)
Dragon	Exeter Street	Crown & Anchor (68)
Draggon	St Martin's Church St.	Draggon (79)
Druid & Five Bells	Salt Lane	Five Bells (95)
Duchess of Albany	Ox Row	Duchess of Albany (80)

THE PUBLIC HOUSES AND INNS OF SALISBURY

Pub Name	Street	See
Duck	Duck Lane	Duck (81)
Duke of Wellington	Chipper Lane	Plough (178)
Duke of York	Milford Street	Duke of York (82)
Duke of York	York Road	Duke of York (83)
Duke William	Catherine Street	Cloisters (51)
Duke's Head	Catherine Street	Cloisters (51)
Dusthole	Tollgate Road	Railway Inn (190)
Eagle	Fisherton Street	Eagle (84)
Eagles	Cathedral Close	Eagles (85)
Elephant & Castle	Brown Street	Elephant & Castle (86)
Elephant & Castle	Ox Row	Duchess of Albany (80)
Elephant & Castle	Petersfinger	Petersfinger Inn (173)
Endless Street Brewery Tap	Endless Street	Salisbury Arms (209)
Engineer's Arms	South Western Road	Cat Tavern (43)
England's Glory	nk	England's Glory (87)
Falcon	Brown Street	Falcon (88)
Falcon	Crane Street	Falcon (89)
Fat Ox	Butcher Row	Market Inn (151)
Faucon	Castle Street	Faucon (90)
Fawcett's Tap	Endless Street	Salisbury Arms (209)
Feathers	Queen Street	Plume of Feathers (180)
Fiddle & Trumpet	nk	Fiddle & Trumpet (91)
Fisher's Stalls	nk	Fisher's Stalls (92)
Fisherton Arms	Fisherton Street	Bar 44 (11)
Fisherton Brewery Inn	Fisherton Street	Bar 44 (11)
Fisherton Tap	Fisherton Street	Lamb (144)
Five Bells	Corn Market	Five Bells (93)
Five Bells	Fisherton	Five Bells (94)
Five Bells	Salt Lane	Five Bells (95)
Fleece	nk	Fleece (96)
Fleur de Luce	Trinity Street	Bird in Hand (18)
Flower Pot	Exeter Street	Crown & Anchor (68)
Flower Pots	Culver Street	Flower Pots (97)
Flying Horse	Catherine Street	Oxford Arms (169)
Four Bells	Wilton Road	Wilton Arms (266)
Fountain	High Street	Fountain (98)
Fox & Goose	nk	Fox & Goose (99)
French Horn	nk	French Horn (100)
Frothblower's Arms	Milford Street	YOYO (270)

– 306 –

CROSS-REFERENCE OF PUBS

Pub Name	Street	See
George	Fisherton	George (101)
George	High Street	George (102)
George	Winchester Street	Old George (165)
George & Dragon	Castle Street	George & Dragon (103)
Gigant Street Brewery Tap	Gigant Street	Huntsman (134)
Globe	Gigant Street	Globe (104)
Glove	nk	Glove (105)
Goat	Milford Street	Goat (106)
Goate	Fisherton	Goate (107)
Golden Fleece	Gigant Street	Globe (104)
Golden Lion	Endless Street	Golden Lion (108)
Grange	St Mark's Avenue	Grange (109)
Grasshopper	Chipper Lane	Plough (178)
Grasshopper	Winchester Street	Grasshopper (110)
Great Western Tavern	Fisherton	Great Western Tavern (111)
Gredire	Catherine Street	Gredire (112)
Green Dragon	Fisherton	Green Dragon (113)
Green Dragon	Rampart Road	Winchester Gate (267)
Green Man	nk	England's Glory (87)
Green Man	nk	Green Man (114)
Grey Fisher	Ayleswade Road	Grey Fisher (115)
Greyhound	Brown Street	Greyhound (116)
Greyhound	Greencroft Street	Greyhound (117)
Greyhound	Ox Row	Duchess of Albany (80)
Griffin	Exeter Street	Crown & Anchor (68)
Half Moon	Bedwin Street	Half Moon (118)
Half Moon	Castle Street	Half Moon (119)
Half Moon	Ox Row	Half Moon (120)
Halfway House	Wilton Road	Halfway House (121)
Hampton Inn	Pearce Way	Hampton Inn (122)
Hand & Flower	Winchester Street	Running Horse (208)
Hard Rock Steam Cafe	Crane Street	Old Ale House (163)
Hatterestaverne	Castle Street	Hatterestaverne (123)
Haunch of Venison	Minster Street	Haunch of Venison (124)
Helme	High Street	Pynnok's Inn (182)
Hobgoblin	Milford Street	Vestry (244)
Hogshead	Fisherton Street	Slug & Lettuce (217)
Hogshead	Wilton Road	Malmesbury Arms (150)
Hogshead Bar	Bridge Street	King's Head (139)

– 307 –

THE PUBLIC HOUSES AND INNS OF SALISBURY

Pub Name	Street	See
Holie Lamb	High Street	Sun & Lamb (224)
Hop Brewery Bar	Milford Street	White Rooms (263)
Hope	Milford Street	YOYO (270)
Horns	Market Place	Horns (125)
Horse	Castle Street	Horse (126)
Horse's Head	High Street	Horse's Head (127)
Horse & Crown	Crane Street	Old Ale House (163)
Horse & Groom	nk	Horse & Groom (128)
Horse & Groom	Wilton Road	Horse & Groom (129)
Horse & Jockey	Exeter Street	Crown & Anchor (68)
Horse & Jockey	Scot's Lane	Horse & Jockey (130)
Horseshoe	High Street	Horseshoe (131)
Horseshoes	Britford	Horseshoes (132)
Horseshoes	Catherine Street	Cloisters (51)
Horseshoes	Fisherton	Horseshoes (133)
Huntsman	Gigant Street	Huntsman (134)
Hungry Horse	Ayleswade Road	Grey Fisher (115)
Hynde	Winchester Street	Hynde (135)
India Arms	Culver Street	India Arms (136)
Joiner's Arms	Milford Street	Joiner's Arms (137)
King's Arms	Fisherton Street	King's Arms (138)
King's Arms	St John Street	Chapter House (45)
King's Head	Bridge Street	King's Head (139)
King & Bishop	Crane Street	Old Ale House (163)
King & Queen	Chipper Lane	King & Queen (140)
King of Prussia	Catherine Street	Cloisters (51)
King of Prussia	Milford Hill	King of Prussia (141)
Labour in Vain	Endless Street	Labour in Vain (142)
Lamb	Catherine Street	Lamb (143)
Lamb	Fisherton Street	Lamb (144)
Lamb	High Street	Sun & Lamb (224)
Lamb	Gigant Street	Globe (104)
Lazy Cow	St John Street	Chapter House (45)
Le Beq's	Milford Street	Vestry (244)
Legge	High Street	Legge (145)
Le Lambe	High Street	Sun & Lamb (224)
Leopard's Head	Salt Lane	Leopard's Head (146)
Lion Commercial Hotel	Milford Street	Red Lion (194)
London Hotel	Fisherton Street	London Hotel (147)

CROSS-REFERENCE OF PUBS

Pub Name	Street	See
London Inn	Bridge Street	London Inn (148)
London Road Inn	Rampart Road	Winchester Gate (267)
Lord Collingwood's Arms	Winchester Street	Anchor & Hope (5)
Lord Malmesbury Arms	Wilton Road	Malmesbury Arms (150)
Lord Radnor Arms	St Ann Street	Radnor Arms (188)
Lyon	Bridge Street	King's Head (139)
Macklin's Tap	Endless Street	Salisbury Arms (209)
Maidenhead	Cheese Market	Maidenhead (149)
Maidenhead	Ivy Street	Queen's Arms (184)
Malmesbury Arms	Wilton Road	Malmesbury Arms (150)
Malt & Hop Brewery	Milford Street	White Rooms (263)
Market Inn	Butcher Row	Market Inn (151)
Marshall's Inn	High Street	Horseshoe (131)
Mason's Arms	nk	Mason's Arms (152)
Maton's Tap	Milford Street	White Rooms (263)
Maxwell's	Water Lane	Cactus Jack's (41)
Mermaid	Blue Boar Row	Mermaid (153)
Milford Arms	Milford Street	White Rooms (263)
Mill	The Maltings	Mill (154)
Miller's Club	Town Path	Old Mill (166)
Mitre	Butcher Row	Market Inn (151)
Mitre	Silver Street	Mitre (155)
Mitre & Crown	Silver Street	Mitre (155)
Moon	Woodside Road	Moon (156)
Mortimer's Bar	Fisherton Street	Mortimer's Bar (157)
Mojito	Salt Lane	Danny's Craft Bar (73)
Nag's Head	Culver Street	India Arms (136)
Nag's Head	Fisherton Street	King's Arms (138)
Nelson's Arms	Gigant Street	Globe (104)
New Inn	New Street	New Inn (158)
New Inn	Poultry Cross	New Inn (159)
New Inn	Tollgate Road	Tollgate (239)
New Inn	Winchester Street	New Inn (160)
New Roebuck	Ox Row	Duchess of Albany (80)
New White Horse Cellar	Rampart Road	White Horse Cellar (261)
NN Bar	Endless Street	NN Bar (161)
Noah's Ark	Milford Street	Noah's Ark (162)
Northumberland Arms	Exeter Street	Crown & Anchor (68)
Northumberland Arms	St Ann Street	Radnor Arms (188)

Pub Name	Street	See
Oddfellows Arms	Milford Street	YOYO (270)
Old Ale House	Crane Street	Old Ale House (163)
Old Bell	Exeter Street	Bell (14)
Old Castle	Old Castle Road	Old Castle (164)
Old Coach House	Milford Street	White Rooms (263)
Old Gate House	Winchester Street	Volunteer's Arms (249)
Old George	Winchester Street	Old George (165)
Old George Tap	Rollestone Street	Brewery Tap (33)
Old Mill	Town Path	Old Mill (166)
Old Roebuck	Butcher Row	Roebuck (200)
One Bell	Fisherton	One Bell (167)
Ox Inn	Ox Row	Ox Inn (168)
Oxford Arms	Catherine Street	Oxford Arms (169)
Ox Row Inn	Ox Row	Ox Row Inn (170)
Packhorse	Ox Row	Ox Inn (168)
Parade Tavern	Blue Boar Row	Parade Tavern (171)
Pelican	St Ann Street	Pelican (172)
Petersfinger Inn	Petersfinger	Petersfinger Inn (173)
Pheasant	Salt Lane	Pheasant (174)
Pilours	nk	Pilours (175)
Plasterer's Arms	Winchester Street	Plasterer's Arms (176)
Plough	Brown Street	Plough (177)
Plough	Chipper Lane	Plough (178)
Plume of Feathers	Fisherton Street	Plume of Feathers (179)
Plume of Feathers	Queen Street	Plume of Feathers (180)
Pot & Limbeck	Trinity Street	Bird in Hand (18)
Prince of Wales Arms	Fisherton Street	Plume of Feathers (179)
Prince of Wales Plumes	Fisherton Street	Plume of Feathers (179)
Prince Regent's Hotel	Catherine Street	Antelope (8)
Princes Arms	Catherine Street	Oxford Arms (169)
Punchbowl	Shady Bower	Punchbowl (181)
Pynnok's Inn	High Street	Pynnok's Inn (182)
Qudos	Castle Street	Qudos (183)
Queen's Arms	Ivy Street	Queen's Arms (184)
Queen's & Plasterer's Arms	Ivy Street	Queen's and Plasterer's Arms (185)
Queen's Head	Ivy Street	Queen's Head (186)
Queen's Head	Milford Street	White Rooms (263)
Quiet Woman	Castle Street	George & Dragon (103)
Radnor Arms	Queen's Road	Radnor Arms (187)

CROSS-REFERENCE OF PUBS

Pub Name	Street	See
Radnor Arms	St Ann Street	Radnor Arms (188)
Rai d'Or	Brown Street	Rai d'Or (189)
Railway Inn	Tollgate Road	Railway Inn (190)
Railway Tavern	South Western Road	Railway Tavern (191)
Railway Tavern	St Ann Street	Railway Tavern (192)
Rainbow	Milford Street	Vestry (244)
Ramme	Bridge Street	King's Head (139)
Rare Joint	Fisherton Street	Deacons (74)
Red Bull	Fisherton Street	Lamb (144)
Red Lion	Fisherton Street	Red Lion (193)
Red Lion	Milford Street	Red Lion (194)
Red Lion	Rampart Road	White Horse Cellar (261)
Red Lion & Cross Keys	Milford Street	Red Lion (194)
Red Lion Tap	Milford Street	YOYO (270)
Red Lyon	Castle Street	Red Lyon (195)
Red Rover	Barnard Street	Red Rover (196)
Retreat Inn	Milford Street	Retreat Inn (197)
Reuben Langford's	Water Lane	Cactus Jack's (41)
Rifleman's Arms	London Road	Rifleman's Arms (198)
Ring of Bells	Salt Lane	Five Bells (95)
Rising Sun	Castle Street	Rising Sun (199)
Roebuck	Butcher Row	Roebuck (200)
'Romsey Arms'	Queen Alexandra Rd.	Royal Oak (206)
Rose	Bridge Street	London Inn (148)
Rose	Crane Street	Old Ale House (163)
Rose	High Street	Crown (67)
Rose & Crown	Harnham Road	Rose & Crown (201)
Rose & Crown	High Street	Crown (67)
Rose & Crown	Winchester Street	Six Bells (216)
Rose & Horseshoes	Catherine Street	Cloisters (51)
Round of Beef	Milford Street	Round of Beef (202)
Royal	High Street	Royal (203)
Royal George	Bedwin Street	Royal George (204)
Royal Marine Rendezvous	Ox Row	Ox Inn (168)
Royal Oak	Culver Street	Royal Oak (205)
Royal Oak	Devizes Road	Royal Oak (206)
Royal Oak	Fish Row	Dolphin (77)
Royal Oak	Milford Street	Royal Oak (207)
Rudder	Rampart Road	White Horse Cellar (261)

– 311 –

Pub Name	Street	See
Running Horse	Winchester Street	Coach & Horses (54)
Running Horse	Winchester Street	Running Horse (208)
Sack Carrier	Rampart Road	White Horse Cellar (261)
Salisbury Arms	Endless Street	Salisbury Arms (209)
Saracen's Head	Blue Boar Row	Saracen's Head (210)
Sarasynhede	Catherine Street	Sarasynhede (211)
Sawyer's Arms	Bugmore	Sawyer's Arms (212)
Shearman's Arms	Fisherton	Shearman's Arms (213)
Ship	Winchester Street	Plasterer's Arms (176)
Shipp	St Nicholas Road	Shipp (214)
Shoulder of Mutton	Bridge Street	Shoulder of Mutton (215)
Silent Woman	Castle Street	George & Dragon (103)
Six Bells	Winchester Street	Six Bells (216)
Slug & Lettuce	Fisherton Street	Slug & Lettuce (217)
Slurping Toad	Cheese Market	Cornmarket (59)
Spire Bar	Bridge Street	King's Head (139)
Splayed Eagle	New Canal	Spread Eagle (218)
Spread Eagle	New Canal	Spread Eagle (218)
Squirrel	Guilder Lane	Squirrel (219)
St Ann Street Brewery Tap	St Ann Street	Baker's Arms (10)
Star	Brown Street	Rai d'Or (189)
Star	Fisherton Street	Deacons (74)
Star & Garter	Gigant Street	Globe (104)
Star & Garter	Winchester Street	Black Horse (25)
Stratford Inn	Stratford-sub-Castle	Stratford Inn (220)
Stone Bridge	Bedwin Street	Royal George (204)
Sugar Loaf	Brown Street	Sugar Loaf (221)
Sun	Bedwin Street	Vine (247)
Sun	Fisherton Street	Sun (222)
Sun	Wilton Road	Halfway House (121)
Sun	Winchester Street	Sun (223)
Sunn	High Street	Horseshoe (131)
Sunny's	Castle Street	Rising Sun (199)
Sun & Lamb	High Street	Sun & Lamb (224)
Swan	Ayleswade Road	Grey Fisher (115)
Swan	Brown Street	White Swan (264)
Swan	Winchester Street	Swan (225)
Swinging Cat	South Western Road	Cat Tavern (43)
Tabard	nk	Tabard (226)

CROSS-REFERENCE OF PUBS

Pub Name	Street	See
Talbot	Trinity Street	Bird in Hand (18)
Talbot	Winchester Street	Anchor & Hope (5)
Tally Ho	nk	Tally Ho (227)
Tarent's Inn	High Street	Angel (7)
Tavern	Endless Street	NN Bar (161)
Thissel	Market Ward	Thissel (228)
Three Cranes	Milford Street	Three Cranes (229)
Three Crowns	Brown Street	Three Crowns (230)
Three Crowns	Town Path	Three Crowns (231)
Three Cups	Winchester Street	Three Cups (232)
Three Flower Pots	Culver Street	Flower Pots (97)
Three Guns	Winchester Street	Three Guns (233)
Three Lions	Queen Street	Three Lions (234)
Three Mugs	Brown Street	Three Mugs (235)
Three Pigeons	Market Place	Three Pigeons (236)
Three Swans	Winchester Street	Three Swans (237)
Three Tuns	Winchester Street	Three Tuns (238)
Tolbott	Winchester Street	Coach & Horses (54)
Tollgate	Tollgate Road	Tollgate (239)
Tom Brown's	Wilton Road	Halfway House (121)
Town House	Bridge Street	King's Head (139)
Trafalgar	Milford Street	Retreat Inn (197)
Traveller's Rest	Milford Farm Road	Traveller's Rest (240)
Tucker's Shears	nk	Tucker's Shears (241)
Two Sawyers	Brown Street	Two Sawyers (242)
Valiant Soldier	nk	Valiant Soldier (243)
Vestry	Milford Street	Vestry (244)
Vestry	St John's Street	Chapter House (45)
Victoria Arms	Wilton Road	Halfway House (121)
Victoria Hotel	Mill Road	Victoria Hotel (245)
Village	Wilton Road	Village (246)
Vine	Bedwin Street	Vine (247)
Vine	Cheese Market	Vine (248)
Volunteer's Arms	Winchester Street	Volunteer's Arms (249)
Waggon & Horses	Brown Street	Waggon & Horses (250)
Waggon & Horses	Fisherton Street	Waggon & Horses (251)
Weaver's Arms	Fisherton	Weaver's Arms (252)
Weaver's Arms	Milford Hill	Weaver's Arms (253)
Wellington Arms	Chipper Lane	Plough (178)

– 313 –

Pub Name	Street	See
West End Inn	Wilton Road	Horse & Groom (129)
Weyhill Tap	Milford Street	Weyhill Tap (254)
Wheatsheaf	Fish Row	Wheatsheaf (255)
White Bear	Catherine Street	Red Lion (194)
White Hart	St John Street	White Hart (256)
White Hart Tap	nk	White Hart Tap (257)
White Horse	Castle Street	Qudos (183)
White Horse	Wilton Road	Halfway House (121)
White Horse	Fisherton Street	White Horse (258)
White Horse	High Street	Horseshoe (131)
White Horse	Milford Street	White Horse (259)
White Horse	New Street	White Horse (260)
White Horse Cellar	Rampart Road	White Horse Cellar (261)
White Hynde	St John Street	White Hart (256)
White Lion	Catherine Street	Cloisters (51)
White Lion	Ivy Street	Queen's and Plasterer's Arms (185)
White Lyon	Fisherton	White Lyon (262)
White Rooms	Milford Street	White Rooms (263)
White Swan	Ayleswade Road	Grey Fisher (115)
White Swan	Brown Street	White Swan (264)
White Swan	Payne's Hill	Dolphin (76)
Wig & Quill	New Street	Wig & Quill (265)
William IV	Milford Street	Vestry (244)
Wilton Arms	Wilton Road	Wilton Arms (266)
Winchester Gate	Rampart Road	Winchester Gate (267)
Windsor Castle	Wilton Road	Village (246)
Wolferstan's Tap	Endless Street	Salisbury Arms (209)
Woolpack	Endless Street	NN Bar (161)
World's End	St Martin's Church St.	World's End (268)
Wyndham Arms	Estcourt Road	Wyndham Arms (269)
YOYO	Milford Street	YOYO (270)

www.ingramcontent.com/pod-product-compliance
Lightning Source LLC
Chambersburg PA
CBHW070959160426
43193CB00012B/1846